Serious Comedy

*The Philosophical and Theological Significance
of Tragic and Comic Writing
in the Western Tradition*

Patrick Downey

ISBN: 1-949716-11-2

ISBN-13: 978-1-949716-11-5

Cover image is "William Shakespeare Between Tragedy and Comedy"
by Richard Westall, 1825.

Cover design by Rachel Rosales, Orange Peal Design

Typeset by Mikael Good

"Well," I said, "since we brought up the subject of poetry again, let it be our apology that it was then fitting for us to send it away from the city on account of its character. The argument determined us. Let us further say to it, lest it convict us for a certain harshness and rusticity, that there is an old quarrel between philosophy and poetry."

—Plato, The *Republic*

Art—to say it in advance, for I shall return to this subject at greater length—art, in which precisely the lie is sanctified and the will to deception has a good conscience, is much more fundamentally sensed by Plato, the greatest enemy of art Europe has yet produced.
Plato versus Homer: that is the complete, the genuine antagonism!

—Nietzsche, *On the Genealogy of Morals*

Both the traditional and current interpretations of Plato may be said to bring out the tragic element in Plato's thought, but they neglect the comic element except were it hits one in the face. Many reasons can be given for this failure. I mention only one. Modern research on Plato originated in Germany, the country without comedy. To indicate why this element of comedy is of crucial importance in Plato I read to you a few lines from the only Platonist I know of who had an appreciation of this element, Sir Thomas More. I quote: "For to prove that this life is no laughing time, but rather the time of weeping we find that our savior himself wept twice or thrice, but never find that he laughed so much as once...." (Dialogue of Comfort Against Tribulation chap. 13). If we compare what More said about Jesus with what Plato tells us about Socrates, we find that "Socrates laughed twice or thrice, but never find we that he wept as much as once." A slight bias in favor of laughing and against weeping seems to be essential to philosophy. For the beginning of philosophy as the philosophers understood it is not the fear of the Lord, but wonder. Its spirit is not hope and fear and trembling, but serenity on the basis of resignation. To that serenity, laughing is a little more akin than weeping. Whether the Bible or philosophy is right is of course the only question that ultimately matters. But in order to understand that question one must first see philosophy as it is. One must not see it from the outset through Biblical glasses. Wherever each of us may stand, no respectable purpose is served by trying to prove that we eat the cake and have it.

—Leo Strauss, "On the Euthyphron"

But then my soul is also gripped with new amazement— indeed, it is filled with adoration, for it certainly would have been odd if it had been a human poem. Presumably it could occur to a human being to poetize himself in the likeness of the god or the god in the likeness of himself, but not to petite that the god poetized himself in the likeness of a human being.... And since we both are now standing before this wonder, whose solemn silence cannot be disturbed by human wrangling about what is mine and what is yours, whose awe-inspiring words infinitely drown out human quarreling about mine and thine, forgive me my curious mistaken notion of having composed it myself. It was a mistaken notion, and the poem was so different from every human poem that it was no poem at all but the wonder.

—Søren Kierkegaard, *Philosophical Fragments*

CONTENTS

ACKNOWLEDGMENTS

UPON the publication of the second edition of *Serious Comedy*, I would like to thank Colin Redemer for his impresario powers and interest in getting this done. He, along with The Davenant Institute and their editors, Onsi Kamel, Rhys Laverty, and Robin Harris, have made this undertaking both possible and pleasant. I would also like to thank the Roosters—you know who you are—for inspiring me to write, and think in terms of writing, in ways I haven't been able to since my graduate studies at Boston College. As the Old Man of the group, and they are all men, I am rejuvenated in your presence. So thank you.

As for the women in my life, I would like to thank my wife Lisa, and my four daughters, Emma, Nora, Catherine and Phoebe. I am a strange man, and yet my wife chose and continues to choose me, while my daughters had me thrust upon them. Thank you, and forgive me. I, at least, am the better because of you.

Again, I would like to thank my late grandfather, Arthur G. Olson, for giving me my first glimpse of my Father in Heaven, and to thank again those two friends from High School, Tom Taylor and now Father Glenn, who gave me early a taste for wit and conversation that I have shared with and through them ever since.

Patrick Downey
February 2022

DONORS

THE republication of *Serious Comedy* was a new kind of project for the Davenant Press. While we have regularly published our own original works and new editions of historic works, this is the first occasion on which we have republished a modern work. Among other things, we discovered that retrieving files from floppy disks in 2021 can be far more difficult than retrieving texts written 500 years ago. The republication of this work would not have been possible without generous donors to our Kindful campaign. All those who gave financially toward the projected are listed below. This book would not be in your hands without them.

Thomas Hall
Ryan Hammill
Mike Lisanti
Marshall Lymburn
Hanif Nori
Elijah Null
Michael Redemer
Tom Taylor

FOREWORD TO THE SECOND EDITION

IN MARCH of 2022 it will be exactly a decade since I first met Patrick Downey.

I was attending a retreat for our college's Great Books Department, where the faculty were asked to discuss potential new additions to the curriculum. As an eager junior faculty member I dutifully showed up, leaving my then very pregnant wife at home.

The retreat started pleasantly enough, with wine and cheese and a discussion of Virginia Woolf's "How Should One Read a Book" carried on in muted but intelligent tones. It wasn't clear if anyone wanted to discuss the essay at all. Many would prefer writing a book of their own, it seemed. But we carried on. The next morning was dedicated to some pedagogical conversations, followed by a discussion of Arendt's *Eichmann in Jerusalem*. This conversation picked up speed a little as we did our duty to the text. Ultimately though, it was a normal conversation and remained forgettably banal. Then a lunch break for which I, at least, was grateful. I was getting bored.

Faculty lingered after the Arendt conversation and broke off into twos and threes to find their way to local provender. Another newish hire and I decided we would light out for a watering hole, eager as we were to stretch our legs over a few miles of easy country. As we walked we found ourselves joined by an older faculty member from the philosophy department. His house was on the way to the bar and he walked some way with us. And in the short conversation we had he made several terse but lively comments. I don't remember what he said, exactly, but I remember walking away from the encounter feeling shocked and mildly offended. I didn't realize then that I'd encountered not just a professor of philosophy but a Philosopher.

That evening, after we had finished the job of thoroughly inspecting the wares at the pub's brass rail, we returned to the conference as the sun set, showing up just in time for the final chat of the evening. The discussion was on Paulo Freire's *Pedagogy of the Oppressed*. I remember being excited for this text because I found it so obviously wrong and knew I would encounter disagreement. I'd been trained to think that teachers had authority, and students went to college out of a desire to gain their knowledge, etc. All the old ways. Of course I knew the approved and appropriate way to voice my objections to the text and to discuss such things (e.g. "I have to respectfully disagree with Freire's conception on this page... if we deployed his methods would we really be caring for the students?"). Early on I got into an argument with a math professor, whom I otherwise found both friendly and clever, about whether when talking about a text we are talking about anything at all.

But then that odd Philosopher I had met earlier weighed in. As he had done on the walk, he said the most outrageous things, violating norms I'd learned were absolutely required in polite company and making vast arguments about the nature of being and its relationship to truth—essential truth— which we needed to place at the center of our institution. If memory serves, he even denounced Freire as a godless Marxist... but these stories do tend to grow in the telling. Suffice to say he had made yet another impression. I remember, the following week on campus, being asked about the retreat and I mentioned, offhand, that there'd been a great debate about Friere. But I was interrupted—my colleague had already heard about the debate ($\Phi\acute{\eta}\mu\eta$ being the fast runner she is) and wanted to assure me that we agreed that mad old Philosopher was way off base. I responded with something like, "Oh I found it fascinating. I think he was on to something." And from the stare I got back I may as well have said "I shall move to Kyrgyzstan and start a harem." It was then, I now know, that I was starting to see the wood for the trees for the first time.

The Philosopher and I rarely interacted over the following few years. Whenever we saw one another he said something that offended me or, more often, offended some sensibility I had been taught to guard by constant repetition from respectable men. Until one day I invited him to join me on a hike and I decided, what the hell, and rather than being offended I began arguing with him. And, truly, we haven't stopped arguing since then. In that capacity he has become my friend.

Aristotle implies that there is no money between friends. Our author takes this to heart and in my presence has never bothered to calculate how to split a restaurant bill, relying on his friends to tell him how much to pay for dinner. But Aristotle also says money is a store of desire. If one friend has something, he makes it freely available to his friend. And if a friend has given something to me I must make every effort to pay it back—not out of a fear of obligation but because I constantly want to give my friend the better end of the deal. As a friend, I have done my part to help return this book to print. I can't help but wonder: is it the author or you, the reader, who will get the better deal? After all, you will get to learn Political Philosophy. All the author gets is money…

Political Philosophy is a little-studied branch of thought in the Christian world. I know of no seminary which offers courses on it and of nearly no Christian scholars besides Downey who write on it theologically. This is partially because it is itself a niche discipline, but is also due to its origins.

It is not inaccurate to describe Political Philosophy, in its modern instantiation, as originating in the work of Leo Strauss (1899-1973). Born in Germany to Jewish parents, Strauss moved to the United States in 1937, after his academic formation in early 20th century Germany, and settled into a small school in Chicago from where he set about reshaping the field of political science into something properly philosophical. His education before he began this monumental task is important for understanding the book you're holding.

Strauss completed his doctorate in 1921 and then, one hundred years ago this year, spent a year in Freiburg attending Edmund Husserl's lectures and those of Husserl's greatest student, Martin Heidegger. Oh to be a fly on the wall in Freiburg in 1922. . . You see it wasn't just Husserl and Heidegger. Strauss attended these lectures among a collection of other first-rate philosophy students, many of whom would go on to massively influential careers of their own.[1] It is unmistakable to anyone who compares Strauss' 1921 dissertation to his post-1922 work that he had undergone a remarkable change.[2] It seems he came to the conclusion that Heidegger had uncovered something profoundly true in his method and possibly also in his metaphysics. In his method, by inquiring into our received understandings of reality (at the highest levels) by asking questions of meaning, being, language, and transmission. In his metaphysics, by arguing openly for a conception of reality and the self which is, at its beautifully decorated heart, minimally an epistemologically based nihilism, unmoored from all traditional and theological constraints.

Strauss, however, had the benefit of seeing what resulted from Heidegger's work both theoretically and practically more

---

[1] Students who were in Freiburg listening in on Husserl and Heidegger's lectures that year include Emmanuel Levinas, Hannah Arendt, Hans-Georg Gadamer, and others. Even those who weren't present were aware of the challenge which Heidegger's phenomenology represented to received ways of philosophizing. It is worth noting that Strauss' dissertation advisor was Ernst Cassirer who would go on to debate Heidegger in 1929; this was an event of some importance in 20th century philosophy. Peter Gordon, in a chapter on this debate in his book *Rosenzweig and Heidegger: Between Judaism and German Philosophy* (Berkeley: University of California Press, 2003), summarizes the outcome of the debate by saying "it was generally agreed that Heidegger was the decisive victor" (279). It is an open academic question whether the quality of the decisive victory was one of style or of substance.

[2] The impression which Heidegger made upon the young Strauss can be seen in an anecdote which Strauss tells about hearing one of Heidegger's lectures. "I left", he says," without understanding a word, but [I] sensed that he dealt with something of the utmost importance to man as man. I understood something on one occasion: when he interpreted the beginning of [Aristotle's] Metaphysics. I had never heard nor seen such a thing—such a thorough and intensive interpretation of a philosophic text. On my way home I visited [Franz] Rosenzweig and said to him that compared to Heidegger, Max Weber, till then regarded by me as the incarnation of the spirit of science and scholarship, was an orphan child" (*Jewish Philosophy and the Crisis of Modernity: Essays and Lectures in Modern Jewish Thought* (Albany: State University of New York Press, 1997, 461).

clearly than Heidegger ever did;[3] theoretically, by witnessing the logical conclusion of Heidegger's intellectual work, the logical conclusions it drove to, and the intellectual fruit his work bore in most of his students; practically... Well, besides looking at Heidegger's late career, feel free to google "German history in the 1940s and 50s."[4] This critical distance helped Strauss to a realization that stayed with him for the rest of his career: philosophy and society are inevitably at odds. This is because society functions on a basis of shared, agreed-upon ways of living and thinking about reality. Philosophy, however, is an ever present attempt to question that account of reality and those ways of living. To put it in words closer to Strauss' own: philosophy requires that we ask certain questions which are philosophically necessary but politically disastrous. This disaster can come in multiple forms but is always suboptimal. It could be that the disaster is the revolutionary destruction of the political community, the very community the philosopher needs in order to continue his philosophizing. Or it could be that the political community (or "the city" in Strauss' parlance) survives the asking of the disastrous question but only by killing the questioner. This is obviously bad for the philosopher but also is bad for the city, which, being unreflective, needed the philosopher's question. In the former case the philosopher sins against his city; in the latter the city sins against the philosopher. In either case, both philosopher and city end up bereft.

What, if anything, can be done to maintain the peace between philosophy and the city? The solution Strauss came to was Political Philosophy itself. Political Philosophy was something Strauss uncovered by applying Heidegger's philosophical method to certain texts which Heidegger overlooked, Strauss saw that there was an older tradition of philosophy which was aware of, and had avoided, the trap into which Heidegger had fallen. He began to see that the

---

[3] For more on this issue read David Tkach's excellent dissertation "Leo Strauss' Critique of Martin Heidegger" and further (and more nuanced) *Heidegger, Strauss, and the Premises of Philosophy: On Original Forgetting* (Chicago: University of Chicago Press, 2011) by Richard L. Velkley.

[4] Not all of this can be laid at Heidegger's feet, but neither can Heidegger be entirely excused.

activity of philosophers must recover a part of the virtue of moderation– moderation relative to philosophy. This particular *philosophical* moderation needed to find a way to discuss precisely those questions which were philosophically necessary but politically disastrous in such a way as to *not harm* those who listened– to keep a sort of hippocratic oath of the philosopher. This is seen at least as early as his book-length interpretation of Xenophon's *Hiero*, which Strauss titled *On Tyranny*, published in 1948, and was preceded by a series of essays later published in a work *Persecution and the Art of Writing*.

In *On Tyranny* Strauss discusses what he has uncovered: "By understanding the art of Xenophon, one will realize certain minimum requirements that one must fulfill when interpreting any Platonic dialogue, requirements which today are so little fulfilled that they are hardly known."[5] In saying this we must wonder is Strauss claiming that these are minimum requirements which must be met when interpreting Plato in order to understand him? Or minimum requirements which must be met in discussing Plato in order to prevent our future non-philosophic readers from being harmed by our answers? This oblique mode of communication is what he is talking about and quite possibly simultaneously deploying. As Kojeve pointed out at the start of his response to Strauss, Strauss was already writing "between the lines."[6] Strauss continues, "Socratic rhetoric is meant to be an indispensable instrument of philosophy. Its purpose is to lead potential philosophers to philosophy both by training them and by liberating them from the charms which obstruct the philosophic effort, as well as to prevent the access to philosophy of those who are not fit for it."[7] For Strauss this is the definitive way to investigate philosophy and, if we are to believe

---

[5] Strauss, *On Tyranny*, 26.

[6] Strauss, *On Tyranny*, 135. It is an accusation Strauss owns up to at the end of his response to Kojeve saying "In our discussion, the conflict between the two opposed basic presuppositions has barely been mentioned. But we have always been mindful of it." (213) i.e. "Yes, Kojeve, we have been communicating in a way hidden from the masses even if they were to read our exchange."

[7] Strauss, *On Tyranny*, 27.

him, he claims this discovery is only a re-discovery, since it was known full well by Socrates and his students. Socrates learned from the comic poet Aristophanes that if he continued doing philosophy without any concern for the city he would not be able to do philosophy for long. Political philosophy, then, is the form philosophy must take if it is to do its essential work. Philosophers must always keep one eye on the public who are not keen on philosophy and see it as a wasteful luxury or a threat. Which it is. As Strauss concludes, "Society will always try to tyrannize thought. Socratic rhetoric is the classic means for ever again frustrating these attempts."[8]

One problem with Strauss' project for anyone who follows in his wake is that, as my friend Professor Marcus Otte has put it, "after Strauss no one can agree what Plato meant by anything!"[9] This is surely too far, but the frustration is understandable. Strauss' writings (which are indebted to Heidegger's method) open up a great many more potential meanings and close down certain simple solutions to the problems of interpreting Plato and many other texts. The deeper problem however is that, in being influenced by Heidegger's method, Strauss never formally rejects Heidegger's metaphysical commitments. And, of course, where Strauss does say the correct and necessary pious things (be they civil or natural pieties) it is not clear whether he is doing this merely for the vulgar reader, whilst intending the *true* philosophers to read his words and actions between the lines. To put it more bluntly than I am supposed to as a trained great-grand-student of Strauss: is Strauss a nihilist? If so, is he importing a method of reading which will pre-determine a reading of Plato and ancient Greek philosophy as, ultimately, nihilistic? If he is, he is doing so in the most agreeable way possible, a way which would not upset the pieties of his readers. For his reading always leaves open the potential that such a nihilistic reading is wrong. He is not a pagan, and so can't be named a virtuous pagan, but *if* he is a nihilist he is a most gentlemanly and virtuous nihilist. To finish off our engagement with Heidegger and

---

[8] Strauss, *On Tyranny*, 27.

[9] Paraphrased from a disputation which took place during the Plato Seminar in the Michaelmas term of 2021 at Davenant Hall.

Strauss we can make a comparison between the Socrates of Aristophanes and the Socrates of Plato. Heidegger, like Aristophanes' Socrates, has his young students secluded in the "new thinkery" looking up at the stars, ignoring the city, and thereby corrupts them. Strauss, like Plato's Socrates, has his young students remain in the marketplace at the heart of the city and there asks them to look for virtue. He may not be entirely innocent of guile, (after all, the search for "knowledge of virtue" remains elusive) but he is not clearly caustic.

Still even in Strauss' formulation the philosophical problem persists once it has been seen and it requires a response. Are our pieties— is our faith— nothing more than an esoteric fig leaf which the wisest of us wear because we know that behind the final door of human knowing lurks an empty and icy cold and meaningless cosmos? If so, the piety could still be sensible because perhaps there is no other way to live *as humans* than as pious men and women in a political community with non-philosophers.

But Christians are committed to more. As Christians, we believe our pieties are sensible in another way entirely. We think we can experience them. We believe they are true, and true in a way which is not objectionable to reason even if not provable by mathematics. Pascal once observed that there is an inverse correlation between the level of certainty we could have about a fact and the importance which knowing that fact would hold for us. For example, we can be absolutely certain who is taller between you and me.[10] Such knowledge isn't worth much. However, it is perhaps impossible to be certain what you should say to your loved ones on your deathbed. Yet if you could know, such knowledge would be worth an inestimable amount. The knowledge of God and of salvation is this kind of knowledge.

Such knowledge is still potentially available in Strauss' framing of the philosophical confrontation between reason and revelation. But it is knowledge which Strauss cannot provide for us—it is never actualized. And it isn't clear whether he expects it will ever be provided. It is precisely here, at the crisis of our existence, where

---

[10] Statistically, I am safe to guess it is me.

the book in your hand is an essential resource.

Downey is one of the only guides I know (and I have only known two) who can take the full weight of the challenge presented by Strauss seriously and can come through the other side offering us a vision of orthodox Christianity that has the blood of life still in it. Christianity is no fig leaf to Downey. It is not wish fulfillment. Nor is it in slavish hock to the political situations of this world. Christianity needs no esotericism because it transcends the central mechanism by which this world punishes philosophers—*death*. In the resurrection of Jesus, Christianity transcends the need for what Strauss calls "the art of Xenophon," which is really, to Strauss, the art of all true philosophers. Strauss can still be useful, but as the Christian transcends the political situation Strauss' readings are no longer essential. The truth of our faith requires an end to the need for hiding our thoughts. Death has been put to death. If true we must speak plainly, and we must become amenable to hearing the truth about ourselves and our world. We must become a whole nation of philosophers. Or as Athanasius said:

> As for Greek wisdom and the grandiloquence of the philosophers, I think that no one needs our argument, as the wonder is before the sight of all, that while the wise among the Greeks had written so much, and were unable to persuade even a few from their neighborhood about immortality and the virtuous life, Christ alone by means of simple words and by means of humans not wise in speech has throughout the inhabited world persuaded whole churches full of human beings to despise death but to think rather of things immortal, and to disregard what is temporal but to consider rather things eternal, and to think nothing of earthly glory but to seek rather only immortality.[11]

This miracle cannot be done by our power. Grace alone can accomplish it. A grace that reaches down into our personal and

---

[11] Saint Athanasius, *On The Incarnation*, trans. John Behr (New York: St Vladimir's Seminary Press, 2011), 100-101.

communal lives right here inside of history and leavens every single thing it touches. In that way this book is a fulfillment of the admonition Peter makes in his epistle that in light of what Jesus has done we must lay aside the hypocrisies and guile which used to mark our lives and instead desire the sincere milk of the Word (1 Peter. 2:1-2). *Serious Comedy* is not itself the milk of the Word, but it can stir up the desire for such nourishment again. It stands, unafraid, as a testament that Christianity, as revealed by God in Scripture, is no second-best to worldly philosophies.

Downey was arguing this back when *Serious Comedy* was first published in 2001. This was before Covid–before even the terror that led to the "war on terror." Since the original publication there has been a turn in our culture.[12] We all feel it. While the turn predates the coronavirus pandemic which marked the start of 2020, the subsequent deaths of however many million from the virus has done nothing to lighten the mood. In light of our tragic turn we must once again answer the questions raised in this book: what kind of story are we in? The various types of stories are all there before us. It could be a serious story which ends in tragedy, perhaps like *There Will Be Blood*. It could be a funny story which nevertheless ends in sorrow, like one of the novels of Michel Houellebecq. It could be a ridiculous story which ends joyfully, perhaps like *Hot Tub Time Machine*. Or, it could perhaps be serious. The kind of story we need to sit up and attend to and study. And while serious, perhaps it is also one that ends in a joy we can't fully imagine but catch glimpses of in every wedding we've witnessed. The story we are in matters, and so too does the author of that story. If the author is merely a man it isn't clear we should ever take it that seriously, as no man can foretell the future.

A final couple of words on the style of the author of this book before I leave you to your task of reading it. You should know about two of the author's theories. The first is the theory of the barrel of monkeys. You've played the old game, I assume. You shake the barrel of monkeys up and then reaching in you grab one

---

[12] Nietzsche helps us see that the return to tragedy is a last gasp of a dying hope. Girard said that once tragedy is unmasked it can never relight the ancient flame.

and linked to it is another and another… this is a most philosophical game. The reason is that whenever you really grab ahold of a part you've already grabbed onto the whole, just as one monkey is linked to the whole barrel-full. This is because the whole *as a whole* is connected to every part. Thus this book unfolds with part linked to sometimes-unexpected-part. I recommend readers grab hold of the parts you understand and keep a tight grip when reading parts that you don't. Connections will come clear with time. The second theory is the theory of philosophical codes. Philosophers, as those who are attempting to grasp the whole, are always trying to express the whole to their students. As such, they can never say enough to do justice to their subject. (Indeed it is not uncommon for someone to ask us to please stop talking.) So instead, every philosopher, particularly ones who leave us completed written works with a beginning, middle, and end, must write in a sort of code. The goal of any philosophical reader then must be to decipher the code. This may not take place after a single reading. In fact, it constitutes the never easy but always pleasant work which no philosopher ever finishes in their effort to pay forward the debt he owes to those who've come before.

Novel arguments and answers to all sorts of questions can be found within and attentive readers will be well rewarded. The book you are about to read resembles nothing so much as the old story of the three blind men wandering in India who come across a strange animal. The first blind man grabs the long nose and feels it moving shouts, "Stand back everyone we've stumbled into an enormous snake!" The second meanwhile grasps a big ear and says, "Don't be daft, it is some sort of sail for a ship." The third blind man grabs a strong stout leg and says, "it is straight and tall. This is no animal we've come across, but a tree!" Meanwhile the apparently wise teller of the tale, the eternal sophist, tempts us with false wisdom that we are on the inside of it all. We know it is an elephant and are meant to reflect on all those things we don't know in our own lives in our blindness. We are, says the sophist, really rather like those blind men. . . It takes professor Downey in this book to point out that none of those four are right. Really all three of them, and the sophist, and even we the reader, are in the same place. And the truly wise person, suppressing a giggle, ought to be shouting "it's a joke!"

Colin Redemer
February 2022

PREFACE TO THE SECOND EDITION

"LIVING OUT OF BOOKS"

LOOKING back on *Serious Comedy* after some 20 years, I can see that it was written to be read by an audience of readers steeped in political philosophy, who both knew and took seriously the ancient quarrel Plato spoke of between "the poets and the philosophers," and were open to seeing the link between that quarrel and the tension between "Athens and Jerusalem," all of which must now be seen in light of the new quarrel between the "ancients and the moderns." The political philosopher Leo Strauss brought all these quarrels to our attention, and set the stage for the question animating this book. If we read in the Bible that Jesus wept but never laughed, and read in the dialogues of Plato that Socrates laughed but never wept, how are we to live our lives in the face of that reading? This is the question of a serious or unserious life in relation either tragic or comic writing, that Plato draws our attention to, again and again, in his most artful dialogues, the *Phaedrus*, the *Republic*, and the *Symposium*.

Although I believe *Serious Comedy* addresses that question thoroughly in light of the three quarrels animating political philosophy, twenty years on, I would ask this same question to an audience of Great Book readers and "romantics" of all sorts, to those who desire to be authentic and yet whose passions and readings guide their entire lives. If we live out of the books we read, are we taking our own lives seriously? Or must a serious life *not* live out of books if it is to be free of the charge of play-acting roles given to it by others? Rousseau, at the origins of Romanticism, puts this as a stark contrast between living within ourselves by authoring our own desires, or the alienation of living outside ourselves,

~~wherein our desires are authored through~~ the "eyes" of others. Or, as Shakespeare's character Hermia put it in *A Midsummer Night's Dream*, "O hell! To choose to love by another's eyes!" To overcome this hell, Rousseau educates his fictional pupil, Emile, by not allowing him to read any books before puberty, apart from the practical *Robinson Crusoe*, so that he will live fully within himself when young, before inevitably learning to live outside oneself with the onset of sexual desire. Our desires, this sort of romanticism argues, must first be "ours," before we can properly desire anything or anyone else. The very word "authentic" implies we should "author" ourselves and not be "authored" by others. Meanwhile, behind all this quest for authenticity, the number one book being ruled out is the Bible. There may well be something about the claim that God has authored the Bible that is the supreme affront to our Romantic desire to author ourselves. Any reader of the Great Books, especially the Bible, must therefore ask themselves this question: are they "living out of books?" The greatness of these books is that, in one way or the other, they all ask this question of their reader: "Are you living your own life or the life given to you by this or any other book?"

In the 19th century, Dostoevsky put this question explicitly before us when he had his narrator in *Notes From Underground* fiercely accuse his readers of the following: "[W]e have grown unaccustomed to life, we're all lame, each of us more or less. We've even grown so unaccustomed that at times we feel a sort of loathing for real "living life," and therefore cannot bear to be reminded of it. For we've reached a point where we regard real "living life" almost as labor, almost as service, and we all agree in ourselves that it's better from a book... Leave us to ourselves without a book, and we'll immediately get confused, lost—we won't know what to join, what to hold to, what to love and what to hate, what to respect and what to despise."

Socrates, Plato's main character in his dialogue the *Phaedrus,* makes a similar, though less accusatory, point. Only the soul and life of a philosopher is worth serious attention, and whatever one writes should only be taken as playful amusements rather than as serious "poems," "laws" or "speeches" (*Phaedrus* 277d-278e). In other words, those who live seriously *don't* take seriously anything written in a book; while those who *don't* live seriously, *do* take seriously what is written in books. Those who do not love wisdom live out of their books and writings, while those who love wisdom do not.

Are Plato and Dostoevsky, then, in agreement? To answer, we must look more closely at what they mean by those who "live out of books." For Plato, the books one might be tempted to live out of were the epic poems of Homer and classical Greek tragedy, that famously, as he says, "educated all of Greece" (*Rep.* 606e). For Dostoevsky, those books were the Romantic writings of the late 18th and early 19th centuries that trafficked in everything "noble" and "lofty." What those "books" both have in common, in the words of the Underground Man, is that they tell us what "to love and what to hate, what to respect and what to despise." We live out of these books because when it comes to love or passion, we seem to live lives of fundamental imitation, and who and what we imitate are the characters and plots we encounter in our written, filmed, or sung "poetry."

As Socrates puts it in the *Ion,* the subject matter of poetry in the widest sense is not just the top to bottom structure of our world, but the models of what we are to love and hate in that world—a world which, inevitably because of those loves and hates, is also one of war. Socrates states:

> "Does not Homer speak of the same themes which all other poets handle? Is not war his great argument? and does he not speak of human society and of intercourse of men, good and bad, skilled and unskilled, and of the gods conversing with one another and with mankind, and about what happens in heaven and in the world below, and the generations of gods and heroes? Are not these the themes of which Homer sings?" (*Ion* 531 c-d).

What Socrates and the Underground Man will not let us forget is that the life we live out of poetry is a life lived through imitation of a world given to us by some other human poet, and that our desire elicited by that poetry is no more our "own" than that poetic world is the "real" world. How, in other words, can we take our own life seriously when we are trained to seriousness through the writings of someone else, the poet, while that poet, in turn, learns his or her seriousness through other poets. Poetry seems to take from us both our desire and reality itself, and enslave us to the desires and world fashioned by others. Like those chained down in the famous Allegory of the Cave, the one thing we cannot see amidst all the projecting shadows is our natural selves. What one *can* see is the apparent world made for us by the artificial images of the poets.

The Underground Man wants his desires back, while Socrates wants back the reality of nature, a nature free from the artificial chains of the poetic caves lit only by fire. Socrates appears to get his wish. The poetic worlds of Plato's dialogues are not to be taken seriously, they are playful and comic, because the poet appears on stage, as it were, and points behind the audience to the real world in which they are all living. If they turn their heads, and see themselves in their poetic chains, they just might possibly climb out of the cave. That is where the life of philosophy lives, in the serious life offstage of asking what virtue truly is, rather than living out onstage the virtuous lives scripted by the poets (cf. *Apology* 38a).

This serious life of inquiry and philosophy offstage and free from books, however, does not seem possible for the Underground Man. Every desire he has, especially the desire to be free from the desire of others, comes to him from his books. All his accusations against his readers redound back to him as the writer. He may want to take his life seriously, but he has presumably read the comedic dialogues of Plato, and all he has gained of self-knowledge is both a superiority to those who have none, and contempt for himself as one whose self-knowledge only leads to digging himself deeper underground. There seems to be no way out for him because there is one Book, unknown to Socrates, but now haunting the Underground Man and his readers, that they cannot let go of, as much as they might try. It is the serious comedy we call the Bible, because it is only living out of *this* book, and this book alone, that will allow this child of the Romantic Enlightenment to take his life seriously.

To see why Socrates can take his life seriously free of books, and why the Underground Man, representative of our modern selves, cannot, we need to read something written by someone who partakes of both, even while explaining the chasm that stands between them. St. Augustine, like the Underground Man, writes in his *Confessions* about his early life in which he was not only educated by Virgil in the same way that Greeks were educated by Homer, but he was also taught what to desire and, concomitantly, what to hate. For, as Socrates in the *Ion* reminds us, the great "argument" of poetry is war. In the case of Virgil, that great argument is the war between Carthage and Rome, but that war gets its start because a rivalry between the gods leads to Desire itself, Cupid, taking the form of Aeneas' young son, climbing onto Dido's lap, and shooting the dart of love for Aeneas into her heart. Dido is now doomed, as are Rome and Carthage, to be eternally locked into a passionate rivalry with the object of her desire. For what does Dido truly love: Aeneas himself, or the god who is hidden within his son? The shame and wrath of Dido is that she somehow knows she is in love with a fiction and a lie, and that the real Aeneas who sails away from Carthage is as much hated as rival as he seemed to be loved when he arrived.

Augustine writes of his past how he too, like Aeneas, arrived at Carthage, and yet, like Dido, promptly fell in love with Love itself: "I was not yet in love, but I was in love with love, and from the very depth of my need hated myself for not more keenly feeling the need. I sought some object to love, since I was thus in love with loving, and I hated security and a life with no snares for my feet" (*Conf.* Bk III.i, Sheed trans.). The god of love, hidden within the story of Dido, just as it was hidden within Aeneas' son, is what elicits Augustine's desire, but since desire deludes itself into thinking it wants something other than its own wanting, it casts about for an object. Once he finds an actual "object", however, all that love turns into the war and conflict of "jealousy, and suspicions and fears, and tempers and quarrels." Again, like Dido, his love turns to hatred and the war within mirrors war without. Desire begats rivalry, and wanting your own wanting drives out whatever you thought you wanted in the first place.

Augustine, in writing of his past, describes for his readers how he was "living out of books," and how his particular book, *The Aeneid*, worked upon him the way tragic theatre works in general.

> "Why is it that men enjoy feeling sad at the sight of tragedy and suffering on the stage although they would be most unhappy if they had to endure the same fate themselves? Yet they watch the plays because they hope to be made to feel sad, and the feeling of sorrow is what they enjoy. What miserable delirium this is….This shows that sorrow and tears can be enjoyable. Of course, everyone wants to be happy; but even if no one likes being sad, is there just one exception that, because we enjoy pitying others, we welcome their misfortunes, without which we could not pity them? If so, it is because friendly feelings well up in us like the waters of a spring. But what course do these waters follow? Where do they flow? Why do they trickle away to join that stream of boiling pitch, that hideous flood of lust? (*Conf.* Bk III.ii Pine-Coffin trans.)

Why indeed? Augustine is asking us why, when we think we are most alive and living for love, we reveal we are only living out of a book, and not living our own life at all. We are speaking lines given to us by a poet, just as Juliet recognizes that Romeo kisses "by th' book," and we realize Romeo has just displaced Rosalind for Juliet. The shame is that the war of the Capulets and Montagues will continue in spite of, as well as because of that love, and all will eventually be "punish'd." Living out of books couples love with hate, models with rivals, and the flush of desire with the blush of shame.

Dante makes explicit what "living out of books" is, in his interview with Paolo and Francesca, caught up forever in the flames of their adulterous passion because they read and imitated the adulterous love of Lancelot for Guinevere:

> On a day for dalliance we read the rhyme
> of Lancelot, how love had mastered him
> We were alone with innocence and dim time.
>
> Pause after pause, that high old story drew
> Our eyes together while we blushed and paled;

But it was one soft passage overthrew

Our caution and our hearts. For when we read
how her fond smile was kissed by such a lover,
he who is one with me alive and dead

Breathed on my lips the tremor of his kiss.
That book, and he who wrote it, was a pander.
That day we read no further.

Dante, *Inferno,* Canto V, 123-135 (Ciardi trans.)

They "read no further" because they now became in life what before what they had merely read in a book. But inevitably the wrath,
shame, and violence of their own version of "falling in love with
love," return. They are slain and so now remain living their "life"
locked together by that "pander" of a book, that, along with Lancelot and Guinevere, forever lock them together in a deathless life of
lust that is not even their own. In that most intimate moment that
joins our lives with that of another, we find that our desire, our
words, and our "love" is not our own, but is rather the imitation
of words given to us out of a book. Nevertheless we desperately
want them to be our own, for those lives to be our lives, and the
fruit of that struggle is shame, rivalry, jealousy and death.

Augustine's *Confessions* might well be seen as a confession of
precisely this. As much as we fight against it and are ashamed of it,
our lives and loves will always "be out of books." To be "in love
with love" is to "live out of a book," so initially his life seems a
mere recapitulation of the tragic seriousness of Virgil's journey
away from Carthage and the lusts of Dido, and towards his hidden
destiny in Italy. The life he lives out of this story becomes, in his
own eyes, however, more and more ridiculous. He is merely play-
acting, and like the Underground Man he knows it and grows more
angry with himself. Nevertheless, as the story continues to unfold,
the true book he is truly living "out of" becomes more and more
explicit, just as the part he must play in that book becomes his
defining question.

The book Augustine discovers he is happily, rather than
shamefully, plotting his life after is the serious comedy of the Bible,
and not the serious tragedy of the *Aeneid.* Rather than externally

moving from Carthage to Italy, Augustine is internally moving from one tree and garden, to another tree and garden. For the journey of the Bible is the movement *from* the Garden of Eden wherein all of humanity eats the fruit of the "tree of the knowledge of good and evil," but it is also is a movement *toward* the Garden of Gethsemane and the beginning of all humanity's access to the obediential fruit on the tree of the cross. In the same way, Augustine's confession is a movement from eating stolen pears in a garden of his youth, to him falling down before a fig tree in a garden outside of Milan.

Eating the stolen pears was not the result of his own desire, but was instead a sort of corporate desire of "friendship unfriendly" wherein he would be "ashamed to be ashamed" not to do the same as everyone else. "Someone cries "Come on, let's do it"—and we would be ashamed to be ashamed! (*Conf.* II.ix, Sheed trans.) Just as there is no speech recorded when Eve gives the fruit to Adam to eat, and hence no reason to eat other than mere imitation; so also is the direct result of that imitation recorded only after Adam and not Eve eats. Then, *both* their eyes are opened, and the shame of that imitation is revealed in their nakedness (Gen. 3:7).

In the same way, Augustine's eyes are opened only after he eats the pears at the urging of his "friends"—but opened to what? What should he do now? Should he try to "really" live his own life, free from the friends, free from the books, that all say "come on, let's go do it?" Unfortunately, he cannot. He is not free. Instead, he immediately proceeds to the "hissing cauldron of lust" that is Carthage, wherein he slavishly imitates and recapitulates Dido, just as he has just slavishly recapitulated Adam. He cannot live his own life, he is enchained to books and lives that he has not chosen for himself; and he, along with all of humanity, is chained to and will inevitably repeat Adam and Eve's lives in the first book of the Bible.

How, then, is Augustine to break the chain of living out of books? The only way, he discovers, is by reading a book! In a garden in Milan, at the climax of his struggle to be free, wherein the chains only seem tighter and stronger as he hears stories within stories told of those who have broken free, he throws himself down at the foot of a fig tree in complete despair, flooding the ground with the tears of pity for no one but himself and his unlived life. He then hears the singing voice of a small child: *"Tolle lege"*, "Take and read." And he knows what it means! He must read the book that will give him back his life in the only way he can have it: through a book. The book in this case was Paul's "Letter to the Romans", but the words he reads are the plot of all readers of the book of the Bible as a whole: "Not in revelry and drunkenness, not in lewdness and lust, not in strife and envy. But put on the Lord Jesus Christ, and make no provision for the flesh, to *fulfill its* lusts" (NKJV Rom. 13:13-4). When he comes to the end of that sentence, he now knows. He must, and he now can, live his life out of *this* book, and this book alone, and "put on" the *persona* or mask of its main character, the Lord Jesus Christ. He must, in other words, live his life out of this book, because in this book alone is one free from the lust, rivalries, jealousies and conflicts that flow from living out of all other books.

Why this should be so comes not from the reader and the reader's life, for as much as we try to (and this attempt goes back to Adam) we cannot author our own lives. There is another Author, however, and it is only by living in complete and happy imitation of the world He has "authored," along with this one book He has also authored, that we can live in a world that is not one of shame, rivalry, lust, and violence. The lives we live in the "book" of nature can now be taken seriously because we have been rescued by the one book that has the same author, the serious comedy of the Bible. It is serious because it concerns our true lives, free from being scripted by anyone else other than the source of our reality and nature, but it is a comedy, because it has the happy ending of giving us back that serious life out of the death of bondage and decay.

Plato's comic dialogues remind us that we cannot take our writing seriously, but the price we pay for that recollection is that our serious life is not particularly our own, and we must resign ourselves to learn the philosophical "art of dying" to our strange existence that gives our particular birth or death no more importance in the face of the eternal ideas or eternal problems than does a particular leaf on a larger tree. The joke of the character Socrates is that he is of no particular importance, no more than the poetic cave of Athens that he dwells in and yet put him to death thinking that it was important. There are just fires, caves, and the sun, and the question why there are both, cannot be answered—they both just are. The natural real world, and the poetic apparent world, are forever side by side, and so even the serious life can only be described as something "written in the soul" because writing will never go away as long as we are alive, and that writing along with all the books we find it in will always undermine the seriousness of our particular life.

Unless, of course, there is something written in a book that *can* be taken seriously. For Augustine and the Underground Man, and for us, their readers, that claim is out there. How we respond to that claim, one way or the other, makes our particular lives what they are, and makes reading and the possibility of living out of books an entirely different matter than in Plato's day. Augustine can happily and shamelessly "take and read" and live his life out of a book as the only way to take his own life seriously. And what one who happily lives out of that book can also see, is what the Underground Man refuses to see. Everything that the Underground Man has narrated to us in his appallingly shameful episode with the prostitute is, in spite of himself, only an attempt to relive the plot of God in rescuing the scarlet woman from her harlotries with other "books" than this one. If the Underground Man could admit that "he can't be good", rather than accusing the "they" who won't let him be good, then he too, like Augustine, could be freed from the shame of the "friendship unfriendly" that prevents him from living his own life. Then he too, along with Augustine, could happily live his own life out of the one book and its Author that he has been unhappily living in all along.

The entire Romantic tradition, one might say, has been the attempt to free oneself *from* the comic Author of the Bible and free oneself *for* a serious life authored by one's own autonomous and creative self. Dostoevsky's Underground Man is rubbing our noses, as it were, in the failure of that attempt, while reminding us why we, unlike Socrates, cannot help but make it. Socrates knew that no writing, much less authorship, can be taken seriously, and that the creativity and the desires elicited by the poet are nothing in the face of the desire to know uncreated nature that, unlike oneself, never dies nor is ever born.

Yet something has happened between the Underground Man and Socrates, and that is the claim that a God has created that nature, and that we can know this because He has also created a poem, Scripture, in which that Poet is its main character, thereby making that poem a comedy that nevertheless asks to be taken seriously. That seriousness is as serious as the claim that this Author came back from the dead, thereby raising the possibility that the reader might also. The individual life and death of a reader would thus be something to take as seriously as the philosophical quest for the knowledge of nature. In the face of that claim, a philosopher must now either affirm it or deny it, but in that affirmation or denial you are willy-nilly a part of that Book, Poem, or Story, because of your response to the possibility of Who may have authored it. You can no longer be a mere reader; this Book reads you and renders your passions here on out either happy or unhappy in relation to it.

This Book, because it is a comedy that brings both audience and poet out upon the same stage, eclipses the serious life of the philosopher, because the most serious question is now what we do on that stage. To deny its Author is to make ourselves our own authors, to author our own desires, and to not live out of any other books other than our own—particularly not that Book! The comical hysteria of Dostoevsky's Underground Man thus mirrors the frustration of discovering that all our self-creative authentic lives cannot be taken seriously, because we know who their author is (i.e. ourselves), and yet we in turn are something entirely authored by everybody else, starting with that Author whom we reject. All our lives are in fact comedies because the poet always breaks the fourth wall and sooner or later reveals him or herself. And what is revealed is a poet who lives out of comedies written by other outed poets. The more conscious we are of this, the less seriously we can take ourselves–yet we still crave to be taken seriously.

Amidst all this frustrated fury of the unfulfilling self-consciousness of our book-haunted world, all Augustine and Dostoevsky (not to mention Kierkegaard and others) attempt to do in writing their own books, is to help us recollect the one Book that is entirely different than all others, including their own. Willy nilly, all of us now live our lives out of books. Which book it is, however, makes all the difference.

With this reissue of my own little book, then, I am only trying to remind us how we might live our lives out of that other Book, and do so by becoming better readers of it. The most unique contribution it makes to ongoing scholarship is to bring out a typological reading of Scripture that is as responsive as possible to the questions set before us by political philosophy. If we ask the questions raised by Plato and Aristotle regarding poetry and the poets, we can best see the unique answer, and structure of that answer, that Scripture provides. The Bible is a comic poem, because its author or poet is also its main character, and Dante's own comedy is but a pale shadow and imitation, envious or not, of the Biblical poem that transformed his world and ours. Because of that Poem, modern political philosophy can never be the same, and all its great exponents who are also poetic writers, such as Machiavelli, Rousseau, Hegel, and Nietzsche, cannot help but obsess over the distinction between tragedy and comedy. In the following pages I have tried to track the source of that obsession, finding its playful source in Plato and Aristotle, and its more serious and oft times angry continuation in the moderns. At the center of it all, however, is that surprising, exhilarating or offensive claim, we see at the heart of Aquinas' answer to the first question of the *Summa*, "Whether, beside philosophy, any further doctrine is required?" His answer, the answer that leads to the happy marriage of Sacred Doctrine to its now humble handmaiden, Philosophy, is entirely based upon the claim that "The author of Holy Writ is God." If that claim is true, then the Bible is a most serious comedy indeed.

Patrick Downey
February 2022

I: INTRODUCTION

"I divine," he said, "that you're considering whether we'll admit tragedy and comedy into the city or not."
"Perhaps," I said, "and perhaps something still more than this."

—Plato, *Republic*, 394d

THE LAST thing the world needs is another book on the difference between comedy and tragedy. A theory of genres that sorts and categorizes various works of literature, bending a little here and accounting for an exception there, is of little interest to me or, I expect, to most readers. Instead, what I am interested in are certain fundamental questions about the way things are and how we should live, questions that usually find their home under the rubric of philosophy or theology. In pursuing these questions, however, I discovered that the issue of comedy and tragedy, in either their opposition or complementarity, would keep appearing again and again. Why is that? Why is it that Plato kicked the tragic poets out of his city in speech? Why is it that he spoke of an ancient quarrel between the poets and philosophers? Why is it that seriousness and playfulness are paired as ways of living a life just as tragedy and comedy are paired as ways of writing a story? Questions like these turned out to be crucial in following the subtleties and ironies of Plato's philosophical writings. Yet when I turned to more modern thinkers such as Hegel, Kierkegaard, and Nietzsche, "comedy" and "tragedy" became, if anything, even more pronounced in their use to explain what these writers were up to. What is it about the dramatic paradigms of stage and audience, with happy or sad endings and laughter or tears, that provided these thinkers with a central image to understand themselves and their undertakings as both philosophers and poets of their own works?

What follows is an attempt to answer some of those questions. Yet, because my interest is not in comedy and tragedy *per se* but rather the philosophical and theological questions that find themselves intimately attached to these terms, what follows is a sort of tracking, if you will, of the trajectory of certain pivotal questions through the Western philosophical and theological tradition. Starting with Plato's "quarrel between the philosophers and poets," certain questions keep coming up in our philosophical tradition that revolve around the tension between living life and writing about it, between the unmade and unfinished project that is our life and the finished and rounded off artifice of writing and reading a narrative, dialogue, treatise or poem. From Plato's *Phaedrus* we get this tension as that between "life" and "writing;" but lives can be playful or serious, just as writings can be either comic or tragic; so Plato's other dialogues will refine this tension in its various permutations and implications.

In our own day, however, the major writing with a claim to be taken seriously is the Bible. Following upon Plato's questions, the philosophical questions it poses for us are twofold. First and foremost is whether the life of faith in the God of the Bible or the life of the philosopher is the right or best way to live. As one influential philosopher puts it, "Whether the Bible or philosophy is right is of course the only question that ultimately matters." The centrality of the Bible in the West has raised anew for us the quarrel between the philosophers and the poets, and yet it also forces our attention on the role of the poet in a way profoundly different than Plato's quarrel with the tragedians. This comes out in the question of whether the Bible should be read as a comedy or a tragedy. If the Bible is indeed a comedy, as I will argue it is, then it may stand in an entirely different relation to the life of the philosopher than what Plato calls the "lie" of the tragic poets. In addition, if this most influential of books is a comedy rather than the more politically influential tragedies of Plato and Aristotle's day, then something profoundly different may have been wrought in our own political scene that must be understood if we are to understand how we differ from the world of the past.

For this reason, just as we must pursue the question of "poets or philosophers," and the "Bible or philosophy," so too must we pursue the "quarrel between the ancients and moderns" if we are to understand ourselves in our often polemical relation to both philosophy *and* the Bible. Not only was one of major founders of modernity a writer of comedies (Machiavelli), but what he deliberately rejected in turning toward the new was the older comedies of Plato and the Bible that spoke of "cities that never were" in a fairytale like fashion. Instead of these romantic comedies, what was needed was the hard-boiled technique of the comic poet applied to everyday life, bringing about through manipulation and deceit what was usually only achieved in the poet's fiction.

"Modernity," however, proved a ferocious business, with an ever renewed need to build upon the death of the old. Before long the "old man" proved to be modernity itself, so the later moderns sought to understand their destructive and critical habits in light of tragedy rather than comedy, for in this way the self-consuming criticism of modern comedy might afford a seriousness lacking in its deliberately youthful self. Modernity "come of age," so to speak, considers itself a "tragic philosophy" because it cannot return to an ancient understanding of philosophy or the Bible without transforming or reinventing both by putting them up on the stage of its own self-conscious artifice.

The crucial question facing late-modernity remains whether or not it can truly take itself seriously, so all the attempts to regain a second naïveté or "re-enchant" the world revolve around the question of taking seriously its own tragedy. Yet because modernity is a quarrel or a question with the ancients rather than a resolution or answer, the possibility still remains of siding with the comedy of the Bible and Plato rather than succumbing to the ferocious comedy of the moderns. If this is to be a live option, however, it requires us to distinguish again between life and writing, and ask whether one can indeed live a serious life while writing comically, as seems to be the case in Plato; or, in the case of the

Christian faith, actually live one's life in terms of the serious comedy of the Bible. The questions remain open for us; the point of this investigation is merely to focus these questions a bit by tracking why comedy and tragedy reappear again and again in accounting for why and what we must decide between.

Nevertheless, this investigation is not without some claims of its own. As already mentioned, one of its burdens will be to argue that the Bible is indeed a comedy rather than a tragedy. To give this claim its proper significance, however, we must start with the claim that Plato's dialogues are self-consciously written as comedies, and this is to be expected from a serious philosopher. Part and parcel of Plato's comedies, moreover, is an account of tragedy; a comic account, if you will, that is comic precisely in its exposure of the "lie" that tragedy must keep hidden if it is to retain the political power it has traditionally wielded. The argument of Plato, seconded by Aristotle, is that tragic narrative functions as a mimetic scapegoat essential to founding and maintaining a political unity in the midst of private individual desires and fears. Tragedy accomplishes this feat as long as it obscures its artificial character, which is to say, it must divert us from the presence of the inevitable tragic poet. Comedy, on the other hand, puts its poet front and center, thereby revealing its artifice and raising the philosophical question of nature by way of contrast. The "nature" revealed through this process, however, is the very need to be lied to we find in tragedy, so the "outing" of the tragic poet is much more the "outing" of the tragic audience as the violent heart of human politics. Exposure, however, is no cure, and Plato's comedies are no more capable of curing the political problem than are tragedies; but there does remain the private consolation of a theoretical life lived pursuing knowledge of the nature covered over in tragedy.

When it comes to the Bible, the claims I make here are at once more radical and more traditional than my arguments about Plato. What makes comedy what it is, is the revealed artifice of the poet. If the Bible is to be a comedy, then, we should find front and center the poet whose revelation makes it a comedy. In modern higher criticism, these poets are the various communities, interests, or cultures that expressed themselves in this collection of writings.

All of these poets, however, are hidden and require the trained technique of the critic to expose them and bring them to light. Such a Bible is a tragedy requiring the modern critical comedy to bring its deceptions to light. Such a reading, I will argue, must read against the grain of the text, for it brings to bear the heterogeneous method of critical analysis that must remake for itself the only object that can be known in this way. To know is to make, so the de facto poets here are the critics; and whatever tragic text remains is undermined by the comic technique used to arrive at it.

What this method leaves out is the manifest comedy of the Bible itself, a comedy that from first to last announces the making of its creative poet who is both main character in the plot and ultimate author responsible for its writing. Until we get to the New Testament, whatever human authors lie behind the text are (with a few exceptions) completely obscured in the light of the main character who is the divine poet of everything. When in the Gospels this character in his role as divine creative logos and human is described four different times and ways by named human authors, the "story" of the Author as plot allows various different "tellings" with no harm to its comic theme. Nevertheless, tragedy is still present, for an overall theme tied in with the "deep" and "sea" is an attempt to reveal the lie found at the heart of human politics that hides us from each other even as it allows us to live in relative peace. The Bible will both reveal and use this "lie" until the end of all things and the beginning of the new, wherein the "sea" will be no more. The scapegoat function of tragedy is here center stage with a scapegoated God, but the scapegoat who reveals the ignorance of his accusers is also the comic poet who reveals the ignorance of his own characters of the very plot of which they are a part.

To read this Bible as do modern critics, is to replace one sort of comedy (the unique and specific comedy of the Bible with its unique and specific claims about its comic poet) with another (the more generic comedy of modernity with its human-all-too-human authors). Nevertheless, this possibility of counter-reading the Bible seems to have been opened up by the Bible itself. For what we have in the Bible is the first truly effective political comedy, and this fact seems to have inspired poets to write comically with tragic political aspirations. Dante, I will argue, was the start of this, but its full flowering in Machiavelli and his political heirs led to the comic and critical turn of mind inherited from the early Enlightenment. What was hid in tragedy is revealed on the political stage of political theater, and technique itself will manage the now manifest violence and selfishness of human desires with a Prospero-like "invisible hand" bringing all alike to a happy end.

That the political and critical methods and techniques of modernity are comic will be argued, but what may need little argument is that they are comic in quite another sense. For all the devices and desires of modernity in its quest after power and protection, the joke is that all of us must die, violently or not, keeping nothing of what we have gained. Cesere Borgia, prime exemplar and model for Machiavelli's new technique, *would* have succeeded had he not gotten sick and died at just the wrong time. Descartes' method will prove its worth by a true test, allowing us to live forever! Modern comedy proves a universal solvent, dissolving even its own claims when its own tools are inevitably turned against itself.

How does one escape this reflexive movement of comedy that inevitably laughs at the past that it puts up on stage, even while finding itself laughed at when that past turns out to be only a stage within a stage of the present? Perhaps there is some final audience that can take itself seriously and bring to a halt the modern comic history that devours the old even as it waits to be devoured in turn. Such, I think, is the attempt of Hegel in his tragic theater of the Absolute. If destruction and violence within comedy can only be mock beatings and boastful ignorance, putting them on stage and watching them from without in their entirety should transform them into a serious "speculative Good Friday" and "Golgotha of absolute Spirit" that retains all the gravity of the historical Good Friday while submitting to no other poet than the audience itself. In other words, since death renders all the endeavors of the early Enlightenment comic and ridiculous, Hegel must provide a serious resurrection to this otherwise merely comic Calvary, and this resurrection is a corporate absolute that in tragic fashion provides a unity by putting violence on stage and leaving behind a stilled and unified audience of spectators. Unfortunately, Hegel is no tragic poet. As a philosopher he cannot help but tell us what he is doing, and tragedy seems only to work if it happens behind our backs. Can the Spirit take seriously what it has made, without forgetting or lying to itself that it is always a Georg, Johann, or Friedrich who is in fact doing that making?

Such, I think, is the discovery of Nietzsche. Lying, self-deception, and forgetfulness are essential to taking oneself seriously à la Hegel, but how can this happen when one's clever individual self has found this out and so cannot do the very thing it must? Nietzsche's first work, *The Birth of Tragedy*, sees this problem even as it seeks to re-do Hegel in Schopenhauerian style, but the later Nietzsche sees more clearly that the entire attempt is a head-on competition with the Christian God to create a comedy that one could take with tragic seriousness. Probity demanded that an individual who does not seek to forget or annihilate himself in his demands for created meaning must take on the prerogatives of a creator-god in direct rivalry with the creator God of the Bible. Hence Nietzsche's "Anti-Christ," who is at the same time "Dionysus," the god of both comedy *and* tragedy. Nietzsche's "eternal recurrence of the same" is his attempt to become the individual god who is not subject to the ridicule of the self-loathing corporate audience of "last-men" who cannot take themselves seriously unless they forget they had individual selves to begin with. Attaining a tragic vision and a true "tragic philosophy" is no easy thing in a modern world of unceasing and unbridled laughter. Can we ever "pronounce holy" this laughter and playfulness and believe ourselves? Such are the problems we are left with if we stay on the road of the moderns and can no longer consider turning back.

In Kierkegaard, however, we have another situation. As a self-styled modern Socrates, Kierkegaard provokes us to recollect both the serious life of the philosopher and the serious comedy of the Bible. By reintroducing the distinction between "life" and "writing" in terms of the comic and tragic, Kierkegaard's writings function as Plato's philosophical comedies—only now a serious existence or life must reckon with the presence of the comic writing of the Bible and the paradoxical challenge that presents to a serious life. Like Nietzsche, Kierkegaard sees the tragic and comic situation inherited from Hegel and the moderns; unlike him, Kierkegaard would bring back to mind that we are not gods but mortals and so remind us of the human predicament of death and limitation embodied in a serious life that cannot fully express itself in anything written. By reminding us of what is the sole prerogative of a creator God rather than us mortals, Kierkegaard also reminds us of the scandalous claim of the Bible that can only be taken seriously if God is indeed its poet and that God has also lived and died among us in a history of his own, rather than our, making.

By the end of this trajectory, three options seem to present themselves. We can lead serious lives but not take writing or what we make seriously—as seems to be the case in the ancient philosophers. Or we can live our lives in the writing and "writer" of the Bible—lives of faith in the poet of the serious comedy of the Bible. Or we can attempt to live in the writings of our own making, taking *them* seriously, while struggling to take seriously our lives apart from them. Such is the comic predicament of modernity. Because of the Bible we inherit the expectation that we can live serious lives in writing; but because we no longer believe in the one divine poet who could make this possible, the joke is always on us for we can no longer take our own comedies seriously.

Perhaps if we were in the position of Plato and Aristotle surrounded by the lies of tragic writing, the situation would be different. But lying and scapegoating have been revealed for what they are along with the outing of the tragic poet and audience. Plato himself, along with the sustained polemic against idolatry in the Bible, would seem to be responsible for this. Can we return, then, to the serious life of a pagan philosopher when the "writing" essential to who we are in the West is no longer a tragedy but a comedy? Perhaps something has unalterably happened to us. Perhaps we are characters in a comedy not of our own making, where we must either get in on the joke or be forever the butt of it. However hard we may laugh or secretly take ourselves seriously, the suspicion remains that the laughter is no longer on our side.

In what follows, these questions and claims will be taken up in three parts. Part I begins with a chapter on Aristotle's account of tragic catharsis in terms of pity and fear. Using Aristotle's *Poetics* is a rather standard starting point for this sort of investigation, but the substance of my argument goes against the grain of the dominant understanding of tragic catharsis and retroactively opens us up to the full political impact of Plato's account of comic and tragic writing. The next three chapters try to tease out this account, primarily through a reading of Plato's major poetic dialogues, the *Republic*, *Phaedrus*, and *Symposium*, along with a few other dialogues. The sixth chapter on "Violence and the Tragic Scapegoat" brings together the account of tragedy in Plato and Aristotle and relates it to the more contemporary arguments of René Girard, Northrop Frye, and Paul Ricoeuer. Chapters 7 and 8 give a relatively summary account of tragedy and comedy, so if the reader is looking for the closest thing to a generic definition, these would be the chapters to begin with.

Part II has to do with the Bible. Chapter 9 argues that there is such a thing, that it has a unity, and that that unity can be understood as either comic or tragic. Help in this endeavor comes from Erich Auerbach and Hans Frei, particularly in their understanding of narrative and figural interpretation. The issue of higher criticism is dealt with here, along with the question of history and "realism" in narrative. The tenth chapter begins with Meir Sternberg's account in his *Poetics of the Biblical Narrative* of how the Bible demands to be read, an account I consider the best of its kind. Nevertheless, Sternberg's "Bible" is only the Hebrew scriptures, so his arguments must be both extended and criticized if they are to apply to the Christian Old and New Testaments. Chapter 11 is a reading of the Bible as a comedy; a reading that is at once figural and argumentative. This reading seeks to bring out the narrative argument implicit in the Bible's type and antitype structure; an argument that elucidates the nature and need for tragedy even as it subordinates and finally does away with that need in an overarching comedy. This reading is perhaps most idiosyncratically "my own" in this entire book, but if there is any "proof" in the pudding of my arguments throughout, it will be found in this chapter. The twelfth and final chapter of Part II is the most strictly theological, for it looks at Aquinas' arguments at the beginning of his *Summa* on the relation between the scripture and philosophy. This chapter deals most explicitly with the question of the "Bible or philosophy" by seeing how Aquinas related these two; but it is also a back-handed confirmation that this question has been properly asked in terms of comic and tragic writing, for it corresponds to the way Aquinas sets up the question at the beginning of his own inquiries. In addition, Aquinas' understanding of the four senses of Scripture in terms of God's authorship of the Bible confirms the central role of the poet in making the Bible a comedy.

Part III tracks comedy and tragedy as it is discussed in modern thought. The first chapter of this part, Chapter 13, argues a transition from the more "ancient" understanding of comedy and tragedy, to what I call the "technological comedy of modernity," by looking at Dante and Machiavelli. Dante points from Aquinas to the moderns, while Machiavelli effects this transition in his *Prince* and *Mandragola*. The fourteenth chapter, on Hegel's "tragic theater," deals with the culmination of a reaction against early modern comedy, wherein Hegel retells and reinvents modernity and Christianity in terms of tragedy. Chapter 15 deals with Nietzsche and his attempt to reincorporate comedy into his tragic philosophy, while the sixteenth and final chapter concludes with Kierkegaard and his return to both the insights of Plato on writing and the comedy of the Bible. All three of these thinkers, Hegel, Nietzsche, and Kierkegaard, use the categories of comedy and tragedy manifestly and in the forefront of their writings, so quite often we find definitions of tragedy and comedy that either diverge or converge with my own. Overall, however, the positions one can take up relative to each narrative form remains constant, and the patterns elucidated by Plato confirm once again the claim that there is very little found in later philosophy that is not a footnote to a position or character found in one of his dialogues. Although this book could very well have started with Kierkegaard, Hegel, or Nietzsche, such a beginning would obscure the fact that a philosophical account of tragedy arose from an ex-tragic poet in a world of thriving tragic poetry—even while it ends in a world filled with little tragic poetry and plenty of "tragic" philosophers. Somewhere along the way, a serious comedy seems to have changed everything.

PART ONE:
COMEDY AND TRAGEDY AT THE
FOUNDATION OF POLITICAL
PHILOSOPHY

II: TRAGEDY AND THE TRUTH: ARISTOTLE'S ACCOUNT OF CATHARSIS

Indeed, [the Greeks] did everything to counteract the elementary effect of images that might arouse fear and pity—for they did not want fear and pity. Giving all honor—and the highest honors—to Aristotle, he certainly did not hit the nail, much less on the head, when he discussed the ultimate end of Greek tragedy.

—Friedrich Nietzsche, *The Gay Science*

AT A climactic moment in *Oedipus the King* the truth finally dawns upon Jocosta, the wife of Oedipus, who he really is. "Oh wretched man, may you never come to know who you are!" With this, she runs off stage and hangs herself. If Aristotle is right, we as the audience should "shudder with fear" and "feel pity" as these events unroll before us. So we do. But does that mean we come to know who we are? Or are those very shudderings and feelings the means by which we fulfill for ourselves Jocosta's dying wish? If that is the case, the very art and power of tragedy would be a "lie," a lie that allows us to live with ourselves and live with each other in the face of the truth seen by Jocosta. Catharsis, the cleansing or purging that Aristotle claims results from this fear and pity, would thus also be a sort of blinding, the psychological equivalent in the audience of the dramatic events on stage. Nevertheless, there is blindness and there is blindness. Teiresias is blind because he sees what others do not, but why is Oedipus blind at the end of the plot? He is blind because he blinds himself. At the very moment he sees the truth, he demonstrates the worth of that vision by plucking his eyes out. He, too, it would seem, agrees with Jocosta. Is tragedy itself any different? When we the audience see the tragic "vision" on

15

stage, is that the last word? Or is that vision only the penultimate
step to our own self-blinding? Perhaps the vision of tragedy keeps
as much distance from us, the viewers, as the stage does from the
audience, and that is exactly how we want it. In other words, the
juxtaposition of vision with blindness in tragedy raises the very
question of its relation to truth, and the answer is not at all obvious.

For Aristotle, at least, the answer lies in his understanding of
the emotions of fear and pity. These two emotions, central to his
definition of tragedy, are also widely misunderstood.

> A tragedy, then, is the imitation of an action that is
> serious and also, as having magnitude, complete in it-
> self; in language with pleasurable accessories, each
> kind brought in separately in the parts of the work; in
> a dramatic, not in a narrative form; with accidents
> arousing pity and fear, wherewith to accomplish its
> catharsis of such emotions.[1]

Provisionally, let us understand catharsis as Aristotle describes it
his *Politics*: "a feeling of relief accompanied by pleasure."[2] What
tragedy essentially relieves us of, then, would seem to be fear and
pity. But what do these terms mean? To answer that we need to
turn to both Aristotle's *Rhetoric* and the *Poetics*, for it is in these two
works, rather than the *Nicomachean Ethics*, that we get an answer.
To see why, consider the following prescription of Aristotle found
in the *Poetics*.

> Since, then, the construction of the finest tragedy
> should be not simple but   complex, and at the
> same time imitative of fearful and pitiable happenings
> (that being the special character of this kind of po-
> etry), it is clear first of all that (1) neither should vir-
> tuous men appear undergoing a change from good to
> bad fortune, for that is not fearful, nor pitiable either,
> but morally repugnant; nor (2) the wicked from bad
> fortune to good—that is the most untragic form of
> all, it has none of the qualities that one wants: it is

---

[1] Aristotle, *Poetics,* trans. Bywater, 49b24-28.

[2] Aristotle, *Poetics*, 1342a14, trans. Carnes Lord.

TRAGEDY AND THE TRUTH

productive neither of ordinary sympathy [philan-
thropy] nor of pity or fear—nor again (3) the really
wicked man changing from good fortune to bad, for
that kind of structure will excite sympathy but neither
pity nor fear, since the one (pity) is directed toward
the man who does not deserve his misfortune and the
other (fear) toward the one who is like the rest of
mankind—what is left is the man who falls between
these extremes. Such is a man who is neither a para-
gon of virtue and justice nor undergoes the change to
misfortune through any real badness or wickedness
but because of some mistake [*hamartia*].[3]

Whatever this "mean" between the two extremes is that allows for
a "mistake" but not an act of viciousness, it does not seem to be
the virtuous mean described in the *Ethics*. In fact, the fear and pity
essential to tragedy seem to be limited to people who are deliberately excluded from the discussion in the *Ethics* because their virtues, whether intellectual or practical, would preclude the key
move in tragedy toward bad fortune.[4] The mean of tragic poetry
excludes by definition both the virtuous man and the philosopher,
and the reason seems to be that the emotions of fear and pity are
feelings of the average man, undisciplined by either virtue or contemplation.[5]

---

[3] Aristotle, *Poetics*, 52b32-53a10.

[4] "For what must essentially happen in the length of time it takes any plot
to develop is a shift that takes place "either probably or necessarily from
bad to good fortune or from good to bad— that is an acceptable norm
of length." Aristotle, *Poetics* 51a13-15. If plot is the "soul" of narrative,
then there are essentially only two plots, comedy and tragedy.

[5] "...argument....cannot exhort ordinary men to do good and noble
deeds, for it is the nature of these men to obey not a sense of shame but
fear." Aristotle, *Ethics* 1179b10. The problems that arise from overlooking the distinction between the "few" truly just individuals and philosophers who are the focus of the *Ethics* and the "many" average folk
motivated by ordinary fear and pity who are the focus of both the *Poetics*
and the *Rhetoric* can be seen in Martha Nussbaum's evident dismay at the
implications of this key section from the *Poetics*:

> One passage remains to be discussed. It is one of the most
> difficult sentences in the *Poetics*, and poses problems for
> any consistent interpretation of the treatise. In *Poetics* 13,
> discussing the types of complex plot that will cause pity

Consider Aristotle's account of the emotion of fear in his *Rhetoric*. "Let fear, then, be a kind of pain or disturbance resulting from the imagination of impending danger, either destructive or painful."[6] This emotion seems common enough, even to the uncommon man. But when Aristotle immediately adds that "not all evils are feared, such as that someone should become unjust or ignorant," it becomes immediately apparent what sort of fear he is excluding—namely, the defining fears of the virtuous man and the philosopher. This, of course, raises the question of whether fear of becoming unjust and ignorant by itself drives out serious preoccupation with these other fears—a question that when asked in connection with the comments on the mean of fear and pity above, leads to the conclusion that these two emotions of tragedy do indeed exclude the desires and aversions cultivated by the life of virtue and contemplation.

Why then are these two emotions central to tragedy? Let us look further in the *Rhetoric*. What people commonly fear is "injustice backed by power," "insulted virtue with power," "rivals for

and fear, Aristotle remarks: "first, it is clear that good men [*epiekeis andras*] should not be shown changing from good to bad fortune— for this is not pitiable or fearful, but disgusting [*miaron*]."... Aristotle's statement is peculiar indeed to anyone who has closely studied all of his statements about the requirements pity and fear and about the goodness of the hero.... The main thing is to realize that whatever we say about this sentence, unless we take one of these escape routes or think of a new one, the sentence is inconsistent with a great deal of evidence in the *Poetics* and other works....(Martha C. Nussbaum, "Tragedy and Self-sufficiency: Plato and Aristotle on Fear and Pity, *Essays on Aristotle's Poetics,* ed. Amélie Oksenberg Rorty (Princeton: Princeton University Press, 1992) 278-9).

The problem here is not with the text, I think, but rather with Nussbaum and others' positive valuation of fear and pity that skews Aristotle's entire argument. The exception in the *Rhetoric* of the fear of acting unjustly or being ignorant is all important in this regard.

[6] Aristotle, *The Art of Rhetoric,* trans. H.C. Lawson-Tancred (London: Penguin Books, 1991), 1382a.

advantages that both parties cannot simultaneously enjoy"; because "the generality of men tend to the bad," and "men, for the most part, do commit crimes when they can," and "there is permanent contention with such people."[7] "Fear," then, "makes men deliberative";[8] but this deliberation, however political, has little to do with practical wisdom or theoretical wisdom. It is the cleverness and cunning that resembles, but is not, the practical deliberation of the gentleman.[9] What we fear, then, is other people—precisely because the nature of their desires is sufficiently like our own to give us good reason to fear them. This account of fear is in full agreement with Glaucon's claim in the *Republic* that society is founded upon the fact that our fear of suffering injustice is stronger than our desire to commit injustice.[10] Stronger, but not by much.

The emotion of fear that makes men deliberative is also at the root of pity. For what we see in the *Rhetoric's* definition of pity is that it is an extension of the emotion of fear.

> Let pity then, be a certain pain occasioned by an apparently destructive evil or pain's occurring to one who does not deserve it, which the pitier might expect to suffer himself or that one of his own would, and this whenever it should seem near at hand. For it is clear that the man who is to have pity must think that he is such as to suffer something bad either in himself or in one of his friends.[11]

The key to pity is thus the deliberation that reckons what one might be likely to suffer himself, thereby making fear the operative emotion even in pity. As we see from the passage in the Poetics, the issue of injustice does not imply that the sufferer has the virtue of justice, it merely implies that someone else acts unjustly. Since there are so many that are unjust, such actions will be much more

---

[7] Aristotle, *Rhetoric*, 1382b.

[8] Aristotle, *Rhetoric*, 1383a.

[9] cf. Aristotle, *Ethics*, 1144a24ff.

[10] Aristotle, *Rhetoric*, 358e.

[11] Aristotle, *Rhetoric*, 1385b.

common than actions that are against those who truly are just. Consequently there is much to pity, especially in a world without justice. Pity must therefore be distinguished from the more distinctively Christian notion of compassion or even philanthropic sympathy, for neither of these emotions involve the interested quality of fear that joins one to the sufferer through calculation.[12]

"In general" then, "whatever men fear for themselves they pity when they happen to others."[13] Pity is therefore the emotion that compounds the immediate feeling of personal fear by extending it to others by means of calculation and imagination; the emotion wherein our own fear of suffering personal acts of injustice begins to fear injustice at large in the city or in the cosmos. This extension of our fears through pity leads us to question whether even the gods themselves are just, since so much of what we fear directly or indirectly through others seems to come from the "unjust" hands of fate.

> [F]or all painful and bitter things that are destructive
> are pitiable, and those that are annihilatory, and those

---

[12] One might add that Aristotle's notion of pity is different from the pity described by Rousseau, since for Rousseau pity is shared in common with animals and so does not involve foresight or calculation, but only the spontaneous fellow-feeling "that precedes... any kind of reflection." *Discourses on the Origin of Inequality from The Basic Writings of Rousseau*, trans. Donald Cress (Indianapolis: Hackett Publishing Company, 1987), 54. Thus when Rousseau relates the image of an imprisoned man witnessing a ferocious animal tearing a child from its mother's breast, the point he seeks to make is the very lack of self-interest involved in the pitying prisoner. He then goes on to relate this to the theater.

> Such is the pure movement of nature prior to all reflection. Such is the force of natural pity, which the most depraved mores still have difficulty destroying, since everyday one sees in our theaters someone affected and weeping at the ills of some unfortunate person, and who were he in the tyrant's place, would intensify the torments of his enemy still more.

This recognition of the ineffectuality of pity shows that however differently defined, he at least agrees with Aristotle that pity is *not* the bond that is capable of holding together society.

[13] Aristotle, *Rhetoric,* 1386a.

20

great evils for which chance is responsible. The painful and destructive things are death, bodily tortures and injuries, old age, disease and shortage of food, and the evils for which chance is responsible are having few or no friends (hence it is also pitiable to be torn from friends and comrades), ugliness, weakness, deformity and the occurrence of an ill from a source from which a good thing was expected . . . These and the like are the things about which men feel pity.[14]

Pity and fear are therefore the emotions appropriate to our encounter with events in life that directly threaten our happiness, especially when that happiness is more of the "blessed" variety that depends upon the gifts of the gods.[15] When we see the gods take away the blessedness that they can also give, we feel unjustly dealt with and so find ourselves in a fearful universe.

Things now get complicated. Why should the tragic poet want to imitate or "re-present" what is not at all pleasant in its initial presentation? If fear and pity are emotions that flow from the frustration of our desire for happiness, why should we want to experience them again? In the case of the comic poet, his imitation makes sense. In imitating our unlimited desire for happiness, he makes a plot wherein desire is satisfied either through questions answered, complications unraveled, obstacles overcome, jokes understood or fools exposed. How then can a tragic poet please us? What he looks to is our frustration, to our fears and pities, and we have more than enough of that.

The answer can be seen in the process of tragic catharsis. The reason Aristotle must mention the emotions in the tragic audience in order to define tragedy is because of the bifurcation and stark contrast between the unhappy events on stage and the happy result in the audience. Unlike comedy wherein the pleasant movement toward good fortune is mirrored in the laughter and pleasure taken by the audience, in tragedy there is a marked contrast between the pain and horror on stage and pleasurable experience of the audi-

---

[14] Aristotle, *Rhetoric*, 1386a.

[15] Aristotle, *Nicomachean Ethics*, 1100a ff.

ence. In fact, this very division of pleasure and pain between audience and stage seems to be essential to tragedy. The tragic plot must therefore be constructed in such a way that it obtains this result. How is it the tragic poet does this? How does he effect this catharsis?

The clue to this mystery can be found in the description Aristotle gives of how we learn through imitation. In proving that all men take pleasure in works of imitation, he asks us to examine our own experience, wherein we find that "there are things which we see with pain so far as they themselves are concerned but whose images, even when executed in very great detail, we view with pleasure."[16] Examples he mentions are drawings of cadavers or unpleasant animals. Yet from these humble examples we see for ourselves the more exalted and mysterious transformation we experience in tragedy. Tragic catharsis is no more and no less than the presentation of mimetic images that cause us initially to fear and take pity, and yet finally cause us to lose, purge, or cast out those unpleasant and painful emotions because of the very pleasure we experience in seeing them as imitated rather than directly experienced. So while this transformation arouses little notice in ordinary instances, in the case of tragedy, the difference between the severity of the painful emotions and pleasure in having them provoked mimetically rather than directly is so great (and so important) that tragic catharsis has become one of the foundational mysteries at the heart of all civilization and religion. Let me elaborate on this.

To begin with, what we see on stage in a tragedy are events that if they happened in real life would not be fearful and pitiful, but rather out and out terrible. For as Aristotle says of Amasius in the *Rhetoric*, he did not weep when his son was taken off to be executed, but did weep when he found his friend begging, "for the latter was pitiable, the former terrible; and what is terrible is different from the pitiable and drives out pity . . . as men no longer pity when what is terrifying is near them."[17] It is not the characters in a

---

[16] Aristotle, *Poetics*, 48b11-13.

[17] Aristotle, *Rhetoric*, 1386a.

tragedy who experience fear and pity, but rather the audience who in their distance can fear and have pity on those events that would be simply terrible if directly experienced.

The first step in understanding tragedy is to see that the portrayed actions are in themselves terrible, as evidenced by the character's terror in undergoing them. Lest this seem obvious, it must be recalled that much of current commentary downplays this violence, bloodshed and general carnage. Even though these events usually happen offstage, they are nevertheless the central events in most tragic plots. This terror points out the difference and distance between the fear and pity generated in the audience and the emotions on stage. In fact, along with the social superiority of the characters, this distance is what allows for the transmutation of emotions that finally occurs through catharsis.

Why these terrible events occur is the question that leads us to the issue of *hamartia*, rendered either as "flaw" or "mistake." What we find in the famous argument of Else is that catharsis does not follow upon the action, but rather precedes it, as the intellectual argument we must give ourselves that allows us to exonerate the hero from culpability for his tragic deeds. According to this argument:

> "[C]atharsis" is a purification of whatever is "filthy" or "polluted" in the *pathos*, the tragic act . . . the "filthiness" inheres in a conscious intention to kill a person who is close kin (father, brother, etc.) An *unconscious* intention to do so, i.e., an intention to do so without being aware of the kinship—as Oedipus did not know that the old man he killed at the crossroads was his father—would therefore be "pure," *katharos*. But the purity must be established to our satisfaction. *Catharsis* would then be the process of proving that the act was pure in that sense.[18]

The problem with this account is that catharsis must precede the action, so to speak, in order to allow us to feel the appropriate fear and pity, which leaves us with fear and pity as the entire point of tragedy. This assumes that these emotions are good in and of

---

[18] Aristotle, *Poetics*, trans. notes by Gerald Else, 98.

themselves. The other problem is that the point of Aristotle's account of calling the hero's action a "mistake" instead of some sort of vicious act is that the hero is precisely not "virtuous" and so needs no exoneration. As we saw in the *Rhetoric*, the emotion of pity and fear is not dependent upon the character of the sufferer of injustice, but only upon the act itself. For all acts of injustice by definition involve unjust suffering; this is why the tragic hero cannot be a "just" person who suffers injustice. For then the attention would fall upon that one character's more personal and rare fears of acting unjust in kind, rather than the more common fears we all share of suffering injustice.

Hamartia, then, has more to do with the mistake or flaw in the hero that corresponds to the mistake or flaw in the political, sexual and religious world around us, a flaw that leads to our personal fear of suffering injustice, and our pity for others who actually do. The flaw of the hero is that he doesn't know his past, that he doesn't know that he is involved in irreconcilable tensions that must explode sooner or later and destroy him. His flaw is essentially ignorance of the deadly consequences of his deeds that inevitably flow from the interconnectedness and violence of the conflicts always surrounding one. The mistake, in other words, is to not know what the audience knows through watching those tragic events—that the world is a fearful and pitiable place.

Oedipus is thus Aristotle's prime example. Oedipus knows that there is a plague, but does not know that he is implicated in it. This ignorance is his flaw. Nevertheless, this ignorance leads him to his fall because he still insists on knowing and will not remain content in his ignorance. In spite of Jocosta's prayer, "may you never come to know who you are," Oedipus persists until he "sees" that he himself is the source of the plague. This terrible vision, however, cannot be borne, so Oedipus must both see and yet not see what he has come to know by tearing out his eyes.

The flaw of ignorance in the tragic character is therefore revealed in the process of the tragic fall, and what is revealed is the fearful universe the audience lives in wherein we both suffer from and yet are complicated in the injustice surrounding us. This knowledge, however, is not the final point of tragedy—for like Oedipus, it cannot be borne without blinding ourselves. The point of tragedy *is* blindness. Its goal is to somehow blind the audience, as a way of living with the knowledge that they themselves are the source of the plague in every city.

In addition to the first step of horrible events on stage, then, the second step in tragedy is the elicitation of the emotions of fear and pity in the audience when they come to know what Oedipus knows. The tragic plot "must be so structured, even without benefit of any visual effect, that the one who is hearing the events unroll shudders with fear and feels pity at what happens, which is what one would experience on hearing the plot of the *Oedipus*."[19] This shuddering comes from uncovering along with Oedipus the true source of all we suffer and fear—that we live in a world that is as unintelligible to us as we are to ourselves. What we discover is a sort of "inverse-insight" that is at the heart of all poetry—that things as a whole do not make sense even though we want and expect them to. Nevertheless, the distance between stage and audience in a tragedy allows us to fear and pity the results of this insight, rather than to suffer it directly through the direct experience of terrible events. In other words, the terrible events are imitated; and through this imitation we learn the violent, because irreconcilable, tensions at the heart of both the family and the polis.

Tragedy therefore "teaches" us the fundamental facts of the "war of all against all" at the heart of society that is later nonpoetically taught by the early modern political philosophers. What we fear and pity is what threatens to destroy us individually and collectively; for self-knowledge leads us to the knowledge that we are a part of that very whole that threatens us all alike. Violence is in the blood, which is why blood relations are central to tragedy; and yet blood must be shed to found and perpetuate a city, for loyalty to the city is in violent competition with loyalty to the blood of family.

---

[19] Aristotle, *Poetics*, 53b4-7.

The paralyzing effect this knowledge has upon the city is exemplified by the plague in Thebes. The plague is somehow a corporate event. Even though only certain individuals suffer from it, the fear of suffering it is felt by everyone and demands some sort of radical cure if the city is to survive and not degenerate into every man for himself. The progressive realization of Oedipus that he himself is the source of the plague, however, also implicates everyone else: for it is they who allowed him to rule because he cured the earlier plague of the Sphinx. When Oedipus learns the truth and proceeds to blind himself, his desire to be cast out from the city shows that Thebes too must now blind itself. And the way the Thebans blind themselves is by thinking that their plague has been cast out along with Oedipus. The fullness of tragic knowledge therefore involves the need to be lied to in order for this knowledge to be borne. To live with this knowledge it must be kept hidden. The paradox of tragedy is that at the height of revelation and clarity, the solution to what is seen involves covering over what is known by lying to oneself and then forgetting that fact. This is the truth behind Nietzsche's argument that "life" involves deception and forgetting.[20]

This pattern can also be seen in the *Oresteia* of Aeschylus. In the *Eumenides* we see Orestes called to account before the jurors of Athens for the murder of his mother. With the Furies as the prosecutor and Apollo the defense attorney, what we see being tried is the cycle of blood revenge that has no end because every act of justice is itself a further injustice. Nevertheless, if this cycle *is* stopped, that too will lead to injustice; for the fear that destroys the city also seems to be the foundation of its very laws.

[The Furies]
Here is overthrow of all

---

[20] "All acting requires forgetting, as not only light but also darkness is required for life by all organisms...without forgetting it is quite impossible to *live* at all. Or to say it more simply yet: *there is a degree of insomnia, of rumination, of historical sense which injures every living thing and finally destroys it, be it a man, a people, or a culture.*" Friedrich Nietzsche, *On the Advantage and Disadvantage of History for Life,* trans. Peter Preuss (Indianapolis, Hackett Publishing Company, 1980), 10.

the young laws, if the claim
of this matricide shall stand
good, his crime be sustained.
Should this be, every man will find a way
to act at his own caprice;

. . .

There are times when fear is good.
It must keep its watchful place
at the heart's controls. There is
    advantage
in the wisdom won from pain.
Should the city, should the man
rear a heart that nowhere goes
in fear, how shall such a one
any more respect the right?[21]

The knowledge of the destructiveness of fear in spite of its necessity is the problem posed by the knowledge uncovered in this tragic trilogy.

Athena, who represents the knowledge of the Athenian audience, must solve this problem with a monumental lie and a massive diversion. Although she agrees that the Athenians must not "cast fear utterly from [their] city" and that "just terrors" lead to righteousness, she also knows that fear and terror destroy the city and law as evidenced in the case of Orestes. [22] Her solution is therefore to exonerate Orestes with the patent lie that man is not born of woman but rather the seed of man alone, vouchsafed by her own divine experience, and then to placate the Furies by using their fury, now turned against outsiders, as the deeply buried heart of justice in the city. The goal of Athena is thus to turn the "spirit of war that turns their battle fury against themselves" into an outward fury against foreigners who commit "injustice" against the city as a whole. The lie of Athena is to placate the furies of interfamilial and civic fear by redirecting and distracting them outward against a common foe whom one can now freely hate.

This my prayer: Civil War

---

[21] Aeschylus, *Eumenides* trans. Richard Lattimore (Chicago: The University of Chicago Press), 1947, 490-525.

[22] Aeschylus, *Eumenides*, 693-700.

fattening on men's ruin shall
not thunder in our city. Let
not the dry dust that drinks
the black blood of citizens
through passion for revenge
and bloodshed for bloodshed
be given our state to prey upon.
Let them render grace for grace.
Let love be their common will;
let them hate with single heart.
Much wrong in the world thereby is healed.[23]

Just as Oedipus must blind himself and blind the city to what they have come to know in order to allow them to live with that knowledge, so too here Athena must lie to the city and distract it with an outward and unifying hatred in order to allow it to continue to live with the destructive knowledge revealed in the pitiable plight of Orestes.

The emotions of fear and pity that result from the knowledge gained through tragic action must therefore be somehow mitigated and covered over again if they are not to destroy the precarious relationship between family and city and citizen to citizen. For fear and pity are dissolving and fragmenting emotions that divide citizen from citizen and lead only to loyalty to oneself. In the case of Oedipus, the covering over of these emotions is accomplished by playing the role of corporate scapegoat who bears upon himself the burden of the plague, in order that by leaving, he can take it from within the heart of the city. The city is thus made one again by purging it of alienation through having only one common alien—the scapegoat. Likewise, Athens must purge itself of internal hatred and strife by having a common hatred of its enemies that allows healing by only shedding the blood of others. Both of these are ultimately no more effective in hiding tragic knowledge than is Oedipus' own blinding, but in the short term, they are the only means that allow one to go on living in peace.

The third and final step of tragedy, tragic catharsis, is thus the true goal of every tragedy. For tragic catharsis is the transmutation

---

[23] Aeschylus, *Eumenides*, 975-87.

that takes place in the audience when the knowledge it gains through the tragic action of the painful emotions of fear and pity is covered over by the accompanying pleasure of learning this through mimesis. What the audience leaves with is pleasure rather than pain, because the mimetic whole of the tragic plot itself functions as the scapegoat, bearing upon its shoulders alone the painful knowledge no longer experienced by the audience. This is why the tragic fall into misfortune and knowledge is desirable and pleasant—because we end up experiencing the mimetic pleasure of a complete and finished plot in spite of its painful content. In other words, we lie to ourselves by distracting ourselves from the painful knowledge tragedy reveals by the very pleasure we get by knowing it mimetically rather than "truly." Mimetic pleasure is how we blind ourselves to tragic knowledge; it is how we make for ourselves a common foe—the tragic plot—in order to hold in common the pleasure we feel as the audience. The more painful the knowledge, the more acute and satisfying the pleasure involved in its mimetic beholding. Yet the greater the pleasure, the more surely we forget the pain that preceded it and disassociate ourselves from its source.

This transition from the painful emotions elicited by tragedy to the pleasurable result is why I must disagree with recent accounts of tragedy that view fear and pity as ends in themselves. That my own emphasis upon the mysterious transition of catharsis is the more traditional one can be seen in a footnote of Else's translation of the *Poetics*, whose arguments have been greatly responsible for reversing this position.

> The usual interpretations of "catharsis" are far too numerous to list here, but they all, or almost all, have in common a focus on the pity and fear which are aroused *in the spectator*. These are to be somehow either "purified" (reduced to beneficent order and proportion) or "purged" (expelled from his emotional system) by the play. Such interpretations are not sustained so much by anything in the *Poetics* itself as by a passage in the *Politics*, 7, 134b38, which speaks of a musical "catharsis."[24]

---

[24] Aristotle, *Poetics*, 98.

The contemporary alternative to this traditional view is to assume that the experience of fear and pity are ends in themselves and somehow intrinsically desirable.[25] In the case of Martha Nussbaum, fear and pity are not only desirable but educational.

> For Aristotle, however, these emotions can be genuine sources of understanding, showing the spectator possibilities that are there for good people. Therefore what more succinct summary of his difference from Plato could there be, than to speak of a "getting clear through pity and fear"? . . . [T]he *katharsis* reference picks up the discussion of the pleasure of learning in Chapter 4. It is not hard to see how it does so, if we stop hearing *katharsis* as a weird and mysterious technical term, and start hearing it in its ordinary sense. For "accomplishing through pity and fear a clearing-up concerning experiences of the pitiable and fearful kind" would be easy to connect with Aristotle's general discussion of getting clear and learning in chapter 4.[26]

The problem with this account is that it overlooks Aristotle's claim that both pity and fear are *painful* emotions. The mystery and goal of catharsis must lie in how these painful emotions are transformed into "the *pleasure* from pity and fear through representation."[27] It is the mimesis (representation) of fear and pity, rather than the emotions themselves, that is the point of tragedy; and that

---

[25] The mistake here is to understand pity as Christian compassion that unites in brotherly love rather than divides through self-preserving calculation. Such an understanding, however, is not surprising in the light of the move we find in Machiavelli's admiring description of the slaying of Remirro de Orca (*The Prince,* Chapter VII) that left the populace "satisfied and stupefied." For Cesere Borgia here used the effects of catharsis to unify the city directly, rather than indirectly, achieving them through tragic catharsis. Politics *as* theater has displaced the theater. This move also coincides with the disappearance of any central or important tragedies in modernity.

[26] Nussbaum, "Tragedy and Self-sufficiency", 281-2.

[27] Aristotle, *Poetics,* 53b12, Nussbaum's translation, quoted from page 282 in the above "Tragedy and Self-sufficiency" (emphasis added).

point, as I have argued, is *not* finally educational. Indeed, just the opposite.

Instead, fear is what must be overcome, for fear (except the fear of becoming unjust or ignorant) is what divides and leads to violence in any community, and as such is a source of pain, even when felt at a distance in pity. Overcoming the pain of fear and pity, then, is the final step in tragedy and the true measure of a tragedy's success. For the greater the fear and pity one might feel from witnessing the events on stage, the greater the feeling of relief and pleasure when that pain disappears and is purged from the audience.

What then is the nature of this pleasure? Or alternatively, what is it the audience takes pleasure in? What it takes pleasure in is the feeling of unity, solidarity and wholeness that it experiences at the end of the play; even though it should be feeling the divisive fears and alienating pity that come from experiencing events that are at the heart of what renders and divides us from one another. It is the pleasure of no longer fearing injustice against oneself or another, of no longer fearing injustice from the gods or fate, of no longer looking over one's shoulder at one's neighbor or even closest family members as a source of treachery and betrayal. In other words, the emotions of fear and pity are the emotions that flow from our encounter with the limits of our desires; and whether limited by other's competing desires, or even our own, those limits must be overcome if we are to have the desire in common that makes of us a community. By seeing our worst personal fears imitated in tragedy, we feel our greatest communal needs satisfied by the resultant pleasure.

The shift from painful to pleasurable emotions in the face of fear or pity is therefore not educational precisely because when we say "this is so and so" to the mimesis of pitiable and fearful events, because of the uniquely horrible nature of those events, the pleasure we take in recognizing them as fearful and pitiable actually obscures what we have recognized. It is as much a knowing as a not-knowing, and the tragedy only works if we do not sift out one from the other. In one sense, then, it is indeed educational—in the sense

that Plato calls Homer the educator of the Greeks.[28] But what it
educates us into is the shadowy world of the cave that cannot discern knowledge from ignorance precisely because politically it cannot afford to. Nevertheless, it is out of that cave that both the rare
philosopher and truly virtuous gentleman must arise.

For when the audience of a tragedy finishes the circuit from
provoked fear and pity to the calm pleasure of fearless and pitiless
unity, what the tragic poet has accomplished is the creation (for
however short a time) of a context wherein the fear of acting unjustly rather than suffering injustice can take root for the first time.
This is why the emotions discussed in the *Rhetoric* and the *Poetics*
deliberately exclude virtue, for it is only insofar as those emotions
are purged that a political entity can arise that provides the background wherein citizens can desire justice for its own sake. In other
words, it is the creation of the appearance of justice through the
mimetic transformation of "showing" rank injustice that provides
the context wherein real justice can appear. Fearing to do injustice
more than suffering injustice is radically heterogeneous with the
fears and pities of tragedy; and yet it is from that soil that this virtuous fear must spring.

Aristotle's virtuous man is fundamentally political, but it is
not he, rather the tragic poet, who is responsible for creating and
preserving the "*polis*" in the first place.[29] The tragic poet, by means
of tragic catharsis, is the one who educates—and so concretely
founds—the city by creating the unifying "appearance of justice"

---

[28] Plato, *Republic,* 606e.

[29] At this point I should contrast Aristotle and Plato with the modern
account, where it is not the poet who founds the city, but rather technology itself, divorced from poetry, and therefore in no need to be hidden.
Whether it be the techniques of Machiavelli's young man who beats fem-
inine Fortuna (chapter 25 in *The Prince*), or Hobbes' "artificial man" and
leviathan of the social contract, modern political thought contrasts nature
with the technological means of founding society. The justification of
modern science because it benefits and aids the human lot that we find
in Bacon and Descartes goes along with this, for the overt founding function of technology as opposed to the covert function of tragedy needs a
defense. And modern philosophy has rushed in to fill the breach— a
breach, opened, however indirectly, by the political repercussions of the
comic, rather than tragic, nature of Christianity.

that is essential even to a band of robbers. When an intelligible whole is lacking even though we still need and desire it, the tragic poet imitates that lack by showing us the unintelligibilities that we rightly fear happening to ourselves and others; and in so doing provides a surrogate wholeness that allows us to live without a truly intelligible whole. Tragic catharsis is in this sense at the heart of both human politics and human religion.

Yet in order to draw this conclusion that tragic catharsis is at the heart of human politics and religion, we have to realize that we are going beyond what can actually be found in the *Poetics*. For what is not discussed by Aristotle that is nevertheless central to Greek tragedy is the role of the gods. In the words of Gerald Else, "Greek poetry was a representation of men *and gods*. One half of this world has disappeared from Aristotle's field of view."[30] This omission of the *Poetics* is, I suspect, deliberate, just as the missing virtue of piety in his *Ethics* may be deliberate. The reason for this would be that he is limiting himself to the perspective of the city and is prescinding from the question of the god or beast that can live without it.[31] In this light, we might say his discussion of the catharsis of fear and pity in the *Poetics* indirectly describes how one transforms beasts into citizens, while the *Nicomachean Ethics* ultimately leads up to the godlike life of *theoria* that is more self-sufficient than anything in the city. The weight of both works falls, however, between these two extremes.

If Aristotle were to discuss the divine element in tragedy directly, he would have to assume the position of the philosopher who fears not the gods but only his own ignorance. This would be in contrast with the fear of injustice appropriate to the gentleman, who even when rising above the common fears in the city, is still dependent upon the context, or whole, created by the tragic poet (if only for the sake of preserving his external goods that makes his life of virtue possible).[32] The theoretical life of the philosopher,

---

[30] Gerald Else, *Aristotle's Poetics: The Argument* (Cambridge: Harvard University Press, 1957), 474-75.

[31] Aristotle, *Politics*, 1253a28.

[32] Plato reiterates this in his description of the guardians as "philosophical dogs" who need either the poets or "noble liars" to tell them who their

however, raises the question of the whole directly, and that question puts him in competition with the gods *and* the poets. The philosopher must expose what the tragic poets hides: that it is the poet who creates both the gods and "fate" as sources of order and benevolence by telling us stories of their chaotic and conflicting desires and downright malevolence. But these are the questions Aristotle does *not* raise in the *Poetics*. To deal with them we must turn to his other writings, or better yet, turn to what are essentially the self-reflectively comic rather than tragic dialogues of Plato.

For as will come out in the following chapters, Plato and Aristotle, I believe, are in essential agreement about the nature of tragedy.[33] In the harshest possible terms, Plato and Aristotle agree that civilization is and must be founded upon a lie, and the result of an effective tragic plot is the creation of that lie. In gentler terms, tragic poets are the makers of a remedy for the ills of the city, but it is a remedy that is just as much a poison, for it does not cure but only covers over for a time the true nature of the disease. This *pharmakon* that both poisons and cures functions the same as the *pharmakos*, or scapegoat, as evidenced in Aristotle's favorite tragic character Oedipus. For Oedipus, who saved Thebes by solving the riddle of the Sphinx, had also already brought about the plague on

---

enemies are-- yet once told, are more loyal to that "knowledge" than to their own private desires. The poet is thus ultimately responsible for the context of all the practical virtues, which is why if the theoretical questions of the philosopher are not raised, the gentlemen's virtues can do no better than the truth of the stories he is told.

This dependence of the practical virtues on the lie of the poets is also the weakness of MacIntyre's argument in *After Virtue*, inasmuch as he attempts to ground the virtues in narrative without ever raising the philosophical question of the truth of those narratives. Without this question as to the truth of narrative in general, one's virtues stand or fall with the goodness of one's chosen narrative— a goodness that *eo ipso* cannot be evaluated. Nietzsche would have the last word here.

[33] Alexander Nehamas calls the assumption "nearly universal" that Aristotle's account of catharsis "constitutes his answer to Plato's charge against the poets," even while calling it into question in his own account of catharsis. "Pity and Fear in the *Rhetoric* and the *Poetics*" in *Essays on Aristotle's Poetics*, 305. I would also call this assumption into question, but on different grounds.

the city, by killing his father, the king of the city. The holy scape-goat who cures is also the cursed scapegoat who sickens. The back-drop to all this, however, is the plague itself, the plague of unjust desires hidden behind a mask of apparent just deeds. For that plague to be truly and finally cured, it would require something that is not a lie, for lying to oneself and others is precisely the nature of the problem. What it would require is the truth. Yet if I am right in my account of Aristotle's tragic catharsis, truth is not to be found here. If it is to be found at all then, perhaps it must be found in the plot largely ignored by Aristotle, but embraced by Plato—the comic plot. If we read Plato's dialogues as comedies, as I think he fully intends for us to do, what should become manifest is a fundamental agreement with Aristotle about the nature of tragic poetry, that simultaneously takes advantage of comic poetry as a way of placing poetry in general in its proper relation to philosophy and the search for truth.

III: PLATO'S *REPUBLIC* ON COMEDY AND TRAGEDY

We always picture Plato and Aristotle wearing long academic gowns, but they were ordinary decent people like anyone else, who enjoyed a laugh with their friends. And when they amused themselves by composing their Laws and Politics they did it for fun. It was the least philosophical and least serious part of their lives: the most philosophical part was living simply and without fuss. If they wrote about politics it was as if to lay down rules for a madhouse. And if they pretended to treat it as something really important it was because they knew that the madmen they were talking to believed themselves to be kings and emperors. They humored these beliefs in order to calm down their madness with as little harm as possible.

—Pascal, *Pensées*

FROM THE very beginning, Plato's life and thought have been wrapped up with tragic poetry. Tradition has it that the young Plato was an aspiring tragedian until the day he met with Socrates—whereupon he promptly went home and burned all his manuscripts.[1] This tradition of a youthful rejection of tragedy is reinforced by the arguments found in his *Republic* wherein Socrates speaks of an ancient quarrel between the philosophers and poets, a quarrel that leads to Socrates kicking out the tragic poets from the city he is creating in speech. Nevertheless, what must not be

---

[1] "Afterwards, when he was about to compete for the prize with a tragedy, he listened to Socrates in front of the theater of Dionysus, and then consigned his poems to the flames with the words:

'Come hither, O fire-god, Plato now has need of thee.'"
Diogenes Laertius, *Lives of Emminent Philosophers,* trans. R.D. Hicks (Cambridge, Mass.: Loeb Classical Library, Vol. 1), III-5.

forgotten is that the *Republic*, along with the other dialogues of Plato, are works of poetry—powerful poetry—so powerful that Nietzsche can describe Plato's dialogues as the life-raft after the shipwreck of high Athenian culture, whereupon all that is great survives, huddling together with Plato as its rescuing captain and guide.[2] Although Plato's dialogues are often read as a compendium of various metaphysical, epistemological and ethical arguments gussied up with dramatic dialogue to make it all go down easier, this approach is to sell Plato quite short. Whatever Plato's youthful aspiration may have been, what he accomplished in later life is the creation of a unique art form that self-referentially makes its own status as poetry one of its major themes. Not only are we to notice that when Socrates speaks harsh words about poetry, we are reading this in a poem; but even more so, we are to notice that when Plato includes characters who are comic and tragic poets, or speaks of the serious and playful writing of tragedy and comedy, both of these moves are juxtaposed to either the philosopher Socrates or a discussion of the unique speech and writing of the philosopher. In other words, Plato is not only writing brilliant poetry in his dialogues, he is also telling us what he is doing as he does so. But why is this? Is Plato just showing off? Is he showing us just how clever he is in the contemporary fashion of modern comedy that knowingly winks at the audience as it goes through the motions? Or is something of a more profound nature going on here?

I believe there is. For Plato, in his usual subtle and ironic fashion, is discussing poetic making in itself; and if we do not think

---

[2] "The Platonic dialogue was, as it were, the barge on which the shipwrecked ancient poetry saved herself with all her children: crowded into a narrow space and timidly submitting to the single pilot, Socrates, they now sailed into a new world, which never tired of looking at the fantastic spectacle of this procession. Indeed, Plato has given to all posterity the model of a new art form, the model of the *novel*- which may be described as an infinitely enhanced Aesopian fable, in which poetry holds the same rank in relation to dialectical philosophy as this same philosophy held for many centuries in relation to theology: namely, the rank of *ancilla*. This was the new position into which Plato, under the pressure of the demonic Socrates, forced poetry." Friedrich Nietzsche, *The Birth of Tragedy*, trans. Walter Kaufman (New York: Vintage Books, 1967), 90-91.

through and get a handle on what Plato has to say on poetic making we will fail to understand what he has to say about politics, ethics, and the philosopher's relation to the city. In other words, my argument is that Plato doesn't just happen to talk about poetry, he *must* discuss poetry if he is to at all adequately deal with all his other major themes. Moreover, if Plato is to discuss poetry, he must speak of it in terms of its two major forms—comedy and tragedy. If we do not pay attention to the tragic form of poetry, we will not understand the appearances and incipient violence that are at the heart of the city. Likewise, if we do not think through comic poetry we will not understand the human passions that motivate the philosopher even while putting him at odds with the city. In other words, comedy and tragedy as the two reciprocal poles of the poetic spectrum of narrative plots are essential to narrating the plot of the philosopher's encounter with the city and politics at large. Socrates, founder of political rather than natural philosophy, is a character we read about in a story, and that same story has the city of Athens as its other major character. Even though one character, Athens, puts the other character, Socrates, to death, what is perhaps most interesting about this plot is that it is a comedy rather than a tragedy. Why it is a comedy rather than a tragedy may well tell us more about what a philosopher is than anything else, and yet why we expect it to be a tragedy may tell us more about ourselves and the city than we could know in any other way. What, then, does Plato have to say about comedy and tragedy?

To begin with, it is not so much what Plato says about comedy and tragedy that is illuminating, it is how he places them into juxtaposition with philosophy. In perhaps his three most literary dialogues, the *Symposium*, *Phaedrus*, and *Republic*, we see a recurring threefold pattern. At its most explicit, in the *Symposium* we see the philosopher Socrates, at the end of a night of drunken revelry, discussing with Agathon, a tragic poet, and Aristophanes, a comic poet, whether one who writes tragedies could not also write comedies, and vice versa. As the conversation proceeds, first the comic poet nods off, and then the tragic poet, until the philosopher alone is left, sober and awake, to begin the new day. Whatever we are to make of these three characters, much light can be shed on them if we relate them to the discussion of serious and playful writing discussed in the *Phaedrus*. For one of the questions this dialogues raises is whether a philosopher should ever write seriously, or whether he should, if he writes at all, write playfully. The seriousness of the tragic poet and the playfulness of comic poets comes to mind in this connection, but if there should be any doubt that philosophy, comedy, and tragedy are at play here, we can turn to the three waves of ridicule that Socrates rides out in Book V of the *Republic*. Each wave is a ridiculous requirement that Socrates claims is needed to found his city in speech, and yet each requirement will also correspond to the inner nature of comedy, tragedy, and philosophy respectively. If we put these three accounts together, what we should have is an in-depth discussion of comic and tragic poetry rivaling anything said in Aristotle's *Poetics*. Let us see if we can make good this claim.

Let us begin by considering Plato's non-"literary" commentary on writing found in his *Seventh Letter*.

> That is why any serious student of serious realities will shrink from making truth the helpless object of men's ill will by committing it to writing. In a word, the conclusion to be drawn is this; when one sees a written composition, whether it be on law by a legislator or on any other subject, one can be sure, if the writer is a serious man, that his book does not represent his most serious thoughts; they remain stored up in the noblest region of his personality. If he is really serious in what he has set down in writing 'then surely' not the gods but men 'have robbed him of his wits'.[3]

What is interesting for us in this quote is the initial light it sheds on Plato's evaluation of his own dialogues. As written, and as poems, none of his dialogues can seem to be taken seriously. This is particularly so in the *Republic* with its own peculiar take on the political foundations of law and legislating. How then are we to take

---

[3] Plato, "Seventh Letter" in *Phaedrus and the Seventh and Eighth Letters*, trans. Walter Hamilton (New York: Penguin Books, 1973), 344.

these writings? Playfully, it would seem. But is playfulness in writing the same thing as writing a comedy? And is serious writing the same thing as tragic poetry? Or to push these questions further, is serious writing comic, with the joke on the writer? Would the only way of not making a joke of oneself be to write playfully in order to guard the serious, if not tragic nature, of one's own life apart from writing?

In order to fully answer these questions, we will have to get a fix on the difference between life and writing that is discussed in the *Phaedrus*, but in the context of the *Republic* we will just need to focus on the distinction between a maker and the thing made. For whatever writing is, it is something made, and for everything made there is the life of the maker apart from the making. In the largest sense, this process of making is called *poesis*, and the thing made is called a poem, just as the maker is called a poet. In a more specialized sense, the knowledge of how to make this thing or that is called *techne*, and it is the *techne* or knowledge of a comic poet or tragic poet that allows them to make, and make well, their comedies and tragedies. The philosopher, however, is the one who causes a problem here, for the question he or she raises is whether there is any particular *techne* or knowledge specific to a philosopher that leads to making something. If so, then a philosopher is ultimately a poet; if not, what are we to make of whatever a philosopher might happen to make? This question is what ultimately lies behind the "old quarrel between philosophy and poetry" Socrates mentions in Book X of the *Republic*.[4] But if we are see the full nature of that quarrel we must see its roots in the discussion of *techne* along with its connection to violence and injustice found in Book I.

The major question that comes up in the *Republic* is that of justice, and while it is indirectly asked of the elder Cephalus, it falls to his son, Polemarchus, to give the first attempt at a sustained answer to Socrates' queries. Under the prodding of Socrates' questions, his answer that "justice is to help one's friends and harm one's enemies" leads to the further conclusion that one must know

---

[4] Plato, *The Republic*, trans. Allan Bloom (New York: Basic Books Inc., 1968), 607b.

how to do so, and such knowledge must be some sort of *techne* that knows how to do either hurt or harm. However, since the art of knowing how to do someone good also involves the knowledge of how to do someone harm, what must be added to this knowledge is when to do what. That knowledge, it seems, is not of any one *techne*, but rather of some overarching knowledge that administers all those various arts to the end or whole that is in question, namely, justice. Justice, in other words, seems to be some sort of architectonic science[5] that is qualitatively different from any one

---

[5] Perhaps this might be a good point to bring out why I am in fundamental disagreement with Nussbaum's arguments on this point even though they cover much of the same ground as my own. At bottom, Nussbaum has fundamentally misunderstood what Plato means by reason because she takes it as a sort of *techne*, even though Plato's ironic use of *techne* as his analogy serves more to distinguish what the philosopher is up to rather than to exemplify it. The architectonic science Plato is aiming at in the *Republic* and other places is thus as qualitatively distinct from *techne* as the "user's art" is from any particular art he may put to use (*Rep* 601d). In fact, it is so distinct, and the distinction is so crucial, that the full force of Plato's ironic presentation of it seems to be that it is only the philosopher who lives his life dedicated to the architectonic form of knowing who can even discern its difference from *techne*. This is why Aristotle will later call this form of knowing *theoria* and thereby connect it up with the description of the "vision" of the ideas described in the *Phaedrus* and *Symposium*. When Nussbaum thus describes Plato's way of knowing in the following, she is essentially projecting modern forms of thought as power and control onto Plato, and thereby missing the distinctive alternative Plato offers to the oftentimes pernicious results that flow from our own modern confusion between theoretical and technical knowing:

> First I shall argue that the Platonic conception of the life of reason, including its emphasis upon stable and highly abstract objects, is itself a direct continuation of an aspiration to rational self-sufficiency through the 'trapping' and 'binding' of unreliable features of the world that is repeatedly dramatized in pre-Platonic texts. Plato's own images for his philosophical endeavor reveal that he himself saw this continuity of aim. But at the same time I shall argue that this ongoing picture of reason is not, in the Greek tradition, the only salient model of reason in its relation to luck. What both *metis* and Platonic self-sufficiency omit is a picture of excellence that is shown to us in the traditional image of *arete* as plant: a kind of human worth that is inseparable and social, a rationality whose nature it is not to attempt to seize, hold, trap, and control, in whose values

techne that it might use, since while an individual craftsman may know how to do something, he doesn't thereby know whether it *should* or *shouldn't* be done. The knowledge of justice is thus akin to the theoretical knowledge of the whole desired by philosophers that will discussed in Book V, inasmuch as it is out of a unified whole that disparate parts gain their meaning and use. In the case of the city, those parts are the various *technai* that must be ordered to truly benefit or protect the whole city, rather than one single part of it to the detriment of another. Polemarchus thus recognizes under the impact of Socrates' questioning that knowledge is needed to act justly in helping one's friends and hurting one's enemies; but Socrates' questions also turn him away from knowledge as *techne* toward some sort of knowledge akin to what Aristotle calls *theoria*. But whether justice can be known in such a way comes into sharp question when Thrasymachus takes over the discussion.

Thrasymachus proposes the bold claim that justice is the advantage of the stronger, a claim that, if true, means that the city is never just as a whole, but is rather "just" only insofar as one part lords it over other parts for its own advantage. Thrasymachus' violent verbal assault mirrors his claim that violence is essential to

---

openness, receptivity, and wonder play an important part. (Martha C. Nussbaum, *The Fragility of Goodness: Luck and Ethics in Greek Tragedy and Philosophy* (Cambridge: Cambridge University Press, 1986), 19).

This entire discussion seems to be entirely misguided, especially in it separation of "wonder," "openness," and "receptivity" from their correlation to the "nature" as object pursued by the philosopher. Rather than nature being something that results from the rational "activity" of making "concepts" found in modern philosophy, nature is precisely the unmade and unnamable that can only be known passively by the philosopher as exemplified in the female image of the midwife. In linking these passive components to tragedy, Nussbaum overlooks a most important component of all her examples of that knowing: that they take place entirely in the man-made and artificial context of theater that is about as organic and "plant-like" as the inner workings of a camera. But that, after all, is the point of both tragedy and photography, to make you forget how you are seeing something in the light of what is seen. Plato, however, cannot forget, because he is more loyal to nature than human artifice since nature cannot be "controlled," "seized," "held," or "trapped" —but only understood.

justice; and that violence, whether through force or fraud, is what makes all the other parts of the city conform to another part as if to a whole. Yet in spite of this onslaught, Socrates asks Thrasymachus a question that reveals a major fissure in Thrasymachus' argument for justice: does that stronger part knows by some sort of *techne* what its advantage truly is? In other words, Socrates asks the question that is key to both the pursuit of advantage and, it would seem, happiness; since what is *truly* to your advantage will also *truly* make you happy. Questions about true advantage are therefore questions as to the whole of life, and so Thrasymachus finds himself in a bind in answering. If he claims his rulers are knowers of their own advantage, then that claim to knowledge undermines the partiality of that advantage; yet if he gives up their claim to knowing their own advantage, his rulers certainly have nothing to learn from Thrasymachus the sophist, and can't even be said to have a particular advantage that is attainable.[6] Thrasymachus, being the man that he is, opts for the first option and

---

[6] David Roochnik in his *The Tragedy of Reason: Toward a Platonic Conception of Logos* (New York: Routledge, Chapman and Hall, Inc., 1990), calls this entire line of argument the "techne-analogy" and explains it as follows:

> Socrates believes that what is good about techne is that it is knowledge. Someone, like Thrasymachus, who affirms the goodness of a techne, has made an important value judgment, namely that knowledge is good. Socrates proceeds to use this judgment against him. Thrasymachus had proposed a version of relativism, which if true (and taken to its most extreme conclusion), would render all values relative. But by declaring techne to be good, as Thrasymachus implicitly does, he elevates techne to the status of non relatively good. This judgment about techne thus contradicts his own relativism. Socrates forces Thrasymachus to acknowledge this contradiction and eventually defeats him. (189)

In the next paragraph, however, Roochnik explains why this is only using techne as an analogy for a nontechnical or architectonic mode of knowledge that I have called *theoria*.

> It should be noted that to say that techne is good does not imply that it is the best or the exclusive mode of knowledge. In fact... it implies something quite different. Since... it is value-neutral, techne is incapable of evaluating itself. If techne is judged good, then the knowledge that is

so plays in Socrates' court until he is bested and blushes in defeat. But the second option is not left wholly unclaimed, for Cleitophon in a pregnant one-line appearance asks whether justice isn't merely the *appearance* of advantage, "what the stronger believes to be his advantage."[7]

Thrasymachus, however, refuses to take up this option, and so is tamed by Socrates because he submits to the imperatives of knowing what *is* rather than mere appearance. So even though Thrasymachus himself drops this suggestion by Cleitophon, the *Republic* does not. In fact, it becomes the mainstay of its argument about the city—that existing cities have only the appearance of justice, and so if justice is to ever be known it must be seen in a city that has never existed and probably never will. The key to the argument of the *Republic*, especially in the light of Glaucon's more

---

> responsible for making this judgment cannot itself be a techne. Techne is thus located in an in-between position. It is superior to ignorance, but some other, higher, mode of knowledge, namely knowledge of what is good, is needed to evaluate it. Therefore, the fact that Socrates believes that techne is good does not necessarily imply he has a techne. He may have a "non-technical" form of knowledge that is capable of judging the goodness of techne. (189)

Roochnik, for his part, does not feel free to call this non-technical knowledge *theoria* and architectonic after Aristotle, because he has to set up what I think is a too-strong contrast between the *logos* of Aristotle and that of Plato. One of the weaknesses of this view is his consequent inability to relate the three classes of the *Republic* with Aristotle's three ways of knowing, and more importantly and crucially for his thesis and mine, his need to argue that Plato is fundamentally tragic in spite of his criticisms of tragedy and explicit use of comic techniques. In other words, if Roochnik is right that the Platonic dialogues constitute the tragedy of *logos*, then why are they so funny? Nevertheless Roochnik is definitely onto something, but by failing to distinguish between life and writing, his arguments which may apply well to life will always be undetermined by the writings themselves and the ironic smile of their hero, Socrates. To read *logos* as the hero, however, as he does, is to read an unwritten story that however important can only be found in the life of the reader. So even if the philosophical life may in fact prove quite tragic, as written of by Plato, it is decidedly comic.

[7] Plato, *Republic*, 40b.

subtle restatement of Thrasymachus' position in Book II, seems to be that what passes for the justice in the city *is* the advantage of the stronger; that one part of the city writes the laws for its own advantage rather for than for all; and that this violence is present precisely because of the absence of any other knowledge than the individual *techne* of each part seeking to acquire what—for this very reason—can only appear to be its advantage. Every city is thus either a timocracy, an oligarchy, a democracy, or a tyranny because it only appears to be just and only appears to be whole; what it truly is, is one part covertly at war with and taking advantage of other parts.

That justice is only an appearance is caused by the lack of theoretical knowledge on the part of the rulers. Put more positively, this lack also explains the need for the ruling part of the city to *appear* to represent the good of the whole, for without this appearance the city would collapse altogether into overt civil war where no part can gain any advantages at all. This positive aspect of appearance comes up in Socrates' description of the city as a "common unjust enterprise" similar to a gang of robbers or pirates who nonetheless must act "justly" to one another if their enterprise is to have any success whatsoever.[8] The appearance of justice in the city is thus neither completely just nor completely unjust, but rather something "in-between" that simultaneously gives reign to the violence of one part against another even as it also seeks to rein that violence in.[9] In the absence of a *true* knowledge of the whole, what cities must have, then, is the *appearance* of knowledge of the whole. And since the whole can only be known through some sort of theoretic vision, the appearance of a whole must be something known through *techne* as an imitation and substitute for that vision. Yet this *techne* that knows only how to make an artificial whole is at odds with itself because what it makes must appear to be the whole known prior to any making (a natural whole that includes within it the maker himself). In other words, the technical knowledge of the maker can't "know" itself without equivocating

---

[8] Plato, *Republic,* 351c.

[9] Plato, *Republic,* 479c.

between these two senses of "knowing," and yet this equivocation is essential to the appearance rather than the reality of justice being a success.

This equivocation is similar to the one found in writing we will see Socrates discuss in the *Phaedrus* , insofar as writing can't "speak" for itself, and yet in that very equivocation and inability finds the key to its success. We may therefore consider the appearance of justice in the city as something *written*, especially when wrought by *techne* in lieu of a true knowledge of the whole. It is for this reason both the *Phaedrus* and Plato's *Seventh Letter* will include laws and legislators together with those who might take their writing seriously, for the regime of this and every other regime are constituted by those who write its laws and what they write. If those laws or the lawgiver take their creation with full seriousness, then they are also taking seriously the city itself with all its appearances of justice rather than truth. Their lives are therefore ridiculous rather than serious because they themselves are the creators of those appearances and are responsible for them. Do they believe their own lies? Can they gain their advantage even though they can't know what it is? Such writers are insane, Plato seems to argue, and "have been robbed of their wits" by what might be called the sober insanity of the men of the city who are themselves no more than a band of fellow-robbers. In a religious context such writers might be called idolators who worship what they themselves have made.

In the context of the *Republic*, however, these serious writers are called the tragic poets, and these poets are the major topic of the *Republic*'s tenth and final book. After completing the founding of his city in speech, Socrates reflects on poetry again by congratulating himself for having refused admittance to the "imitative," which is to say, the type of poetry directly presented to an audience without the overt presence of narration. Narration here means *mimesis* rather than *diegesis*, or the "showing" associated with drama rather than "telling" of, say, a novel.[10] He narrows down this focus

---

[10] Plato, *Republic,* 392ff. Socrates also seems to associate mimesis more with tragedy than comedy when he says:

further from poetry in general to drama and then to tragedy in the following aside:

> Between us—and don't denounce me to the tragic poets and all the other imitators—all such things seem to maim the thought of those who hear them and do not have knowledge of how they really are as a remedy [*pharmakon*].[11]

Socrates' complaint recalls the ambiguity of writing as a *pharmakon*, which will be further discussed in the *Phaedrus* and Book V. The problem here, however, is not with the *pharmakon* or remedy per se, but rather with people's ignorance of how tragedy functions *as a pharmakon*. The following sections are therefore a lover's quarrel between Homer, "the first teacher and leader of all these fine tragic things," and Socrates, who in spite of his friendship and respect for Homer must still speak the truth.[12] Socrates therefore explains both how tragic poetry "maims the thought" and how one might rightly use this pharmakon and yet still remain aware of what one is doing.

Socrates goes about this by comparing the process of knowledge involved in making a couch with what Glaucon calls a "wonderful sophist" who seems to be capable of producing much more than mere couches. The *techne* of couch-making seems to involve two elements: first, "looking to the *idea*" of what is made by the craftsman; and second, the making of something that imitates and conforms to that idea.[13] Socrates depicts the idea of a couch itself as being produced by a god, while the couch produced by a

---

"If the poetry nowhere hid himself, his poetic work and narrative as a whole would have taken place without imitation... Now, I said, understand that the opposite of this comes to pass when someone takes out the poetry's connection between the speeches and leaves the exchanges."
"That I understand, too," he said. "That's the way it is with tragedies."
"Your supposition is most correct." (Plato, *Republic*, 393c-394b).

[11] Plato, *Republic*, 595b.

[12] Plato, *Republic*, 595b.

[13] Plato, *Republic*, 596b.

craftsman is an imitation of that ideal couch: but both, the idea and the produced couch, are contrasted in turn with the imitation of a couch in a painting. Why is it Socrates uses a couch as an example here? It seem peculiarly inappropriate, especially when the "idea" of a couch would seem to be something produced by the craftsman himself rather than the gods. The idea of a tree or a cat, something natural rather than artificial, seems a much more likely candidate to be produced by a god.

Perhaps the contrast Plato is drawing our attention to here is the political one between the life of the producer and his product. A producer, who in his desire for god-like wisdom and knowledge of the whole, is the first principle of anything he makes, and yet as the source of anything made, must be understood as prior to both the making and the made. What is produced by the gods is either the architectonic whole of nature, or the apparent whole created by the serious but less than divine making of the lawgivers. *Techne*, if it is to truly be a part of the architectonic whole of nature, must therefore be a form of *mimesis*, or imitation, of something that is known or striven for in theoretic vision of what *is*,[14] just as our divine capacity to know is higher than and logically precedes our capacity to make.

Besides this imitation by *techne* of an idea, there is the further imitation of *techne* as imitation exemplified by the painting of a couch—an imitation of an imitation. This second-order imitation reaches its peak in the "wonderful sophist" who has not only the *techne* "to make all implements but also makes everything that grows naturally from the earth, and he produces all animals—the others and himself too—and, in addition to that, produces earth and heaven and gods and everything in heaven and everything in Hades under the earth."[15] This master imitator "of that of which these others are craftsman" is finally labelled as "the maker of tragedy" who is "third from a king and the truth."[16] But why a maker of tragedy, and in what way is he an imitator at a third remove from

---

[14] Plato, *Republic*, 597a.

[15] Plato, *Republic*, 596b.

[16] Plato, *Republic*, 597e.

the truth? Or to put this question another way—the way it has been traditionally asked by defenders of poetry ever since—how can Plato give such a crude and condescending account of poetry, especially when he of all people should know better?

Well, perhaps the very crudity or ridiculousness of these examples are our clue, for when Socrates likened imitation at a third remove to holding a mirror up to everything that can be seen,[17] what is not reflected, and indeed can't possibly be reflected in this mirror, is the "heaven and gods" and "everything in Hades under the earth" mentioned earlier.[18] The discrepancy between what a mirror reflects and what the "wonderful sophist" can make shows that the poet's imitation is of an altogether different "nature" from holding up a mirror. Far from just imitating natural things or things made, poetry creates a whole in which all these things and more find their place; and that whole is artificial rather than natural. The maker of tragedy is thus a maker of an artificial whole that substitutes for the reality of the unknown whole of nature. This artifice stands at a third remove from "what is," insofar as a maker of tragedies does not find his principle in his life as a seeker after divine wisdom, but instead emulates the knowledge of the craftsman who fully knows only what he makes and yet is as a god to his own creation. In other words, the tragic poet takes the analogy of *techne* too seriously by supposing that the whole can be understood in the same way—by the making of it. If the tragic poet does *not* know his ignorance of the whole, if he takes his poetry too seriously, he then becomes "some wizard and imitator" who is "all-wise," rather than the philosopher who in putting "knowledge and lack of knowledge and imitation to the test," can't already be said to actually "know."[19]

The philosopher and the tragic poet are thus *both* ignorant insofar as they do not know the whole. The tragic poet, however,

---

[17] Plato, *Republic*, 596d.

[18] One might even say that the seriousness with which Rorty criticizes this analogy in his *Philosophy and the Mirror of Nature* (Princeton, NJ.: Princeton University Press, 1979), may flow from his not getting this joke.

[19] Plato, *Republic*, 598d.

is given credit as a knower by those who are educated by him. In the case of Homer, this is all of Greece, for it has learned the architectonic concerns of "the management and education of human affairs" from him.[20] He and the Greeks in general are thus tempted to take his poetry seriously—for how could he teach what he does not know? But if he "knows," he would seem to know the various *technai* he writes about. But he does not seem to be concerned with that sort of knowledge. Socrates puts it this way:

> "Do you suppose that if a man were able to make both, the thing to be imitated and the phantom, he would permit himself to be serious about the crafting of the phantoms and set this at the head of his own life as the best thing he has?"
> "No, I don't."
> "But, I suppose, if he were in truth a knower of these things that he also imitates, he would be far more serious about the deeds than the imitations . . ."[21]

But since the poet does take seriously, very seriously, his imitations, the real complaint of Socrates concerns perhaps not the imitation, but rather this seriousness. This interpretation gets reinforced when the poet is further criticized in terms that could hold as well for Socrates himself—that he does not know any particular crafts such as medicine or generalship and does not even found a school. When Socrates thus concludes the discussion by saying that "the imitator knows nothing worth mentioning about what he imitates; imitation is a kind of play and not serious; and those who take up tragic poetry in iambic and in epics are all imitators in the highest possible degree," the essential criticism seems to be directed specifically against the seriousness of the tragic poets rather than against their lack of concern with technical knowledge—especially when we remember that Socrates himself is not ultimately concerned with technical knowledge either. [22]

---

[20] Plato, *Republic,* 606e.

[21] Plato, *Republic,* 599a-b.

[22] Plato, *Republic,* 602b.

In fact, during the course of this argument Socrates sneaks in another triad to explain imitation that is much different from imitation at a third remove, and yet brings out the essential source of the conflict behind it. "For each thing there are three arts—one that will use, one that will make, one that will imitate."[23] Here we can see much more clearly that the chief issue is the architectonic art, the user's art par excellence, which in the individual is the quest for true happiness and in the city is the quest for the best regime. For this *techne* is not really a *techne* at all, just as imitation is not truly an imitation of what is made but rather an imitation of the user's art. The quarrel between these two is therefore over who is truly the architectonic knower and teacher—the poet or the philosopher. Yet to even ask this question shows that the tragic poet is the *de facto* teacher of the user's art for the city, which is why he takes himself and is taken so seriously. But if we are not knowers of the true architectonic art, if we are only ignorant seekers of it who know only our own ignorance, then our poetry cannot be serious but can only be playful. It must, in other words, be comic poetry.

Rather than being less than and at a third remove from the ideas, the point of the division between the ideal and the imitative seems to be that the tragic poet is the *de facto* founder and educator of the actual polis. The city's blending of the natural and the conventional is therefore directly a result of this poet's ability to create the mimetic architectonic whole wherein every part will have its place. The serious business of the city thus flows from the serious poet as the carver of the images in the allegory of the cave that cast the shadows of "artificial things" by which the city lives and knows.[24] The men behind the wall holding up the images casting the shadows are not just poets, they are tragic poets, and so if we are to understand the workings of the city we must understand and see through the workings of tragic poetry. Just as in the first book the justice of the city was shown to be that of a band of robbers,

---

23 Plato, *Republic,* 601d.
24 Plato, *Republic,* 515.

so too in the last, the tragic poet is shown to be both the founder of that city and the teacher of its justice.[25]

Justice is therefore no more present in the city than knowledge of the whole is present in the individual. Given that absence, then, and given the need to live in cities and that need to live without knowledge of the whole even while making some sort of substitute for it, one must therefore write and one must imitate. The most important question, then, is *how* one writes and *how* one

---

[25] The preceding argument must be contrasted with Eric Havelock's intriguing but ultimately misleading account of why Plato attacks the poets. What he argues in his *Preface to Plato* (Cambridge: Harvard University Press, 1963) is that Plato's target is an "oral culture" and the state of mind that flows from being educated by public performances rather than private readings of Greek poetry. Since Greece at that time was only minimally literate, he argues, the major educational task of cultural preservation had to take place by means of memorization and repetition which could only succeed poetically. The Greek poets were therefore essentially encyclopedists performing a didactic function. This assumption of an "oral culture" therefore becomes the key to his solution of the mystery of Plato's attack on poetry. "If Plato could deal with poetry as though it were a kind of reference library or as a vast tractate in ethics and politics and warfare and the like, he is reporting its immemorial function in an oral culture and testifying to the fact that this remained its function in Greek society down to his own day" (43). Havelock sees correctly here the educational role of poetry, but what he misses is Plato's emphasis on education's connection to knowledge of "the whole" rather than merely disparate technical parts.

The argument is missed because Havelock can only understand an "aesthetic" function for poetry rather than the constitutive role it plays in the Bible, Homer, Virgil, Goethe, and Shakespeare for their respective community of *readers*. One might imagine his objecting on the grounds that Homer, the Bible and Virgil are foundational precisely because they arise out of only newly literate cultures, but the circularity of this claim should be manifest. The overwhelming fact he is overlooking is that this oral culture is a construct of historicist scholarship, while the fact of reading and writing is incontrovertible. So in the case of Plato, he seems to forget entirely the impact Socrates' arguments on "writing" in the *Phaedrus* may have on the related issues of "mimesis" in the *Republic*. "In all of these discussions, over and over again, the relationship of the student or the public to poetry is assumed to be that of listeners, not readers, and the relationship of the poet to his public or his constituency is always that of a reciter and/or an actor, never of a writer" (38).

imitates. Seriously—where the gap between our need and its temporary satisfaction is covered over—or playfully—where the gap is made manifest and so not forgotten. Neither one closes the gap, but it is only in the gap exposed and made thematic in comedy, Plato seems to say, that the philosopher can live.

This is why the *Republic* is ultimately more a defense of the philosopher than the founding of a city. For such truly serious business can only be written of in jest. But what does this mean—to write in jest, to write playfully and not take imitation seriously? What it means is to write comic poetry, not because comic poetry is more pleasant or beneficial to the city in itself, but rather because comedy opens up the possibility of the life of the philosopher even though it is just as far from its actuality as is tragedy. The philosopher quarrels with the tragic poets precisely because philosophy is something one lives rather than makes. Yet this quarrel itself must be expressed in a comic poem. The comic poem of the *Republic* is thus itself the chanting of the "counter-charm" that would prevent us from falling back into love with tragic poetry "which is childish and belongs to the many."[26] Comedy can also allow knowledge of how it really is as a *pharmakon*,[27] because it is the poetry that cannot be "taken seriously as a serious thing laying hold of truth";[28] and so it does not exclude the serious life of the philosopher that can alone seriously contemplate such a possibility.

Another way of verifying that the quarrel between the philosopher and the poet in this book is actually a quarrel with tragic poetry by means of comic poetry would be to point out that along with the myth of Er, the only other topic discussed in Book X concerns the effects of tragedies and comedies within the city.[29] But in order to make full sense of this discussion, we will need to draw upon the *agon* between the philosopher and the waves of comedy and tragedy seen in Book V; for it is there that all three,

---

[26] Plato, *Republic,* 608a.

[27] Plato, *Republic,* 595b.

[28] Plato, *Republic,* 608a.

[29] Plato, *Republic,* 605b-606c.

the comic poet, the tragic poet, and the philosopher, are indirectly and yet crucially distinguished.

In Book V of the *Republic* Socrates is again grabbed by Polemarchus and compelled to begin his argument anew. This new beginning he will call his "female drama" as opposed to his earlier "male drama" of initially founding his regime of guardians. The reason this new approach is a female drama is threefold: first, because it deals with the key themes that arise from Aristophanes' female drama, *The Assembly of Women*; second, because it deals with the problem of erotic things such as sexuality, family and philosophy in relation to the city; third, and most important for my own argument, because it is here that Socrates analyzes what is going on in tragic and comic drama within the confines of his own drama that has a philosopher as its poet. It is in Book V, then, that we find Plato's most extended discussion, however indirectly, of both comedy and tragedy and why both are crucial in grasping the philosopher's relation to the city and writing.

This female drama brings up all the themes that must continually be abstracted from if Socrates' city in speech is to have any chance at real existence, so in bringing them up here, Socrates is also showing why his city is ultimately impossible.[30] In his earlier male drama he could unite the city against its foes in the guardians who as "philosophical" attack dogs could distinguish friend from foe and thereby fulfill Polemarchus' earlier definition of justice as doing harm to one's enemies and help to one's friends. In this female drama, however, Socrates must go beyond this armed camp of male camaraderie and their craftsman to the question of how the city perpetuates itself—to the question of genesis and Eros. For what we have here is the unavoidable conflict in any city between the city as a whole and its common good, and the loyalty to one's own and the private goods that because of their connection

---

[30] "The abstraction characteristic of the *Republic* is the abstraction rom the body. The characteristic political proposal is complete communism. But the body constitutes the absolute limit to communism; man cannot, strictly speaking, share his body with anybody else, whereas he can well share his thoughts and desires with others." (Leo Strauss, *The Rebirth of Classical Political Rationalism: An Introduction to the Thought of Leo Strauss* (Chicago, Chicago University Press, 1989), 164).

to the body cannot be shared. In fact, the problem of justice in the city grows out of this very tension, for as we have seen from Thrasymachus, the desire to gain advantage grows out of one part taking itself for the whole, and the ultimate "parts" of every city are the body and its offspring that because of their intrinsic partiality are always at incipient war with every other part. So while in the male drama a man might sacrifice and thus share his body in war against a common enemy, in the female drama the problem is that he will not share the body of his wife. It is this drama, then, that Socrates must rewrite if the city is to hold all things in common.

The presence of Eros in the city thus raises the question as to the very possibility of justice in the city, especially when in its divine passion for eternity discussed in the *Symposium*, what it gives birth to (whether it be manic deeds (sexuality), children (family) or philosophical speeches) all challenge the temporal justice of the city and undermine an individual's loyalty. So while in the *Symposium* the drunken private party centers around speeches in praise of Eros, in the *Republic* Eros is described as the most unjust passion of all that reaches its height in the rapaciousness of the tyrant.[31] What the *Republic* must do then is speak of Eros in term of its absence, which is to say, abstract from it, just as the *Symposium* speaks of its presence. And so while the *Symposium* will end with an overt discussion of comedy and tragedy by Socrates with the tragic poet Agathon and the comic poet Aristophanes, the *Republic* will have at its heart the more subtle challenge of the three waves of ridicule that covertly have to do with comedy, tragedy and philosophy. In addition, while Socrates will argue in the *Symposium* that the good tragic poet could also write comedy, in the *Republic* it is in the context of a female drama modeled after Aristophanes' comedy, *The Assembly of Woman*, that Plato will write his own comic account of tragedy, comedy and philosophy.

The reason we know that Aristophanes' *Assembly of Women* is the correlate of Socrates' female drama is because in it we find a proposal of laws by women that instantiate the very same things Socrates will also argue for: namely, the political equality of women

---

[31] Strauss, *Rebirth of Classical Political Rationalism,* 562ff.

and the sharing of all things in common including wives and children.[32] Where the joke comes in is that in order to bring about this complete sexual equality, separate laws must be passed that go against the natural sexual inequality between youth and age and ugliness and beauty. For example, the law that demands one must sleep with old hags before gaining sexual access to youthful beauties constitutes one of the key jokes of this piece, because such highly and laughably unnatural means must be used to bring about this "natural" inequality. The "naturalness" of equality is thus rendered highly suspect.[33] What Socrates does in subjecting himself to the first "wave" of ridicule, then, is make these same proposals as to the natural equality of men and women, but then dispute with the comic poet as to how one can ascertain what is truly natural, since what "nature" is, it seems, is at the heart of the comic. [34]

For the way comedy works, Plato seems to argue, is to contrast the ignorant actions of its characters with the "true" knowledge of what is natural held in common by the playwright and his audience. The comic poet must therefore create a direct

---

[32] "Plato's *Republic* may be said to be the reply *par excellence* to Aristophanes. The political proposals of the *Republic* are based on the conceits underlying Aristophanes' *Assembly of Women*. The complete communism, communism not only regarding property but regarding women and children as well, is introduced in Plato's *Republic* with arguments literally taken from Aristophanes' *Assembly of Women*. There is this most important difference between the best city of the *Assembly of Women* and that of the *Republic*. Plato contends that complete communism requires as its capstone or its foundation the rule of philosophy, about which Aristophanes is completely silent. This difference corresponds to a difference indicated in Plato's *Banquet*. According to Aristophanes the direction of eros is horizontal. According to Plato the direction of eros is vertical." Strauss, *Rebirth of Classical Political Rationalism,* 125.

[33] "By making us see in this simple way the difference between worthy and unworthy designs, the poet teaches the just things. Yet since the designs—as distinguished from the ends by themselves, like peace—are in all cases laughable, he teaches us the just things by making us laugh. The designs are laughable because they are (more or less obviously) impossible; by making a part of the audience think about why a given design is impossible, the poet addresses the wise as distinguished from the laughers (1155-56)." Leo Strauss *Socrates and Aristophanes* (Chicago: Chicago University Press, 1966), 278.

[34] Leo Strauss, *Rebirth of Classical Political Rationalism,* 457.

bond with his audience, whether explicitly as in Aristophanes' many appeals to audience (or at least to those wise among them);[35] or implicitly by means of a character whose wink at the audience includes us as those in the know. Comedy is thus a contest between ignorance and knowledge. What we know is what is natural, what is possible; and who we laugh at are those who pay no heed to the Oracle's advice to know thyself and so fail to know the limits of their own nature.[36] Yet how a comedy brings about this laughter is absolutely crucial, for oddly enough this ignorance of nature is "revealed" by artificial means, by the poet's ability to create the unnatural context on stage that can bring out a common understanding of what is natural between him and his audience.

So just as in the *Assembly of Women* the unnaturalness of equality between the sexes is exposed by the artificial laws needed to bring it about, so too in a comedy does the poet's artifice expose the essentially unnatural and even ludicrous character of his own task.[37] The comic hopes to establish what is natural by means of

---

[35] ....But you judges, first
I want a word with you, to put you all right—
Let the serious wiseheads choose me because of my serious
    side,
The jokes being mere additions not too profuse for them.
Let the wags also choose me for the witticisms I provide,
The other part being but a mere excuse for them.
The clearly I must win the suffrage of one and all.
"Assembly of Woman" in *The Complete Plays of Aristophanes*, ed. Moses Hadas, (New York: Bantam Books, 1962), 461.

[36] "Socrates: You can use this to understand the nature of what we find comical.
Protarchus: Go on.
Socrates: There is a certain type of worthlessness which, to put it briefly, gets its nature from a certain state of mind. Specifically, I mean that there is a worthless condition which is the opposite of the instruction in the Delphic inscription.
Protarchus: Do you mean "know yourself," Socrates?"
Philebus, trans. Robin Waterfield (New York: Penguin Books, 1982), 48c.

[37] Leo Strauss describes the ludicrous political position of the comic poet as follows:

the artificial, but such an attempt always opens him up to the same sort of ridicule he has himself so richly ladled out, especially if he fails. His only defense, and the goal of all comedians, is thus to have the last laugh on his side, for the consensus (if only for the moment) of laughter is what converts the artificial into the natural. The question for the comic poet, then, is, can his artifice save him from ridicule? Which is to say, can and must nature be discovered through artificial means?

Socrates' answer would seem to be, "no." Nevertheless, as much as Aristophanes, he too runs the risk of appearing ridiculous in claiming the natural equality between men and women in terms of argument rather than jokes. For his argument will have the very same structural weakness of Aristophanes' comic jokes insofar as it too attempts to reveal that what is taken to be natural in comedy is actually conventional—which is why the comic is as changeable and capricious as Aristophanes' plot outlines and Athenian politics.[38] So rather than our laughter revealing what is truly natural, Socrates argues that laughter is merely mistaking nature for what *seems* natural because of the strength of social convention. The power of convention is thus the same power as the social ostracism of comic ridicule and its attendant shame, even though in a comedy that power is exposed and consequently weakened by its overt use. Socrates thus takes what would likely appear to his audience

---

In a word, justice as Aristophanes understands it consists in preserving or restoring the ancestral or the old. The quality of a comedy, on the other hand, depends very much on the inventiveness of the poet, on his conceits being novel. Aristophanes may have been an unqualified reactionary in political things; as a comic poet he was compelled to be a revolutionary. Strauss, *Rebirth of Classical Political Rationalism,* 109.

[38] To gain the populace we need
Some plan extravagantly clever;
And you must do the deed.
The audience is rather sick
Of plots antiquely patterned; so
Produce one new and striking—quick
Before they go.
Plato, *The Assembly of Women,* 438.

to be the most ridiculous aspect to his proposal—the naked gymnastics of women and men together—and argues that the naked gymnastics of men, which is the pride of the Greeks, could just as easily have been made a subject of comedy at an earlier time or among another people.[39]

In his own time, however, Socrates makes a common argument with *his* audience as follows:

> But, I suppose, when it became clear to those who used these practices that to uncover all such things is better than to hide them, then *what was ridiculous to the eyes disappeared in the light of what's best as revealed in speeches.* And this showed that he is empty who believes anything is ridiculous other than the bad, and *who tries to produce laughter* looking to any sight as ridiculous other than the sight of the foolish and the bad; or, again, he who looks seriously to any standard of beauty he sets up other than the good.[40]

The heart of ridicule, and thus the heart of comedy, is the ability to make things appear "ridiculous to the eyes"; and as his example shows, such ability to produce laughter has nothing to do with knowledge of nature—of what is by nature best or beautiful—but rather only with knowledge of what is conventionally taken to be beautiful and good. Yet convention is known to be such precisely in its changeability. Just as the innovativeness of the comic plot saves itself from ridicule by gaining our laughing consensus as to what is natural and hence truly ridiculous, so too does Socrates' innovative proposal as to the equality of women save itself from ridicule by arguing for a better understanding of what is natural and is possible.

> Mustn't we then first come to an agreement whether these things are possible or not, and give anyone who wants to dispute—whether it's a man who likes to play or one who is serious—the opportunity to dispute whether female human

---

[39] Plato, *Republic,* 452c.

[40] Plato, *Republic,* 452d-e, (emphasis added).

nature can act in common with the male class in all deeds or in none at all, or in some things yes and in others no, particularly with respect to war?[41]

The "man who likes to play" is, of course, Aristophanes the comic poet, so by "disputing" with him Socrates is also asking him not to "mind his own business" but rather to be serious.[42] But for a comic poet to do this, according to Socrates own definition, would be manifestly unjust.[43]

The philosopher, on the other hand, makes it his business to know nature; and so in this first wave of ridicule Socrates is exposing the nature of the comic poet and what his *techne* consists of, and he does so by both imitation and argument. By thus subjecting himself to ridicule, Socrates also ridicules the comic poet who is always subject to ridicule. In asking ourselves why this is so, however, we can now come to see in what comedy consists.

For comedy is the imitation of the discovery of nature; or one might say, the imitation of inquiry's satisfaction in an insight. Keeping in mind, then, both what is imitated and the imitating, Socrates first wave brings out the desire to know and the fear of ignorance, coupled with the shareable pleasure of discovery—but in terms of nature, shame and communal laughter, and ridicule. In fact, it is because the first experiences listed are the lived reality of our human life that the comic poet is able to imitate them by means of the second with his distinctive *techne*. In choosing Aristophanes' *Assembly of Women* to bring his point home, however, Plato is looking over his character Socrates' shoulder and reminding us that what is especially unique to the comic poet is that he cannot keep hidden his artifice and imitation—that he must always make the role of artifice and contrivance essential to his plot. In other words, we can never forget about the comic poet in his poem because laughter is always shared, and if we don't share it *with* him we can

---

[41] Plato, *Republic,* 452c.

[42] Plato, *Republic,* 462a-c.

[43] Plato, *Republic,* 433a.

only laugh *at* him. A successful comedy is thus always a joint venture between poet and audience. In the same way, Plato would have us realize, if playful writing is to succeed it must be an explicit and complicit exercise between the writing and the reader. The reader must join in, and his decision to do so is the central part of the play.

The first wave, the wave of comedy, is thus survived by drawing attention to the overt manipulative character of comic poetry that can just as readily establish or undermine our consensus as to what is possible or beneficial. The problem with this consensus, however, is that it does not last. Very little can be founded upon it because he who laughs today can be laughed at tomorrow, and so the contrived quality of comic consensus cannot be hid any more than it can be counted upon for anything permanent in the city. In founding his own city in speech Socrates' argued for consensus as to the equality of men and women is therefore not enough; for the final goal of equality between male and female guardians does not turn out to be the principle of the matter, but rather the need for children whose parents are both of the same nature, and for that the guardians must include females. In other words, as we shall see in the second wave, the point of this mock argument for equality is for the sake of a program of eugenics rather than the nature of woman *per se*.

It is in the second wave, then, that Socrates deals with what is truly beneficial for the city, but the price he pays is to give up speaking of possibility altogether, which is to say, he must ignore the very question of nature. Therefore when Socrates makes the following proposal that—

> All these women are to belong to all these men in common, and no woman is to live privately with any man. And the children, in their turn, will be in common, and neither will a parent know his own offspring, nor a child his parent.[44]

—he follows it with this further observation:

---

[44] Plato, *Republic,* 457c-d.

> As to whether it is beneficial, at least, I don't sup-
> pose it would be disputed that the community of
> women and the community of children are, if
> possible, the greatest good . . . . But I suppose
> that there would arise a great deal of dispute as to
> whether they are possible or not.[45]

Glaucon, however, would dispute both; so Socrates must rest content only with the first and consequently only argue benefit. For
what Socrates is doing with this second wave is exposing how
tragic poetry seeks to bring about the greatest good for the city—
but a good that is entirely divorced from nature. Socrates will
therefore use this proposal to show what the city needs above all
else and yet also the essentially artificial means by which it must be
supplied. What follows, then, is a comic account of the role of
tragedy that with a mock serious proposal exposes the artifice behind the serious concerns of tragedy—concerns that both require
this artifice, and yet also require, in contrast with comedy, that it
remain hidden.

To begin with, the reason why Socrates can assume that the
community of wives and children would be best for the city is what
we have already seen come out in his discussion of justice with
Thrasymachus—that faction, the partiality that afflicts the city and
makes one part seek to take advantage of the other parts, flows
from the "erotic necessities" of marriage and children that lead to
private loyalties in conflict with public ones. Not only does the
entire erotic desire for beauty lead to the tragic conflict epitomized
by the excessively unequal beauty of Helen, but the subjective
beauty of one's own children or siblings in contrast to others leads
to the family and clannish conflicts at the root of civil war. In other
words, in every city the essentially private nature of the body and
its erotic necessities threaten to tear it apart, and so must somehow
be controlled, mitigated, suppressed, and repressed.

The body politic is therefore always sick, and its disease, we
might say, is the body private. In this light, Socrates will describe
the greatest good and the greatest evil in the city as follows:

---

[45] Plato, *Republic,* 457d.

"Have we any greater evil for a city than what splits it and makes it many instead of one? Or a greater good than what binds it together and makes it one?"

"No we don't."

"Doesn't the community of pleasure and pain bind it together, when to the greatest extent possible all citizens alike rejoice and are pained at the same births and deaths?"

"That's entirely certain," he said

"But the privacy of such things dissolves it, when some are overwhelmed and others overjoyed by the same things happening to the city and those within the city?"

"Of course."

"Doesn't that sort of thing happen when they don't utter such phrases as 'my own' and 'not my own' at the same time in the city, and similarly with respect to 'somebody else's?'"

"Entirely so."

"Is, then, that city in which most say 'my own' and 'not my own' about the same thing, and in the same way, the best governed city?"

"By far."

"Then is that city best governed which is most like a single human being?"[46]

Yes. Unfortunately the city is not like a single human being, so it must be made to be so. But how? This is where the tragic poet comes in, for he is the one who in fact makes it so by educating the city into whatever appearance of unity it might possess.

By describing how he would bring about this beneficial community of women and children, Socrates is thus also comically giving an account of the role the tragic poet plays in the city; yet since it is a comic account, Socrates can't help admitting that his plan is not possible and so is entirely contrived and artificial. Nevertheless, contrivance is the means by which the city gains the appearance of unity, but as he will comically show, the contrivance of

---

[46] Plato, *Republic,* 462a-c.

tragedy only works if it remains hidden. The contrivance of tragedy, in other words, is the contrivance of the lie, but a lie that in this case proves eminently useful.

In keeping with the image of a sick body politic, Socrates brings us back to our old friend, the word *pharmakon* (here translated as both "drug" and "remedy"), when he says that someone so gravely ill needs strong medicine, "and when there is also a need to use drugs, we know there is need of the most courageous doctor."[47] However, because Socrates is not yet dealing with the possibility of this cure but only with what the cure would consist of, he will tell us only how the drug works but not yet who the doctor that can properly administer it might be. For what this drug is, is the "lie"; and what makes it a lie is precisely its need to keep the role of this doctor and his goals hidden. "It's likely that our rulers will have to use a throng of lies and deceptions for the benefit of the ruled. And, of course, we said that everything of this sort is useful as a form of remedy . . . . And all this must come to pass without being noticed by anyone except the rulers themselves if the guardians' herd is to be as free as possible from faction."[48] The benefit of the lie, then, is to reduce faction and this lie seems to function in the same way as the *pharmakon* of writing we see in the *Phaedrus*. For what this lie does is create an artificial whole that regulates marriages, births, relations and mores, as a clear substitute and overlay for what is nonetheless going on naturally. And perhaps the most important means by which this wholesale substitution can take place is to have this overt manipulation be perceived as chance, for when chance determines our choices it takes on the same authoritativeness as the mysteries of nature we call "fate." Socrates describes this essentially tragic transmutation of manipulation into fate as follows: "I suppose certain subtle lots must be fabricated so that ordinary man will blame chance rather than the rulers for each union."[49]

---

[47] Plato, *Republic,* 459c.

[48] Plato, *Republic,* 459c-e.

[49] Plato, *Republic,* 460a.

We thus see why this second wave is the comic account of tragedy, for this theme of fate will be the common rubric in which the issues of incest, war, burying of bodies, etc.—all the common themes of tragedy—will find their place. "Fate" is therefore the contrived lie of the tragic poets wherein the irreconcilable tensions in the city will find an aesthetic or cathartic unity. This unity will only work on the condition that it is seen as somehow natural, as fate rather than manipulation, and for that to occur the tragic whole must be seen as the true whole of reality and so the city with all its tensions must absorb into itself all of nature. So in contrast with comedy that appeals to a common understanding of what is natural *apart* from the city in order to mock at what is unnatural within it, in tragedy the city is conflated with nature in order to reconcile its audience with the conflicts between the city and the demands of their own bodies.

How a tragedy does this, Socrates seems to argue, is to create an entire system of artificial relations that takes up the fears and desires on the natural level and apply them to objects appropriate only on its own level of convention. So, for example, in the case of incest, the fear of sleeping with a relation (and perhaps also the desire) is calmed by an artificial and arbitrary delimitation of brothers and sisters designed to both recognize that fear and yet divorce it from its natural object.[50] Likewise, the respect of the young for the old would still be recognized as a necessity, but no longer as enforced by the family and for the sake of the family, but rather for the sake of the city and enforced by the city. All the pleasures and pains found naturally in individuals and their families would not be done away with, but would be redirected by means of a corporate lie into a common fund of pleasures and pains in order to drive out faction.[51]

---

[50] Plato, *Republic*, 461b-e.

[51] Havelock at least has this right, that the point of the poetry Plato is criticizing is the identification the audience has with the poem. Although he sees it as the identification of the oral memorizer to his poem, what I would argue he is describing is the cathartic identification of the tragic audience, whether read or heard, with the poetic activity in its entirety— which is to say, the corporate unity that takes into itself the direction and return from stage to audience. "This then is the master clue to Plato's

By mentioning Homer, Hesiod, and the themes of the great tragic poets in this second wave rather than Aristophanes and the threat of ridicule we saw in the first wave, Socrates implies that it is the tragic poets who are the *de facto* liars who actually perform this function. The tragedian, then, is the one who creates a corporate lie that takes upon itself the fundamental and conflicting pains and pleasures within the city. And yet because these passions now find their place within the artificial world on stage rather than in the audience, if a tragedy is successful and keeps this separation between stage and audience believable, it has the cathartic effect of driving out faction from the latter by locking it safely within the artificial bounds of the former. One might even say that tragedy functions as a sort of scapegoat, Derrida's *pharmakos*, in the sense that all the sins of faction within the city are made fearfully and awe-fully manifest, but only on stage as divorced from their true source in the audience. [52] The function of this scapegoat "mechanism" can only work, however, if this function is kept quiet, and the best way to keep such a thing quiet is the lie of the half-truth that distracts us from self-knowledge by knowing it only in another. [53] *Oedipus the King* was thus rightfully viewed by Aristotle as the epitome of the tragic plot in the sense that the knowledge Oedipus gains of who he is simultaneously fulfills for the corporate audience Jocosta's prayer "may you never come to know who you are." The fulfillment of both of these desires is essential to every

---

choice of the word *mimesis* to describe the poetic experience. It focuses initially not on the the artist's creative act but on his power to make his audience identify almost pathologically and certainly sympathetically with the content of what he is saying." Havelock, *Preface to Plato*, 45. The corporate unity effected by tragic poetry also accounts for what Havelock describes as the disappearance of the "I" which is essential to the didactic success of poetry. "[T]he poem's structure, rhythm, syntax, and plot, its very substance, have all been designed for a situation in which 'I' do not exist. They all provide the machinery of self-identification, the magic of the spell, the drug that hypnotizes. Once I end my absorption in the poem, I have ended the poem too." Havelock, *Preface to Plato,* 217.

[52] Derrida's use of this term in his essay, "Plato's Pharmacy," will be taken up in more detail in the next chapter.

[53] This term is René Girard's and will be discussed in later chapters.

scapegoat, and when done deliberately, it is the unique sort of lie mastered by the tragic poet.

As if to reinforce this diversionary technique of the tragic lie, when Glaucon presses Socrates on the possibility of all that has preceded, Socrates sidesteps the question with a further and extended discussion of various themes found in tragedy. But when this tactic no longer works, Glaucon will repeat his question: "Is it possible for this regime to come into being and how is it ever possible?"[54] In order to finally answer this question, however, Socrates must return from the artificial world of the tragic lie to the world of nature; for the only thing that would make this sort of scheme possible would be if the liar also had a certain type of nature—the nature of the philosopher. The third wave of ridicule Socrates now faces turns out to be the greatest; for it turns out that nothing in his city is natural at all, and its possibility depends entirely upon the absurd claim that philosophers must become kings or vice versa—a highly unlikely possibility.

What Socrates finally does, then, in order to face this third and greatest wave, the wave that questions the possibility of his entire regime in speech, is not to answer it all, but rather to defuse it. For what he does is demote speech in the light of deeds by asking: "Can anything be done as it is said? Or is it the nature of acting to attain to less truth than speaking?"[55] This demotion, however, can be taken in two ways. The first is to take "speaking" in the sense of Socrates and Glaucon as joint founders of an imaginary city, whereby any actual founding would inevitably be less. But the other way would be to take "speaking" as the actual existing regimes that Socrates is indirectly criticizing and yet also explaining as the appearance of unity in cities created by the "speeches" of the tragic poets. The deed that is less than these "speeches" (think of the serious written speeches of the lawmaker in the *Phaedrus*) is the private life of the philosopher, whose deed of living a life devoted to wisdom must inevitably seem less than and even threatening to the mimetic whole created poetically.

---

[54] Plato, *Republic*, 471c.

[55] Plato, *Republic*, 473a.

The first sense comes to the fore when we get the answer that Socrates' city in speech could only come about when "the philosophers rule as kings or those called kings and chiefs genuinely and adequately philosophize."[56] But when we shift our attention to why this is the case, to what it is about the philosopher that would alone make a just city possible, the second sense comes to the fore. The nature of the philosopher, in other words, is the key to the question of the just city and Socrates' ultimate and final defense against all these waves is to show "that it is by nature fitting for [the philosopher] to engage in philosophy and to lead a city, and for the rest not to engage in philosophy and to follow the leader."[57]

The private Eros of the philosopher is therefore as much, if not more, of a threat to actual cities as the Eros of bodies and family. However, in contrast with the injustice of the familial Eros that would take its part for the whole, the philosopher's Eros must be shown to be the only possibility of true justice since its desire is for the whole itself rather than one part. So even though the demand of living a life devoted to that knowledge of the whole will always seem less in the eyes of the poets who must create out of the partial Eros connected to the body, the center of Socrates' entire argument is to show that the erotic desire of the philosophic life is the one true source of justice, whether public or private, and so also the true source of happiness.

The city as audience to the appearance of justice created and taught by the poets is therefore itself an imitation of the lives of the philosopher who is the audience, so to speak, of the whole known in *theoria*. It is in this sense, then, that Socrates contrasts the erotic life of the philosopher who "is a desirer of wisdom, not of one part and not another, but . . . all of it," and "who is willing to taste every kind of learning with gusto, and who approaches learning with delight, and is insatiable," with what he calls the "lover of sights." [58] The lover of sights is the one who "just as though they had hired out their ears for learning—run around to every chorus

---

[56] Plato, *Republic*, 473c.

[57] Plato, *Republic*, 474c.

[58] Plato, *Republic*, 475b-c.

at the Dionysia, missing none in the cities or the villages," and seem to Glaucon to love learning just as much as the philosopher. [59] But to Socrates these lovers of sights are only *like* the philosopher, and the relation between the lover of sights and the "lovers of the sight of truth" is the key to the relation between appearance and truth, between opinion and knowledge.[60]

For what you have in all cities is only the appearance of justice, because true justice, which is sought by the philosopher, when

---

[59] Plato, *Republic*, 475d.

[60] Compare the above argument on the importance of the "lover of sights" with the following one by Eric Havelock:

> Now who is the sight-seer? As introduced, he is portrayed as a kind of theatre-goer who perpetually makes the rounds of the Dionysiac choruses both metropolitan and provincial. But why, we should ask, does Plato in seeking to define the new intellectual standards of the Academy imply that the obstacle to their achievement is simply a habit of attending the theatre? This seems more frivolous than the deep seriousness of his purpose required. Theatre-goers in our culture are a sophisticated minority of the better educated. The whole passage makes it clear on the other hand that Plato's target is the average man of average mind. In what sense was the average Greek mind a theatrical mind? The answer can be found only by supposing that Plato's real target here is poetic performance, by which the cultural tradition was stored kept alive, and memorized, and with which the living memories of the audience had to identify. In short, though here as sometimes in Book Ten he focuses on dramatic performance because it is the most contemporary form of the tradition, his target (as in Book Three also) is 'the poets and Homer', the epic performance no less than the tragic. It is not poetry as it might be read from a book that he is attacking. It is the act of memorization through identification from the poem itself, and which constitutes a total act and condition of mimesis." Havelock, *Preface to Plato*, 243-4.

Havelock is right to see that the point of this passage isn't comedy and tragedy strictly in the dramatic sense, but by condescending to these "lovers of sights" as "average men" rather than true competitors with the philosopher, he misses the importance of the ease by which poetry can be confused with philosophy, and consequently the true nature of their competition.

shown in community "with actions, bodies . . . looks like many."[61] The role of the philosopher who alone by nature could rule a city justly, is therefore played in actual cities by both the comic and tragic poets who educate the citizenry into the manifold appearances of justice they must live by. The citizen must then be the lover of the sights created for them by the poets, and because of the changeable quality of those sights "can in no way endure it if anyone asserts the fair is one and the just is one and so on with the rest." The challenge Socrates poses to this audience and so fundamentally to the poets themselves is, "'Now, of these many fair things, you best of men,' we'll say, 'is there any that won't also look ugly? And of the just, any that won't look unjust? And of the holy, any that won't look unholy?'"[62] The problem with poetry, in other words, is that it will always be either comic or tragic, that tragedy will provide food for comedy even as comedy will fall into tragedy, because as the "wanderer between, seized by the power between" it is never a whole unto itself but can only imitate that whole by means of the movement both within itself and from one to the other.[63] Socrates must therefore ride the first two waves of comedy and tragedy before getting to the wave of philosophy. Yet even in this wave the philosopher as the lover of truth rather than opinion does not have what he loves, so he can only speak of it in terms of opinion. The philosopher must therefore speak of what he seeks either comically or tragically, and as the joke of his entire shifting of gears from an impossible city to a possible philosopher indicates, he has chosen to speak of this city in speech comically. For what comedy brings to our attention is Socrates the poet playing within his own play the role of Socrates the philosopher who must defend himself against the accusations of the city.[64]

---

[61] Plato, *Republic*, 476a.

[62] Plato, *Republic*, 479a.

[63] Plato, *Republic*, 479d.

[64] In the context of Aristophanes, Strauss explains this self-referential quality to comedy in contrast to tragedy as follows:

> Hence, whereas the destruction of the dramatic illusion is fatal to the tragic effect, it may heighten the comic effect. Aristophanes is then able in his comedies to speak to the

What these three waves tell us about Socrates' "female drama," a drama that seems to last until the end of Book VII and climax in "the allegory of the cave," is that it is a comic drama that tells of the philosopher's relation to the tragic city. Or to put this another way, since in the opinionable world things keep changing into their opposite and so comedy changes into tragedy and vice versa, and since this movement is an imitation of the whole the philosopher is seeking, Plato as a writer will choose to write comic dialogues that contain within themselves the constant back-drop of the tragic poem of the city that is nevertheless overcome through laughter and irony.[65] For comedy, as we saw in the first wave, presupposes some sort of preestablished fixation, prejudice, habit, or convention acted upon as natural, that can be laughed at and revealed as ignorance when contrasted with the "nature" created in the comic consensus. Comedy is thus always subversive of the conventions taken for nature in tragedy and the comic plot primarily consists of the movement from one to the other. Tragedy, on the other hand, is the establishment of these conventions and so must take whatever temporary "discoveries" of nature that arise from comedy and transform them into a permanent structure independent of the discoverers. The tragic plot is thus primarily of the individual falling from a high place of knowledge or power into

---

audience directly; his chorus or his characters may address not only one another but the audience as well. It is even possible that the hero of a comedy, e.g., Dicaiopolis in the *Acharnians*, reveals himself to be the comic poet himself. Strauss, *Rebirth of Classical Political Rationalism,* 109.

So while we may not find Plato himself making an appearance in his dialogues, his generic equivalent, the "philosopher," is to be found in Socrates who in his ironic prominence as questioner, erotic master, mythmaker and speaker rather than writer, cannot help but make us aware of the loud absence of the one person who would seem to be both his equal and peer—and perhaps superior as poet—Plato himself.

[65] "Comedy rises higher than any other art. It transcends every other art; it transcends in particular tragedy. Since it transcends tragedy, it presupposes tragedy....Comedy rises higher than tragedy. Only the comedy can present wise men as wise men: men like Euripides and Socrates, men who as such transcend tragedy." Strauss, *Rebirth of Classical Political Rationalism,* 108.

the dissolving and collective abidingness of fate. And so on they go, one turning into the other, their only stability being the pattern of the movement itself.

If there is to be a plot to philosophy, then, which is to say, if the philosopher is to write, he must write a comic plot and his hero must be the *eiron* or self-deprecator rather than the *alazon* or boaster of tragedy. Nevertheless, the *alazon* must still remain as a presence in any comedy, but now as a figure of fun rather than of fear and pity. And so the boasting we find in the comedies of Plato is the boasting of the city, and the irony of the hero, Socrates, is that even at its best the city is like a cave in comparison with the sun-lit world in which the philosopher dwells. As Allan Bloom puts it in his commentary on the *Republic*:

> In the light of the splendor of the soul's yearning after the whole, the city looks very ugly. This is the true comedy—taking the city with infinite seriousness, beautifying it with every artifice, making it a veritable Callipolis, and then finding that compared to the soul which was supposed to be like it, it is a thing to be despised. This fair city, the goal of so many aspirations, now looks like a cave, and its happy citizens like prisoners. . . . From the point of view of the city, the philosopher looks ridiculous; but from the point of view of the whole, the citizen looks ridiculous. Socrates asks which of the two contexts is the more authoritative. Aristophanes' comedy is the human comedy, Socrates the divine.[66]

What makes Socrates' (and more importantly, Plato's) comedy divine as opposed to the human comedy of Aristophanes is, however, nothing intrinsic to the comic plot or structure itself, but rather something extrinsic that is only "opened up" by that structure. And what that possibility is, is the actual life of the philosopher, whether it be Socrates, Plato, or any given reader. Take away the life of the reader, and all you have is an extended shaggy dog

---

[66] Alan Bloom, "Interpretative Essay" in *The Republic of Plato*, trans. Bloom, 408.

story to which the punch-line never comes—for we alone can supply it. If we do supply it, however, the "divinity" that we discover is not something that can be found in poet, poem, or character, but only in that which is divine in ourselves and in its sun-lit splendor puts the artificial lights of our cave to shame. Or, that divinity may well be the divine poet Himself, which is the argument of Christian faith in its belief in the comic nature of Scripture.

If we compare this divine comedy of Plato with the more recognizable *Divine Comedy* of Dante, what we see is the intrinsic logic of comedy itself. For if in Plato comedy can only allow us to turn away from poetry itself to the unmade whole of nature we share in through our desire to know that whole, the only way one could stay within poetry and still have the satisfaction of knowing that whole would be if the maker of the comic poem was also the maker of whole of nature. In the case of Holy Scripture, viewed by both Aquinas and many Christians as authored by God, the creator of the whole of nature, that demand is satisfied. The plot of Scripture is therefore not surprisingly a comedy, and getting the joke in this case is believing its author and main character is also the author of nature. Yet either way, be it the divine comedy of Plato or the divine comedy of the Bible, the common opponent is the lie of tragedy that covers over the fact that the gods it worships and the justice it contrives are made by human hands.

With this account of the three wave of Socrates' "female drama," we can now return to the description of comedy and tragedy that I deliberately neglected in Book X. In this final discussion of the "imitative" Socrates returns to the strategy and themes he uses in discussing the three waves to explain why the imitative is either comic or tragic. This strategy, as we have seen, consists of indirectly describing what is going on in actual cities by means of describing what would ideally happen in Socrates' city in speech. In the same way, his ideal political proposals also indirectly describe what actually goes on in poetry. Both cities, then, real and ideal, are contrasted with the philosopher who as private, stands in relation to the city as higher to lower, as reality to appearance, and as whole to part. In the light of this strategy, Socrates' following complaint against the imitative will also turn out to be a factual description of what *mimesis* accomplishes and how it does so, even though this very knowledge is what sets the philosopher apart from and above the poet.

To begin with, Socrates outlines the imitative, or *mimesis*, in terms of two fundamental possibilities consisting of a character's actions and feelings—a description that we will later see essentially repeated by Aristotle in his *Poetics*:

> Imitation, we say, imitates human beings performing forced or voluntary actions, and, as a result of the action, supposing themselves to have done well or badly, and in all of this experiencing pain or enjoyment.[67]

The imitative, then, seems to consist of either the tragic plot of painful action ending badly, or the comic plot of pleasurable action ending well. The reason for these plot movements seems to be similar to the opinionable world wherein ideas are "everywhere mixed with actions, bodies and one another,"[68] but here elaborated in terms of the faction found in every soul:

> Then, in all this, is a human being of one mind? Or, just as with respect to the sight there was faction and he had contrary opinions in himself at the same time about the same things, is there also faction in him when it comes to deeds and does he do battle with himself?[69]

This faction in the soul of the individual that seems to take up into itself the same faction that is at the heart of the city will therefore be our guide to what is going on in tragic *mimesis*. For the faction in the soul and the tension in the city both stand in the way of true justice, and since each individual is always its own faction within the city, the constant war between the private individual and the city is the most fundamental faction of all, and the one most in need of overcoming. Without the unique soul of the philosopher, however, this faction is impossible to overcome. So what Socrates

---

[67] Plato, *Republic*, 603c.

[68] Plato, *Republic*, 476c.

[69] Plato, *Republic*, 603c-d.

does by putting the "decent man" in conflict with the effects of tragic *mimesis* is to show how both the decent man and by implication a tragedy deal with faction in essentially the same way; even though both are doomed to failure because each is in opposition to the other and both are in conflict with nature.

By taking the example of the decent man whose son dies suddenly, Socrates brings out how his very decency puts him in conflict with his natural desire to mourn and his civic duty to keep a lid on it. His desires as a private father thus seem incompatible with his desires as a public citizen, so what must come to bear is something to subordinate one desire to another. What this "something" is Socrates calls "law and argument," *logos* and *nomos*, in the sense that the law of the city that "presumably says that it is finest to keep as quiet in misfortune and not be irritated" must impose its demands on the individual by means of some sort of argument that would persuade the father that "human things" such as his son are not "worthy of great seriousness" in the light of the city.[70] Whatever this argument for the law is, then, it seems to have the same sort of characteristics we saw in the second wave, for it must argue that "one must accept the fall of the dice and settle one's affairs accordingly" and do away with this "lament by medicine."[71]

These arguments by what Socrates calls the "calculating part" of the soul must apply the same sort of deceitful medicine to the other parts of the soul that the ruler applies to create the eugenically best marriages among the guardians. Such arguments, however, do not persuade to truth but only to belief in the concocted laws of the rulers. Because of this manipulative character, the *logos* of the rulers must be of an entirely different order than those of the ruled, and so we see why putting the "calculative" as the highest part fits perfectly with those souls fit to be *ruled* but neglects entirely what is highest in the souls of those who are by nature fit to *rule*—the philosophers. The individual argument that would make a decent man decent is thus at odds with the corporate "argument" of tragic *mimesis* that must provide the medicine needed

---

[70] Plato, *Republic*, 604b.

[71] Plato, *Republic*, 604c-d.

by everyone else in the city.[72] Nevertheless, both are medicinal, pharmacological, and artificial; which is to say, neither is natural and both have more to do with the carved idols of the cave rather than the sun-lit whole gazed upon by the philosopher.

In the following synopsis of the effects of tragedy, then, what we see is how tragedy, even while performing on a corporate level what goes on individually in the decent man, partakes of the same flaw that will inevitably lead to the breakdown of both.

> If you are aware that what is then held down by force in our own misfortunes and has hungered for tears and sufficient lament and satisfaction, since it is by nature such as to desire these things, is that which now gets satisfaction and enjoyment from the poets. What is by nature best in us, because it hasn't been adequately educated by argument or habit, relaxes its guard over this mournful part because it sees another's sufferings, and it isn't shameful for it, if some other man who claims to be good laments out of season, to praise and pity him; rather it believes that it gains the pleasure and wouldn't permit itself to be deprived of it by despising the whole poem. I suppose that only a certain few men are capable of calculating that the enjoyment of other people's sufferings has a necessary effect on one's own. For the pitying part, fed strong on these examples, is not easily held down in one's own sufferings.[73]

The flaw in both the decent man and tragedy is the need to use force against nature in order to become civilized—corporately or individually. Yet if this "holding down by force" is not the crude violence of physical beating, then what is it and how is it different and yet the same in both personal discipline and tragedy? What is

---

[72] The difference between the "decent man" and what Aristotle calls the gentleman in the *Nicomachean Ethics,* corresponds, I think, with the difference I argued in the first chapter between the gentleman who fears "being unjust" and the not-exactly-virtuous-hero of a tragedy who Aristotle insists must not. cf. *Poetics* 52b32--53a10 and *Rhetoric* 1382a.

[73] Plato, *Republic*, 606a-b.

the same is *nomos*, a sort of artificial nature or second nature like habit that supplants rather than fulfills the initial nature. What is different, is how this law or habit gets created. In the individual it is created by argument, but argument used in the ironic sense that led Socrates earlier to call attack-dogs "philosophical" because they distinguish friend from foe independently of any expected rewards or punishments.[74] This is why calling the calculating part of the soul "what is by nature best in us" also seems questionable, when all it calculates is how to obey laws given to it by another for better or worse. The decent man, in other words, creates out of the faction in his soul the appearance of unity by giving one part dominion over the rest, but at the price of not knowing which part that should be apart from laws and conventions established by others. The implied violence of these sorts of arguments is the violence of technical rhetoric that can always make the weaker argument the stronger because it can never know "which is which" out of its own resources.

The "argument" of tragic *mimesis*, on the other hand, is the corporate indulgence in pleasures that must be submerged individually. Ultimately, these two are at odds, but without a knowledge of the whole that can alone satisfy all these desires justly, this conflict must be hidden for the sake of the short-term prosperity of both. Since the desires held down in the decent man are not eliminated by argument but only repressed, such repression must have the outlet that tragedy supplies. The decent man therefore cannot be deprived of this satisfaction by "despising the whole poem" because to do so would be to despise what is natural in himself; and yet by indulging in this vicarious satisfaction he indirectly admits and subtly undermines the poetic "habit" created in his own soul. Tragedy is therefore essentially a case of both knowing and not knowing that one must keep in tension if it is to work, and the distance created by the poet between the audience and the factions revealed on stage maintains this volatile yet foundational tension. Tragedy is thus always courting its own demise, but until that happens it is the dramatic manifestation of the need for the city to be

---

[74] Plato, *Republic*, 376aff.

lied to and yet believe its own lies. Again, the reason for this is because the body of the body politic is sick, is composed of factions at war with each other, and yet must still compose some sort of workable peace if it is to function at all and so must administer the *pharmakon*/drug of tragedy that cures by means of further sickening.

From Socrates' earlier definition of imitation, then, what must be highlighted here is that even though the experiences of pain or enjoyment are real enough, one can only "suppose" whether the actions turn out well or badly. Tragedy and comedy with their sad or happy endings are thus only the appearance of good and bad when seen apart from the whole of true good and evil that they can at best only imitate. The difference between tragic imitation or comic imitation, however, has to do with the overtness of the comedic competition with the city and the audience's identification with the comic poet rather than the poem. In the following summary of the temptation of comedy, then, what we should notice is that what argument "held down by force" in the passage on tragedy, is here held down by the shame of buffoonery, and that the result of comic shamelessness is to join forces with the private shamelessness of the poet.

> Doesn't the same argument apply to the laughing part? If there are any jokes that you would be ashamed to make yourself, but that you enjoy very much hearing in comic imitation or in private, and you don't hate them as bad, you do the same as with things that evoke pity. For that in you which, wanting to make jokes, you then held down by argument, afraid of the reputation of buffoonery, you now release, and, having made it lusty there, have unawares been carried away in your own things so that you become a comic poet.[75]

By indulging the pitying part of one's soul the private individual ran the risk of producing "a bad regime in his soul,"[76] yet here,

---

[75] Plato, *Republic*, 606c.

[76] Plato, *Republic*, 605b.

when indulging the laughing part, the risk run is merely reputation, which of course is merely "keeping up the appearances" that the joke reveals to be just that. What happens "unawares" to the laughing part, then, is that it becomes itself the comic poet, and that however corporate the laughter in the audience may seem, you as the private individual must stay private because your laughter is always at the expense of the conventional whole, and so you must be "carried away in your own things" in order to even "get it." You as that part of the audience that gets the joke therefore become the comic poet himself inasmuch as his subversive poem cannot be completed without you.

This, then, brings us full circle back to the "old quarrel between and philosophy and poetry"[77] and my argument that this quarrel is not with the comic poets but rather with the tragic poets. For the reason Socrates immediately turns from these two descriptions of the corrupting effects of tragedy and comedy to his accusation against Homer and the tragic poets, rather than, say, Aristophanes, is because Homer has been the *de facto* educator of Greece and the supplier of arguments for the city. The major flaw of Homer as educator, however, is that he cannot overcome the intrinsic tension between the individual and the city and so even while educating the decent man is also undermining and corrupting him. Tragedy must therefore make a defense for itself as to why any city should tolerate its presence, but such a defense would ruin whatever effectiveness tragedy has in the first place. Comedy, glaringly absent at this point, *can* give a defense; and that defense is the ironic defense given in the entire *Republic* by Socrates, who in defending himself and the overriding importance of the individual over the city, is also defending the role of Plato, the comic poet. It is comedy, then, especially the comedy that points to the higher possibility sought by the philosopher, that condescends to defend itself before the city even while subverting it entirely in the light of something higher. The tension between the city and the individual can only be resolved, it seems, when the individual knows within himself the whole that includes the city; and that resolution comes

---

[77] Plato, *Republic*, 607b.

about only when the individual "becomes" the comic poet, and the comic poet also happens to be a lover of wisdom.

The upshot of this argument is that there are three types of comedy, two of which are essentially human and only one of which is truly divine. The first sort of human comedy is that of Aristophanes, which will lead into the "technological" comedy of modernity described by Hegel. The second sort of human comedy is what Bloom here calls "divine" in contradistinction from the merely human comedy of Aristophanes, and that is the comedy written by and for philosophers that consists of the comedic juxtaposition of the philosophical life to the tragedy of the *polis*. This juxtaposition is itself merely a human comedy, but it does open up a possibility of the serious life of philosophy that is divine in comparison. The only truly divine comedy (and as we will see later, Dante's *Commedia* does not qualify) is that found in Scripture insofar as one believes that God as the poet of creation is also the author of this narrative. For when the *logos* through which all things were made shows up as the main character in the center of this story, we are dealing with the central defining characteristic of comedy, which is the poet's own explicit and overt appeal to become a part of his poem. Whether this comedy is truly divine or not is of course a question of faith—but that is precisely its point. Before laying this out in detail, however, we should flesh out more fully the "divine" comedy of Plato.

IV: PLAYFUL AND SERIOUS WRITING IN PLATO'S *PHAEDRUS*

THE *Phaedrus* is an odd dialogue. Surrounded by the constant chirping of cicadas, it is one of the few that takes place outside the walls of the city, and the conversation seems to veer widely from contradictory speeches to wild myths and images, to a final, relatively prosaic condemnation of writing versus speaking. While the section on writing will be of most concern here, some of the earlier events should shed light on our discussion.

Consider, for example, the two speeches Socrates gives on Eros. Having earlier scorned the erotic lover in his first speech, Socrates reverses himself entirely by recanting the first speech and praising the madness of erotic passion. He recants after he receives his daemonic sign, a sign, he explains, that only speaks to him negatively.[1] The negativity of this sign thus seems akin to the poverty of Eros discussed in the *Symposium*, and its daemonic nature shows forth Socrates' knowledge of his need for the divine. Socrates' second speech is therefore made in honor of the gods. It is also made to prevent him from becoming blind like Homer, a blindness the poet Stesichorus avoided by exonerating the beautiful Helen from her responsibility for the Trojan War in the following palinode:

---

[1] "This voice, whenever it comes, always *dissuades*. In this utterly abnormal nature, instinctive wisdom appears only in order to *hinder* conscious knowledge occasionally. While in all productive men it is instinct that is the creative-affirmative force, and consciousness act critically and dissuasively, in Socrates it is instinct that becomes the critic, and consciousness that becomes the creator—truly a monstrosity *per defectum*!" Friedrich Nietzsche, *The Birth of Tragedy* trans. and edited Walter Kaufmann (New York: Vintage Books, 1987), 88.

> False is this tale. You never
> Went in a ship to sea,
> Nor saw the towers of Troy.[2]

Although in Homer the beauty of Helen is responsible for the violence and betrayal of the Trojan War, Socrates argues that such beauty can lead to a different "type of madness," one that is "the greatest benefit that heaven can confer on us."[3] Yet before this can be proved "we must form a true notion of the nature of soul, divine or human, by observing it both in its passive and its active aspects."[4] Socrates begins, therefore, with the active aspect of the soul which as self-moving is as immortal and as unchanging as what *is*. This active element is known in terms of what it is not, the passive aspect, that is moved through its seeking of this active "prime origin of motion." Although Socrates can say that soul is immortal because of the passive aspect's dependence upon the self-moving aspect, what he cannot describe is the soul's nature, of "which only a god is capable." So as with all the things we give birth to, things that only imitate the intelligible whole of reality, here too he will only "say in shorter compass what it resembles."[5]

What the soul resembles, Socrates poetizes for us, is "a winged charioteer and his team acting together."[6] In the case of the gods' chariots, their horses act together in harmony, while our own team acts in disharmony because the ruling element of the charioteer must control two horses, one well-behaved and another stubborn and unruly. Socrates thus distinguishes two sorts of living beings, the mortals and immortals, even though in the case of the immortals, "there is not a single sound reason for positing the existence of such a being, but because we have never seen or formed an adequate idea of a god, we picture him to ourselves as a being of the same kind as ourselves but immortal, a combination of soul

---

[2] Plato, *Phaedrus*, 243.

[3] Plato, Phaedrus, 245.

[4] Plato, *Phaedrus,* 245.

[5] Plato, *Phaedrus,* 246.

[6] Plato, *Phaedrus,* 246.

and body indissolubly joined forever."[7] The immortal gods, then, whether or not they in exist in reality—or perhaps precisely in their nonexistence—exist for Socrates' purposes as a means to speak of that in us which strives after the unchanging and deathless whole that explains our own death and change. Socrates is thus creating a narrative to explain our life in quest of happiness with its manifold produced and yet inevitably inadequate satisfactions by portraying two different circuits through the heavens—the blessed and happy circuits of the gods and our own troubled and more erratic circuit.

With the god's circuit, what we see is a description of the life of *theoria* that rises above the circuit of genesis to view the intelligible whole that does not move at all, but rather motivates that movement and gives it its highest happiness:

> Now the souls that are termed immortal, when they reach the summit of the arch, go outside the vault and stand upon the back of the universe; standing there they are carried round by its revolution while they contemplate what lies outside the heavens. But of this region beyond the skies no mortal poet has sung or ever will sing in such strains as it deserves. Nevertheless the fact is this; for we must have the courage to speak the truth, especially when truth itself is our theme. The region of which I speak is the abode of the reality with which true knowledge is concerned, a reality without color or shape, intangible but utterly real, apprehensible only by intellect which is the pilot of the soul.[8]

The story told here may describe the life of the gods, or the life of the one truly wise, but as for the love of such wisdom and the life lived in pursuit of this god-like happiness, it is better portrayed, along with lesser forms of that pursuit, as follows:

> But of the other souls that which is likest to a god and best able to follow keeps the head of its charioteer above the surface as it makes the circuit, though the

---

[7] Plato, *Phaedrus,* 246.

[8] Plato, *Phaedrus,* 247.

unruly behavior of its horses impairs its vision of reality. A second class sometimes rises and sometimes sinks, and owing to the restiveness of its horses sees part, but not the whole. The rest, in spite of their unanimous striving to reach the upper world, fail to do so [and] depart without achieving initiation into the vision of reality, and feed henceforth upon mere opinion.[9]

And again, lest we forget: "the reason for their eagerness to behold the plain of truth is that the meadow there produces fit pasturage for the best part of the soul, and that the wings by which the soul is born aloft are nourished by it."[10] The driver of our chariot (the soul) is the intellect that wants to be truly happy, and if allowed to steer, directs the soul to its highest level where it encounters unchanging Being, which gives it its truth *and* happiness.

How do we account for this desire, this push toward what we do not have and can't yet know, with the expectation that it will satisfy the entangled and confused desire for happiness *and* pleasure that we know all too well? Socrates accounts for it by means of recollection, by putting this entire narrative of the soul in the past tense as a means to account for how we seem to know and yet not know what we want, and for how we can possibly recognize it for what it is when we get it. Recollection, in other words, is the mimetic explanation of our desire for happiness and the truth. Why should we want the truth unless we had somehow known what is true and real and then somehow forgotten it to the point where we are not sure which is which and yet can't stop caring? The madness of Eros is thus praised because it quickens the soul to a radical wakefulness and recollection, a recollection of the soul's past vision of the Beauty of Being that was the highest possible happiness inasmuch as "beauty was once ours to see in all its brightness. . . . and to be initiated into that mystery which brings, we may say with reverence, supreme felicity."[11]

---

[9] Plato, *Phaedrus,* 248.

[10] Plato, *Phaedrus,* 248.

[11] Plato, *Phaedrus,* 250.

Yet all these things—recollection, the soul as a chariot on a circuit of the heavens, talk of the immortal gods themselves—are only likenesses, only poetically produced imitations of something that has somehow been understood by their producer. Socrates' admission that this entire story is only a "resemblance" raises the question of the truth of resemblances themselves, especially when this entire speech stands in direct opposition to another speech produced right before it, by the same producer! In other words, the relation between *techne* as the ability to make speeches, especially opposing speeches, and the evident desire we all have in our lives to be truly happy, must be raised precisely because of that desire. This is why Socrates uses his two speeches as an appropriate segue into the entire issue of the writing of speeches, of writing itself, and of all things made in general in relation to our quest for the essentially unmade and natural. By turning their conversation from the madness of lovers to the questionableness of writing, the characters written about by Plato speak of themselves as characters, Plato as writer, and ourselves *as* readers.

The issue of writing, then, not only makes thematic the relation of Plato's dialogues to the life of the philosopher, but also our own life's relation to reading about this sort of thing *vis-à-vis* our own actual orientation toward truth and happiness. As obscure as the use of the term writing may seem, its use in the *Phaedrus* raises for us most concretely the tension between the questions we ask about the good life and the mimetic and produced sort of answers we give ourselves that allow us to live with that question still unanswered. The issue of life and writing in the *Phaedrus*, particularly in the light of the distinction between playful and serious lives and writing, should provide a means of asking what is the writing of our lives, and what we are to do with the as yet, and perhaps ultimately, unwritten remainder. For that question, as oddly put as it is, is *the* question that Plato would say makes life worth living and may well help put us on the road toward true happiness.

Socrates begins his discussion of writing by telling a story that he introduces as follows: "Well I can give you a tradition handed down from men of old, but they alone know the truth. If we could find that out for ourselves, should we have any further use for human fancies?"[12] From the very beginning of his discussion, Socrates tips his hand, for this passage summarizes the essential issue behind any writing, namely, that we write because we lack the truth, and that if we had the truth we wouldn't need to write. In the absence of the truth on the nature of writing Socrates treats us to a story instead.

The story takes place in Egypt, and concerns two divine characters, one Thamus and his chief inventor, Theuth. One of Theuth's inventions—among others such as calculation and dice—was that of writing, and since he submitted all his inventions to the king for approval, he presented writing to the king with these words:.

> Here is an accomplishment, my lord the king, which will improve both the wisdom and the memory of the Egyptians. I have discovered a sure receipt [*pharmakon*] for memory and wisdom.[13]

To which replied the king:.

> Theuth, my paragon of inventors . . . the discoverer of an art is not the best judge of the good or harm which will accrue to those who practice it. So it is in this case; you, who are the father of writing, have out of fondness for your offspring attributed to it quite the opposite of its real function. Those who acquire it will cease to exercise their memory and become forgetful; they will rely on writing to bring things to their remembrance by external signs instead of on their own internal resources. What you have discovered is a receipt [*pharmakon*] for recollection, not for memory. And as for wisdom, your pupils will have the reputation for it without the reality: they will receive a quantity of information without proper instruction, and in consequence be thought very knowledgeable when they are for the most part quite ignorant. And because they are filled with the conceit

---

[12] Plato, *Phaedrus,* 274.

[13] Plato, *Phaedrus,* 274.

of wisdom instead of real wisdom they will be a burden to society.[14]

Thamus the king, we may presuppose, is wise because he can judge
what is harmful and beneficial. In judging that the *pharmakon* of
writing is a poison rather than a remedy (*pharmakon* has both these
meanings), he is also saying that, from the perspective of wisdom,
writing suffers from the temptation inherent in all things produced
by us, namely, that as mimetic wholes they will replace the quest
for the true whole of reality. Theuth, in contrast, by presupposing
that we already have wisdom and only need to improve upon it,
shows that he only possesses what he has himself made, and so is
more attached to what is his own rather than either truth, benefit
or wisdom. In other words, it is Theuth's attachment to writing as
his *own* invention that brings out the poisonous temptation of all
poetic creations—that just as with bodily offspring, we are more
attached to them because they are our own rather than because
they are necessarily true or good.

Writing thus suffers from the temptation built into the nature
of genesis that we see in the *Symposium*. Procreation in the beautiful
can ultimately stand in the way of contemplating the beautiful in
itself, but it can also lead up to that vision as in the stairs of ascent.
What then makes the difference? Does writing always lead to forgetting with its function being to poison, or can it sometimes be a
remedy or medicine that leads to our ascent beyond ourselves?

Socrates begins to ask this question by concluding from his
story of Theuth that it is great folly "to suppose that one can trans-
mit or acquire clear and certain knowledge of an art through the
medium of writing, or that written words can do more than remind
the reader of what he already knows."[15] In addition, he compares
writing to mute paintings, that when asked what they mean,
"simply return the same answer over and over again. Besides, once
a thing is committed to writing it circulates freely among those who
understand the subject and those who have no business with it."[16]

---

[14] Plato, *Phaedrus*, 275.

[15] Plato, *Phaedrus*, 275.

[16] Plato, *Phaedrus*, 275.

The problem of writing, in other words, is that presumably unlike spoken instruction, "it cannot distinguish suitable and unsuitable readers"[17] and cannot rescue itself from the misunderstandings of those who do and do not "understand the subject" as one can in speech—a situation Socrates likens to a parent coming to the rescue of its child.

This seemingly offhand analogy of parent and child takes on greater significance when Socrates uses it to distinguish what by implication is the illegitimate brother, namely writing, with the "legitimate brother" who *can* have its parent come to its rescue. This legitimate brother, who we are led to infer by contrast is the spoken speech of instruction, is now for the first time described—yet still only in terms of writing. It is "the kind that is written on the soul together with understanding; that knows how to defend itself, and can distinguish between those it should address and those in whose presence it should be silent."[18]

Notice that in spite of the contrast between these two brothers, both turn out to be "written" and both bear some sort of relation to genuine understanding. The illegitimate brother's weakness is that it cannot distinguish between its readers who "understand the subject," and those who don't, while the legitimate brother must be written on the soul "together with understanding," a relationship that seems to provide the "parent" who can rescue it from unsuitable readers. The point, however, is that if in contrast to this illegitimate brother we were to simply assimilate the legitimate brother to its father, the "understanding," we would be making an essential mistake.

It would be a mistake, I think, along the same lines as equating the lover of wisdom with one who is truly wise. For the deliberate use by Socrates of "writing on the soul" to describe what is seemingly not writing at all, but rather speech, may well tip us off (if we are in fact "suitable readers") that Plato has everything here to say about writing, but very little about speech. In other words, since one might naturally assume from the apparent drift of the

---

[17] Plato, *Phaedrus,* 275.

[18] Plato, *Phaedrus,* 276.

analogy that writing would be best described in terms of speech, when Socrates instead remains silent about speech directly and only describes it in terms of writing, we as readers should be forewarned that there might be two ways of following this argument: one that gets the point (joke shall we say?), and one that doesn't. For both brothers, in spite of the overt attempt to get us to think in terms of speech, are emphatically forms of writing.

Or to put this differently, it is Phaedrus who draws the analogy, and not Socrates, when he exclaims: "You mean the living and animate speech of a man with knowledge, of which written speech might fairly be called a kind of shadow."[19] When Socrates answers "Exactly," we may well wonder if he is not silently covering over the fact that Phaedrus has gotten the terms of the comparison exactly backwards. Be that as it may, Socrates draws the subject back to writing again through the roundabout of playful and serious farmers.

Socrates asks whether a sensible farmer would take his good seed and sow it "in sober earnest in gardens of Adonis at midsummer, and take pleasure in seeing it reach its full perfection in eight days? Isn't this something he might do in a holiday mood by way of diversion, if he did it at all?"[20] If the farmer is serious rather than playful, would he not "follow the true principles of agriculture and sow his seed in soil that suits it,"[21] and wait patiently to harvest it eight months hence? The object of the analogy is then revealed when Socrates asks further:

> "And are we to say that the man with real knowledge of right and beauty and good will treat what we may by analogy call his seed less intelligently than the farmer?"
> Phaedrus: "Of course not."
> Socrates: "Then when he is in earnest he will not take a pen and write in water or sow his seed in the black fluid called ink, to produce discourse which cannot

---

[19] Plato, *Phaedrus,* 276.

[20] Plato, *Phaedrus,* 276.

[21] Plato, *Phaedrus,* 276.

defend themselves viva voce or give any adequate account of the truth."

Phaedrus: "Presumably not."

Socrates: "No, indeed. It will be by way of pastime
that he will use the medium of writing to sow what
may be styled gardens of literature, laying up for himself as well as for those who follow the same track
aids to recollection against the time when the forgetfulness of old age may overtake him, and it will give
him pleasure to see the growth of their tender shoots.
And when other men resort to other diversions, and
indulge themselves with drinking-parties [*symposia*]
and kindred pleasures, he on the contrary will amuse
himself, I think, with the sort of pastime that I am
describing."[22]

Here then we have an account of contrasting approaches to writing
that follows the same pattern as the relation between the two
brothers, and retroactively, so to speak, serves to illumine that relation. Whereas at first the point here may seem to be that the man
with "real knowledge of right and beauty and good" would never
write seriously, on second thought, that main point may well be
that he would write playfully, "by way of pastime," if he writes at
all. In addition, sowing his seeds in ink in this way would be a way
of amusing himself rather than attending symposia where people
might, for example, amuse themselves by making speeches about
Eros.

Whoever he is, then, what we can say of this man who has
real knowledge of right, beauty and good is that if he writes anything it will be written playfully, as a pastime to amuse himself rather than something done seriously. Whether this man is truly a
god or whether he knows these things only because he knows he
doesn't know them, the one clue we do have as to his identity is
that he would write discourses rather than attending symposia.
This seems an odd sort of contrast until we reflect on the fact that
we are reading this in a discourse written not by Socrates (who as
far as we know never wrote anything but a few fables but by Plato

---

[22] Plato, *Phaedrus*, 276.

his student. [23] And one of the things we notice about this Plato is that, in another dialogue he wrote, the *Symposium*, there is a description of a drinking-party in which a philosopher, many poets, speech-writers and statesmen are present, but Plato is not among them; nor could he be, because of its recollected back-dating. Is he referring to himself here, in jest? We have good reason to think so, especially when the topic of writing draws our attention more to Plato who alone does all the writing here rather than to his Socrates who only speaks.

The little joke of Plato may well be continuous with the joke of the two brothers, and the point may well be the same—that the issue is not actually writing versus speaking, but rather serious writing versus playful writing and the relationship each has to its respective readers. The question then is the connection between understanding and reading and understanding and writing, and the possible disconnection that can take place in serious writing. The analogy of spoken instruction that can distinguish and rescue its sons from misunderstanding among its hearers may well be a positive prescription for that kind of writing that *is* able to rescue itself from inadequate readers—playful writing.

Nevertheless, when Phaedrus seems to take the point that amusing oneself writing dialogues about justice is finer than attending symposia, Socrates again seems to return to the image of spoken instruction.

> Quite so, my dear Phaedrus. But finer still is the serious treatment of these subjects which you find when a man employs the art of dialectic, and, fastening upon a suitable soul, plants and sows in it truths accompanied by knowledge. Such truths can defend themselves as well as the man who planted them; they are not sterile, but contain a seed from which fresh truths spring up in other minds; in this way they secure immortality for it, and confer upon the man who possesses it the highest happiness which it is possible for a human being to enjoy.[24]

---

[23] Plato, *Phaedo,* 60d-61b.

[24] Plato, *Phaedo,* 276d-277a.

As readers we can guess that this highest happiness concerns the life of Socrates and his actual hearers; yet as readers we have only this written dialogue that we know is not and cannot be the real thing. Our only approach to whatever Socrates is talking about here must therefore be through writing. Likewise, whatever actually went on in the lives of Socrates or Plato, our only access to it is indirectly through our own lives as readers. When we thus read about this life lived in pursuit of happiness, the issue facing us rather than Phaedrus is whether that writing is serious or playful; for that may be our most important clue in knowing whether we are dealing with a serious pursuit of true happiness or just a playing at pursuit that mistakes its own productions for what it truly seeks. For if Plato is here arguing that it is the serious pursuer who will write playfully while serious writing is a sign that the writer is only playing at his pursuit, then playful writing, the writing Plato implies we are now in fact reading, would be the best clue that we are dealing with a serious pursuit and serious writing would be the best clue we are not.

Socrates therefore concludes his case to Phaedrus both positively and negatively. Negatively, he says that "Lysias or any other writer, past or future, who claims that clear and permanently valid truth is to be found in a written speech, lays himself open to reproach."[25] Such serious writing would be a sign that one is not living a serious life and is unable to distinguish between "dream and waking reality about right and wrong, good and evil, a condition which cannot escape censure, even though the populace as a whole may be loud in its praise."[26] Positively, Socrates argues, one ought to write in such a way as to avoid taking for true what are only imitations of the truth, because one realizes that

> a written composition on any subject must be to a large extent the creation of fancy; that nothing worth serious attention has ever been written in prose or verse—or spoken for that matter, if by speaking one means the kind of recitation that aims merely at creating belief, without any attempt at instruction by

[25] Plato, *Phaedo,* 277.

[26] Plato, *Phaedo,* 277.

> question and answer; . . . whereas lucidity and finality
> and serious importance are to be found only in words
> spoken by way of instruction or, to use a truer phrase,
> written on the soul of the hearer to enable him to
> learn about the right, the beautiful and the good; fi-
> nally, to realize that such spoken truths are to be reck-
> oned a man's legitimate sons, primarily if they
> originate within himself. . . . to believe this, I say, and
> to let all else go is to be the sort of man, Phaedrus,
> that you and I might well pray that we may both be-
> come.[27]

Only in the actual life of Socrates or Phaedrus it would seem, or
any given reader, can we hope to find the desire for happiness and
the truth. Only in the cultivation through concrete question and
answer do we have any hope of attaining it.

In what lies before us, however, this sort of dialectic cannot
be found at all, for this entire dialogue is itself something written
and we are neither speaking nor hearing, but only reading, the
words of fictional characters. At best we can only be dealing here
with the illegitimate son rather than the legitimate one of "spoken
truth." Nevertheless, it is only in our own questions as readers arising from our desire for happiness, along with the answers that are
known as such precisely because they satisfy the criteria we alone
can give for what happiness truly is, that we can possibly find those
legitimate sons fathered by true justice, beauty, and the Good that
make for true happiness. The legitimate son, in other words, can
only come to birth in our concrete life as readers, and the father of
both this legitimate son we find in life and the illegitimate sons
found in the fictional characters in writing—serious or playful—is
that which truly *is* and makes all these sons possible.

So once again, when at the height of his praise of spoken instruction, we find Socrates using the "truer phrase," of "instruction
written on the soul of the hearer," we find our attention directed
away from speech to writing. And when we further see that Socrates calls his literary discussion with Phaedrus a case of "amusing
ourselves" rather than the serious pursuit of dialectic that he has

---

[27] Plato, *Phaedo,* 277d-278a.

just described and prayed for, then I think we should take him at his word and not take the ostensive distinction between the two sons seriously.[28] Instead, we might consider that when a distinction between speech and writing is made *in writing*, "getting the joke" may well consist of distinguishing only between two different kinds of illegitimate sons—both of which are written, yet one is serious and one is playful. In other words, the joke is that *both* sons here are bastards, and that whoever and wherever the legitimate son may be, all we can be dealing with here in this written dialogue is one of the bastard sons wearing his name-tag. This imposter we will call playful or comic writing, and it is this sort of writing by Plato that we are now reading. Comic writing is that sort of writing that turns back in upon itself and imitates the missing legitimate son by pointing to ourselves as readers and laughing at us when we forget we are reading a written dialogue against writing. If the joke is to not be on us, we must recollect ourselves, and attend to the serious business of living a truly happy life after we put the book down.

Serious writing, the writing that forgets even the possibility of a legitimate heir, would seem to be the true target of criticism here. For Socrates' final charge to Phaedrus is to claim the following as the substance of the message they have received from their conversation, a message that should be delivered to Lysias, Homer and other poets, and writers of laws:

> If any of them had knowledge of the truth when he wrote, and can defend what he has written by submitting to an interrogation on the subject, and make it evident as soon as he speaks how comparatively inferior are his writings, such a one should take his title not from what he has written but from what has been the object of his serious pursuit.[29]

Since, of course, this interrogation is impossible, what seems to make serious writing serious is that it *doesn't* interrogate the reader, it doesn't redirect our attention away from itself and toward

---

[28] Plato, *Phaedo,* 278.

[29] Plato, *Phaedo,* 278.

our own life, or the life of the writer, as what is truly worthy of serious attention. If we can therefore say the philosopher is the one who knows that the life lived in pursuit of the truth is worth more than any writings about the truth, and yet if we can never interrogate anything a philosopher has ever or will ever write because it will always answer the same thing back, perhaps the true philosopher will have to write the sort of playful writing that demands us to interrogate ourselves.

The one who writes seriously, on the other hand, "the man whose most precious production is what he has composed or written, and who has devoted his time to twisting words this way and that, pasting them together and pulling them apart, may fairly be called a poet, or a speech-writer or a maker of laws."[30] What makes these men serious writers is that their writings are precious to them, the world of their own creation is worth as much attention as their own lives, for somewhere in the midst of all their written words they expect to find the truth.

Yet how can we know this about them, especially when all we have are their writings, which cannot be interrogated to reveal the life of their writers? How we can know is the serious nature of their writings, a seriousness that draws all attention to itself and so obscures the essential role of the reader in his reading. It is writing that passes for wisdom itself apart from our loving or seeking it, just as the laws must seem wise on their own without directing our attention to the wisdom of the lawmaker or judge. Serious writing, in other words, is essentially the writing of the tragic poet who, in contrast with the comic poet, cannot make a stage appearance or directly address his audience without ruining the dramatic effect of his tragedy. Serious writing is writing that must lie about its true inability to speak truth rather than opinion, precisely because it *must* be taken seriously.

This equation of serious writing with the dramatic effects of tragedy and playful writing with the dramatic effects of comedy brings out why the quarrel between the poets and the philosophers in the *Republic* parallels the *Phaedrus's* dispute between speech and

---

[30] Plato, *Phaedo*, 278.

writing. For there too, the seeming quarrel with all poets is really with the tragic poets, just as here the distinction is between playful versus serious writing. The point of Plato's dialogue on writing is therefore not to go around asking whether authors are serious or playful, but rather to distinguish between playful and serious writing—because there is no life behind writing that we can interrogate except our own. And yet since our own life is *the* essential issue for philosophy, to distinguish between playful and serious writing is to judge both by means of the effect they have upon us the reader. Plato, in other words, is distinguishing between comic writing and tragic writing because each has a distinct relationship to its reader as a result of its structural rather than real relation to its writer or poet (the real relation is authorship *per se*, while the structural is the relation of the narrative to its narrator, implied author to reader, etc.). In the larger issue of the relation between life and writing, then, we find that comedy and tragedy are the two most important terms for dealing with that relation because each has a distinct and separate relation to a possible audience. It comes as no surprise, and in fact serves as a confirmation of this reading of the *Phaedrus*, that comedy and tragedy play a leading role in Plato's other major dialogues and are invariably juxtaposed with the issue of the life of the philosopher and his relation to poetry, the body, and the city. Already we have seen this confirmed in our reading of the *Republic*, but before turning to the *Symposium* and other dialogues we should perhaps see how this argument stands up to Derrida's justly famous essay covering similar ground.

In "Plato's Pharmacy," Derrida gives a backhanded confirmation of my reading of the *Phaedrus* when he declares that "the conclusion of the *Phaedrus* is less a condemnation of writing in the name of present speech than a preference for one sort of writing over another."[31] I am not sure I could have summarized my own point any better. And yet the problem with Derrida's argument is that he arrives at it not by reading Plato as either playful or even ironic, but instead by letting the text "deconstruct" itself—which is exactly what ironic and playful texts tend to do. When Derrida

---

[31] Jacques Derrida, *Dissemination,* trans. Barbara Johnson, (Chicago: The University of Chicago Press, 1981), 149.

arrives at this declaration by noting the metaphorical subversion of calling speech "writing on the soul," what he misses is the possibility that such subversion may well be deliberate and in fact a comic clue as to which type of writing is preferred and why. Derrida therefore draws the right conclusion that what is being spoken of is two kinds of writing, but by not giving Plato credit for knowing that this is his point as well, his recognition of its truth gets its importance all wrong.

In the following paragraph, for example, what is dead on and what misses the point are so intertwined that sorting each out should prove well worth doing:

> According to a pattern that will dominate all of Western philosophy, good writing (natural, living, knowledgeable, intelligible, internal, speaking) is opposed to bad writing (a moribund, ignorant, external, mute artifice for the senses). And the good can be designated only through the metaphor of the bad one. Metaphoricity is the logic of contamination and the contamination of logic. Bad writing is for good a model of linguistic designation and a simulacrum of essence. And if the network of opposing predicates that link one type of writing to the other contains in its meshes all the conceptual oppositions of "Platonism"—here considered the dominant structure of the history of metaphysics—then it can be said that philosophy is played out in the play between two kinds of writing. Whereas all it wanted to do was to distinguish between writing and speech.[32]

What Derrida has got right here, is that philosophy *is* played out in the play between two kinds of writing. But what is wrong is the failure to acknowledge that these two kinds of writing are actually comic writing and tragic writing—something Derrida's spiritual mentor, Nietzsche, did not overlook and which gave him a much better take on reading Plato.[33] In the words of Stanley Rosen, Derrida's major mistake is that of overlooking the distinction between

---

[32] Derrida, *Dissemination*, 149.

[33] So, for example, Nietzsche's first work in which he begins his life-long quarrel with Socrates, concerns the birth of tragedy and has at its center

"text and life," or "writing and reading,"[34] by downplaying the controlling irony that this entire discourse is itself something written.

---

the figure of Socrates who presides over its death; and yet in his later "Attempt at Self-Criticism" of that same work he will end with the admonition: "Laughter I have pronounced holy: you higher men, *learn*—to laugh!" Nietzsche, *The Birth of Tragedy*, 27.

[34] "Derrida is unable to countenance the doctrine of the author's intention because he cannot distinguish between the text and life. In other words, he cannot distinguish between reading and writing." Stanley Rosen "Platonic Hermeneutics: On the Interpretation of a Platonic Dialogue" in *Proceedings of The Boston Area Colloquium in Ancient Philosophy*, vol. 1, 1985, ed. John J. Cleary (Lanham, MD: University Press of America, 1986), 288. This article by Rosen has had a great influence upon the reading of Plato being used here and its relation to Derrida, so it would be useful to summarize this aspect of his argument in the following:

> …Derrida states the central problem of the Platonic dialogues in a forceful way by attributing to Plato a preference for speech over writing because of his adherence to a metaphysics of presence. In my view, this takes us to the heart of the matter, but it almost exactly inverts the correct inferences to be drawn from the Platonic corpus....I shall attribute an intentional self-deconstruction to Plato, as an intrinsic feature of his presentation, not of Being, but of the absence of an epistemic speech about Being. (272)
> …Once more on Derridean grounds, we can therefore take Socrates' criticism of writing as play in the *Phaedrus*, together with Plato's own disownment of writing in general, and his dialogues in particular, in his *Letters*, to justify the following conclusion. Since speech is writing and writing is playful, not only is there no serious writing, but there is no speech. I mean by this that what Derrida call "phonocentrism" is entirely absent from the Platonic dialogues. On the basis of the evidence that he himself cites, *there is for Plato nothing but writing*. (274)
> …Throughout the dialogues, ostensibly technical discussions are regularly designated as playful. If we are allowed to include myths, like that of the *Timaeus*, as playful discourses, and recall that a serious discourse would be about eternal or divine things, then it is safe to say that the dialogues are entirely playful. But where everything is playful, including the distinction between the serious and the playful, then the playful becomes serious. (283)

If we connect up this last conclusion with the first comments about reading and writing, then what seems to follow is that Plato's intention is to take the lives of his readers with the utmost seriousness by writing in a

This irony, if recognized, draws attention not to itself as writing but rather to the reader, just as verbal irony reveals the hearer even as it hides the dissembling speaker.[35] In other words, when we read of the distinction between life and writing in something written, the irony should direct our attention to our own lives as readers; keeping in mind that whatever limitations and vulnerabilities our lives might be subject to, they are not subject to the same sort of deconstructing as is a text. The two kinds of written texts distinguished by Plato are thus two different *virtual* relations to *actual* readers and this difference is best exemplified by the dramatic differences between tragedy and comedy.

---

consistently playful manner. The alternative to this approach, taken by the tragic poets, would be to write in such a way that the reader takes what he reads with the utmost seriousness: a seriousness that requires one to forget, so to speak, the role of author in relation to reader (or their structural surrogates) as much as possible.

An example of this seriousness in action that also leads to an entirely different approach to Plato can be found in the beginning of Martha Nussbaum's *The Fragility of Goodness*. "It occurred to me to ask myself whether the act of writing about the beauty of human vulnerability is not, paradoxically, a way of rendering oneself less vulnerable and more in control of the uncontrolled elements in life" (xv). It is also no surprise that the hermeneutical investigations of Heidegger and Gadamer in their easy dismissal of the role of authorial intent gained their impetus from the tragic orientation of Nietzsche.

> "In oratorical discourse there frequently occurs a figure of speech which bears the name of irony and whose characteristic is this: to say the opposite of what is meant. With this we already have a determination present in all forms of irony, namely, the phenomenon is not the essence but the opposite of the essence....The ironic figure of speech cancels itself, however, for the speaker presupposes his listeners understand him, hence through a negation of the immediate phenomenon the essence remains identical with the phenomenon....In all these instances irony exhibits itself most nearly as conceiving the world, as attempting to mystify the surrounding world not so much in order to conceal itself as to induce others to reveal themselves." Søren Kierkegaard, *The Concept of Irony: With Constant Reference to Socrates,* trans. Lee M. Capel, (Bloomington: Indiana University Press, 1965) 264-268.

When Derrida does finally recognize that Plato is in fact arguing for playful writing and so explicitly deals with the all-important irony that this discussion occurs in a written dialogue, he again fails to distinguish between life and writing:

> The opposition *spoude/paidia* will never be one of simple symmetry. *Either* play is *nothing* (and that is its only *chance*); either it can give place to no activity, to no discourse worthy of the name—that is, one charged with truth or at least meaning—and then it is *alogos* or *atopos*. Or *else* play begins to be something and its very presence lays it open to some sort of dialectical confiscation. It takes on meaning and works in the service of seriousness, truth, and ontology. Only *logoi peri onton* can be taken seriously. As soon as it comes into being and into language, play *erases itself as such*. Just as writing must erase itself as such before truth, etc. The point is that there *is* no *as such* where writing or play are concerned.[36]

What Derrida overlooks here is that Plato is distinguishing between a playing at life and playful writing. So while Derrida's description may apply to the play that can pass for living as opposed to the seriousness of real life, it does not apply to specifically playful writing which functions in a distinct manner from the serious writing of tragedy.[37] A serious life that writes playfully is thus not "playing at play," but rather seriously playing—as in the case of Plato—the game of writing philosophical comedies.

What of serious writing then? In what way can the writing of the poets, speechwriters and lawgivers be said to be tragedies? Derrida unwittingly gives us a good account of this sort of writing on his own, since it is this sort of writing he seems to think Plato is

---

[36] Derrida, "Plato's Pharmacy," in *Disseminations*, 156.

[37] Examples of what I mean by playing at living would be Kierkegaard's "Aesthetic Stage" of existence or Pascal's account of "diversion". In connection with this, what I think is misguided about Bigelow's *Kierkegaard and the Problem of Writing*, (Tallahassee: The Florida State University Press, 1987), is that although his analysis may apply at the level of Kierkegaard's description of the aesthetic stage it fails to account for the other stages, particularly Religiousness B.

engaged in. For serious writing seems to function in the same way that Derrida describes the *pharmakon* and all the pharmaceutical terms that go with it, especially the *pharmakos*, or scapegoat. Derrida discerns this quality of tragic writing when he penetrates to what he calls another level of the "Platonic reserves" and discovers that this "pharmacy is also, we begin to perceive, a theater. The theatrical cannot here be summed up in speech: it involves forces, space, law, kinship, the human, the divine, death, play, festivity. Hence the new depth that reveals itself to us will necessarily be another scene, on another stage, or rather another tableau in the unfolding of the play of writing."[38] Yes, this is a theater; but there are two kinds of theater, both of which have the same elements of lust, violence, incest etc., but one leads to laughter and the other does not. Plato knows all these elements are there in his writings in all their pharmaceutical duality, but he deliberately places his philosophical hero, Socrates, in a comedy with its laughter and irony—rather than a tragedy.

When Derrida describes what he calls "patricidal writing," he is describing something akin to the Sophoclean tragedy of *Oedipus the King*:

> In effect, the father's death opens the reign of violence. In choosing violence—and that is what it's all about from the beginning—and violence against the father, the son—or patricidal writing—cannot fail to expose himself, too. All this is done in order to ensure that the dead father, first victim and ultimate resource, not be there. Being-there is always a property of paternal speech. And the site of a fatherland.[39]

On the other hand, when he describes Plato as writing out of the death of Socrates, or of Socrates representing the father or elder brother to Athens in the form of a gadfly, what he is describing has more in common with the laughable father-beatings and mock violence of Aristophanes' *The Clouds*.[40] Both stories center around

---

[38] Derrida, "Plato's Pharmacy," 142.

[39] Derrida, "Plato's Pharmacy," 146.

[40] Plato, *Apology,* 30c-31b.

the theme of patricide, father and sons, and the internal realities of the polis; but seriousness and playfulness make all the difference and so to substitute one for the other has a huge effect upon an actual, living audience.

Patricidal writing, we might say then, is writing *tout court*; but such patricides can be either in jest or deadly serious, and this difference goes to the heart of both the family and the *polis*. For what we have in Derrida's entire description of the pharmacy, of the undifferentiated power that allows *pharmakon* to be translated both as poison and as remedy, is what "writing" means in the broadest sense—whether it be *techne*, *mimesis*, *poesis*, or *genesis*. Unfortunately, this latter "pharmacy" of terms is limited by Derrida to what I will call tragic writing.

When he describes that type of writing he is quite accurate, but he is wildly off base when he encounters Plato's own choice to write playfully. Take, for example, Derrida's description of the "pharmaceutical nonsubstance" as the

> prior medium in which differentiation in general is produced, along with the opposition between the *eidos* and its other; this medium is *analogous* to the one that will, subsequent to and according to the decision of philosophy, be reserved for transcendental imagination, that "art hidden in the depths of the soul," which belongs neither simply to the sensible nor simply to the intelligible, neither simply to passivity nor simply to activity. The element-medium will always be analogous to a mixed-medium. In a certain way, Plato thought about and even formulated this ambivalence. But he did so in passing, incidentally, discreetly . . . [41]

Yes, Plato did formulate this discreetly—by writing playfully. But in choosing to write as a comic poet he was also able to distinguish writing (as the ultimate "nonsubstance") from the life of the reader wherein true substance may be found in the vision of *theoria*. Moreover, Derrida's analogy between the pharmacy and the transcendental imagination is not strictly an analogy at all, but rather talk

---

[41] Derrida, "Plato's Pharmacy," 126.

about the same thing under different terms. This is possible inasmuch as Kant's *a priori* productive power collapsed *theoria* into *poesis*, thereby widening the break the moderns had already made from the ancients by eliminating *theoria* and claiming knowledge of only what we have ourselves made. The *pharmakon* has thus truly been in modern thought the "bottomless fund," "(the production of) difference," "the differance of difference . . . that holds in reserve, in its undecided shadow and vigil, the opposites and the differends that the process of discrimination will come to carve out," and the fund from which "dialectics draws its philosophemes."[42] The dialectical reversals, pyrotechnics and self-immolations of Hegel's and Marx's philosophemes will later amply bear this out, yet in Plato at least, those "philosophemes" are found only in the playful writing of his dialogues. So Derrida is quite right to say of them that in the dialogues "the order of knowledge is not the triumphant order of forms or ideas, as one might be tempted retrospectively to interpret it; it is the antidote."[43] In other words, the playful writing of the dialogues has a function, but no certain content; and that function is to direct our attention to our own life apart from writing which is the only place true knowledge can be attained. In contrast, Hegel's triumphant order of forms or ideas has the duplicitous content of tragic writing that when exposed, does indeed have the unending deconstructive quality that Derrida describes so well.

Serious writing, then, covers over the distinction between life and writing, ignoring one's ignorance because in it one takes what one makes for what one knows. Yet this ignorance is the ignorance at the heart of the city and seems to be a condition for its very existence. When Derrida sees Plato equating *logos* with *nomos*, then he overlooks that it is the makers of laws (*nomoi*) rather than the philosophers who write seriously and so are the ones founding the regimes and writing the laws that preserve them, even though they can't fully know what they are doing without theoretical knowledge. [44] One might say of them that they only know what

---

[42] Derrida, "Plato's Pharmacy," 127.

[43] Derrida, "Plato's Pharmacy," 138.

[44] Derrida, "Plato's Pharmacy," 146.

they are doing after they have done it—which would be the truth behind the claim that "the just is the legal." By playing at lawmaking, Plato is thus uncovering this cover-up, knowing what he is doing—lying—and saying as much. And as he implies in Book V of the *Republic*, the role the lie plays in the city is the role the scapegoat plays in uniting and making the city one by excluding the "other."

So when Derrida follows the chain of signifiers found in Plato's text, "*pharmakeia-pharmakon-pharmakeus*" until he finally arrives at the word "strikingly absent from the 'Platonic text'," namely, the *pharmakos* or scapegoat, we find that he has arrived at the heart of Plato's analysis of the city and tragic writing.[45] For the lie at the heart of the city is epitomized by the scapegoat function of tragic writing that must hide the means by which it succeeds if it is to do so. The scapegoat, in other words, is what effects the appearance of justice in the polis, and Derrida's description of the *pharmakos* bears this out.

> The city's body proper thus reconstitutes its unity, closes around the security of its inner courts, gives back to itself the word that links it with itself within the confines of the agora, by violently excluding from its territory the representative of an external threat or aggression. That representative represents the otherness of the evil that comes to affect or infect the inside by unpredictably breaking into it. Yet the representative of the outside is nonetheless *constituted*, regularly granted its place by the community, chosen, kept, fed, etc., in the very heart of the inside . . . Beneficial insofar as he cures—and for that venerated and cared for—harmful insofar as he incarnates the powers of evil—and for that, feared and treated with caution. Sacred and accursed. The conjunction, the *coincidentia oppositorum*, ceaselessly undoes itself in the passage to decision or crisis. The expulsion of the evil or madness restores *sophrosune*.[46]

---

[45] Derrida, "Plato's Pharmacy," 129.

[46] Derrida, "Plato's Pharmacy," 133.

But the philosopher is not moderate, he is mad; and as we have seen in Socrates' palinode and Diotima's initiation, this madness seeks to break free from writing altogether into the life of *theoria*. The mad philosopher therefore only plays with writing, and so quite self-consciously offers himself up as the scapegoat for the city—as with Socrates—or plays at writing its laws, or telling it its lies. But rather than letting Derrida, who seems to completely abstract from the political except for this and a few other passages, explain the scapegoat to us, we should stick to Plato himself on this matter, particularly in the political writing par excellence, the *Republic*.

V: THE *SYMPOSIUM'S* EROTIC STRIVING IN LIFE AND WRITING

AS WE can see from the *Phaedrus*, the overarching backdrop for a discussion of comedy and tragedy might be called "the problem of writing." Somewhere, between our unlimited desire to know and to live what is truly the good life and the limited fulfillment of that desire in the life we actually do lead, is where we will find this problematic. We might also have called this the problem of "narrative," "*techne*," "*mimesis*," or "*poesis*," but the term "writing," because it includes all these others, brings them together in their contradistinction from "life." Life, as we must live it, invariably involves the quest to know and live what is truly the good life of happiness; nevertheless, all of us must face the fact that what makes that knowledge and life possible is something independent of us of which we are mostly ignorant. Writing, on the other hand, seems to be something we *can* know since we make it ourselves, so the temptation of writing and all things made by ourselves is to substitute themselves for the truth we are seeking and provide the whole within which our desire for happiness can be satisfied. And since writing in the widest sense is written as a means to satisfy our desires, the challenge writing presents to our desire for happiness is that this desire too can only be satisfied by something we make, which would mean the truth itself must be something "written."

To clarify this further, let us interpret writing in terms of Aristotle's "*techne*." In Book VI of the *Nicomachean Ethics* he contrasts *techne* with *theoria*. *Theoria* deals with the knowledge of what has always existed and can only be contemplated in the passive vision of theory, while *techne* deals with what actively comes into existence and has the principles of its genesis in its producer and not in itself as product.[1] *Techne* thus brings into being things that have the cause of their being outside themselves in their maker; and yet that maker, as much as he may be responsible for supplying the principle to what he makes, does not possess his own "principle" (or what makes of something an intelligible whole), but rather must discover it through what he sees in the contemplation of *theoria*. With *techne*, then, what we make is an intelligible whole because of its source in ourselves as intelligent makers. Since we can't help desiring the intelligible whole that gives the truth to our own lives, and yet since we are for the most part ignorant of that whole, the ability to make intelligible wholes we see in technical knowing presents itself as a form of knowing that avoids our ignorance and seems to satisfy our desire for the truth. The intelligible wholes of things made are thus a sort of imitation, or "*mimesis*," of the intelligible whole sought by *theoria*. They are what might be called "mimetic wholes," in the sense that their intelligibility, inasmuch as it has its source in their producers, is always an imitation, at a second remove, from whatever intelligibility has previously been discovered by the intelligence of their producers—an intelligence that spontaneously seeks an intelligible wholeness prior to making anything at all.

What little intelligible sense we have discovered about our world may well seem meagre and not altogether clear or unquestionable, yet since our decision to make this or that product must be derived from that unclear intelligibility, the clearer knowledge of *how* to make something must always be subordinated to the not so clear knowledge of *what* to make. To put this another way, what is immediately most clear to us and manifestly intelligible, a mimetic whole, is entirely dependent upon what is always less clear

---

[1] "All art [*techne*] is concerned with the realm of coming-to-be, i.e., with contriving and studying how something which is capable both of being and of not being may come into existence, a thing whose starting point or source is in the producer and not in the thing produced. For art is concerned neither with things which exist or come into being by necessity, nor with things which produced by nature: these have their source of motion within themselves." Aristotle, *Nicomachean Ethics*, trans. Ostwald (New York: Macmillan, 1986), 1140a10-16.

and much harder to fathom, the intelligible whole sought by intelligent inquiry that provides the context for all *mimesis*. Hence the temptation for a mimetic whole to stand in for the less accessible quest for an intelligible whole, a temptation that becomes a necessity if the quest for the true whole is deemed quixotic.

Connected with this problematic is a more overarching one, that in keeping with our use of Greek terms we might call "genesis." Genesis has to do with the problem of coming into being in general, either through the coming into being of our products, or the coming into being or going out of being of ourselves, the producers. Birth and death are in this way intimately connected with making and destroying. For Aristotle and Plato, we who are seeking the theoretical vision of an intelligible whole that *is*—that stays the same and never comes into existence or goes out of existence—are seeking that vision as the unchanging context that will give the truth to our ever-changing attempts to live the best life of happiness. Because we are mortal and come into being we find that the questions we ask about the best life cannot be fully answered precisely because we do come into being—because we have bodies, are limited in time and space, have more questions than our time or ability can answer.

The fact of our own genesis, then, leads toward thought about nature (*physis*) that stays the same in the midst of all genesis; and the way we know *physis* is through *theoria*. But the fact of genesis also leads toward thought about what has its genesis through our own hands, the products of *techne*, because such knowledge puts us in the position of immortal gods to our mortal creations. Coming into being, genesis, therefore strives after Being—mortality strives after immortality—but there are two ways of doing so: *techne*, which seeks to "overcome" genesis by means of further genesis; and *theoria*, which hopes to supersede genesis in the knowledge of what it does not yet have but only seeks.

So whereas *theoria* refers to the contemplation of the enduring processes of nature that stay the same even in the midst of change, *techne* refers to the knowledge needed to bring something into being artificially—a knowledge of the process of *poesis*, or what Socrates in the *Symposium* calls "the entire process of turning a thing from non-being into being."[2] Both terms, then, *techne* and *poesis*, refer to something conventional, or what is artificially brought into being; in contrast to nature which brings *itself* into being, and in its cyclical pattern of rebirths continues to stay what it *is*, namely, Being.[3]

Writing, that has so far been described in terms of *techne*, *mimesis* and *poesis*, can also be fleshed out by the narrative about Eros which Diotima relates in the *Symposium*. Prior to recalling this tale, Socrates criticizes the tragic poet Agathon's eulogy to Eros for failing to see that Eros is not itself beautiful, but rather only strives after the Beautiful. Eros, Socrates argues, suffers from that same sort of emptiness or ignorance we have already found to be at the heart of living: that we strive after a passive vision of what we do not possess in order to make happily complete and good the life we do possess. For Eros, striving after that vision is the striving after beauty, and it is only in the light of that beauty that it can attain the Good. Eros is daemonic, "intermediate between mortal

---

[2] Plato, *The Symposium of Plato*, trans. S. Groden (Boston: University of Massachusetts Press, 1970), 205c.

[3] Heidegger in his essay "The Question Concerning Technology" (Martin Heidegger, *The Question Concerning Technology and Other Essays*, trans. William Lovitt, (New York: Harper & Row Publishers, 1977) seems to get this backwards in a way that undermines his entire claim about "technology" having its origins in the thought of Plato. For what he does in the following passage is directly assert exactly what Plato and Aristotle denied, namely, that nature, or *physis*, is the same as *poesis*, a denial that was at the heart of their entire thought, even as its affirmation is at the heart of all modern thought. "*Physis*, also, the arising of something from out of itself, is a bringing-forth, *poiesis*. *Physis* is indeed *poiesis* in the highest sense." (10) This passage makes one suspect that Heidegger's entire thought is more a response to modern thought rather than ancient thought, to which his description does indeed apply; but by extending this description to Plato and Aristotle he shows himself, at the very least, a poor student of the original "epoch" of philosophy. By conflating these two terms Heidegger also makes it difficult to truly understand modern thought, for modernity defined itself precisely in terms of this difference and knew that in so doing it was breaking with the "ancients". So, for example, Chapter 15 of Machiavelli's *The Prince* brings out the directness of the modern's repudiation of the ancients, while chapter 25 connects it to the knowing of technique and mastery over nature rather than the theoretical grasping of what cannot be changed in nature.

and immortal," because it is only in striving after what it isn't, the immortal, that it satisfies its mortal craving for the attainment and perpetuation of happiness. To know one's emptiness in the light of this erotic striving is thus to be daemonic oneself, for we will also know this striving cannot ultimately be satisfied by anything made. As Diotima puts it, "one who knows of such things is a daemonic man, while one who is versed in any other skill, be it craft or any handiwork, is just a workman."[4]

Diotima's following story about Eros thus functions as the link between life and writing, both by distinguishing and uniting them, since "being in the middle, it fulfills both, and in this way unites the whole with itself."[5]

> That's a rather long story to recount, she answered, but I'll tell it to you. When Aphrodite was born, the gods were feasting, a group of them, including the son of Invention, Resource. And when they had dined, Poverty came along begging since there was a party going on. So she stood there at the doors. Now Resource, having gotten quite drunk on nectar—there was no wine then—had gone out to Zeus' little garden, and in his discomfort fallen asleep. Here Poverty schemed, since she herself was without resource, to have a child by Resource; and she lay with him and thereby conceived Love [Eros]. For this reason Love has been Aphrodite's attendant and servant, because he was conceived on the day of her birth, and at the same time is by nature a lover of beauty because of Aphrodite's being so beautiful.
>
> Therefore, as the son of Resource and Poverty, Love finds himself in this situation: first of all, he is always impoverished, and far from being tender and beautiful, as most people think, he is harsh and rugged, barefoot and homeless; always lying unsheltered on the ground, he is lulled to sleep on doorsteps and in the open roads. Possessing his mother's nature, he is always in need. But, then again, through his father he turns out a schemer for beautiful and good things,

---

[4] Plato, *Symposium*, 203a.

[5] Plato, *Symposium*, 202e.

is courageous, bold, and intense, an awesome hunter always devising some machination or other, eager for understanding and inventive; he is a lover of wisdom throughout his life, and a brilliant wizard, healer and philosopher![6]

Let us see if we can understand this story in terms of the "whole" we have been talking about. Poverty, the mother of Eros, would be the emptiness at the heart of life that requires what it does not possess, while the father, as the son of Contrivance, is the Resource that provides the temporary substitutions to sate Poverty's insatiable longings. Life, we might say, is forever scheming through writing, through "devising some machination or other," to fill its emptiness, and since such scheming is always only partially successful, each success will lead to a new failure. Inasmuch as one strives after complete success, after happiness, and will be content with nothing less, that one will be a philosopher—a lover of wisdom who lives for what he doesn't have. On the other hand, inasmuch as one is content to curb that striving by means of a mimetic rather than the intelligible whole known through wisdom, that one is a wizard conjuring up images that temporarily heal the wound at the heart the way a drug may mask the symptoms but provides no cure. Because of his mixed parentage, Eros is always both—every bit the philosopher as the wizard.

Eros, in striving after the good life, desires not only good things, but the preservation and maintenance of those good things that make for a good life. As Diotima briefly puts it, "Eros is for the good to always belong to oneself."[7] But how does this desire actually work? It works by means of "procreation in a beautiful thing," by genesis in the light of the vision of the Beautiful.

> You see, Socrates, all humans are pregnant physically and spiritually, and when we reach our prime, our nature desires to give birth. Nature is not capable of giving birth in the ugly, but only in the beautiful. Now

---

[6] Plato, *Symposium*, 203b-d.

[7] Plato, *Symposium*, 206b.

this is a divine act, and this pregnancy and birth impart immortality to a living being who is mortal.[8]

At this point Diotima cautions Socrates that Eros is not love of the Beautiful per se, but rather of "giving birth and procreation in the beautiful,"[9] for with this distinction we get at the heart of the problem of genesis and all things connected with it—that we love our own and the things we have generated through our bodies or abilities first and foremost, and the vision of the beautiful appears to be only the means to that end, the end that the "good be eternally one's own."[10]

In sum, we desire not only to be happy, but to be happy forever, which is why we want that happiness to be in the context of Being—to be true and hence enduring happiness. Yet because that whole stays the same even while our pursuits of happiness within it are endlessly malleable, what we find is that in our seeking true happiness we come closer to reaching that goal when happiness takes on the same quality of permanence sought in Being. The desire for truth functions in this context in the same way as a vision of beauty. Both are a passive encounter, a vision or *theoria*, that brings forth in us active productions or procreations that seek to imitate as much as possible the beauty of what was seen. Human making, genesis, or procreation in the Beautiful is thus the same as *mimesis* of the intelligible whole; and so whether it be the sexual desire leading to progeny that gives to one's seed immortality, or honor's desire for an eternal name, or an artist's for an enduring work of art, "the mortal partakes of immortality . . . in the body and in all other respects," because it strives after true happiness. [11]

We are all, then, pregnant with happiness, but we need some sort of vision of beauty to bring that happiness to birth. And the greater that vision, the greater the happiness; so Diotima, as a sort of midwife to Socrates, initiates him into the mysteries of beauty that will lead to ever greater births, until the greatest birth of all is

---

[8] Plato, *Symposium*, 206c.

[9] Plato, *Symposium*, 206e.

[10] Plato, *Symposium*, 207a.

[11] Plato, *Symposium*, 208b.

achieved—true happiness. What we see in this ascent, however, is that each time one gives birth, what is born is itself beautiful and so partakes in the vision of the beautiful in the same way *mimesis* partakes in what it imitates. Therefore, what is born can in turn give rise to still further births, until one reaches the highest stage of all wherein birth is abandoned altogether as the goal in the light of the vision of the Beautiful in itself, which "is eternal, and neither comes into being or perishes"[12] and so can no more be born than it can die. The life that no longer seeks to give birth and procreate in the beautiful, but rather seeks the Beautiful in itself and for its own sake "is the life worth living for a man, lived in the contemplation [*theoria*] of the Beautiful itself."[13] The paradoxical yet true satisfaction of Eros is thus to get beyond Eros altogether, to get beyond what is produced and comes into being and contemplate Beauty itself, in the same way that the desire for true happiness is only fully satisfied when it spends its time contemplating the very whole that would make it "true" happiness to begin with.

The life of the philosopher is therefore the happiest because he is the one who knows this, who in knowing his daemonic nature knows that it is the immortal in him, the contemplation of the beautiful in itself, that can alone truly make him happy. Yet mortal nonetheless, he must go back and forth between his two parents, and so only imitate and strive after the happiness of the gods through the poetic births and deaths of his own mixed nature— for he is, after all, only a lover of wisdom and not truly wise.

What Diotima's narrative of Eros and her ladder of ascent illustrates for us is thus the complex relation of *techne, mimesis, poesis,* and *genesis,* with our life lived in pursuit of the best life of happiness. Where then is "writing" in all this? Writing is what we are now reading: it is Diotima's narrative, Socrates' speech on Eros, as well as Plato's dialogue entitled the *Symposium.* It is what comes to birth, an expression of what is striven after in the *theoria* of Beauty. In the widest sense, it is what is given birth to in the Beautiful. In this specific case, it is one of the many "beautiful and magnificent

---

[12] Plato, *Symposium,* 211a.

[13] Plato, *Symposium,* 211d.

speeches and discursive thoughts in unstinting philosophy" given birth from out of the philosopher's contemplation of the "the vast sea of beauty," which includes all the Platonic dialogues, that as written, are not themselves the intelligible whole of Beauty, but rather only a mimetic whole given birth out of an inchoate vision of the whole. [14] Even then, this vision is not of Beauty in itself, the highest stage of ascent that leaves genesis altogether, but only the vision of the beauty of all things as a changing whole rather than the vision of the unchanging intelligible whole of what is beautiful by nature—Being. Philosophy, whether in speech or in a written dialogue, must therefore be distinguished from the "life" of the philosopher that seeks not to give birth at all, but instead desires to contemplate the whole responsible for the birth of everything else, whether by nature or convention. Writing that knows itself must therefore know something beyond anything "written," taken in its widest sense, and the writing that can do that must understand itself in terms of the relation between the writings of the comic poet and the tragic poet—Aristophanes and Agathon.

The importance of the two poles of serious and playful writing as the penultimate backdrop to the philosopher's erotic ascent comes out obviously at the end of the dialogue when Socrates' last conscious drinking partners are Aristophanes and Agathon, with whom Socrates argues that the same man should know how to make comedy and tragedy; and that he who is by art a tragic poet is also a comic poet.[15] While he is making this argument, however, first Aristophanes and then Agathon fall asleep and Socrates walks home, sober and awake, as the sun rises.

If we examine these two characters' earlier speeches on Eros we should be able to see how Plato would exemplify what makes each of these artists what they are. If Plato, in so doing, also shows that he is the one whose art is capable of doing both, then that should only further reinforce our confidence that he knows what he is doing in writing the decidedly comic rather than tragic *Symposium*. For the fact that his Socrates never gets to directly question

---

[14] 210d, translation from Stanley Rosen's, *Plato's Symposium*, 2nd Edition (New Haven: Yale University Press, 1987), 267.

[15] Plato, *Symposium*, 223d.

Aristophanes' speech and yet still frames both the beginning and the end of Agathon's speech with questions, seems to indicate that tragedy rather than comedy requires philosophic questioning to be fully exposed, whereas comedy may well stand sufficiently revealed on its own. Let us start with Aristophanes' speech to see why this might be the case.

Aristophanes prefaces his speech with an expression of his fears that remind us of the goal of comedy laid out by Socrates in the first wave of Book V in the *Republic*—that he, the comic poet, must be laughed *with* but not *at*. "[F]or in what is about to be said I am not afraid to say laughable things—for that would be a gain and native to our Muse—but only things that are laughed at."[16] Just as Socrates in Book V braved the fear of appearing ridiculous in order to make his own female drama of comic arguments to compete with Aristophanes', here too Aristophanes himself will set it as his comic task to steer between these two closely related results. What the comic poet must accomplish we know from the start, and so he must fully confess to us if he is to elicit our sympathy and support.

Aristophanes, the character, will say this on his own behalf, but what Plato, the poet, seems to say comes out in his ordering of the incidents prior to Aristophanes' speech. For earlier, when Aristophanes was set to take his turn around the table and give his eulogy to Eros, he was beset with a fit of sneezing leaving Erixymachus, the physician, to take his place after receiving some medical advice on how to stop himself. It is only after Erixymachus finishes giving his speech exalting the role of *techne* in Eros that Aristophanes can now proceed—with his sneezing cured by Erixymachus's medical techniques and his mastery over his own speech now in question. What this laughable ordering seems to imply is that the comic art of Aristophanes is less than the purely technical art of Erixymachus, and that the techniques of comedy that make us laugh are ultimately subject to and dependent upon the technology at large in the city that allows it to continue. Comedy thus appears to be very close to technology and perhaps, without

---

[16] Plato, *Symposium*, 189b.

philosophy, indistinguishable from it. No wonder Aristophanes worries that Erixymachus will have the last laugh.[17]

The reason technology is so close to comedy will come out further in Aristophanes' speech. For what the comic poet praises in Eros is his power—Eros' power to be philanthropic and a healer of mankind's illnesses that results in our greatest possible happiness. Yet to explain why this is so, Aristophanes must teach us to "understand human nature and its afflictions."[18] How he does so is to make up an entirely contrived history of mankind that, while being entirely incredible, still makes plausible sense of human behavior. Aristophanes is thus doing what we see Socrates accuse the comic poet of in the first wave—using highly artificial means to bring out and explain human nature. The very artificialness of these means, the comic "technique," is why Erixymachus and his pursuit of technique for its own sake rather than nature (i.e. technology) threatens always to supplant comedy. One might even say that comedy, because of the intrinsic instability of pursuing nature by artificial means, lends itself to a vulnerable openness to either higher or lower things: an openness that can be either a Trojan Horse for an all-dominating technological understanding of the whole that finally stops even caring about nature (modernity), or the preferred medium by which higher concerns such as the pursuit of the truth and nature can express themselves without getting trapped by or forgetting the limitations of expression. Another relation to comedy comes about, however, when the possibility of a divine rather than human comic poet is raised; but that possibility will only come up in the unique context of the Bible.

With Aristophanes, however, we find that the gods themselves are a creation of the comic poet and that they are as equally

---

[17] "Erixymachus. . . is a spokesman for 'technicism'. . . it is Plato's opinion that poetry cannot maintain its independence, either as the 'legislator for mankind' (Agathon) or as as the *defensor pacis*, the bulwark of political justice. The poetic interpretation of Eros, if not subordinate to that of philosophy, finally becomes absorbed by, and so subordinate to, the claims of technicism. In this specific context the hiccoughs with which 'chance' afflicts Aristophanes is forced to yield to Eryximachus in word and deed." Rosen, *Plato's Symposium*, 91.

[18] Plato, *Symposium*, 189d.

in need of artifice as is the poet; for their need is to both control the arrogance of humanity and yet still maintain their lucrative traffic in sacrifices. In other words, just as the gods must lower the standing of the circle-men and yet still satisfy the demand for praise and service, Aristophanes must level all his characters to the common need of the audience to laugh. The gods therefore contrive a solution, they cut the circle-men in half, and it is that cut—a "contrivance" of the gods—that now constitutes our nature. Whether straight, lesbian or homosexual, our erotic nature is now to seek out our other half, to become whole again; and so it is in Aristophanes' speech that we find most overtly presented the mimetic desire to imitate the whole explicitly represented within the action and thought of the plot itself. The comic desire for a happy ending is therefore the erotic "desire and pursuit of the whole," which is also the desire for "our ancient nature."[19] The position this puts the comic poet in is thus similar to the role of Hephaestus, the god of invention, who stands over us, the audience, with his tools and asks "What is it that you want, human beings, to get for yourselves from one another?"[20] What we want is our wholeness, our true nature, but all the comic poet can supply is laughter and a happy ending within the confines of his poem—i.e., contrived substitutions for the real thing.[21]

---

[19] Plato, *Symposium*, 193c.

[20] Plato, *Symposium*, 192d.

[21] What we see in Aristophanes' speech is therefore something very similar to the account of nature we see in the writings of Rousseau, in the sense that we have an account of nature that is entirely fictional and yet is used to account for the deepest yearning in the soul as desire to return to this nature. Nonetheless, because of the constitutive role of artifice in our very nature (Rousseau's "perfectability") such a return is impossible and we can at best only create new encounters that imitate it (which seems to be the major goal of education in *Emile*) In Aristophanes and Rousseau, then, we see a deeply conservative role for their poetic endeavors in the sense that the greatest possible happiness is not that of the gods, but is instead only that happiness found between the poles of our lost nature and the punishment of being cut in two, and a possible future second cutting which is threatened if we become too satisfied and too arrogant with what we have become (Plato, *Symposium*, 190d).

Happiness is thus always limited, and limited by the boundaries of convention which we have no choice but to live with. One
must contrast this with the unlimited happiness of the philosopher,
who, because his happiness is solely in terms of nature cannot be
constrained by the limits of convention—a lack of limits that inevitability gets him into trouble with the city. Yet Aristophanes, as
the artificer of this entire story, however conservative its content
may be, is putting himself above that content to the level of the
gods; and in so doing stands as a sort of alternative city, subversive
of it even as he seeks to conserve it. This comes out directly when
in his discussion of homosexuality he makes the argument that
while the city may consider marriage and procreation natural, at
least in the case of the half-men "they are pederasts and. . . naturally pay no attention to marriage and procreation, but are compelled to do so by the law."[22] Again, just as Socrates did in the first
wave of his female drama, Aristophanes argues that what is taken
to be natural in the city is truly conventional and the poet by his
art is best able to reveal this. However subversive this revelation
may be within the context of the comic poem, because of that very
context, because of the comic poet's vulnerability and need of his
audience's indulgence, comedy itself is relatively harmless, politically ineffective, and ultimately conservative. To be politically effective the poet would have to hide his artifice, he would have to
obscure the difference between nature and convention and make
the audience feel that it is entirely dependent upon the poem rather
than vice versa.

This, as we shall see, is the effectiveness of Agathon. The
beauty of his speech that ends in spontaneous applause rather than
laughter is the power that makes tragedy able to both found and
preserve the city. When in his speech we see him exalt the youth
and innovativeness of Eros it will truly be the exaltation of the
innovation of the city itself—the laws and virtues of which seem
new in relation to the primordial chaos and violence prior to its
founding. Agathon's praise of Eros is thus essentially praise of his
own tragic Muse. Nevertheless, because Agathon is praising his

---

[22] Plato, *Symposium*, 192b.

own creative process rather than the actual tragic product—the tragic poem whose victory at the Dionysia is the excuse for this entire symposium—his speech is given "partly in playfulness, partly in measured earnestness."[23] Agathon's speech is therefore in praise of his own power as a tragedian that playfully comments upon what he accomplishes in his serious work. In contrast with the comedian, however, such commentary cannot itself be incorporated into that work, but must instead lie outside of it if it is not to spill the beans, as it were, of the tragedian's effectiveness. When Agathon begins his speech by claiming to direct his attention to what Eros is rather than what goods he causes, we can also take this as Agathon directing attention to his own god-like power as distinct from its embodiment within his creation.[24]

When Agathon says that Eros is "the youngest of gods and ever young" rather than the oldest as claimed by Phaedrus, we must see what he means in relation to the contrast between Eros and the gods of Necessity spoken of by Hesiod and Parmenides.[25] For under the rule of Necessity there were "castrations and bindings of each other, and many other acts of violence amongst the gods," whereas "had Eros been among them; there would have been friendship and peace, just as there is now since Eros became king of the gods."[26] If we keep in mind the actual content of tragedies, however, be they of Homer, Aeschylus or presumably Agathon himself, filled as they are with the very violence Agathon says Eros has no part of, what we must conclude is that the erotic power of tragedy is precisely to rid the audience of this violence and lead the audience into the peace and friendship of which he is speaking. The youth of Eros is the youthful part of the city that is

---

[23] Plato, *Symposium*, 197e.

[24] This is very similar to the position of Nietzsche, who in commenting on his god-like powers of creation can be very witty and speak of laughter, and yet must still maintain that the act of creating is serious business that must be believed soberly as the truth if it is to be effective. His laughter, in other words, is always a sort of "meta-laughter."

[25] Plato, *Symposium*, 195c.

[26] Plato, *Symposium*, 195c.

always founded and preserved against the backdrop of violent origins exemplified in such stories as the fratricide of Romulus and Remus.

Eros as the young god, then, is very similar to other young gods such as Marduk, the slayer of his mother Tiamat, who founded and ordered the now peaceful society out of her slain body.[27] The youthfulness of order out of chaos, peace out of violence, the Olympians out of the Titans, is thus also the eternal amnesia of youth that forgets not only its use of the old's tactics in turning against them, but also its continuing dependence upon old in order to ever again become the new.

It is Agathon's Eros, then, the eros of tragedy, that out of ugliness, faction and bloodshed brings forth beauty, harmony and peace. That this Eros has nonetheless turned the gods of Necessity's own weapons against them, comes out when he admits that in spite of being peaceful and harmonious, "lack of harmony and Eros are always at war with one another."[28] The peace, beauty, harmony and virtue of Eros, precisely because of this youth, always comes with the history of their opposite; and that history is of the transmuting power of the tragic poet who turns the painful passions, violence and faction on stage into the cathartic pleasure, peace and unity of the tragic audience.

The tragic Eros is in this way the source of justice in the city—who "neither commits injustice nor has injustice done to him"—because as the origin of justice himself is also prior to it.[29] This Eros is "beyond good and evil" because he is prior to it. What makes him prior is that he is the foundational source of the very laws themselves, and when the just is the legal—which must be the case precisely because of Eros' newness—he can no more commit injustice than have it happen to him. What is old, then, in contrast with the youth of laws, is violence; and so here too Eros not only keeps up appearances, but actually creates them.

---

[27] This is the Babylonian creation myth, the *Enuma Elish*.

[28] Plato, *Symposium*, 196e.

[29] This is essentially the argument of both Glaucon and Hobbes that justice comes on the scene only after the formation of the "social contract."

For it is not by violence that Eros is affected, if he is
affected at all—for violence does not touch him; nor
does he act with violence, for everyone of his own
accord serves Eros in everything. And whatever anyone of his own accord agrees upon with another of
his own accord, the 'royal laws of the city' declare to
be just.[30]

Everyone of his own accord does indeed follow Eros in a tragedy,
as can be seen in the cathartically unified audience, but violence is
nevertheless at the heart of every tragic plot that we see on stage.
This ambivalence toward violence is seen in the city as well, for
while all are in accord that violence not be done to them, there is
not quite the same unanimity against doing violence to others, especially in the communal violence directed against any sort of
scapegoat.[31] In the light of this structural ambivalence, the positivity of the laws that "declare to be just" is thus the same positivity
of tragic success that we see in a cathartically unified audience that
has thrown out its private alienation. The appearance of justice
created by Agathon's Eros is therefore the very same justice of
Socrates' band of robbers, but here those appearances are directly
tied to the aesthetic power of Agathon's muse who is the master
at creating beautiful and abiding appearances.

As to moderation (for Agathon in his tragic role of educator
of the city is giving us a list of his own cardinal virtues), we see the
same pattern of the tools of its opponents being used against themselves, for the greater pleasure of Eros dominates all lesser pleasures. Likewise with courage, "in dominating the bravest of all the

---

[30] Plato, *Symposium*, 196c.

[31] This is essentially the point of Glaucon's argument in Book II of the
Republic when he brings his argument against justice to a climax by claiming that true justice leads to a humiliating death whereas the appearance
of justice preserves one's life. The difference between these two possibilities is the heart of Glaucon's "social contract," so it no surprise that the
duality of the "scapegoat mechanism" that is the origin of all good and all
evil is essentially the mechanism behind the creation of Hobbes' "sovereign," for the scapegoat embodies this duality of both fear and desire described by René Girard in terms of "mimesis."

rest, he must be bravest."[32] When it comes to wisdom, however, Agathon comes right out and equates it with his own poetic power as a tragedian, since the wisdom of Eros is seen in his own *poesis* that makes "poets of others too." The wisdom of Eros is therefore the wisdom of inspiration, the power of the Muses that is equated with the power of nature inasmuch as "the making of all animals is nothing but Eros' wisdom, by which all the animals come to be and grow."[33] The wisdom of tragic Eros is thus the power of making, the *techne* of *poesis*, that leaves no room for the theoretic knowledge of nature because even the animals are the result of its making.

This conflation of *poesis* with *physis*, or nature, is in fact the very essence of its power and purpose, for this wisdom must presuppose something in the past that it has overcome and transformed, an ugliness that the beauty of Eros has transfigured.

> So it is plain that, when Eros came to be among them, the affairs of the gods were arranged out of love of beauty—for there is no eros present in ugliness. But before that, as I said at the start, many awesome events took place among the gods, as is said, through the monarchy of Necessity; whereas since the birth of this god all good things have resulted for gods as well as for human beings from loving the beautiful things.[34]

Such beauty has not existed forever; it is not the beauty of the whole, but is rather the beauty of a partial whole carved out of the larger and prior whole of ugliness by poetry. The ugliness of Necessity can therefore never be eliminated from the presence of poetic beauty, for it is the very movement out of necessity that constitutes this sort of beauty. Necessity and ugliness are therefore the unavoidable and constant themes of tragedy, and the beauty of the tragic poem that portrays the necessity of fate on stage is the beauty of tragic catharsis that transmutes this pain and ugliness

---

[32] Plato, *Symposium*, 196d,

[33] Plato, *Symposium*, 197a.

[34] Plato, *Symposium*, 197b.

into the pleasure and beauty experienced by the tragic audience. The tragic poet is thus the maker of the appearances of justice and beauty in the *polis* par excellence, because his wisdom is the wisdom that substitutes for the wisdom arising out of a vision of the whole sought by the philosopher. The philosopher's wisdom is the vision of *theoria* which is the vision of beauty in itself rather than beauty created out of ugliness.

In the following lines of verse, Agathon evokes an image that focuses this entire poetic process of bringing peace, order and beauty out of discord, ugliness and chaos.

> Peace among human beings, on the open sea calm
> And cloudlessness, the resting of winds and sleeping
> of
> > care.[35]

All these images evoke an almost mesmerizing stability that lulls us into forgetting what we cannot stop thinking—that all this peace is a mere bubble surrounded temporally and spatially by the raging storms of the sea, wind, and awakened care. The peace this Eros brings is like the little bubble of order and civilization surrounded by the larger chaos of Tiamat, the sea-goddess recently killed by her young son, Marduk. Like the eye of a hurricane, this strangely beautiful calm is only an appearance that gains its authoritative power precisely in its seductive ability to lull into forgetful sleep the cares that preceded it and now indirectly lend it its power.

Here, then, we have Agathon the tragic poet revealing his poetic gift and the elusive and yet essential peace and beauty it brings about. For the tragic catharsis he leaves with his audience, as we see from Socrates' second wave, is the power that makes the city one. As Agathon puts it, by emptying us of our alienating and estranging private desires and filling us with the poetic attachment to a unified audience his tragic Eros is the source of everything corporate in the city. "He empties us of estrangement, he fills us with attachment; he arranges in all such gatherings as this our coming together with one another: in festivals, in dances, in sacrifices he

---

[35] Plato, *Symposium*, 197c.

proves himself a guide; furnishing gentleness, banishing wildness."[36] With this mention of guiding at sacrifices, we can also see
that we are not too far here from the sacrificial scapegoat, which
in its duplicitous duality both masks and reveals the violence at the
heart of the city by bearing on its shoulders the burdens of estrangement and wildness even while returning us to attachment
and gentleness. The scapegoat functions, in other words, by means
of deception; but a deception that if made manifest, if made too
conscious and explicit in its cathartic functioning, fails.

Nevertheless, comedy's job *is* to reveal this function, and so
following up upon Agathon's unanimous applause, Socrates comically claims Agathon should rather be laughed at for having misunderstood what it is to eulogize Eros.

> For in my stupidity I believed the truth had to be told
> about anything that was given a eulogy . . . . But it was
> not this after all, it seems that was meant by the fair
> praising of anything, but the attribution to the matter
> at hand of the greatest and fairest things possible re-
> gardless of whether this was so or not. And if the
> praise were false, it was of no importance anyway; for
> the injunction was, it seems, that each of us should be
> thought to eulogize Eros, and not just eulogize him.[37]

In other words, what Socrates the comedian must reveal with his
joking is that Agathon's entire eulogy was a pack of lies. In the
same way, in his role of philosopher, Socrates own eulogy of Eros
will begin by questioning Agathon in order to manifest the tragedian's complete ignorance of Eros' true nature. What Socrates
does by framing both the beginning and the end of Agathon's
speech with questioning is uncover tragedy's lying character, a
character that cannot be exposed by the tragedian himself—even
when speaking "partly in playfulness."

The philosopher, then, as we also see from the third wave in
the *Republic*, knows both why the tragic poet must lie and what that

---

[36] Plato, *Symposium*, 197d.

[37] Plato, *Symposium*, 198d-e.

lie consists of, but such knowledge in no way diminishes the tragedian's beauty. In fact, as we see from the *Symposium's* conclusion, the philosopher seems to be the one person capable of writing both comedies and tragedies, for he alone understands the reason for the beauty and appeal of both. Socrates, then, if he wanted to be a poet at all, could be either a comic poet or a tragic poet. Plato, who we know *did* want to be a poet, chose to write comedies. For comedy, as much as the philosopher is capable of writing both comedy and tragedy, would seem to be the philosophical narrative of choice.

This is why even though Socrates may poke fun at Aristophanes, his only true competitors and the object of his quarrel with poetry are the tragic poets. In Book II of the *Republic* we see him kick them out from his own city, and then still feel compelled to take them on again in Book X; but throughout we see that they, and not the comic poets, are the ones who pose the problem of justice in the city. In similar fashion, we see in Plato's *Laws* that its own speeches on politics, precisely because they are to be read comically rather than seriously, are the direct competitors with the speeches of the tragic poets:

> Athenian: As for what they call the 'serious' poets, our tragic poets . . . [we will say when asked for admittance to our city] 'Best of strangers, . . . we ourselves are poets, who have to the best of our ability created a tragedy that is the most beautiful and best; at any rate, our whole political regime is constructed as the imitation of the most beautiful and best way of life, which we at least assert to be really *the truest tragedy*. Now you are poets, and we too are poets of the same things; we are your rivals as artists and performers of the most beautiful drama, which true law alone can by nature bring to perfection—as we hope. So don't suppose that we'll ever easily, at any rate, allow you to come among us, set up your stage in the marketplace, and introduce actors whose beautiful voices speak louder than ours.'[38]

---

[38] Plato, *The Laws of Plato*, trans. Thomas Pangle, (Chicago: The University of Chicago Press, 1980), 817b-e (emphasis added).

The admission of this passage is that all laws are founded and maintained by the tragic poets, and that these old men in founding their own better city in speech are only writing the "truest tragedy," and so must kick out the lesser creators who are their rivals in creating the "drama" that is the *polis*. But what it also does is equate all laws (*nomos*, "conventions") with the offspring of the tragic poets who create the laws as the only way of perfecting the city which is inherently imperfectible. Hence the inherent scapegoat and cathartic quality of all tragedy—it can only keep the forces that tear the *polis* apart at bay by letting them into its innermost courts. Here we also see clearly the source of the equation Derrida makes between *logos* and *nomos* that he sees throughout Plato—they will always be connected when Plato playfully imitates the serious writing of the tragic poets. But this dialogue *is* only an imitation, and a comic imitation at that, of tragic writing. The "truest tragedy" is true then because it is an "imitation of an imitation"—a confession that is decidedly comic.

So when we turn to what is said in the *Laws* about the comic poets, we see that this dialogue does not itself compete with them or need to drive them out from its city in speech, because in admitting comedy into the city it is also secretly forging its own passport.

> Athenian: . . . but it is necessary to look at and get to know what pertains to shameful bodies and thoughts, as well as those who turn themselves to laughter provoking comedies—through speech and song, dance and the comic imitations all these contain. For someone who is going to become prudent can't learn the serious things without learning the laughable, or, for that matter, anything without its opposite. *Yet one can't create in both ways if one is to partake of even a small portion of virtue*, and indeed one should learn about the ridiculous things just for this reason—so that he may never do or say, through ignorance, anything that is ridiculous, if he doesn't have to. The imitation of such things should be assigned to slaves and to strangers who work for hire. There should never be any seriousness whatsoever about these things, . . . in fact, these imitations should always manifest something

new. Let the play that provokes laughter, the play we call "comedy" be thus ordained in law and argument.[39]

How this passage smuggles comedy into the serious world of the city can be seen if we contrast the lines in italics with the end of the *Symposium*. What leaps out at us is the irony and play of Plato in prohibiting for political and moral reasons what Socrates almost boastfully implies the philosopher alone can do. By dividing up the creative roles between masters and slaves, with the slaves alone creating comedy for the sake of the virtue of their masters, what we have is the political role that the philosopher must always play *vis-à-vis* the city. And what this also implies is that the philosopher is quite capable of writing a serious political "drama" that is every bit as good or better than the tragedian's; and this is precisely because what from the perspective of the city can and must be viewed as a serious effort, from the perspective of the philosopher is simultaneously viewed as a playful comedy.

The more overt claim of the *Laws* to compete with and replace the tragic poet in all things "serious," is thus playfully undermined by the more subtle and seemingly less important establishment of an apolitical sort of comedy in the midst of the city. The nature of this concern comes through clearly when the Athenian Stranger backhandedly defends the role of "charm" in the arts:

> Athenian: So then pleasure would be a correct criterion only for something which wasn't produced to provide some benefit, or truth, or similarity, nor of course harm, but was produced only for the sake of what accompanies these, the charm. And when it is accompanied by none of the other things, it would be very noble for someone to call the charm "pleasure." Kleinias:. You are speaking now of harmless pleasure only.

---

[39] Plato, *Laws,* 816-817a (emphasis added).

> Ath: Yes, and this is what I call "play"—when something doesn't do any harm or any benefit worthy of serious consideration.[40]

"Play" has now been defined as quite harmless and in fact pleasurable and charming, but this is all because of its disconnection from "benefit," "truth" or "similarity"; which is to say, because it has no pretensions to express the real "object" of Plato's concern we will see in his *Seventh Letter*.[41] 'Play' is therefore quite safe to allow into the city, and so Plato's *Laws* secretly forges its own invitation. Yet apart from gaining its own admission, this discussion in the *Laws* also suggests what the proper concern of a philosopher might be apart from the city. For when "pleasure" is set out as the correct criterion of "charm," and when we realize that Socrates is notorious for his charming ways, we might also suspect that along with writing and speaking out of playfulness, the philosopher might also have as his proper study pleasure itself; even if only because when or if one ever has "truth accompanied by knowledge" he would possess "the highest happiness which it is possible for a human being to enjoy."[42]

If this is indeed the case, that the lover of wisdom's proper study is play and pleasure rather than politics and its respective seriousness, then perhaps we could say the *Philebus'* discussion of pleasure and pain is more properly "philosophical" because it is concerned with the issues of pleasure and pain. In fact, one of the more definite conclusions Socrates seeks to make in this dialogue is that "in laments and tragedies and comedies—and not only in those of the stage but in the whole tragi-comedy of life—as well as on countless other occasions, pains are mixed with pleasures."[43] The issue of comedy and tragedy is thus right at home in this question of pleasure and pain, just as it was central to the question of politics in the *Laws*. But in this case there is an opposing emphasis, for while the speeches of the *Laws* were almost in their entirety

---

[40] Plato, *Laws,* 667d-e.

[41] Plato, *Seventh Letter,* 342-343.

[42] Plato, *Phaedrus,* 277a.

[43] Plato, *Philebus,* 50b.

meant to be a substitution for the role tragedy usually plays in a regime and so treated comedy with a sort of benign neglect, in the case of the *Philebus* the opposite is the case. The question that arouses Socrates' interest here is comedy even to the point of admitting that he has "concentrated" on the mixture of pleasure and pain in comedy.[44] But it is the way he does this that should interest us, for while it is assumed by Socrates and Protarchus that in a tragedy "while they are weeping they're enjoying themselves," in the case of comedy, Socrates must prove that pain is even present in the first place.[45]

Socrates goes about this proof in an odd sort of manner, so odd that we might almost get the idea that he is arguing for a slightly different point altogether. For what he argues overtly is that pain is mixed in with pleasure in comedy because "when we laugh at what is comical in friends—when, that is, we mix pleasure with spite—then we are tempering our pleasure with pain. For we agreed some time ago that spite is a painful condition of the soul; but we also agreed that amusement is pleasant, and on those occasions they both occur simultaneously."[46] But the way Socrates has made the point that laughing at friends involves spite is via the division that follows:

> Socrates: If you describe as comical those who are not only deluded but are also weak and unable to retaliate when mocked, you will be right. As for those who *are* able to retaliate, however, and are strong, if you call them frightening and dangerous, you couldn't describe them more accurately. You see, self-ignorance accompanied by strength is not just disgraceful, it's dangerous too: anyone who comes into contact with it, or anything like it, is threatened. But the nature of ignorance in weak men made us classify it as comical.[47]

---

[44] Plato, *Philebus, 50c.*

[45] Plato, *Philebus,* 48a.

[46] Plato, *Philebus,* 50a.

[47] Plato, *Philebus,* 49c.

In other words, Socrates argues that enjoyment of the misfortune of the strong is not spite and so involves no pain, while enjoyment of misfortune and ignorance in the weak or those who are friends does involve pain, precisely because they are, or could be friends, and spite is defined as the pleasure at the misfortune of friends.

But why is the issue of strong and powerful ignorance raised at all here—how often are comedies directed at people whose potential ridiculousness is not available to all and so quite easily and safely mocked? As a possible answer, Plato hints here at the need for comedy to take place in a context of friendship, wherein the objects of ridicule have been pacified and will not retaliate when mocked. In other words, without the precondition of friendship with the city, there is no possibility at all for aphilosophical comedy. The twin role of comedy is thus to dissemble the apolitical seriousness of the philosopher; but also—by means of laughter, and as a precondition for more laughter—to make friends with the city.[48] Otherwise, philosophy, because of its inherent inability to defend itself straight off by means of the first 'four' mentioned in the *Seventh Letter*, will not survive long enough to find the few naturally good souls who can discover the serious truth lying behind philosophy's comic exterior.

If we put the respective concerns of the *Laws* together with the *Philebus*, what we have are two ways of arguing for why philosophical comedy is the *techne* by which philosophy will both live in, and affect, the city. The serious existence of the philosopher requires that he express himself playfully, and it is also this serious existence that allows him to understand and choose both what is involved in comic and tragic expression, and why he must choose comedy as his own. But what is the "serious existence" of the philosopher, what is it that makes the life devoted to the love of wisdom a serious one? Perhaps the best way to see what a serious life

---

[48] "The classics did not regard the conflict between philosophy and the city as tragic. Xenophan at any rate seems to have viewed that conflict in the light of Socrates' relation to Xantippe. At least in this point there appears then something like an agreement between Xenophan and Pascal. For the classics, the conflict between philosophy and the city is as little tragic as the death of Socrates." Leo Strauss, *On Tyranny*, (Ithaca, NY: Cornell University Press, 1963), 221.

would be is to get an indirect fix on it by means of serious writing. In other words, perhaps there is something we see in tragic writing that brings out an essential element to any tragic life, however much that life may express itself comically.

In order to bring out this element, let us look again at the *Philebus*. In the context of a discussion of desire in the soul, and its relation to the pleasures and pains in the soul, Socrates draws a distinction between two sorts of combinations of pleasure and pain in relation to desire that bespeak the essence of both comedy and tragedy. In what I take to be a description of comedy, Socrates describes a situation in which "someone who is expecting replenishment feels pleasure thanks to his memory but, since he is also experiencing the lack at the same time, is simultaneously feeling pain."[49] The comic element here is the expected happy ending or punchline, that will pull the sting from whatever complications or digs had preceded it. On the other hand, in a covert description of what goes on in tragedy, Socrates describes a case wherein someone, although he is "experiencing a lack, he has *no* hope of replenishment coming his way. Isn't it then that his pain would be doubled?"[50] By answering yes to this question, Protarchus is also indirectly admitting that he can see no way that pleasure can be found in the latter, even though he will later assume that tragedy involves both pleasure and pain.[51] What this seems to imply is that Protarchus, who is not a philosopher, can apprehend that the *techne* of tragedy involves pleasure *and* pain, but he cannot conceive how a painful condition in the soul that involves a desire that is not fulfilled could also involve a pleasure. Socrates, for his part, seems to bank on this lack in Protarchus, and so feels no need to either argue here for the pleasure involved in tragedy or, on the other hand, for the pleasure that might accompany the 'serious' soul of the philosopher.

The pleasure experienced by the serious philosopher, in other words, might be just as mysterious and yet self-evident to Socrates

---

[49] Plato, *Philebus*, 36b.

[50] Plato, *Philebus*, 36b-c.

[51] Plato, *Philebus*, 48a.

the philosopher, as the pleasure in tragedy is to Protarchus. Since the pleasure involved in tragedies is somehow related to the objectification of the inability to satisfy the competing desires of the individuals in the *polis* (how this "somehow" works seems to be as unknown to the tragic poet as his audience), there must also be some sort of pleasure connected to the lack of satisfaction involved in the subjective desires of the philosopher.

The question raised by the philosopher is therefore how his pain is not "doubled" in desiring to know the truth and the nature of the whole, while also having little to no hope that he can satisfy that desire. Or to put this another way, what is the pleasure in not only knowing you are ignorant, but also in having no hope of changing that condition? Although Protarchus can't seem to provide one, the explanation Socrates seems to give in the fifth book of the *Republic* of why tragic audiences "enjoy themselves even while they're weeping," is that in the lie of the tragic "poem" the audience is told a story that makes objective sense out of what can have no subjective sense in the immediate world of the *polis*. The pleasure, then, is the pleasure of refounding some sort of communal order in the midst of individuated bodily chaos, and the transformation from pain to pleasure parallels the transformation of chance into fate. For the lover of wisdom, then, what seems to make him a "serious man" is that his desire to not rest content with the pleasures of tragedy that ease but do not satisfy his thirst for the knowledge of the whole can only be satisfied by abstracting from the very locus of his desiring in his own individuated soul. So while the pleasures of serious writing arise out of an escape from the factional body into the communal world of the tragedy, the pleasures of the serious man seem to arise out of the escape from his individual body into the noetic vision of true existence in the soul.

This seems to be what Plato is describing in his *Seventh Letter* when he explains why the serious man would never write anything "serious." The explanation seems to hinge on his distinction between the four sensible and psychic means of coming to know an object (name, definition, representation and knowledge, understanding and true belief, with the last three classed as one), and the existing object itself as the end. As Plato puts it:

> [U]nless a man somehow grasps the first four, he will never attain perfect knowledge of the fifth. Moreover, owing to the inadequacy of language, these four are as much concerned to demonstrate what any particular thing is like as to reveal its essential being; that is why no intelligent man will ever dare to commit his thoughts to words, still less to words that cannot be changed, as is the case with what is expressed in written characters.[52]

By setting out the two possibilities of coming to know either likeness or true reality, with no guarantee of one as opposed to the other by the noetic means at one's disposal, Plato seems to be implying that there is some sort of major disjunction that makes this ambivalence possible. As we see in the case of someone who actually does come to know reality rather than mere likeness, what seems to make the difference is pure chance, and chance as we have seen in the case of tragedy becomes bearable only if transmuted into fate. [53] Yet if in tragedy this transmutation takes place by means of poetic craft, how is it to take place for the philosopher?

Perhaps what we might say of the philosopher is that in desiring to know the whole of reality he comes to discern that the elements of chance and contingency *cannot* be known, and if put together with what *can* be known (nature), they are both together the "whole" and as such constitute "fate." The knowledge of the whole for the philosopher is therefore the knowledge of what cannot be known, in the same way that the tragic vision of the audience is of what cannot be reconciled. So just as we might say the "lie" of the tragic poet is the falsely intelligible whole of the tragic work, so we might say the tragic pleasure of the philosopher is the discovery of the falseness of an intelligible universe as a whole. Yet

---

[52] Plato, *Seventh Letter*, 343a.

[53] Plato, *Seventh Letter*, 343a.

THE *SYMPOSIUM*'S EROTIC STRIVING

why should this discovery be in any way pleasurable? Possibly because the discovery of what isn't intelligible is simultaneously the discovery of what truly *is* intelligible. The seriousness of the philosopher is therefore different from the usual seriousness of the tragic poets because his seriousness involves an awareness of what not to take seriously, and so involves a knowledge of what is only play. The fact that Plato chooses to write comedy and not tragedy would therefore seem to indicate that what he *does* know is that poetic creation is essentially tied into that element of the whole that is unintelligible and cannot be fully known.[54]

Yet there is also another element to this choosing of comedy over tragedy that comes to the fore when discussing the life of the philosopher versus his writing. And that is the issue of the philosopher's relation to the gods. Whereas before, in taking up the question of writing in Plato we had Derrida looking over our shoulder, in the question of the relation of the philosopher to the gods, we have the visage of Leo Strauss. Strauss, who seems to see directly the elements in Plato that Derrida stumbles onto indirectly or by misdirection, is fully aware of Plato's comic intent in his dialogues and so follows the irregular line of the joke and laughter rather than the straight path of seriousness. Which is to say, Leo Strauss has understood Plato's writings in a way unrivaled since Kierkegaard's day; for in both we see a recognition that philosophical *writing's* only rival is tragic poetry, and the only rival to the philosophical *life* is the life devoted to the gods, i.e., piety. Yet the nature of this rivalry, especially in the light of the philosophical seriousness that knows the limitations of its knowledge, is such that it can

---

[54] On a different but related topic, namely the irrationalities of persuasion as opposed to reason, Strauss makes a similar point in commenting on Xenophon's Socratic dialogue *Oeconomicus*: "Yet as Xenophon says, he could do this 'in the speeches'; he could refute or silence all men who argued against him but could not induce all of them to obey him. It suffices to remember his accusers and condemners. This 'tragic' limitation of Socrates' power of speaking is, as it were, foreshadowed by its 'comic' limitation, by Socrates' inability to persuade Xanthippe." Leo Strauss, *Xenophon's Socratic Discourse*, (Ithaca: Cornell University Press, 1970), 176-7.

never be resolved into one or the other, any more than appearances will fully give way to truth. The attitude the philosophical life must bear to the religious life is therefore one of a serious grasp of both its intrinsic unintelligibility and yet its unavoidable demand for attention and respect. Perhaps the best way of seeing this relationship comes out in this description Xenophon gives of Socrates' attitude toward their mutual connection:

> With respect to becoming a . . . farmer . . . or a general, he held that such studies can be acquired by human thought. However, he said that the gods reserved the most important parts of them for themselves and of these parts nothing is clear to human beings . . . He said that those who suppose that nothing of such things belongs to the domain of the divine but all are within the capacity of human thought are possessed by madness. But they are also possessed by madness who inquire of diviners concerning things that the gods have given to human beings to judge on the basis of study . . . He said that what the gods have given human beings to accomplish by study must be studied; what is not clear to human beings should be inquired about from the gods by means of divining; for the gods give to those who happen to be in their grace.[55]

The relation of the divine and human thus seems to intimately revolve around the permanent relations that can be studied and repeated, and the instabilities of chance that can neither be predicted nor fully understood. Yet without understanding the relationship between both elements, some of the most important disciplines in the city—farming and generalship—would lose their point. The city therefore seems to stand in need of the mutual moderation of knowledge that knows its own limits, and relations with the divine that do not encroach on human knowledge. Nevertheless, in spite of the moderate sensibleness of this proposal, cities seem to be filled with just this sort of madness—the madness of the tragic poets who in their creations present a knowledge of

---

[55] Xenophon, *Memorabilia*, trans. E. C. Marchant (Cambridge, MA: Harvard University Press, 1923), I i 7-9.

the whole city based upon divine inspiration that covers over what can truly only be known apart from it. On the other hand, the temptation to madness on the philosopher's part is to not seek divine guidance at all in understanding what cannot be understood in its own right, and it is this form of madness that Plato sees epitomized in the sophists.[56]

Let us take another look at this first sort of madness by concentrating on inspiration rather than writing. Perhaps the best place to do this will be to look at the *Ion*, Socrates' dialogue with a performer of Homer's poetry. The complaint against Ion is that he claims for himself the ability to perform Homer well because he shares in his "art and knowledge," while Socrates insists that Ion only shares in Homer's inspiration rather than his knowledge. Socrates is, in other words, trying to cure Ion of the madness of claiming his divine inspiration as some sort of knowledge. At one point Socrates almost persuades him with a speech that Ion admits lays "hold of my soul." But this speech, that "the poet is a light thing, winged and sacred, able to make poetry because he is inspired and out of his mind and intelligence is no longer in him," while pleasing Ion's vanity, cannot exorcize the very madness that it describes. [57] For in agreeing that inspiration is a form of madness, Ion also gleefully proclaims the mystery of the pleasure and pain in his performances, wherein "if I set them to crying, I shall laugh myself because I am making money, but if they laugh, then I shall cry because of the money I am losing."[58] In other words, Ion's madness is not the madness brought on by the gods, but is rather the madness brought on by the audience in the city, and his alienation from their reaction is the alienation the liar has from his lie. Socrates subtly brings this out when he follows this observation of Ion's with his own:

> Socrates: You know, then, that this spectator is the
> last of the rings which I said get their power from one

[56] cf. Plato, *Lesser Hippias.*

[57] Plato, *Ion*, trans. Allan Bloom, *The Roots of Political Philosophy: Ten Forgotten Socratic Dialogues.* (Ithaca, NY: Cornell University Press, 1987), 534b.

[58] Plato, *Ion*, 535e.

another through the Heraclean stone? And you the
rhapsode and actor are the middle, and the top is the
poet himself, but the god through all these draws the
soul of human being wherever he wishes transmitting
the power from one to the other . . . And one poet is
suspended from one Muse, another from another.
And we name this "being possessed," and it is very
nearly that, for he is held.[59]

The power of magnetism in the inspiration of the poet, when coupled with the very sober profit-making calculations of Ion, opens
the possibility that Socrates means the very opposite of what he
says, and that the magnet of madness works out from the audience
and they are in fact the creators of the source of power in both the
poets and the gods.

In other words, just as Ion must serve his audience in order
to succeed rather than serving his "Muse," so also, we might say,
the gods and their poets must serve the city if they are to succeed
as well. This would be the truth behind the traditional equation of
vox dei and *vox populi*. We have already seen how this seems to fit
the role of the tragic poets, inasmuch as the city demands to be
lied to for the sake of its own survival; and it is the tragic poet who
supplies these lies to bind the city together mimetically rather than
in truth.

How, then, would this look if we applied it to the gods? Perhaps we should ask what would make Ion different, what would
make him laugh when his audience laughed and cry when they
cried? The answer, I think, is that Ion would have to be a comic
poet, for it is only in comedy that the co-conspiracy of poet and
audience to create a shared world of manipulated emotions is explicit and the poet knows which way the power of the magnet
flows. But that is also why comedies do not usually take the gods
very seriously. In that light, consider the *Euthyphro*. In this dialogue
as well as the *Ion*, we see Socrates compare his interlocutor with
Proteus the sea-god. Socrates is therefore putting himself in the
position of Menelaus who had to hold down Proteus the shape-
changer in order to find what sacrifices were due to Zeus in order

---

[59] Plato, *Ion*, 536a-b.

to escape from Egypt. The question of both these dialogues might well be said to be the question of what sacrifices the philosopher owes to the gods. The specific question of *Euthyphro*, however, is, "Do the gods love piety because it is pious, or is it pious because they love it?"[60] What, then, is the connection between these two questions?

To attempt an answer, we might say that if the gods were philosophers, they would love piety because of its nature, because it is pious; but if that were so, then all gods would love the same thing. But since they don't, since the gods are continually quarreling with one another and demanding differing acts of piety; they are not philosophers and so are more like poets who love what they make precisely because they have made it.[61] In other words, the gods suffer from the central affliction of the city, which is the unshareability of the body and one's own creations. What is true by nature can be shared by all, but what is true by fiat can only be shared by those loyal to the creator of that "truth." If the gods are therefore not philosophers, Proteus can give no answer to the question of Socrates/Menelaus because there is no answer by nature that would satisfy.

Yet there might be a mimetic answer that would satisfy, and that would be the comic action of the dialogue itself. For in this dialogue we see a discussion that moves in a circle between different definitions of piety that imitates the human traffic in goods and services based on supply and demand rather than actual worth. The definition of piety as "the art of carrying on business between gods and men," because of this circularity of definition, seems to get turned on its head and end up meaning that men traffic with the gods for their own good rather than that of the gods.[62] This is also the answer that we have seen the Proteus, Ion, give to Socrates as well. Piety as well as tragic poetry seems to be essential to the city and are in fact directly created because of this need; and yet

---

[60] Plato, *Euthyphro*, trans. Lane Cooper, *The Collected Dialogues of Plato*, eds. Edith Hamilton and Huntingdon Cairns (Princeton: Princeton University Press, 1961), 10a.

[61] Plato, *The Republic*, 330c.

[62] Plato, *Euthyphro* 14e.

Plato in his dialogues never denies the reality of this need—and thus the gods—any more than he would deny that Homer and not Socrates was the educator of the Greeks. The seriousness of the philosopher is therefore reflected in the fact that he is not an atheist, but his playfulness is reflected in his comic arguments that the gods are in fact as mad as the city, and the tragedy of the city and of the gods is one in the same. Nevertheless, humans cannot live outside the city and so the gods are as real as is the city; and the purpose they serve is to satisfy the ultimately unsatisfiable demand to both control and understand what cannot be understood or controlled—chance.

Consider the following quotation from Strauss concerning the mention of farming and generalship found in the *Euhtyphro* as well as the *Ion*:

> Whether the outcome of the use of generalship and of farming be good or bad depends upon chance. Chance is that which is in no way controllable by art or knowledge, or predictable by art or knowledge. But too much depends on chance for man to be resigned to the power of chance. Man makes the irrational attempt to control the uncontrollable, to control chance. Yet he knows that he cannot control chance. It is for this reason that he needs the gods. The gods are meant to do for him what he cannot do for himself. The gods are the engine by which man believes he can control chance. He serves the gods in order to be the employer of gods, or the lord of gods.[63]

In other words, the serious understanding of the philosopher is also an understanding of the serious need of the city. Yet as understanding, it also sees that the attempts to satisfy that need cannot be taken seriously, and so one can only engage with those who take the attempt seriously in a playful way. Serious living leading to playful writing therefore reflects a true knowledge of the limits of what can be known, whereas serious writing on its own reflects an ignorance of those inherent limits.

---

[63] Strauss, *Rebirth of Classical Political Rationalism, 203.*

In the light of this, if we were to read the Bible as one of the fundamental books of serious writing in our own civilization, rather than that of Greeks, then we might agree with Thomas More when he said: "For to prove that this life is no laughing time, but rather the time of weeping we find that our Savior himself wept twice or thrice, but never find that he laughed as much as once."[64] Likewise, if we assume the Bible is serious and a tragedy, then we can also see why Strauss brings out the fundamental question facing philosophy in our day as follows:

> If we compare what More said about Jesus with what Plato tells us about Socrates, we find that "Socrates laughed twice or thrice, but never find we that he wept as much as once." A slight bias in favor of laughing and against weeping seems to be essential to philosophy. For the beginning of philosophy as the philosophers understood it is not the fear of the Lord, but wonder. Its spirit is not hope and fear and trembling, but serenity on the basis of resignation. To that serenity, laughing is a little bit more akin than weeping. Whether the Bible or philosophy is right is of course the only question that ultimately matters. But in order to understand that question one must first see philosophy as it is. One must not see it from the outset through Biblical glasses. Wherever each of us may stand, no respectable purpose is served by trying to prove that we eat the cake and have it.[65]

I have quoted this passage in length because it brings out the essential concern in this initial discussion of Plato on writing, as well as leading us into the later concerns of narrative, and the nature of the particular narrative of the Bible in relation to philosophy.

In other words, *if* the Bible is in fact a tragedy (i.e., serious), then in choosing between the Bible and philosophy one is indeed choosing whether the intelligible or the unintelligible aspects of the universe are of the highest order and demand upon us. In the light of philosophy, then, choosing the Bible would be choosing to be

---

[64] Thomas More, *Dialogue of Comfort Against Tribulation*, chap. 13, quoted from Strauss, *Rebirth of Classical Political Rationalism,* 206.

[65] Strauss, *Rebirth of Classical Political Rationalism*, 206.

a plaything of the gods and is therefore not ultimately a serious choice. Yet in the light of the writing of the Bible itself, this choice is ultimately the only serious thing one can do. Nevertheless, this sort of question is at a stalemate because the philosopher cannot prove that this is not so, and he knows it, in the same way as he knows the limitations of the whole—hence he must respect both choices. But is this stalemate truly the last word?

For *if* the Bible is *not* a tragedy, and is in fact a comedy, then both the nature of this choice and the relation of living according to the Bible and the philosophical life must be reconsidered. In later chapters I will argue precisely this. Yet always in the background, the cogency of Plato's account of the philosophical life and Strauss' reading of it remains as a foundation that demands of this entire endeavor that it not be a case of having one's cake and eating it too.

VI: VIOLENCE AND THE TRAGIC PLOT AS SCAPEGOAT

DRAWING out the connection between violence and tragedy may seem a bit harsh, especially in the present scholarly climate where catharsis is viewed as educative and peaceful conflict viewed as the norm. Yet, as I have tried to argue, Plato and Aristotle did not view it this way. For both of them, factional violence is a continuing threat to every regime, and tragedy was the predominate, if ultimately ineffective, means of dealing with that threat. Tragedy, as the *pharmakon* that both poisons and cures, was emblematic of the city that contains the seeds of its own destruction in the very means by which it is preserved. More precisely, the tragic plot is the *pharmokos*, or scapegoat, that bears this factional violence in the action on stage in order to separate it off and purge it from the now apparently unified audience. Lest this claim seem idiosyncratic, or relevant only to the superseded world of classical politics, I will bring together three contemporary theorists and show how they converge on essentially this point. René Girard as an anthropologist on religion, Northrop Frye in his "poetics" of literature, and Paul Ricoeur in his symbolic archaeology all confirm in the context of their own theories the intimate connection between tragedy, violence, and the laws and religions at the foundation of society. Although I will not agree fully with any of them, there should prove enough overlap between all three to indicate they are all onto something, and that "something" is no less than what Plato was onto long ago when he quarreled with the tragic poets and the city.`

In Girard we get the claim that the transformation of human violence through mimesis is the foundation of all civilization and religion, and that essential to this process is the obscuring and forgetting of how it works. Theater and religion are therefore inextricably bound.

> There is no true science of religion, any more than there is a science of culture. Scholars are still disputing about which cult Greek tragedy should be ascribed to. Were the ancients correct in assigning tragedy to Dionysus, or does it rightfully belong to another god? Undoubtedly this is a genuine problem; but it is also, I think, a secondary one. Far more important, but far less discussed, is the relationship between tragedy and the divine, between the theater in general and religion. . . . Any phenomenon associated with the acts of remembering, commemorating, and perpetuating a unanimity that springs from the murder of a surrogate victim can be termed "religious."[1]

Girard and Plato would seem in complete agreement about the connection between tragedy and the gods, the connection between mimesis and the essential foundations of human religion and society. Where Plato might take exception to much of Girard's argument, however, is his claim "that these imitations had their origin in a real event."[2] Apart from this telling move, what Girard describes is essentially the founding role of tragic catharsis. Let us see, then, what Girard has to say about the "scapegoat mechanism" that makes the contagion of human violence livable.

At the basis of all religious systems Girard finds what he calls the "surrogate victim." What he means by this term is exemplified by the ritual cannibalism of the Tupinamba tribe, wherein the victim was first captured, then made a member of the community, and later both scourged and honored, prior to being finally eaten after a mock escape. Girard describes what was being accomplished through all this as follows.

---

[1] René Girard, *Violence and the Sacred*, trans. Patrick Gregory, (Baltimore and London: The Johns Hopkins University Press, 1979), 315.

[2] Girard, *Violence and the Sacred*, 309.

> They were trying to reproduce an original event that actually took place, to recover the unanimity that occurred and recurred around the person of the surrogate victim. If the prisoner was treated in two contradictory ways, if he was sometimes vilified and sometimes honored, it was because he represented the primordial victim. He was hated insofar as he polarized the as yet untransformed violence; he was revered insofar as he transformed the violence and set in motion the unifying mechanism of the surrogate victim.[3]

What Girard describes here is something very similar to the workings of tragedy in the movement from the bad things connected with fear and pity, and the very good things connected with the catharsis of those emotions. Tragedy as a whole seems to have the double nature Girard gives to the surrogate victim, inasmuch as tragedy elicits the fear and pity that "polarizes" the violence in the city, and finally unifies that polarity by means of the victimization of the hero on stage.

The final result of cathartically purging fear and pity in tragedy is thus exactly what the surrogate victim is intended to accomplish. Girard thus finds both Aristotle's notion of catharsis and Plato's dual use of the *pharmakon* that both poisons and remedies to be especially apt expressions for the working of the scapegoat mechanism, or *pharmokos*.

> The Greek term for an evil object extracted by means of a similar ritual is *katharma*. This term was also used as a variant of *pharmakos* to designate a sacrificial human victim . . . . The word *katharsis* refers primarily to the mysterious benefits that accrue to the community upon the death of a human *katharma* or *pharmakos*. The process is generally seen as a religious purification and takes the form of cleansing or draining away of impurities. Shortly before his execution the *pharmokos* is paraded ceremonially through the streets of the village. It is believed that he will absorb all the noxious influences that may be abroad and that his death

---

[3] Girard, *Violence and the Sacred*, 276.

will transpose them outside the community. This is a mythical representation of what does in fact *almost* take place. The communal violence is indeed drawn to the person of the surrogate victim, but the final resolution cannot be described as the expulsion of some substance. The interpretation thus approaches the truth but fails to attain it because it fails to perceive three essential facts: the mimetic nature of reciprocal violence, the arbitrary choice of the victim, and the unanimous polarization of hostility that produces the reconciliation.[4]

The reason the scapegoat only "almost" purges the body of an alien substance is because the scapegoat mechanism is a massive diversion and deception. Girard is thus attempting to expose the deception and lay bare its true workings in the same way Plato, and, to a lesser extent, Aristotle were. Since I believe it is essentially the same deception operative throughout, let us examine in more detail the inner workings of this mechanism laid bare by Girard.

The first of the three essential facts that must be seen rather than hidden is the "mimetic nature of reciprocal violence." Violence always breeds more violence because of human nature's grounding in learning through imitation; we not only learn to desire what others desire, but for that very reason, find ourselves in potentially violent competition over the same things. The mimetic nature of violence leads to a certain "doubling" wherein everyone becomes the twin of everyone else because what one hates and fears in the other are the very things manifested in oneself. This reciprocity of violence therefore has no limit except for its complete triumph and the consequent elimination of all differences; but it is precisely this chaotic confusion that provokes the need *and* the opportunity for its solution.

> The universal spread of "doubles," the complete effacement of differences, heightening antagonisms but also making them interchangeable, is the prerequisite for the establishment of violent unanimity. For order to be reborn, disorder must first triumph; for myths

---

[4] Girard, *Violence and the Sacred*, 287.

to achieve their complete integration, they must first
suffer total disintegration.[5]

Reciprocal violence is thus the cause behind the emotions of fear
and pity central to tragedy, for the violence exhibited in tragic action brings out the mutual fear of injustice based upon self-
knowledge described by Aristotle in his *Rhetoric*. The violent action
on stage of the hero who is outraged at the *other's* violence, is an
overt manifestation of the civil war that threatens to tear the city
apart, just as are the chaotic "bindings and castrations" of the older
gods of Necessity described by Agathon. Yet it is the very mimetic
representation of this violence that provides the opportunity of
getting rid of this spreading contagion of violence.

For Girard, however, mimesis is the cause of the problem,
rather than the means to the cure, which is why he subordinates
tragedy to the anthropologically primordial event of arbitrarily
choosing a victim. For in choosing a victim who is no less and no
more guilty than everyone else, the unchecked violence of all gets
checked by attaching itself to one focal point who is alone guilty,
thereby rendering everyone else innocent. This victim thus receives all the violence upon himself that would otherwise be mutually suffered by all. The arbitrariness of this victim is correlative
to the fact that all are mutually guilty, thereby leaving everyone as
suitable for victimization as another. Yet once hit upon, this arbitrary selection, because it leads to the return of difference and order, is itself seen as no longer arbitrary but rather the primordial
act of divine and human order.

The arbitrariness of the victim must therefore be hid at all
costs. If revealed, the entire function of being a scapegoat is rendered ineffective. Girard is thus indirectly echoing the arguments
of Plato in Book V of the *Republic*, wherein the noble lie that makes
the city one is intimately involved with converting what seems like
mere chance events into the foundation of all order. Chance is thus
not merely chance, but rather "Fate"; and it is the role of the tragic
poet to make what seems arbitrary evidence of the will of the gods.

---

[5] Girard, *Violence and the Sacred*, 79.

Plato's rulers, however, know why this lie is needed and hence engage in it deliberately; but for this noble lie to work, it must seem like a lottery. For lotteries are sacred rites, and "Chance can always be trusted to reveal the truth, for it reflects the will of the divinity."[6]

Plato and Girard are thus both in agreement that "hiding and deceit" are essential to founding and ordering civilization, and that hiding is the source of all belief in the divine and gods. Where they differ is over the central role the poet plays in all this. For Plato, the poet is himself this "liar" who founds the city and preserves it in its appearances, but for Girard, the poet is merely another manifestation of an underlying phenomena of which the poet himself is only dimly aware. Girard will thus use Aristotle's account of tragedy merely as a means to illustrate his own thesis.

> On closer inspection, Aristotle's text is something of a manual of sacrificial practices, for the qualities that make a "good" tragic hero are precisely those required of the sacrificial victim. If the latter is to polarize and purge the emotions of the community, he must at once resemble the members of the community and differ from them; he must be at once an insider and outsider, both "double" and incarnation of the "sacred difference." He must be neither wholly good nor wholly bad. A certain degree of goodness is required in the tragic hero in order to establish sympathy between him and the audience; yet a certain degree of weakness, a "tragic flaw" is needed, to neutralize the goodness and permit the audience to tolerate the hero's downfall and death . . . . The spectator may shudder with "pity and fear," but he must also feel a deep sense of gratitude for his own orderly and relatively secure existence. Every work of art might be said to partake of the initiatory process in that it forces itself upon the emotions, offers intimations of violence, and instills a respect for the power of violence; that is, it promotes prudence and discourages hubris.[7]

---

[6] Girard, *Violence and the Sacred*, 313.

[7] Girard, *Violence and the Sacred*, 291-2.

Girard overlooks, in this startling affinity between his thesis and the prescription laid down for the tragic hero, that philosophy may well have caught onto this deception much earlier than he did, and that in exposing the lies of tragic poetry may well have been attempting to do exactly what he is trying to do.

The difference between Plato's exposure and Girard's, however, would be that Plato is attempting to understand violence and mimesis in the light of the intelligibility of the whole, whereas Girard, as a modern, views intelligibility as somehow itself founded upon the very mechanism he is describing. In other words, by quarreling with the tragic poets Plato is saying that it is mimesis itself that hides the truth, and that the truth it hides is our own intelligent discovery of the unintelligibilities we all find ourselves in, of which violence is itself only a central part. Girard, on the other hand, is trying to uncover some sort of "*ur*-event" that accounts for everything that follows, and *not* trying to find a constant founded upon essential features of human nature that respond to as well as create our history.

This fundamental divergence between Plato and Girard can be seen in Girard's obscuring of the difference between tragic and comic poetry. Consider what he says of *Oedipus the King* in the following.

> In *Oedipus the King* the public's attention is insidiously diverted from the community's efforts to rid itself of the *pharmakos* to the *pharmakos* itself, with whom the poet and poetry tend to side.[8]

Plato would agree. In fact, it is the entire point to his criticism of the poets; but only if we remember that it applies only to the *tragic* poets. For what constitutes the deception of the tragic poets is that they must hide themselves and their role if their poems are to meet with success. It is they who must distract their audience from "how" they are accomplishing tragic catharsis to "what" they accomplish. And that entails hiding the central role of their own poetic artifice. This is not the case, however, in comic poetry. The

---

[8] Girard, *Violence and the Sacred*, 293.

comic poet must invariably reveal himself and his role as the satis-
fier of the audience's desires if he is to at all succeed. In comedy
the process of artifice and its relation to our desires is its primary
theme, and so it cannot allow for the diversion from itself to its
"product" that Girard is speaking of here.

This is why Plato chooses to write comically, as I have argued
earlier. For Plato recognizes that he must himself engage in artifice
and poetry if he is to write anything at all, but the choice of writing
playfully rather than seriously allows him to keep before our eye,
unhidden, precisely that which Girard is so concerned to uncover.
Plato thus has the advantage over Girard of being able to place his
own writings in the context of mimesis, an advantage that allows
him not to forget that the only primordial event he can be sure of
is that of telling a story or acting out a ritual, since even his putative
"*ur*-event" is itself a story. Girard is a victim of the very deception
he uncovers, because he takes his own story of this early event as
not a story at all, but some sort of deduced, established, or demon-
strated fact.[9] Unlike Plato, he is not attending to the "likely story"
character of his own myth-making and so overlooks the preemi-
nent role myths take in what he is describing. Plato avoids this sort
of criticism by admitting its intractability, and by writing comically
as the only way to expose tragedy.

---

[9] Girard's use of a factual ur-event to ground his theory is remarkably
similar to Rousseau's ambiguous use of the state of nature as both "history" and useful "hypothesis." Consider the troubling transition in the
following quotes from the beginning of Rousseau's *Discourse on Inequality*:

> "Let us begin, then, by setting aside all the facts, for they
> are irrelevant to the problem. The investigation that may
> be made concerning this subject should not be taken as
> historical truths, but only as hypothetical and conditional
> reasonings, better suited to casting light on the nature of
> things than to showing their real origin, like those the phys-
> icists put forward everyday with regard to the formation of
> the world...."O man, whatever may be your country, and
> whatever opinions you may hold, listen to me: Here is your
> history, as I believe I have read it, not in books by your
> fellow men, who are liars, but in Nature, who never lies.

Daniel Rousseau, *The Essential Rousseau,* trans. Lowell Bair (New York and
Scarborough: Ontario, New American Library, 1974), 144-5.

When Girard thus accuses Plato of indulging in the very sort of scapegoating he is criticizing by kicking out the tragic poets, he is just not getting the joke. Of course it is the same thing! Only this time, not to be taken seriously. The claim that "the Platonic rejection of tragic violence is itself violent, for it finds expression in a new expulsion—that of the poet," is to mistake the mock-violence of comic beatings for the serious violence of tragedy. [10] Since philosophers are the last ones to want to rule, they will be the last ones to kick anybody out anywhere. By quoting Derrida approvingly in his criticisms of Plato and philosophy as "an attempt at expulsion . . . perpetually renewed because never wholly successful," Girard merely shows that he, like Derrida, has confused the modern project of philosophy with that of Plato.[11] For the essential difference between Plato and the moderns is on this very issue. Plato chooses to write comically and so make manifest the deceptive qualities of writing, whereas the moderns write seriously and so openly embrace, even while still covering over, the deceptive means of tragedy for the founding of society.

In this light, the primordial event of Girard differs very little from the founding of the "Leviathan" described by Hobbes. By finding the "unity of all rites," Girard has created for us the myth behind all myths; but that still leaves him every bit the mythmaker. Unless he examines the nature of mythmaking itself, he is no different from the tragedians who distract us from their brilliance and mythmaking by the realism and believability of the myths they make. The stories they tell seem be to something that really happened, or are perhaps even more real than what did happen. If Girard would just wink at us when he lays out for us his "likely story," we might then be free to pursue the truth of ourselves as myth-makers, rather than just our myths.

Yet even apart from that wink, Girard has indeed uncovered in our own day the equivalent of what Plato was uncovering in his. The role of violence, scapegoating, and deception, and their founding function in human society and religion, seems to confirm that

---

[10] Rousseau, *Essential Rousseau*, 295.

[11] Rousseau, *Essential Rousseau*, 296.

Plato was indeed onto something, and that this something had everything to do with what we find in tragedy. Plato is generally vilified today for his hostile attitude toward the poets, but from Girard we get an entirely different voice confirming that the concerns about violence, lying, and the dangers of imitation are very real and intimately involved in making us who we are. At the very least, then, the work of independent anthropological work of Girard should convince us to reevaluate Plato and consider seriously his claims about violence, politics, the gods, *and* writing.

If René Girard can be said to found an entire anthropological theory upon the effects of tragic poetry, in Northrop Frye's *Anatomy of Criticism* we find an extension of Aristotle's attempt to write a "poetics" that takes poetry solely on its own terms. Although there are many rich and fascinating aspects to this poetics, what I find most illuminating of my own concerns is his account of the four archetypal plot possibilities, or *mythoi*, that correspond to the four seasons. And yet, just as all four seasons move between the two poles of the winter and summer solstice, so here also all four *mythoi* can be reduced to two—the movement up to comedy, and the movement down to tragedy. Irony and Romance are thus transitional types that must be understood as subspecies of either comic or tragic movement. What I will concentrate on here and later, then, will be Frye's descriptions of the two *mythoi* of comedy and tragedy.

Frye distinguishes fictional modes from thematic modes, and divides fictional modes into "two main tendencies: a 'comic' tendency to integrate the hero with his society, and a 'tragic' tendency to isolate him."[12] This division would seem to support my own arguments as to the twin poles of comedy and tragedy. The role of both "action" and "character" is echoed by the role he gives to both hero and society, wherein integration or isolation are the comic and tragic directions that correspond to Aristotle's happy or sad endings.

Comedy and tragedy thus have to do with what he calls "internal fiction"; but, as he says, "besides the internal fiction of the

---

[12] Northrop, Frye, *Anatomy of Criticism: Four Essays*, (Princeton: Princeton University Press, 1957), 54.

hero and his society, there is an external fiction which is a relation between the writer and the writer's society."[13] By extension, then, it would seem that if the internal fiction moves between the twin poles of comedy and tragedy, so then ought the external fiction. In this light we might say that Aristotle dealt primarily with the internal fiction when he described the difference between comic and tragic poetry, whereas Plato's additional discussion of the difference between playful and serious writing concerns what Frye would call the external fiction. Both, however, would involve the twin poles of the comic and tragic, so perhaps Frye's very distinction between fictional and thematic modes might prove ultimately redundant.

Consider the following account of the "external fiction" wherein Frye describes the thematic mode of the writer in relation to the writer's society.

> [C]learly there is no such thing as *a* fictional or *a* thematic work of literature, for all four ethical elements (ethical in the sense of relation to character), the hero, the hero's society, the poet and the poet's readers, are always at least potentially present. There can hardly be a work of literature without some kind of relation, implied or expressed, between its creator and its auditors. When the audience the poet had in mind is superseded by posterity; the relation changes, but it still holds. On the other hand, even in lyrics and essays the writer is to some extent a fictional hero with a fictional audience, for if the element of fictional projection disappeared completely, the writing would become direct address, or straight discursive writing, and cease to be literature.[14]

The thematic mode thus parallels the comic and tragic bipolarity with the bipolarity of a writer who either writes "as an individual, emphasizing the separateness of his personality and the distinctness of his vision," or on the other hand, the poet who is "a spokesman of his society, which means, as he is not addressing a

---

[13] Frye, *Anatomy of Criticism,* 52.

[14] Frye, *Anatomy of Criticism,* 53.

second society, that a poetic and expressive power which is latent or needed in his society comes to articulation in him."[15] When the intrinsic connection between the obscuring qualities of serious writing and the low profile of the tragic poet is brought out, however, both modes can be understood as either comic or tragic, for the relation between the poet and his poem, even within the poem, is what constitutes the essential difference between comedy and tragedy.

In addition to the internal or external fiction of modes, Frye also discusses what he calls *epos*. What he includes under this term is character and setting, and in order to understand the significance of this term, he refers back to the noble or base characters that we have already seen in Aristotle; and rather than interpreting these Aristotelian terms in the usual modern way as either good or bad, he reminds us that

> Aristotle's words for good and bad, however, are *spou-daios* and *phaulos*, which have a figurative sense of weighty and light. In literary fictions the plot consists of somebody doing something. The somebody, if an individual, is the hero, and the something he does or fails to do is what he can do, or could have done, on the level of the postulates made about him by the author and the consequent expectations of the audience. Fictions, therefore, may be classified, not morally, but by the hero's power of action, which may be greater than ours, less, or roughly the same.[16]

In light of these characters' powers of action, then, he divides them five ways depending upon whether they are superior in kind (myth), superior in degree (romance), superior in degree to other men, but not to his natural environment (high mimetic), superior neither to other men nor to his environment (low mimetic), and inferior in power or intelligence to ourselves (ironic). Since characters are an element in any plot, Frye can therefore divide up each plot as being predominantly either mythic, romantic, high mimetic,

---

[15] Frye, *Anatomy of Criticism*, 54.

[16] Frye, *Anatomy of Criticism*, 33.

low mimetic, or ironic. This determining element of *epos* is so important that Frye will also argue that literature has in fact had a tendency to move down this scale through time, and the fundamental plots at the level of the gods get displaced into lower levels until finally in our own day we see the ironic mode transform itself into a mythic mode that presumably would start the process all over again. As he puts it, "reading forward in history, therefore, we may think of our romantic, high mimetic and low mimetic modes as a series of *displaced* myths, *mythoi* or plot-formulas progressively moving over toward the opposite pole of verisimilitude, and then, with irony, beginning to move back."[17]

Although this account of *epos* in terms of "lightness" or "weight" is very close to what we have already seen, there is a key difference here that is distinctively emblematic of more modern thinking—translating *spoudaios* and *phaulos* in terms of relative power. *Spoudaios* and *phaulos* correspond to what I have been discussing under the terms of seriousness and playfulness, and these two categories are, at least in Plato and Aristotle, political categories and have to do with an individual's relationship to the city (i.e., his political or social standing). Thus someone who takes political things with the highest seriousness would be "heavy" and bear the gravity of position and responsibility, whereas taking such things lightly makes one free to play with such things and not to take on the burden of political responsibility.[18] Seriousness and playfulness are thus directly connected to nobility and baseness, for what makes the noble noble is their political standing in the eyes of those who matter, while the baseness of the base is their primary concern with such nonpolitical concerns as sex, money and comfort. If we add the element of wisdom to this—which may come into either conflict or concurrence with political nobility and baseness, and so ties in with the thematic elements connected with the narrator—we can say that Frye's understanding of character based upon

---

[17] Frye, *Anatomy of Criticism,* 52.

[18] A modern instance of a writer using these two terms in their political sense along with their corresponding lightness and heaviness, can be found in the corpus of Milan Kundera, especially *The Unbearable Lightness of Being* and *The Book of Laughter and Forgetting.*

power sets it apart from his more accurate account of plot in terms of society. If he were thus to interpret character according to political, which is to say social, standing, there would be a much greater congruence between the characters and action. This is especially so in the light of his two "main tendencies" having to do with movement into or out of society; a movement that must always have political implications, one way or the other, for the characters. What he calls "displacement" might then be better understood in the light of changing politics and philosophy, rather than some sort of intrinsic momentum of literature on its own.[19]

Turning directly to Frye's description of the tragic plot, the first thing we notice is that in contrast to the wish-fulfillment quality of comedy it "guarantees, so to speak, a disinterested quality in literary experience. It is largely through the tragedies of Greek culture that the sense of the authentic natural basis of human character comes into literature."[20] This disinterested and "realistic" quality of tragedy reminds us of the qualities of tragedy we have already noted in their contrast to comedy, such as its predictability and seemingly autonomous presence on the stage. But what it also means is that while in comedy the emphasis falls on the narrator, in tragedy, because of its "disinterested quality," the emphasis falls on the plot. In other words, "the source of the tragic effect must be sought, as Aristotle pointed out, in the tragic *mythos* or plot-structure";[21] and what this structure tends to consist of is an individual or individuals who by their movement out of society "lead up to an epiphany of law, of that which is and must be."[22]

Although the action of tragedy reveals the necessity and inevitability of law, this law is also revealed as a brute fact in the sense

---

[19] The intrinsic relation of comedy to technology because of the comedic emphasis upon contrivance, when seen in the light of modern philosophy's wedding of theory to *techne*, would thus account for why literary forms have become increasingly forms of comedy rather than tragedy. Thus Frye's last level of displacement, irony, he will himself call an aspect of comedy.

[20] Frye, *Anatomy of Criticism*, 206

[21] Frye, *Anatomy of Criticism, 207.*

[22] Frye, *Anatomy of Criticism*, 208.

that "it simply happens, whatever its cause, explanation or relation-
ships. Characters may grope about for conceptions of gods that
kill us for their sport, or for a divinity that shapes our ends, but the
action of tragedy will not abide our questions."[23] Note that it is the
characters that grope about for these answers rather than us; for
we are spectators and not active participants in a tragedy—hence
the disinterestedness. The one over-riding interest within the plot
itself Frye describes as a two-part movement from the hero's violation of some sort of law, and the consequent vengeance upon
that violation. "The hero provokes enmity, or inherits a situation
of enmity, and the return of the avenger constitutes the catastro-
phe."[24] The action of a tragic plot, precisely in its realism and disinterestedness, is for the sake of the society the hero leaves behind
rather than for the sake of the hero himself; so we as audience
submit to its inscrutable decrees in the same way the comic narrator submits to us.

However, in explaining the action of tragedy Frye seeks to
avoid what he calls two "reductive formulas," one of which is that
"all tragedy exhibits the omnipotence of an external fate" and the
other the claim that the act that starts the "tragic process going
must be primarily a violation of *moral* law."[25] The first formula is
reductive because it

> confuses the tragic condition with the tragic process:
> fate, in a tragedy, normally becomes external to the
> hero only *after* the tragic process has been set going.
> The Greek *ananke* or *moira* is in its normal, or pre-
> tragic, form the internal balancing condition of life. It
> appears as external or antithetical necessity only after
> it has been violated as a condition of life, just as jus-
> tice is the internal condition of an honest man, but
> the external antagonist of the criminal.[26]

---

[23] Frye, *Anatomy of Criticism,* 208.

[24] Frye, *Anatomy of Criticism*, 208-9.

[25] Frye, *Anatomy of Criticism*, 209-10.

[26] Frye, *Anatomy of Criticism*, 209-10

One might say the hero is thus the one who bears on his shoulders inquiry's move from past satisfactions toward its new encounter with the limits of the inverse-insight. The hero as the stand-in for inquiry's frustration, then, brings out the move from past insights as an internal organizing factor, represented by the hero's eminent status, to an external, frustrated demand, exiled from, yet unable to leave alone or go beyond, his past home from which he was separated. Yet Frye's connection of what I have called "intelligibility" with "law," especially when we remember law's connection to *nomos*, convention or custom, reminds us that tragedy is mimetic, and that the imitation transforms the nature of what it imitates. Yet in tragedy this transformation hides its tracks behind the very inevitability and inexorable quality of the "law" that is revealed in the tragic process.

The tragic poet, in the very process of having his hero discover (*anagnorisis*) that he was responsible for his own reversal (*peripety*) into a process of lawful causation, must exert all his power "to avoid the sense of having manipulated that situation for his own purpose."[27] In contrast with comedy, the effect on his plot of the tragic narrator hiding himself, Frye describes as follows: "just as comedy often sets up an arbitrary law and then organizes the action to break or evade it, so tragedy presents the reverse theme of narrowing a comparatively free life into a process of causation."[28] The tragic hero thus usurps (and therefore hides) the narrator's role of causing the action by taking upon himself the responsibility for what follows next, but this taking on of responsibility is not necessarily what Frye calls a "moral" flaw; instead the *hamartia* of the hero is more connected with the hubris of going beyond law itself and becoming a law unto himself; and yet even in going beyond the law the hero only reveals the law for what it is. "Aristotle's *hamartia*, then, is a condition of being, not a cause of becoming."[29] Tragedy thus questions the law even as it must submit to it, and so tragedy "seems to elude the antithesis of moral

---

[27] Frye, *Anatomy of Criticism*, 211.

[28] Frye, *Anatomy of Criticism*, 212.

[29] Frye, *Anatomy of Criticism*, 213.

responsibility and arbitrary fate, just as it eludes the antithesis of good and evil."[30]

What Frye is describing here is what I have earlier discussed under the rubric of tragedy as a scapegoat. The scapegoat (whether viewed as the hero or the tragedy as a whole) bears the burden of our knowledge of the law's arbitrariness and consequent inability to free us from our limitations, but also hides that knowledge from us by reasserting the priority of those laws by being cast out or destroyed by means of them. Frye sees this connection, albeit in the opposite manner of Girard, by viewing tragedy as a "mimesis of sacrifice." As Frye would have it:

> Anyone accustomed to think archetypally of literature will recognize in tragedy a mimesis of sacrifice. Tragedy is a paradoxical combination of a fearful sense of rightness (the hero must fall) and a pitying sense of wrongness (it is too bad that he falls). There is a similar paradox in the two elements of sacrifice. One of these is communion, the dividing of a heroic or divine body among a group which brings them into unity with, and as, that body. The other is propitiation, the sense that in spite of the communion the body really belongs to another, a greater, and a potentially wrathful power.[31]

Frye is here needlessly disconnecting narrative from political desires and then reconnecting them up again as a mimesis of those desires when he could instead bring out the intrinsic role mimesis plays in the political formation itself. For the sense of rightness in tragedy is the overwhelming need to create out of our divisiveness a political unity (communion with a divine body); and yet the sense of wrongness is that the achievement of political unity requires some sort of violent or deceptive sacrifice in order to attain it (the potentially—for the hero, actually—wrathful power).

Between Frye and Girard, then, we have all the pieces to make the argument that the tragic plot itself functions as the scapegoat. In the case of the tragic hero as the internal scapegoat, he

---

[30] Frye, *Anatomy of Criticism*, 213.

[31] Frye, *Anatomy of Criticism*, 214.

gives a description that hits off perfectly the ambivalent nature of the *pharmakos*, whether it be this internal hero or the external "lie" of the tragic poem itself.

> We may call this typical victim the *pharmakos* or scape-goat.... The *pharmakos* is neither innocent nor guilty. He is innocent in the sense that what happens to him is far greater than anything he has done provokes, like the mountaineer whose shout brings down an ava-lanche. He is guilty in the sense that he is a member of a guilty society, or living in a world where such in-justices are an inescapable part of existence. The two facts do not come together; they remain ironically apart. The *pharmakos*, in short, is in the situation of Job. Job can defend himself against the charge of hav-ing done something that makes his catastrophe mor-ally intelligible; but the success of his defense makes it morally unintelligible.[32]

The moral intelligibility of mimesis as a *pharmakos* is thus inacces-sible precisely because it is an imitation of, and *not* the intelligibility of, insights themselves. As with Job, the answer to Job's entreaties appear out of a whirlwind only in the form of further questions; and we must wait for an adequate answer until we get to the com-edy of the Gospel of John, where the "*logos*" no longer speaks out of a whirlwind but face to face. Is the righteousness of Job any-thing else than perhaps this very willingness (as opposed to the tragic poets) to wait for that answer without cursing God in the meantime?

Be that as it may, because the tragic narrative hides its process of coming to be in the characters and plot, the description of plot in terms of law and character have also been ways of describing the function of the narrative itself—as a means of both founding and preserving human society. As we have seen, one of the major problems facing any human association is the vagaries of contin-gency and novelty normally associated with "time." In tragedy, time is connected with the inevitability of fate and stands over and against the human—it is what must be made "human" by means

---

[32] Frye, *Anatomy of Criticism*, 41-42.

of the tragic process itself. But the resulting human time is the re-assertion of the old or ancient time, with the attempt at rising above that time or escaping it having been cast out with the hero. The time of tragedy is thus cyclical and the reassertion that there is, and can be, nothing new under the sun. It is the fall into time; but the time one falls into, of course, is the time that always was and will be. As Frye describes it:

> [T]ime *begins* with the fall; . . . the fall from liberty into the natural cycle also started the movement of time as we know it. In other tragedies we can trace the feeling that *nemesis* is deeply involved with the movement of time, whether as the missing of a tide in the affairs of men, as a recognition that the time is out of joint, as sense that time is devourer of life, the mouth of hell at the previous moment, when the potential passes forever into the actual, or, in its ultimate horror, Mac-beth's sense of it as simply one clock-tick after an-other. In comedy time plays a redeeming role: it uncovers and brings to light what is essential to the happy ending.[33]

In contrast with tragic time, then, comic time is the new time that delights in its novelty as the font of creation. This is why the end of comedy is the triumph of the young, even while the result of tragedy reasserts the old. Comic time is the time it takes to pull off a new creation, while the ancient quality of tragic time covers over the creation of the plot under cloak of the scapegoated hero. Trag-edies are thus essentially traditional while comedies are always modern. The overwhelming predominance of comic forms in modern theater, even when they attempt tragic themes, may thus arise from the self-conscious modernity of "modern" thought. This may also explain why Frye's displacement has been a move-ment toward increasingly comic and ironic figures rather than ones suited to tragedy. Yet before we can investigate more thoroughly the nature of comedy, we must finish up this discussion of tragedy by taking a look at the work of Paul Ricoeur.

---

[33] Frye, *Anatomy of Criticism*, 213.

In the *Symbolism of Evil*, Paul Ricoeur lays out for us four different types of myths that can again be reduced to two. The two
Ricoeur emphasizes are the "myth of creation" and the "Adamic
myth"; while he views a third, the "tragic vision," as an intermediate type, and the fourth, the "myth of exile," as "marginal" and
"solitary." As one might expect, these first two myths are direct
opposites of each other, and thus purer types, because one is a
distinctly tragic narrative and the other is distinctly comic. So even
though Ricoeur will call one of his types the "tragic vision," it is
the cosmogonic myth of chaos that he presents most clearly as a
narrative plot that moves in a contrary fashion to the comic narrative of the Adamic myth; and he sets up his major contrasts between this myth and the Adamic myth. Ricoeur does not use the
terms tragic or comic directly in the contexts of these two myths,
but I think an examination of them both in the light of the preceding accounts of comedy and tragedy should make this relation
clear.

In the following succinct account of the myth of creation, we
can see that this first typology has primarily a dual structure, a
structure that Frye has pointed out as characteristic of tragedy.

> [In] the drama of creation, the origin of evil is coex-
> tensive with the origin of things; it is the *"chaos" with
> which the creative act of the god struggles.* The counterpart
> of this view of things is that *salvation is identical with
> creation itself*; the act that founds the world is at the
> same time the liberating act. We shall verify this in the
> structure of the cult that corresponds to this "type"
> of the origin and end of evil; the cult can only be a
> *ritual reenactment* of the combat at the origins of the
> world. The identity of evil and "chaos," and the iden-
> tity of salvation with "creation," have seemed to us to
> constitute the two fundamental traits of this first
> type.[34]

In this twin identification of evil with chaos and salvation with creation, we can see the same dual structure of tragedy that Frye describes as a two-part movement wherein the hero's violation of

---

[34] Paul Ricoeur, *The Symbolism of Evil*, (Boston: Beacon Press, 1967), 172.

some sort of law is also at the same time the re-assertion of the inevitability and inviolability of that law. So just as the tragic plot is the narrative *par excellence* of the founding of the city, so also is the myth of creation the myth of the foundation of the cosmos. What is significant in both of those foundations, however, is that the role of chaos, or its agential manifestation in the form of violence, is part and parcel of the reassertion of order or law.

Ricoeur says of this myth that it is by "disorder that disorder is overcome"; and the key example he uses to illustrate this comes from the *Enuma Elish*, wherein the older gods are slain in order to make room for the new order of the slayer god, Marduk. [35] In a description of this battle that is reminiscent of Derrida's description of tragic writing as a form of parricide, Ricoeur gives an account of this creative act/murder as follows:

> Thus the creative act, which distinguishes, separates, measures, and puts in order, is inseparable from the criminal act that puts an end to the life of the oldest gods, inseparable from a deicide inherent in the divine.[36]

If we replace the order of gods to man, with father to son, we can see a further confirmation of this in the *Enuma Elish*. For in this account man's creation is itself dependent upon this form of parricide; "man is made from the blood of an assassinated god, that is to say from the life of a god, but from his life ravished by a murder."[37]

This point brings us to a seeming distinction between the tragic plot and the myth of creation: that the hero in a tragedy moves out of society and ends with his defeat, whereas the myth of creation seems to end with a young god who defeats the old. Marduk, for example, who seems to be the hero of the *Enuma Elish*, does not seem to function as a tragic hero because his end is one of triumph with the entire cosmos forming around him, rather

---

[35] Ricoeur, *The Symbolism of Evil*, 179.

[36] Ricoeur, *The Symbolism of Evil*, 180.

[37] Ricoeur, *The Symbolism of Evil*, 180.

than the end of exile or being cast out from the society of the cosmos. It must be kept in mind, however, that this is a story about the gods rather than men. Whereas, in a human tragedy the hero serves the purpose of reasserting the divine order and fate precisely by falling from it (and in so doing, becoming subjected to it), in the case of stories about the gods themselves when there is no difference between this divine order and the ultimately triumphant god, then the representative role of hero and order must both be personified in the form of different gods. The role of the tragic hero is thus played by the older rather than the younger gods. In this sense Tiamat, and her "tragic fall," is the simultaneous establishment of the new reign of another and newer god, Marduk. Because this tragedy has gods as characters, the reassertion of law and order (fate) at the end of a tragedy is in this case embodied by the new god who triumphs over the old god. One might say that Marduk, precisely in his youthfulness, functions as the founder of the traditional political order of the myth's audience. The newness of Eros in Agathon's speech is an example of this; in his very youthfulness he founds the justice of the city. What makes the theogonic plot tragic, then, is that the function of the plot is to bring about the destruction of one element while also reasserting the supremacy of another—and one cannot be accomplished without the other. Another way of putting this might be to say that in a tragic plot about the gods, the triumph of Marduk is what the fulfillment of prophecies, *nemesis*, and so on, are in a human tragedy, whereas the murder of Tiamat is what the fall of Oedipus would be. So just as the gods, fate or *nomos*, ultimately triumph in a tragedy, in dealing with the divine world directly, one particular god must triumph and that triumph must also involve the violent fall of another.

The two-faced nature of the scapegoat who both curses and saves the city is therefore divided in a theogony between two gods. This plot is a tragic one nonetheless, because the function of tragedy is to found the very order it seeks by leaving behind the chaos it hopes to avoid within the confines of the plot itself. The story of Marduk's triumph is thus also the story of Tiamat's dismemberment, and what this story covers over is that chaos is as primordial as order. Marduk thus "personifies the identity of creation and destruction." "Violence," therefore "is inscribed in the origin of things, in the principle that establishes while it destroys."[38] That principle, I would say, is also the principle and the essence of the tragic plot.

If we might restate Plato's objection to tragedy at this point, this principle which inscribes violence into the very center of the city also conflates nature with chaos and the unintelligible, and so renders them both indistinct. What replaces a clear apprehension of either is therefore the mimetic product itself, that in telling the story of a theogony makes for itself a cosmogony. The creation that Ricoeur speaks of as also being "salvation" is therefore the creation of this very narrative. Salvation in this sort of myth ultimately comes by means of "technology," insofar as mimetic *poesis* is also a form of *techne*, but the nature of tragic "making" is that it covers over this technological salvation in the plot of the story. Although I don't think Ricoeur has made this connection directly, indirectly he indicates it by connecting the "ritual reenactment" that must go along with this myth to make it effective for a community. The ritual is itself just another form of mimesis, and without the mimetic narrative it reenacts or imitates, it would be without effect. "Thus the turn from the cosmic to the political is effected within the divine sphere itself; a pact with the earth, with men and history, is written in this attribute of Sovereignty."[39]

Ricoeur starts off his discussion of the tragic vision by claiming for Greek tragedy that it is "the sudden and complete manifestation of the essence of the tragic."[40] Yet I have already argued that his myth of creation is itself essentially tragic. What then is the difference between these two? The difference, I think, is merely that one deals primarily with gods, while the other involves the interaction between gods and men. The tragic vision is described as both a vision of man and a vision of the divine, and it is the later vision that is problematical. For what is seen in this vision of the divine

---

[38] Ricoeur, *The Symbolism of Evil*, 182-83.

[39] Ricoeur, *The Symbolism of Evil*, 194.

[40] Ricoeur, *The Symbolism of Evil*, 211.

is an "insupportable revelation" which, if thematized, "could only be the scandalous theology of predestination to evil."[41] Because of this vision of the divine, then, the theology of Greek tragedy is "unacceptable to thought" and so can only be "tied to a spectacle and not to a speculation."[42]

What Ricoeur seems to be getting at with these descriptions is the essential connection of tragedy to an image of the limits of the intelligibility of the whole; and so the connection of "vision" and "spectacle" is to be found more in their counterfeiting, and hence spurious, connection to the "speculation" and "vision" of theory. In other words, Ricoeur is describing the essential mimetic function of tragedy that makes an image of the limits of intelligibility. Plato talks of this as the lying nature of tragedy, but Ricoeur puts it differently: "This connection with a spectacle, then, would be the specific means by which the *symbolic* power that resides in every tragic myth could be protected"; which is to say, the lying nature of tragedy is protected precisely by its function, its "symbolic power," that proves effective at lying only if it covers over the fact that it is a lie within its own content, its "spectacle."[43] This need of tragedy to protect itself makes of tragedy both a "warning" and an "invitation"; a warning against what Ricoeur characterizes as Plato's attempt to "unmask" its scandalous theology, and an invitation to "take into account the invincibility of the spectacle" in any movement from theater to theory."[44] In other words, with this warning and invitation Ricoeur is tipping us off that ultimately his own philosophy must be tragic because the need for a "lie" cannot be expunged, and (in contrast to Plato) must enter into the very heart of *theoria*.

Be that as it may, when Ricoeur describes tragedy in the following, we can see that he, Derrida, and Plato, are all converging on a central characteristic of tragic writing:

[41] Ricoeur, *The Symbolism of Evil*, 212.

[42] Ricoeur, *The Symbolism of Evil*, 212.

[43] Ricoeur, *The Symbolism of Evil*, 212.

[44] Ricoeur, *The Symbolism of Evil*, 213.

No doubt such an evasive theology cannot be worked out with precision, since, in order to express primordial incoherence, speech must become out of joint and obscured, as Plotinus says of the thought of nonbeing, of the "lying essence."[45]

This is a clear statement of why tragedy is connected to lying, because it expresses the attempt to think "nonbeing." But the question that must be asked is whether this "primordial incoherence" is some residue of chaos that ultimately cannot be understood or ordered and as such is coterminous with the whole, or whether this incoherence is a "surd" of temporary and temporal irrationality that enters into the whole within the larger context of an even greater rational whole. In other words, the question is whether rationality is ultimately finite and limited and thereby forced to deal with a primordial incoherence and the need to "lie" as the flip-side of this finitude; or whether rationality is unlimited and the need to lie is not because of finitude but rather because of a guilt brought about not because of, but only within the context of, finite creatures with infinite desires. Or as Ricoeur himself puts it, if the ethical moment in evil is to appear (for as he says "ethical denunciation and reform is not the business of tragedy, as it was to be the business of comedy")[46] and tragedy is to give way to the comic Adamic myth, then "guilt must begin to be distinguished from finiteness."[47]

If we take tragedy and comedy as direct expressions (as opposed to the indirectness of Plato's reversal) of finite existence in relation to the intelligibility of the universe (which I will later argue can only happen in one case—if God is indeed the author of the Bible), then we can say that tragedy must ultimately claim that evil is a result of finitude, whereas comedy must argue that evil is a result of some sort of fault and consequent guilt on our parts alone. Ricoeur, I think, would tend to agree with this except for his conflation of mimesis with insight, which is to say, his Kantianism. But

---

[45] Ricoeur, *The Symbolism of Evil*, 219.

[46] Ricoeur, *The Symbolism of Evil*, 219.

[47] Ricoeur, *The Symbolism of Evil*, 222.

to bring out what I mean here, I must first argue that his "tragic" vision is ultimately no different from his myth of creation.

While giving a somewhat detailed account of *The Persians* and the *Oresteia*, Ricoeur says of them that "without a doubt" they are the same theology as found in the myths of creation "non-thematized."[48] So just as the creation of the cosmos is coextensive with chaos, and the triumph of the god of order is the downfall and carving out of that order from the female body of the god of chaos, so also in these tragedies "[t]he Erinys pursue the guilty because, if I may venture to say so, *she* is the guiltiness of being."[49] The theme of both myths, then, seems to be that Being itself is guilty; but whereas in the myth of creation this guiltiness is the foundation of the cosmos upon the corpse of chaos and guilt, in Greek tragedy this guiltiness is discovered in the conflict between this divine "guilt" and the hubris of the hero. In other words,

> the freedom of the hero introduces into the heart of the inevitable a germ of uncertainty, a temporary delay, thanks to which there is a "drama"—that is to say, an action the outcome of which, while it is taking place, is uncertain. Thus delayed by the hero, fate, implacable in itself, deploys itself in a venture that seems contingent to us.[50]

This seeming contingency is what Plato describes as the transformation of chance into fate in the case of the noble lie, and thus by extension, in every tragedy.

But does this differing role of the hero in Greek tragedy make it any different from what is essentially tragic in the myth of creation? I think not, because this transformation of chance into fate shows that the contingent events of the hero in the plot are the means by which fate triumphs as the last word, and the only difference between a tragedy with a hero and a tragedy with gods is that fate is not embodied in a character in the former while it is in the latter. In both cases, however, the essential role the myth or

---

48 Ricoeur, *The Symbolism of Evil*, 220.

49 Ricoeur, *The Symbolism of Evil*, 220.

50 Ricoeur, *The Symbolism of Evil*, 221.

narrative itself plays in transforming the contingency of temporality into the seeming order of a divine "fate" is covered over—either by the anonymity of the poets of these creation myths, or the dramatic "spectacle" whereby "the ordinary man enters into the 'chorus' which weeps and sings with the hero; the place of tragic reconciliation is the chorus and its lyricism."[51] Identifying through ritual reenactment with Marduk is thus no different than identifying with the chorus rather than with the hero—who we weep for, I would say, but not "with." For ritual reenactment and identifying with the chorus are both, I would say, forms of tragic catharsis. The final society represented by the chorus is therefore no different from the political society represented by Marduk, and both myths are essentially tragic because the function of the narrative to itself bring about this society is hidden within the plot or spectacle.

So just as the myth of creation equates that very creation with salvation itself, in Greek tragedy we must say that "salvation, in the tragic vision, is not outside the tragic but within it."[52] In other words, salvation in both of these tragic narratives comes from the scapegoat mechanism of their mimetic nature. The tragic tendency to hide its mimetic and created nature is thus also the tragic function of making out of its own creation a foundation whereby we can both know and not know that the foundation of human society is based upon something unintelligible.

> Such is the deliverance which is not outside the tragic,
> but within it: an aesthetic transposition of fear and
> pity by virtue of a tragic myth turned into poetry and
> by the grace of an ecstasy born of a spectacle.[53]

The spectacle is itself salvation, then, just as the reenacting of the story of creation is; but this salvation will only work if we keep our distance from it, and cast the knowledge of how it "works" out into the desert of aesthetic distance and keep within the gates only its salvific results.

[51] Ricoeur, *The Symbolism of Evil*, 231.
[52] Ricoeur, *The Symbolism of Evil*, 229.
[53] Ricoeur, *The Symbolism of Evil*, 231.

This scapegoating technique is, in fact, so effective, that while he can see its operation in the case of Greek tragedy, Ricoeur completely overlooks it, and thus "falls for it" in the case of theogony. For one of the reasons he calls the tragic vision a "transitional" type is that he sees it ultimately transforming into a myth of creation in order that "holiness" might win out over "primordial badness." As he puts it:

> Thus it is "epic" that saves "tragedy" by delivering it from the "tragic"; the "wicked god" is reabsorbed in the suffering of the divine, which must attain its Olympian pole at the expense of its Titanic pole.[54]

Such a transformation of "primordial badness" into the "suffering of the divine," only works as a solution if one rests content with the story and doesn't raise the question as to why it is that some gods suffer while others do not. In other words, such a story works as a solution to the problem of evil only if one doesn't ask who or what stands behind the story—if one doesn't ask about the poet behind the story. Yet this aesthetic requirement for the effectiveness of this myth is precisely what Ricoeur admits is required in the "tragic" vision.

Why doesn't Ricoeur see this in the myth of creation? Perhaps because the entire phenomenology of religion that he relies upon, deriving from German idealism, is itself based upon a tragic narrative and a technological historicism; wherein the creations not of the poets per se, but of human consciousness, are intrinsically salvific. And yet in his more lucid moments Ricoeur does admit that this form of idealism has its roots in the myth of creation, which he says "anticipates typologically the most subtle ontogeneses of modern philosophy, especially those in German idealism."[55] But he fails to connect to this observation that, as in the "tragic vision," such idealism takes its aesthetic creations all too seriously, as does, I think, Ricoeur himself. Ricoeur's Kantianism, whereby

---

[54] Ricoeur, *The Symbolism of Evil*, 228.
[55] Ricoeur, *The Symbolism of Evil*, 177.

he can call his entire project a "transcendental deduction" of symbols,[56] leads me to believe that what he is doing is basically a "learned theogony" as described in the following:

> The tragic is invincible at the level of man and unthinkable at the level of God. A learned theogony, then, is the only means of making tragedy invincible and intelligible at the same time; it consists, in the last resort, in assigning the tragic to the origin of things and making it coincide with a logic of being, by means of negativity.[57]

What makes his thinking a "learned theogony" is that his relation of symbol to thought is almost an exact replay on the level of philosophic discourse of the theomachy between the old gods of the first naiveté with the newly triumphant gods of the second. Standing between them is the unavoidable limitation and intellectual violence of criticism, but out of this primordial "evil" the good of resurgent order comes about when these dynamic battles between symbols give rise to thought.

In this sense, Ricoeur's thought brings us full circle, from Plato who claimed that tragedy can only be revealed and understood in the light of philosophy to the more contemporary position that philosophy can only be understood in the light of tragedy. Oddly enough, attendant upon this change is the inability of our culture to write anything but comedies.[58] Philosophy itself, along with its nostalgia for long-dead cultural myths and "first naivetés," now finds itself alone as the tragic voice crying out in the wilderness of modern technological comedies. A genuine second naiveté, however, is impossible when the need for the deception and forgetfulness that makes it possible is overwhelmed by our comic and self-conscious suspicion we have become habituated to as moderns. The only other option to nostalgic pining, then, is belief in the Christian comedy that allows no deception or forgetting. But

---

[56] Ricoeur, *The Symbolism of Evil*, 355.

[57] Ricoeur, *The Symbolism of Evil*, 327.

[58] On this see George Steiner's *The Death of Tragedy*.

if this belief is not to collapse into another form of doomed naiveté, it must be allied with a philosophy that knows the limitations
of both comedy and tragedy, and strives for the truth higher than
poetry in any form. For unless Christian faith believes in the God
greater than anything that can or could be made, the God it comes
to know through both his creation and the unique "poetry" of the
Bible, is merely an idol.

VII: TRAGEDY

How is it that a man wants to be made sad by the sight of tragic sufferings that he could not bear in his own person? Yet the spectator does want to feel sorrow, and it is actually his feeling of sorrow that he enjoys . . . . But how can the unreal sufferings of the stage possibly move pity? The spectator is not moved to aid the sufferer but merely to be sorry for him; and the more the author of these fictions makes the audience grieve, the better they like him. If the tragic sorrows of the characters—whether historical or entirely fictitious—be so poorly represented that the spectator is not moved to tears, he leaves the theater unsatisfied and full of complaints; if he is moved to tears, he stays to the end, fascinated and reveling in it.

—Augustine, *Confessions*

PERHAPS at this point a concise account of tragic narrative might be in order. There are, I think, three key components to any narrative: plot, characters and narrator. Since narratives are fundamentally either tragic or comic, each of these components will themselves tend toward the tragic or comic pole. The plot of a narrative will tend either toward sad or happy endings, characters will tend either toward characters greater than or less than the audience, and narrators will tend toward either covertness or overtness. To summarize the nature of tragedy I will need to take each of these in turn and show how they work together to make a tragedy: starting with the narrator, for it is his role that is central and determines all the rest. The narrator, after all, is the one who makes a "narrative" what it is.

NARRATOR

The narrative transaction in its totality involves a narrator, the narrative, and the narratee. The narrator, however, determines the other two; for it is he who stands both within and without narrative as the mediator between the outside poet who must concretely bring it into existence, and the inside presenter of the story who determines the possible relations one can take up to it. The narrator thus determines the various possibilities of the narratee *vis-à-vis* the narrative, for the narratee stands both inside the world of the narrative and outside it as well.

Framing the inner workings of action and character, then, are always the narrator and narratee who are both "inner" and "outer" to the text, so to speak, because they mediate the virtual world of the narrative with the concrete world of the poet and the poem's auditors or readers. The possible relations an audience or reader can take up to a narrative text are thus structured within the text itself by the reciprocal relationship between the narrator and narratee.[1] The best example of how a narrator must somehow always

---

[1] How the narrator and narratee stand both inside and outside the narrative must be understood in the light of the problem of temporality. For narrative is primarily an imitation of our insights into our own and others temporality, which is to say, our lived experience of time. Because these insights are into "temporality" rather than "time" as something measurable, the temptation to view temporality as something measurable must be replaced by the "human time" of temporality that always has its basis in the lived presence of a subject to himself; who, as questioning, transcends the limits of that immediate presence into the lived temporal events of others. In other words, the insight into the image of our own temporality also involves the transcendence into the images of others in a common temporality, or what we would call "time." Time is thus intrinsically social in a way that temporality is not, and is found only in the implicit interaction of different subjects in the same way that measured time is seen only in the implicit relation of the measure and measured. What this means is that insights into temporality that involve temporal events, rather than the mere givenness of temporal presence, must involve a social time wherein different subjects determine the events and the different events determine the subjects. There must be, in other words, a social time that remains constant throughout all the differing temporal reference frames by which all its members must approach it; and such a social time is made possible by the transcending quality of insight that can move from the

limitation of the images related only to oneself, to the higher images of the subjects related amongst themselves. A fundamental quality of insight is then its ability to understand an intelligibility across temporal reference frames. And yet, because the insights that concern us here are insights into our own and others temporality, the transformation from one temporality to that of others is implicit in any such insight. (On this see Bernard Lonergan's *Insight*, especially Chapter Five.)

What this means for narrative is that as an imitation of our insights into temporality, it must somehow imitate the ability of an insight to transcend the particular temporal reference frame of the inquirer into the various temporal reference frames of others and/or society. It must, in other words, not only imitate the intelligible structure of the insight, but it must also imitate the inevitable temporal status of the intelligence, which as temporal, always takes part in the common intelligibility of temporality as "time." The way narrative does this is through the essential presence of the narrator, who either covertly or overtly, mediates the events of the plot to the reader. The narrator is thus the presence in any narrative that by mediating the temporal events of the narrative through his own reference frame, allows us as readers to assimilate the narrative events to our own. The narrator thus allows the reader and the narrative to share a common time, in spite of the many differing temporalities involved. So however ordered the events in a narrative might be in their own interaction, the narrator must present them to us the reader in the one particular order that allows us common access to them in their own order. The narrator is thus the element in all narrative that allows access to a narrative across all the various temporal reference frames of a narrative's readers, including even the actual author himself in a later reading. The particularity of the narrator therefore frees a narrative from the particularity of its author or its readers. For by acknowledging the essential need for a particular frame of reference, his own, and yet by incorporating the ability to move across reference frames within the narrative itself, the narrator allows for the text to function as a sort of relative absolute, in the same way that human time is itself only a relative absolute—relative in both cases to the intelligence's presence to itself. To use a distinction borrowed from Aristotle, there are two ways to understand something, either in relation to me and my coming to understand it (*via cognescendi*), or in relation to itself apart from how I came to understand it (*via essendi*) (*Ethics* 1095b). The function of a narrator is to allow us to move through the *via cognescendi* in reading or viewing a narrative, and yet still have something at the end of this process that we can share with others because of the *via essendi*.

What the narrator mediates to us across time are the events of the narrative, which is to say, the characters and events in their mutual implication that go together to make up the sense of a narrative. In other words, the mutual implication of event and character is the mimetic image of our insights into the social time we are all a part of, in the same way

be present in any narrative can be seen in the case of the "showing" of drama. Presenting a drama on stage wherein the characters speak directly to one another with no overt narrator describing the action might seem to question whether a narrator is present at all in such a production.

But if we remember that drama begins at one point—usually after the curtain rises—and ends at another, follows a script, and must have a director, we can see that the story is being told somehow by someone even though it is hard to focus on who that is or how it is being done. Yet if an actor directly addresses the audience, or if a character who claims to be the playwright or director speaks to the characters *as* characters or ourselves *as* audience, focusing on the role of the narrator in bringing before an audience the play becomes easier. The fourth wall between stage and audience is broken in such a case, thereby thematizing it and making known to us that someone is always doing the "showing" to us even when we are absorbed in the "show." In such a case we become thematically aware that the world on stage is an artificial world because it thematizes the artificer. This breakdown of the fourth wall happens predominantly in comedy, nevertheless it serves to show that tragedy is no less artificial and that the fourth wall in tragedy is functioning at its best when entirely unnoticed. This also brings out why the hidden quality of the narrator is essential to tragedy, for correlative to this hidden narrator is the audience's forgetfulness

---

that in measured time there is the mutual implication of the measure and the measured. There are thus no events that take place outside of some sort of social context, just as there is no social context apart from the events that take place within it. The "characters" in a narrative are thus every bit as essential to a narrative as the action they take part in. So even if Aristotle mentioned the possibility of a tragic plot apart from characters, the fact that he correlated base or noble characters with comic or tragic plots shows that he was somehow aware of an intrinsic connection between characters and events. Likewise, the connection between base and noble authors, and comic and tragic plots showed an awareness of a connection between the nature of the mediator of a narrative and its particular type, even though as I will argue , the degrees of overtness in the narrator is the essential connection and the character of the actual author is more problematic. But either way, all three of these—event, character, and narrator—take part in the division of narrative into comedy and tragedy.

of themselves *as* audience. The overt narrator of a comedy, even if only the overtness of a happy ending wherein the audience knows its desires are being manipulated along with the plot, thus reveals the covertness of the tragic narrator who must still manipulate without drawing attention to himself.

A disguised, hidden, covert, or masked external narrator is thus the heart of all tragedy. It is a "heart," however that is rarely noticed, for its notice is the death of tragedy. What goes along with this hidden narrator, then, is the forgetful audience. For by concealing his manipulations and presence, the tragic narrator prevents his audience from thematizing themselves and their response to what they see going on. The predominance of spectacle in tragedy, with its all-absorbing terror and bombast, serves to distract the audience from itself until the play is over. The cathartic calm afterwards is the fruit of this distraction, for the result of the audience's total absorption in the spectacle is its total release when finished into the unified pleasure of the cathartic transference. This must happen behind the audience's back, so to speak, if it is to happen at all. The thematization of the audience or the poet in any way would break the spell, and the serious (rather than playful) casting of a spell is the point of all tragedy.

This hidden quality of the narrator in tragedy also brings out why the issue of writing in the broad sense used by Plato can also be described as tragic or comic. For everything written has a writer and a reader, and the relationship the writer and reader have to something written can either be made thematic or ignored. To ignore it is to write seriously or tragically; whereas to thematize it is to be playful or comic. Plato chooses the latter and thus writes comically in order to criticize the former, especially as epitomized by the tragic poets.

The fact that Plato can move from discussing "writing" in an undifferentiated way to the concrete narrative form of tragedy brings out the centrality of the narrator and the self-consciousness of the poet's artifice in distinguishing between comedy and tragedy. This is also why the tragic narrative has its center of gravity in drama in a way comedy does not, for the dramatic medium lends itself to a hidden narrator in a way, for example, the modern novel does not. Yet even apart from drama, the claim to divine inspiration as in "Sing goddess, the anger of Peleus's son," masks the narrator behind his Muse and thereby gives a serious quality to his work it might otherwise lack. Homer and his individual artifice are irrelevant in the light of the divine power emanating from the gods that connects together the poet, the rhapsode, and his audience.

If we turn to the narratee directly, what we see in tragic narrative is that by not thematizing the narrator the narratee's existence apart from the narrative (the "outside" aspect) is left cloudy, thereby allowing the narratee to feel the concrete world is somehow continuous with the narrative world. One can move from one to the other without a break (the break of self-consciousness), which allows the poetic world and the real world to become one and the same.

This is why tragic narratives alone can serve as the foundational myths of a culture or *polis*, for the movement from absorption on stage to cathartic release is at one with the movement from threatening chaos to restored order at the beginning of things. Tragedy is thus the narrative that allows the audience to become part of the cyclical whole of a cosmos founded upon surrounding chaos. Thematize the narratee's independence from the narrative and you have also thematized the individual's independence from whatever political and religious whole he is a part of. Tragedy may not produce philosophers, but it is a sure cure for alienation.

CHARACTERS

In a tragic narrative the characters are on a higher level than the audience in order to keep the distance that is essential to the tragic effect, and to allow the audience to become absorbed in the action and the character's plight without necessarily "identifying" with them. If the audience (who we may assume are always the "many" rather than the "few" who might be on the same level as characters) identifies with the characters, the problem is that the terrors undergone by the characters on stage will also terrify the audience. A terrified audience feels neither pity nor fear because the intensity of this emotion drives out all others. But if the characters cannot be identified with because of their superior position then one is free to experience these emotions along with their cathartic release. The higher quality of tragic characters thus preserve the distance between stage and audience that is finally the key to tragic catharsis, for it is the very separation between the pain and terror experienced on stage and the pleasure felt by the audience that is at its heart. The distance between the higher characters and lower audience is thus correlative with the hidden narrator, in the sense that it goes along with feeling of the world on stage (the narrative) being an independent world undetermined by the audience or a poet's desires or manipulation.

The high quality of tragic characters also leaves room for a fall. Yet this fall is not a sort of democratic leveling, but rather a fall from individuation into the corporate unity the play ends with and leaves behind through catharsis. Fear and pity are individuating emotions, and so just as the audience must cast these emotions out, so too must the hero fall from his individual and hence ignorant hubris into the corporate knowledge of "fate." When the characters in a tragedy are gods rather than men, however, although the characters are obviously higher than the audience, there is no tragic fall because there is no human ignorance. Instead, what you have is the overthrow of the old gods by the young, with the young gods standing in for the order and justice participated in by the audience, and the old gods the continually threatening disorder and chaos. What is young among gods is thus what is old or ancestral among men. Higher than all tragic characters, then, whether gods or men, is the overarching presence of Fate, who is shared in alike by characters and audience and gives the point to all tragedy. Fate revealed on the distant stage somehow allows it to be also something immediate, consoling and shared.

PLOT

In the tragic plot we find, above all else, the fall from good fortune to bad. If the plot concerns men, the move is to bad fortune by the hero. If the plot is divine, the bad fortune happens to the older gods. Either way, the painful and often violent events that occur are amazingly removed from the pleasure the audience takes in them. The tragic plot of the fall, in its seeming incongruity with what an audience might want to happen, is the *telos* of tragedy; for the mimetic transformation of this pain to pleasure is what tragedies are all about. The distance between an audience of people who personally desire happy endings for themselves, watching or hearing a story with an unhappy ending, is thus continuous with the distance between themselves and the characters and the hiddenness of the narrator or poet. Tragedy works precisely in the gap between stage and audience. Comedy works by eliminating that gap, by giving the audience exactly what it wants. But tragedy works by keeping its distance, and the greatest distance of all is between the unhappy ending and the satisfied audience.

Reversal and recognition within the plot thus correspond to the reversal and recognition between stage and audience, albeit in an inverse manner. When the hero's fortune reverses from good to bad, this corresponds to the reversal from painful events on stage to the pleasure in the audience. The recognition of the hero which removes the tragic flaw of his ignorance, however, leads to the recognition in the audience that its own ignorance of what is revealed in the tragic plot—all the violent, unjust and malevolent deeds of gods who seem to kill us for their sport—is desirable and in fact necessary if the audience is to go on living in a world that appears to make sense. The audience thus recognizes what is fearful and pitiable in the plot's events, only in order to cast out these emotions that go with that recognition when the curtain falls. In the hero's recognition, the audience recognizes its overwhelming need not to know—to blind itself. It is in this sense that the tragic plot functions as the scapegoat, for what happens on stage with the characters is intended to free the audience from the fear of those very same events. This distance set up by the hidden narrator, higher characters, and plot reversals and recognitions serves to cast what is seen on stage away from and out of the audience. Yet in that very distance, the world is created and the order restored whereby the audience must live. The distance between the two is thus the very source of the order of what is; and so the resultant bifurcation at the heart of being is paralleled by the eternal violence between the older and younger gods. Theogonies are thus always also cosmogonies. The narratee's ability to become absorbed in the narrated world is thus predicated on this very distance between stage and audience, for this distance is not one of self-consciousness or alienation, but rather one of division and return dear to that dismembered god of theater, Dionysus.

VIII: COMEDY

ALTHOUGH comic narrative is relatively neglected in that part of the *Poetics* handed down to us, between the discussion by Plato and the few comments by Aristotle, along with the contemporary accounts of Frye and Ricouer, we should at least have enough to get our bearings. Narrative, we might say, is an imitation of the inverse-insight into the whole—the insight that the whole is not completely intelligible to us. While tragic narrative imitates the "inverse" nature of this insight, as a sort of fall into the limits of the intelligible, in comedy we will find the imitation of unlimited inquiry that leads to this inverse-insight in the first place. As an imitation of our unlimited inquiry rather than its satisfaction, comic narrative provides an image that can itself seem to satisfy that inquiry. Yet since our inquiry into the whole leads to an inverse-insight rather than an insight proper, comedy must bring out this limitation by overtly announcing to us the artificial nature of its satisfactions. It does this by self-consciously reflecting the fact that inquiry's satisfactions must be artificial and mimetic when they are not found naturally. The hallmark of comedy is thus self-conscious artifice, which means the poet himself is, in one way or another, always thematic and central to a comedy.

Yet since the poet is always correlative to the role of the audience (i.e., hidden poet, hidden audience; overt poet, self-conscious audience), the results of comedy are manifest as the directly present success of laughter and "getting the joke." The comic audience that corresponds to the overt poet is thus the one who makes the discovery (*anagnorisis*) that the poet is trying to bring about the reversals of his plots and jokes (his success is thus always the audience's also). Contrast this with tragic narrative, wherein the

185

hidden poet has the hero do the recognizing rather than the audience in order to allow the audience its own inverse response of a sort of blinding "catharsis." Whereas tragedy imitates the inverse-insight by inverting the relation between plot and audience, in comedy the relationship is direct in that what the poet reveals we have to discover. When Aristotle connects the origins of comedy to "phallic songs," he is thus bringing out the erotic element of comedy that makes of it a communal satisfaction of desire between poet and audience that climaxes in the "revel" of laughter and celebration. Yet this is exactly what makes Aristotle speak less highly of the comic poet who indulges in the base imitations rather than the noble imitations of tragedy.[1] For the comic poet leaves the audience with what it already has—its private desires—rather than raising them to the higher level of tragedy wherein the audience's base fears are cast out and it is thereby elevated to a higher public level—the level of the political.

Comedy is in this sense almost "subpolitical," for it satisfies the disparate and individual desires of its audience one by one. While some may get this joke and some may get that joke, sooner or later everybody will get laughed at in turn and they will not all find it funny. Comedy is in this sense individualizing, for only individuals have desires, just as it is only the individual who can inquire into the nature of the whole. Just as every joke might not be funny to everybody, so too is a happy ending only happy if the individual wants it to be. The "outsider" who refuses to laugh is thus always a part of the "inside" of comedy.

With regard to characters, the low quality of the comic character corresponds to the possible identification between poet and audience. Comic characters are either equal to or lower than the many in the audience in order that they can be identified with or even condescended to. The reason for this Aristotle describes in the following:

> Comedy is as we said it was, an imitation of persons
> who are inferior; not, however, going all the way to

---

[1] Aristotle, *Poetics*, 48b24-28.

full villainy, but imitating the ugly, of which the ludicrous is one part. The ludicrous, that is, is a failing or
a piece of ugliness which causes no pain or destruction; thus, to go no farther, the comic mask is something ugly and distorted but painless.[2]

The key here is that comedy is painless. Whereas in tragedy the
painful suffering of the noble characters must be transmuted into
pleasure in the audience by means of catharsis, in comedy the base
and ugly characters need no transmutation for the audience's
recognition of itself in them is always pleasurable. This pleasure is
the pleasure of insight itself and its imitation, the pleasure of saying
"I know that type, he's just like my neighbor!" What is funny in
comedy, then, is always the pleasure of satisfied inquiry, of recognition—the pleasure of seeing ourselves in the mirror held up and
pointed to by the comic poet.

This is also why comic narrative moves from bad fortune to
good.[3] For comedy starts off with the complications or trouble that
leads us to inquire and ask "what is it?" or "how will it work out?"
but since its job is to imitate those very inquiries, it imitates them
by showing what it is we want when we ask them—the pleasure of
happiness and good fortune. Nevertheless, comedy does not actually satisfy those inquiries, for they still remain unsatisfied outside
the context of the mimetic world of the comic plot. The happy
ending of comedy is in this sense different from tragedy: because
comedy accomplishes what we want it to accomplish, we also
know we and not the poem itself are responsible for its success.
Comedy can thus make no claim to be an expression of the real
world independent of our desires, for it is merely an expression of
those desires and a discovery of them rather than a discovery of a
genuine satisfaction to them. In tragedy the unhappy ending that
nevertheless brings pleasure convinces the audience that it is somehow receiving its pleasure from the nature of things. In comedy,
the happy ending, along with the base characters, and overt narrator, remind the audience that its pleasure is the result of a private

---

[2] Aristotle, *Poetics*, 49a33-40.

[3] Aristotle, *Poetics*, 51a13-15.

transaction between itself and the poet, and not a public pleasure shared in equally by everyone.

The key to comedy is thus its overt contrived quality that brings out the fact that our inquiry into the whole must be satisfied artificially because it is not satisfied naturally. The job of the comic poet is to bring this point home, in small ways and large. But the point is always the same—that artifice stands in the gap between our unlimited desires and our limited satisfactions. The various contrivances and manipulations of Plato's Aristophanes brings this out, just as does his laughable proposal of men exercising naked with women. Comedy is an artificial imitation of intelligible nature that must stand in for it as long as it the "real thing" is not available. Since Aristotle has little to add to the account of this already given by Plato, we should now turn to the work of Northrop Frye whose emphasis on comedy is inversely proportional to Aristotle's emphasis on tragedy.

By taking various generic examples from Greek New Comedy, Frye describes what normally happens in comedy as follows:

> [A] young man wants a young woman . . . his desire is resisted by some opposition, usually paternal, and . . . near the end of the play some twist in the plot enables the hero to have his will. In this simple pattern there are several complex elements. In the first place, the movement of comedy is usually a movement from one kind of society to another. At the beginning of the play the obstructing characters are in charge of the play's society, and the audience recognizes that they are usurpers. At the end of the play the device in the plot that brings hero and heroine together causes a new society to crystallize around the hero, and the moment when this crystallization occurs is the point of resolution in the action, the comic discovery, *anagnorisis* or *cognitio* . . . . The appearance of this new society is frequently signalized by some kind of party or festive ritual, which either appears at the end of the play or is assumed to take place immediately afterward.[4]

---

[4] Frye, *Anatomy of Criticism*, 163.

From this description we can see that all of the major elements described in connection with tragedy are implicitly included here as well. Yet the constellation of narrator, character, and plot arrange themselves differently in a comic plot and Frye brings out the crucially different comic role of each.

Turning first to the narrator, even though Frye does not mention him explicitly, it is his role that permeates and organizes the rest. For example, what we see in the society that crystallizes around the hero, which leads in turn to some sort of party or festival that can occur on or off the stage, is the overwhelming implied presence of the narrator in his correlation to a thematized narratee. It is the satisfaction of the audience's desires for a happy ending, happy on stage and in the audience, that constitutes the narrator's "overtness." And it is this overtness that makes the co-creative aspect of the audience manifest, since the celebration at the end is as much the audience's as the characters. Comedy is thus brought close to the audience—even to the point of confusion—because the comic narrator is uniting the desires of character and audience, thereby making their frustration our own, so that their triumph will also be ours. The laughter and satisfaction of a comedy is thus found in the deliberate breaking down of the fourth wall by means of the narrator. Frye describes this essential element—in contrast with tragedy—as follows: "The resolution of comedy comes, so to speak, from the audience side of the stage; in a tragedy it comes from some mysterious world on the opposite side."[5] He goes on to say "the tendency of comedy is to include;" and it is the narrator who is doing the including, whether by means of character, plot, or more importantly, by means of the self-conscious manipulation by which he seduces the audience into joining in through teasing and laughter rather than the tragic means of subterfuge. [6]

---

[5] Frye, *Anatomy of Criticism*, 164.

[6] Frye, *Anatomy of Criticism*, 165.

The "willing suspension of disbelief" (with emphasis upon the consciousness of this willing), is thus essential to comedy; precisely in order that we may let the narrator surprise us with the exact nature of his particular plot twist. In Frye's words:

> [C]omedy regularly illustrates a victory of arbitrary plot over consistency of character. Thus in striking contrast to tragedy, there can hardly be such a thing as inevitable comedy, as far as the action of the individual play is concerned. That is, we may know that the convention of comedy will make some kind of happy ending inevitable, but still for each play the dramatist must produce a distinctive "gimmick" or "weenie," to use two disrespectful Hollywood synonyms for *anagnorisis*. Happy endings do not impress us as true, but as desirable, and they are brought about by manipulation. The watcher of death and tragedy has nothing to do but sit and wait for the inevitable end; but something gets born at the end of comedy, and the watcher of birth is a member of a busy society.[7]

Even though we as the watchers of comedy are as busy as the narrator, we nevertheless both know and expect him to be the director of our business. From this passage we can also see the difference it makes when the narrator hides himself, for in that case, we as audience become more passive, and find the realism and consistency of the characters convincing us that what we are seeing is inevitable, apart from either us or the narrator.

The central and obvious role of the narrator in comedy also brings us before the question of creativity in a way that we do not find in tragedy; for the comic narrator raises the question of "nature" in the very self-consciousness of his artifice. In *A Natural Perspective: The Development of Shakespearean Comedy and Romance*, Frye elaborates on this issue by relating both comedy and tragedy to the cycles of nature:

> The mythical backbone of all literature is the cycle of nature, which rolls from birth to death, and back

---

[7] Frye, *Anatomy of Criticism*, 170.

again to rebirth. The first half of this cycle, the movement from birth to death, spring to winter, dawn to
dark, is the basis of the great alliance of nature and
reason, the sense of nature as a rational order in which
all movement is toward the increasingly predictable .
. . . Comedy, however, is based on the second half of
the great cycle, moving from death to rebirth, decadence to renewal, winter to spring, darkness to a new
dawn . . . . This movement from sterility to renewed
life is as natural as the tragic movement, because it
happens. But though natural it is somehow irrational:
the sense of the alliance of nature and reason and predictable order is no longer present. We can see that
death is the inevitable result of birth, but new life is
not the inevitable result of death. It is hoped for, even
expected, but at its core, it is something unpredictable
and mysterious, something that belongs to the imaginative equivalents of faith, hope and love, not to the
rational virtues. The conception of the same form of
life passing through death to rebirth of course goes
outside the order of nature altogether.[8]

Frye's connection here of the miracle of spring to comedy, and the
inevitability of autumn to tragedy, provides an overarching image
for the differences between those two movements of narrative. Yet
we can also see in comedy's and tragedy's varying connection to
"reason" where the limitations of his theory arise. The reason I
describe narrative as an imitation of *insights* into action, rather than
an imitation of the "images" themselves, is to clarify that narrative
is as closely related to understanding as is nature, and both therefore are equally dependent upon the illumination of insight. The
unpredictability of a plot twist and the eternal surprise of spring
are thus both the respective artificial and natural images of the passivity of coming to understand anything in the first place. Yet as
"images," nature and narrative are equally inadequate to express

---

[8] Northrop Frye, *A Natural Perspective: The Development of Shakespearean
Comedy and Romance*, (New York: Harcourt Brace Jovanovich, 1965), 119-
122.

the fullness of insight, and so the only thing "inevitable" is the incompleteness of our images manifested most mimetically in autumn and tragedy.

In the light of Frye's undifferentiated image and insight, consider the following claim: "Man understands reality only through the medium of some fiction that he has created, whether a verbal or a mathematical fiction. Any sort of reality that lies beyond or outside such human fictions is pure alienation, and inaccessible to us."[9] What this argument is founded upon is the conflation of insight with its mimetic image, and what goes along with this, the confusion of the philosopher with the poet. Frye has, like Aristotle (although for different reasons), limited himself to a political account of narrative; but instead of choosing to emphasize tragedy, he has, in a thoroughly modern way, tended to emphasize comedy.[10]

One of the felicitous results of this counter-emphasis has been Frye's application of Aristotle's terms to the context of comedy, namely, "peripety" which he defines as "reversal," and "anagnorisis" which he defines as "recognition." "Reversal" he says, "is primarily something the dramatist does to his plot; recognition is the response to it on the part of other characters and of the audience."[11] Both terms, therefore, bring out the essential role of the narrator who is, so to speak, both inside and outside the plot, thereby enabling a response to his role both internally among the characters and externally among the audience. The flip-side of this is that the narrator, through his contrivances, allows the reactions of the audience to be embodied in characters, who, even while inside, also represent possible reactions outside of the plot.

---

[9] Northrop Frye, *The Myth of Deliverance: Reflections on Shakespeare's Problem Comedies*, (Toronto: University of Toronto Press, 1983), 84.

[10] In Frye's case, the difference is the undue influence of Kantian philosophy, wherein the "categories" lend themselves to an increasingly poetic understanding, and a comic *poesis* at that. Nietzsche's comic ridicule of Kant's categories is thus well in keeping with this same tradition wherein *poesis* swallows up theory.

[11] Frye, *Myth of Deliverance*, 7.

For example, since the comic plot is the movement into a shared community, there must be presupposed the element of un-shareability, or in Frye's terms, "individuality," that precedes and enters into the new community of the comic happy ending. If this movement takes place on stage, there must also be the corresponding movement between the play and audience, and so the narrator must bring the recalcitrant individual responses of the audiences into the newly created communal world of laughter and festivity. However good the comedy, then, there is

> still a contrast between the individualizing movement of the identity of awareness and the incorporating movement of a social identity. This contrast corresponds to a split in the mind of the spectator in the audience. The comedy moves toward the crystallization of a new society; everybody, including the audience, is invited to participate in this society and in the festive mood it generates; it is usually approved by the dramatist, and the characters who obstruct it or are opposed to it are usually ridiculed. Part of us, therefore, if we like the comedy, feels involved with the new society and impelled to participate in it, but part of us will always remain a spectator, on the outside looking in . . . [therefore] in any well-constructed comedy there ought to be a character or two who remain isolated from the action, spectators of it, and identifiable with the spectator aspect of ourselves.[12]

This character is the fool or clown, and it is his shoulders that bear the potential ambivalence of the audience. The narrator thus guarantees complete unity in his end product only by including even possible dissension in the final recognition of the characters and audience.

What then of the reversal? How can that be something that happens inside to the characters in the plot and yet something we also know is done outside by the dramatist? The most obvious way for this to occur, and one of earliest, is to have the poet himself appear on stage to plead and cajole his audience to reward him for

---

[12] Frye, *A Natural Perspective*, 91-92.

making it laugh. Aristophanes made a point of doing this, but even in Shakespeare we can readily see that Prospero and the Duke in *Measure for Measure* are stand-ins for the very thing the poet does with the play as whole. They are, in other words, the ones doing the "reversing," and what they do to the other characters can also be done by the narrator to his audience.

Yet both these characters, fool and poet, must be found in relation to the hero who as the central character is mediating the inside and outside. The hero is the central focus of the audience because in a comedy the "hero's character has the neutrality that enables him to represent a wish-fulfillment," and wish fulfillment is exactly what we expect when we go to a comedy.[13] The hero must therefore be both neutral and young, for he is the embodiment of the novelty we won't see fully consummated until the end of the play.

The hero and the direct or indirect presence of the poet are therefore both *eiron* figures, which is to say, self-deprecators, because their self is incomplete apart from the completion of the play.[14] But what stands in the way of these ironic characters is the *alazon* (or boaster) and the *senex* (or father-figure), who represent the resistant matter the comedy starts with and overcomes. These two are the heart of the illusions the poet is determined to dispel, and so we can see through them how comedy is imitating the inquiry into images (illusion, appearance, phantasm) by emphasizing the resulting "dispelling" of that image through insight. The comic narrator's imitation of the unlimited desire for insight is therefore a contrived plot twist; for it is the plot twist that defeats the old and brings about the new, and it is in the plot twist that we find the mimetic image of the surprising "aha!" event of insight.

The comic plot is therefore the movement across time of the characters from a state of illusion to reality. If there is any doubt of the intimate connection between desiring insight and the movement of a comedy, Frye clears it up by equating the movement of comedy with the movement from opinion to knowledge.

---

[13] Frye, *Anatomy of Criticism*, 167.

[14] Frye, *Anatomy of Criticism*, 173.

Thus the movement from *pistis* to *gnosis*, from a society controlled by habit, ritual bondage, arbitrary law and the older characters to a society controlled by youth and pragmatic freedom is fundamentally, as the Greek words suggest, a movement from illusion to reality. Illusion is whatever is fixed or definable, and reality is best understood as its negation; whatever reality is, it's not *that*. Hence the importance of the theme of creating and dispelling illusion in comedy: illusions caused by disguise, obsession, hypocrisy, or unknown parentage.[15]

Comedy has this quality because what it is primarily imitating when imitating the insights into human action is the gaining of new insights into those actions—hence comedy's concern with all things new and youthful and the equation of its own consequent "newness" with reality.

If we recall Socrates' own "female drama" in Book V of the *Republic*, which was his competition with the comedies of Aristophanes, the argument made there was that his comedy was truly a comedy because it showed forth what was "really" natural, whereas Aristophanes' putative "nature" was merely artificial. From this dispute we can see that both agree that comedy makes some sort of claim about reality, or better, "nature." Yet what Plato brings out is the paradox that comedy shows forth this reality by the most unreal and artificial of means; and so we might say the need for a plot twist to imitate our desire for an insight into the whole of reality should draw us to the nature of that desire itself rather than its imitation in comedy. Be that as it may, Frye, in elaborating the constellation of tendencies we find in comic narrators, characters, and actions, has brought out the quality of comic narrative as an imitation of the "inquiry aspect" to our insights into human action.

At this point we can now consolidate what has been said in Part I about comedy and tragedy and relate it to the question raised by the narrative of the Bible. To do this, I will return to Ricoeur and his description of what he calls the "Adamic myth" and its

---

[15] Frye, *Anatomy of Criticism*, 169-170.

account of the human origins of evil. In this myth, what we are dealing with is a new "system" wherein creation is

> good from the first; it proceeds from a Word and not from a Drama; it is complete. Evil, then, can no longer be identical with a prior and resurgent chaos; a different myth will be needed to account for its appearance . . . . History too, then, is an original dimension and not a "reenactment" of the drama of creation. It is History, not Creation, that is a Drama. Thus Evil and History are contemporaneous; neither Evil nor History can any longer be referred to some primordial disorder. . . .neither can Salvation any longer be identified with the foundation of the world; it can no longer be an aspect of the drama of creation reenacted in the cult; it becomes itself an original historical dimension like evil.[16]

The Adamic myth therefore does not just happen to be contrary to the tragic myth of creation described earlier; rather, it comes into existence in the Old Testament as directly opposed to that myth. And the way it opposes this tragic myth is to tell a comic myth that takes part in the threefold quality of comedy that Frye describes as the movement "from threatening complications to a happy ending and general assumption of post-dated innocence."[17] Hence the change wrought by this type comes about with the "idea of the 'fall' of man that arises as an irrational event in a *creation already completed*," because this already completed creation is essentially good, and with this goodness as the meaning of "nature," provides the backdrop for the ensuing comic action. [18]

What this action consists of is the initial action of the "fall," which is wholly anthropological rather than cosmological, and the resulting final act which represents salvation as the counterpart to this fall. There is therefore "a new peripeteia in relation to the primordial creation; salvation unrolls a new and open history on the

---

[16] Frye, *Anatomy of Criticism*, 203.

[17] Frye, *Anatomy of Criticism*, 162.

[18] Frye, *Anatomy of Criticism*, 172.

basis of a creation already completed and, in that sense, closed."[19] So whereas the tragic myth of creation is concerned to bring out the mimetic image of unintelligibility, and this process consists of a separation and limiting of what is intelligible (order) from what isn't (chaos), the Adamic myth is comic because the final order it brings about is not itself limited but rather the unlimited (nature) that is discovered at the end to be what has already been there from the beginning. As myths, both concern the *"Beginning* and the *End* of fault,"* but the essential difference between these two is that the Beginning of fault in tragedy is simultaneously the End, in the manner of a circle, while the Beginning of comedy is like a line that descends *from* a circle and then returns in the form of an ascent to its End. The circular image in each is different because of its different relation to the linear image of time; tragedy casts it out and closes ranks about the circle; comedy indulges it by finally including the line within the circle. So when Ricoeur talks of the historical nature of the Adamic myth he is reiterating Frye who says of the comic plot that time is its ally while in tragedy time is the enemy. The time it takes for the *peripeteia* to take place is the time it takes for the events in the myth to "imitate" the creation already completed, and so the very "newness" of these events brings out that a different sort of "creation" is being imitated—the creation that partakes more of the unlimited desire of inquiry than the frustration and satisfaction of the inverse-insight itself.

Since the complicating events that precipitate the action in this myth seem to bring about a limitation that goes contrary to unlimited desire, Ricoeur calls these complications "the irrational event of the fall." Irrational, that is to say, in the light of the "rationality" of unlimited desire of inquiry which can only rest content with a happy ending. Frye would describe this "irrationality" by saying comedy is the movement from illusion to reality, *pistis* to *gnosis*: but either way the point held in common is that this sort of plot will brook no limits because of its connection to an unlimited origin—creation.

---

[19] Frye, *Anatomy of Criticism*, 298.

This assumption in comedy of some sort of normative knowledge is why Plato connected comedy with the claim to a knowledge of nature. The joke of a comedy is ignorance of nature, while the joint laughter at its end is the reaffirmation of a knowledge of nature. For this nature, comedy always argues, was of course true even before the ignorance manifested in the action. Of course this nature is rendered highly questionable because of the artificial argument for it in a narrative, but the question of nature is at least directly raised in a comedy, while it is covered over in a tragedy.

Another way of saying this is that a comic myth raises the question of the myth-maker, and in Ricoeur that question is the issue of "creation." In Ricoeur's "myth of creation" we have seen that creation is co-equal with salvation; but the flip side of this is that evil is "co-extensive with the origin of things." The upshot of this, however, is that the "creation" in this sort of myth is also the creation of the evil within it, and so the inevitable question as to who created such a combination in its entirety, the whole, cannot be answered any more than one can ask who created the gods. One can only reiterate the creation itself, or as Ricoeur puts it, "reenact it by ritual," because tragedies express the need to be lied to by means of an image substituting for an answer to an unanswerable question. Creation in the Adamic myth, however is "perfect," which is to say, an answer to all questions. Yet against this backdrop a new question is raised because of the fall that is only answered in the last act, but this answer is related to what was answered from the very beginning. So when Ricoeur says of the Adamic myth that "the problematics of evil are separated from the problematics of creation," we can see that the problem of evil which is ultimately solved at the end of the myth leaves us with the remaining problem of the Creator. The Adamic myth therefore generates a central concern with the Creator in the same way all comedies raise the issue of the poet.

The central concern of this myth, then, is who its author is. If its author turns out to be ultimately a human poet rather than the Creator who is the poet of his own creation, the function of this sort of myth is radically altered. If this poem is ultimately of human rather than divine creation, then the human creator must partake of a different nature than his own work, since the problem of evil obviously resides in himself and does not originate for the first time within his own plot.

Claiming human origins for myths about the gods brings out what Plato has in mind when he describes the reversal between a serious life and the writing of playful works that we saw in earlier chapters. A human creator of comedy, insofar as he knows himself apart from his writing, knows he is "tragic" because his creation of a salvific world is coextensive with his chaotic existence in evil as creator. If he creates a tragic myth, however, he can either take his creation seriously and become unconsciously comic by equating his creation with the creation of the gods. Or he can avoid this by *not* taking his creation seriously, draw attention to himself, and thereby transform his tragedy into a comedy. Either way, the very nature of myth as something poetically created, and the ultimate object of its concern with creation *vis-à-vis* evil or chaos, puts us in the position of dealing with this reversal. On the other hand, if the Adamic myth is authored by the same poet who created the world, then a new relation comes about between writing and existence, or in this case, reading and existence, that reopens the question of the relation between poetry and the gods not considered by Plato.

This turn to the question depends, however, on reading the Bible as a comedy rather than a tragedy. And so in contrast to Leo Strauss's and Thomas More's reading of the Bible as a tragedy rather than a comedy, what Ricoeur has done in illustrating the Adamic myth by the Old and New Testaments as a three-part comedy in contrast to the two-part tragic action of the creation myth, is to make a good argument for considering Christianity as essentially a comedy rather than a tragedy. And what is more, he makes this strong argument at the level of myth, or plot. So it is in the narrative structure itself, rather than in the laughing or weeping of Christ, that the Christian narrative would seem to function differently from tragic narratives. Such an argument still leaves us with the overwhelming question of the author of this comedy, but by clarifying the narrative structure of the work in question we can see more clearly what must be asked and bring to bear Plato's quarrel with the poets in a more illuminating way. Ultimately it will mean rethinking philosophy's relation to Christian theology, but before doing that we must solidify the claim that the Bible is in fact a comedy. This concern will be taken up directly in Part II.

PART TWO:
THE BIBLE AND ITS COMIC NARRATOR

THE ROWING ENDETH

I'm mooring my rowboat
at the dock of the island called God
This dock is made in the shape of a fish
and there are many boats moored
at many different docks.
"It's okay," I say to myself,
with blisters that broke and healed
and broke and healed—
saving themselves over and over.
And salt sticking to my face and arms like
a glue-skin pocked with grains of tapioca.
I empty myself from my wooden boat
and onto the flesh of The Island.
"On with it!" He says and thus
we squat on the rocks by the sea
and play—can it be true—
a game of poker.
He calls me.
I win because I hold a royal straight flush.
He wins because He holds five aces.
A wild card had been announced
but I had not heard it
being in such a state of awe
when He took out the cards and dealt.
As he plunks down His five aces
and I sit grinning at my royal flush,
He starts to laugh,
the laughter rolling like a hoop out of His mouth
and into mine,
and such laughter that He doubles right over me
laughing a Rejoice-Chorus at our two triumphs.
Then I laugh, the fishy dock laughs
the sea laughs. The Island laughs.
The Absurd laughs.

Dearest dealer,
I with my royal straight flush,
love you so for your wild card,
that untamable, eternal, gut-driven ha-ha
and lucky love.

—from *The Awful Rowing Toward God* by Anne Sexton

IX: THE COMIC UNITY OF THE BIBLICAL NAR-RATIVE

IS THE narrative of the Bible comic or tragic? Unfortunately, before we can ask that question we must first ask if there is such a thing as a "Bible" in the first place.[1] In our academic age the text has so disappeared under its professional interpretation that to speak of "the" Bible is quite likely to provoke scandal, especially among those who can confidently use this word merely to identify their own academic department. Between the Enlightenment impulse to break something down into its parts in order to reconstitute it and know it through this making,[2] and the historicist impulse

---

[1] In the promisingly titled collection *Tragedy and Comedy in the Bible* (*Semeia* 32, Decatur, GA: Scholars Press, 1985), the preface states: "While some theoretical discussion appears here. . . what is offered in these studies is detailed consideration of specific texts rather than attempts to work out a full-fledged theory of tragedy and comedy as applicable to the biblical material." Unfortunately, the problem with this offering is that it leaves one in the dark as to what comedy and tragedy is, how either might apply to the Bible, and above all, what the Bible as whole is that could be either comic or tragic. My own offering below, while running the risk of arrogance in the face of such modest aspirations, can only defend itself by noting that if the distinction between comic and tragic narrative is at all important, then it should have something to say not about this or that narrative strand within the Bible but rather the narrative of the Bible itself. Otherwise, it is a mere game of classification and of no philosophical, theological or historical importance.

[2] This habit of analysis was deliberately inculcated by Bacon and later Descartes with full awareness of its implicit hostility to the traditional reading of both the Bible and nature. Bacon begins the move in the following: "Now what the sciences stand in need of is a form of induction which shall analyze experience and take it to pieces, and by a due process

to use the present as mere data to reconstitute the much more interesting development that led to it,[3] the "Bible" studied in the

of exclusion and rejection lead to an inevitable conclusion" (Francis Bacon, *A Selection of His Works*, ed. Sidney Warhaft, (New York: Macmillan
Publishing Company, 1985), 314). Descartes follows it up with his own
elaboration of the four fundamental rules of procedure that, with a few
variations, have become second nature to all higher critics:

> The first was never to accept anything as true that I did not
> know evidently to be so; that is, carefully to avoid precipi-
> tous judgment and prejudice; and to include nothing more
> in my judgments than what presented itself to my mind
> with such clarity and distinctness that I would have no oc-
> casion to put in doubt.
>
> The second, to divide each of the difficulties I was
> examining into as many parts as possible and as is required
> to solve them best.
>
> The third, to conduct my thoughts in an orderly fash-
> ion, commencing with the simplest and easiest to know ob-
> ject, to rise gradually, as by degrees, to the knowledge of
> the most composite things, and even supposing an order
> among these things that do not naturally precede one an-
> other.
>
> And last, everywhere to make enumerations so com-
> plete and reviews so general that would be sure of having
> admitted nothing. (Rene Descartes, *Discourse on Method*,
> trans. Donald Cress (Indianapolis: Hackett Publishing Co.,
> 1993), 11).

Doubting the *prima facie* wholeness of something, breaking it into
pieces, and applying a uniform method that both reassembles and gives
the very unity and order that can now be found in this newly constituted
thing, is so much a part of contemporary biblical criticism that it is not
even noticed anymore that the Bible it professionally speaks of is deliberately different from the one its methodological doubt was initially applied to.

[3] The primordial example of the historicist impulse can be found in the
Second Discourse when Rousseau, in order to explain present inequality

> shows its origin and progress in the successive develop-
> ments of the human mind;. . . [a] development [that] re-
> quired the chance coming together of several unconnected
> causes that might never have come into being. . . . [and
> considers] the various chance happenings that were able to
> perfect human reason while deteriorating the species. . .
> [and] finally bring man and the world to the point where
> we see them now. (59)

world of professional academic criticism bears shockingly little re-semblance to the Bible read by the many in human history who have not shared those impulses. Where those impulses originate, as I will argue in the later chapters, can be found either in the dis-tinctively modern comedy of the early Enlightenment, or the later tragic philosophy deriving from Rousseau and climaxing in Hegel and Nietzsche. Keeping in mind what we have already argued for with regard to comedy and tragedy, however, we should now be able to ask whether the Bible is a comedy or tragedy without pre-supposing either of those orientations in our answer. The Bible, I will argue, has its own unique claim to comedy that must be dis-tinguished from the comedies of Plato *and* the modern comedy of the early Enlightenment. When the Bible is nevertheless read as a tragedy, what we are usually reading is a narrative expression of a tragic philosophy that owes more to that philosophy than to its own narrative exigencies. For the Bible is definitely a comedy, I will argue, and comedies put certain demands on us as readers that a genuine tragedy can never do.

To start with the nonacademic and lived reality of most of us, the Bible that might be either comic or tragic is the one found in any motel room across America. This Bible starts with Genesis and tells of the beginning of the world and ends with Revelation that tells of its demise and the beginnings of a new one. This Bible is typically bound together as a whole and so its external closure mir-rors its internal one. To speak of the Bible as a unity is primarily to speak of a narrative unity, for all its various books in all their di-versity are tied together around a common plot that has a begin-ning, middle, and end, and this plot is mediated to us as readers by means of the entire "Bible" or "book." This mediation process in its entirety is the biblical narrative, and it is connected to the dis-tinctive narratives of its various books as whole to parts. Implicit in any narrative is some sort of narrator, and, as I have argued ear-lier, the narrator is the central determining factor in distinguishing comedy from tragedy. To determine if the Bible is comic or tragic,

---

Just as Nietzsche's text disappears under the interpretation, in historicism the present publicly available data of the Bible disappears under the pro-fessionally available history that is said to explain it.

then, we must first examine this narrative structure to see what it says of its narrator.

At this point, a number of troubling questions arise, particularly for one schooled in the modern enterprise of biblical criticism. "What do you mean the 'biblical narrative'?" I can see various narratives within the Bible, each of which has a more or less evident narrator, but to call the Bible as a whole a narrative is a bit of a stretch. And what of the Old Testament itself, isn't that the whole "Bible" to the Jews? The unity of the Christian Bible and the Hebrew scriptures may each be that of a unified canon, but it seems doubtful that either can be a unified "narrative," especially in the absence of a single narrator.

A response to these questions will prove somewhat complicated, but the initial move is the reminder that I have been using narrative and narrator throughout in a much broader sense than a particular telling of a story by a particular teller. I have instead used these terms in the more comprehensive sense of a poet and his or her poem, made to convey a world of thought and deed to a narratee, which is itself taken in the broad sense of a hearer or reader who must make out the meaning of that poem in terms of both what is being said and how. Making out "how" a narrative is being narrated is the discernment of the "narrator," and it is within that discernment that we find the dual possibilities of comedy or tragedy. Particular narrators such as John in his gospel or Nathan telling the story of the ewe lamb to David are thus all on a continuum of telling and hearing, a continuum that is always anchored by some sort of ultimate narrator or poet who mediates the poem as a unity to its audience. Since poems are something made, there is always some sort of physical closure to them that fixes that unity, and that closure becomes the first clue a reader or hearer has in organizing all the particular tellings on that continuum into a narrative whole that makes it variously either a comic or tragic poem.

To speak of the biblical narrative, then, is to speak either of what has been canonized as the Hebrew scriptures or the Christian Bible, including or excluding the Apocrypha. Yet to determine the limits set by either canon is not yet to determine the narrative, it is only to determine the limits of the body of data that can lead to the discovery of that narrative. Otherwise the canonizers would be the narrators in the same way publishers or bookbinders would be authors. The canon of Hebrew scriptures and the canon of the Christian Bible are thus two different narratives, implying different narrators. In the case of the latter narrative, however, it includes the former and subordinates its narrative in the same way all final narratives subordinate internal ones.

If the canonizers are not to be the narrators of the Bible, then their canonical decisions must somehow be in response to a perceived unity that they discovered rather than "put" into these various books. If we are not to presuppose that those decisions were based upon mere power plays arising from the human will to dominate, and if we are not to presuppose that those decisions were made with no reference to the content of the books so canonized, then I think we can best understand why they determined that these books fit together by trying to discover how in fact they do fit together. In other words, the best data we have to understand the canonization process is the result of that process, just as the best way to find unity is to look for unity. If we no longer look for unity we will, of course, never find it. If we presuppose that whatever putative unity one does find was imposed from without and thus an expression of external power relations, we can only discover it as a claim extrinsic to the text itself. Instead, if we do look for unity in the text itself, the question of whether that unity is artificial, imposed, or an expression of the human-all-too-human, or whether it is instead a unity made by God and so a result of "domination" in its only rightful sense, may well turn out to be the central question being asked by that unity.[4] Keep in mind, however, that the unity of a central claim or question is not necessarily

---

[4] Whether unity or an "ending" is something we must ultimately make for ourselves and thus a fiction, or rather something actually to be found in reality without our making, is the heart of the differing notions of rationality between the ancients and the moderns. Consider this epigraph from Nietzsche in Frank Kermode's *The Sense of an Ending* (New York: Oxford University Press, 1966): "What can be thought must certainly be a fiction." On such a view, reasoning and knowing can only be a making, and so we must all know as a god knows. One has already sided with the

the unity of an answer nor the validation of that claim. The final truth of the Bible might very well turn out to be different than the truth it claims for itself, but the truth in each case would be in response to a different question. Getting a joke is not the same as finding it funny, for each is a response to a different question; but we must necessarily "get it" before we can laugh at all. Let us then ask what unity the canonizers of the Christian Bible found that fit these various books together in the way we might find them in our motel room.

The first clue we have is that the Bible is divided into two halves, the second half presupposing some sort of unity in the first half by calling it "the scriptures."[5] Not only are the narrated events of Jesus' life said to fulfill these scriptures, but the structure of the narratives of that life often imitates significant parts of those scriptures, particularly the beginning of the world (Genesis and the Gospel of John) and the beginnings of Israel (Matthew and Exodus). In addition to the Gospels, there is also the Acts of the Apostles that narrates the story of the twelve disciples with an historical interest clearly inspired by the history of the twelve tribes of Israel. Along with these narrative sections of the second half, there are also the various epistles often written by important characters mentioned in the Gospels and Acts, just as in the first half many of the non-narrative writings have some connection to major characters mentioned in the narrative sections. Not only does the second half of the Bible speak of and imitate the first in some way, but it also makes claims about the status of the first half, claims that are not also, initially at least, self-referential.[6] From all this and

---

serpent in this account, so inevitably a reading of the Bible is from its inception a counterreading.

[5] cf. John 5:39 "You search the scriptures, because you think that in them you have eternal life; and it is they that bear witness to me" (RSV).

[6] cf. 2 Timothy 3:14-17 "But as for you, continue in what you have learned, and have firmly believed, knowing from whom you learned it and how from childhood you have been acquainted with the sacred writings which are able to instruct you for salvation through faith in Christ Jesus. All scripture is inspired by God and profitable for teaching, for reproof, for correction, and for training in righteousness, that the man of God may be complete, equipped for every good work" (RSV).

more (for example, the almost constant reference to passages and themes from the Old Testament found in the New), one might be safe in surmising that there existed a tacitly unified canon in and around the time of the early church, roughly the same one that was officially canonized in early Judaism, and even more roughly what has come down to us as the Old Testament found in our motel rooms.

How these "scriptures" became a first half, and how they became an "old" rather than "the" testament can best be seen in the results of putting Revelation at the end of the second half.[7] By ending with a proleptic account of the end of all things and the beginning of something entirely new, The Revelation of John attaches an end to the beginning of Genesis, and makes possible the enclosure of written narratives of earlier events under one common rubric or central and overarching story or plot.[8] The written Gospels about how Jesus fulfilled scripture can now themselves be "scripture" after a fashion, and it is that possibility that we find in the canonized New Testament. What was canonized was that which fit into this story and plot, and since everything written since the time of Jesus could conceivably fit into this story, the New Testament canon does not have the same sort of closure found in the old.

In other words, the silence in the New Testament about its own status as written, juxtaposed with its loud claims about the status of Jesus in relation to the writings of the Old Testament (i.e., fulfilling the writings inspired by God), gives a unity to the Christian Bible that is at once a unified writing understood and internally certified as itself part of a unified plot that goes beyond and includes that writing. The unity of the Bible is at once the unity of various writings unified as writings, and the claim that it is even more so the unity of a story plotted by God and so coterminous

---

[7] The question of how one could justify adding anything to the scriptures we today find as the Hebrew Bible without violating its own intrinsic integrity will be taken up in my criticism of Meir Sternberg.

[8] The distinction between story or plot, and narrative, along with an explanation of why it is important at this point, will be taken up later.

with history itself in its entirety. As such it includes inspired writings, but it also goes beyond those writings through an odd process
called "fulfillment." To call this unity the unique comic unity of
the Bible will be the burden of what follows, so let me try to elaborate on this puzzling situation with the help of three writers who
speak of the "narrative" of the Bible as some sort of unity distinct
from its various narratives or books: Erich Auerbach, Hans Frei,
and Meir Sternberg.

The reason I will turn to these three thinkers alone is that for
all the decades of immense labor in the field of biblical criticism,
the results of that labor are of little help in answering the questions
I am asking. Because of the methodological presuppositions mentioned above (analysis, reconstruction, and historicism) that preclude studying a Bible that has not been reconstructed out of its
critical parts (a "bible" that makes the critic its *de facto* narrator),
higher criticism has had little to say about the Bible as a whole.
More recently there has been much work done among Bible critics
that claims to be a literary rather than historical and source criticism of the Bible. That is all for the good, yet apart from people
who come from different fields than biblical criticism such as com-
parative literature or theology, all this work still presupposes that
its largest unit of investigation is a particular book or narrative such
as Luke-Acts or the Deuteronomistic narrative. To speak of the
biblical narrative *per se*, would be to either break with the entire
field's presuppositions (hence it is left to "hobbyists" outside the
field), or to transgress disciplinary boundaries into "theology."[9]

---

[9] A particularly illustrative example of why there is no discussion of the
biblical narrative itself apart from narratives in the Bible among the more
"literary" of biblical critics, can be found in J.Cheryl Exum's *Tragedy and
Biblical Narrative* (New York, Cambridge University Press: 1992). When
speaking of writers such as Steiner and Frye who "can extract from the
Bible a unified and coherent view of reality only by excluding alternative
interpretations of the Biblical literature," she says: "Such explicitly 'final'
readings as Frye's and implicitly comprehensive readings as Steiner's and
Kurzweil's can always be challenged by close reading of particular texts."
(8) Indeed they can. In fact, the unity and integrity of most anything can
be challenged by breaking it into pieces. And yet in the case of higher
criticism in the Bible, this habit is inscribed in its foundation, just as hostility to faith is inscribed in Enlightenment foundations. In the case of the

Brevard Childs alone seems to have run this risk, but the historicist habit still remains in the need for higher critical readings to set the stage for canonical formation—the unity of the Bible is a unity made out of something else, and that making can't help but compete with what was made.[10] When one speaks of the Bible as "canon," emphasis is placed upon human decisions and institutional judgments. When one speaks of the Bible as a narrative, the emphasis is placed upon the possibility of divine making and divine emplotment in its juxtaposition with human making and idolatry. To call these "theological" rather than "biblical" or even "literary" concerns is merely to beg the question.

If we look outside the guild of biblical critics, then, we do find a strand of scholarship that might prove of help in examining the biblical narrative in its totality. This is the strand inaugurated by Erich Auerbach's *Mimesis*, and then celebrated and critically defended in Hans Frei's *The Eclipse of Biblical Narrative*. In his work Frei explains this approach as a shift from a historical concern with

---

Bible, the question is whether such particularity does not betray a hostility to the Bible as it stands and a refusal to accept what it claims rather than a genuine argument (or reading that) it is claiming something else. One does not need to side with Job's three friends in order to maintain that "the suffering, the misery, the evil, and the inexplicable in the world are part of an inscrutable, larger plan for the good" (1), one merely needs to see that this is in fact what the Bible, rightly or wrongly, is at great pains to argue by means of its entire narrative. To say that "dissenting voices are repressed or ignored in the interests of an overarching view" (8) is as wrongheaded as saying Thrasymachus and Cleitophon are being repressed or ignored in the *Republic*. They are an essential part of the story when they could easily not have been. And yet there they are, because a whole is that which orders and is greater than the sum of its parts. Literary criticism of parts of the Bible that are not parts of a literary reading of the whole Bible, is just another example of the protean adaptability of higher criticism in face of whatever intellectual fad comes its way. Higher criticism it is, and higher criticism it remains. And what makes it "higher" is that it stands above and violently interrogates its material in the same way modern science is said to "constrain and vex" (Bacon), "master and possess" (Descartes) and "constrain nature to give answer to questions of reason's own devising" (Kant).

[10] cf. Brevard Childs, *Introduction to the Old Testament as Scripture* (Philadelphia, PA: Fortress Press, 1979) and, *The New Testament as Canon: An Introduction*, Philadelphia, PA: Fortress Press, 1984.

issues lying outside the text to a narrative concern with the direct issue of the biblical text itself. Yet as we shall see, raising the question of the narrative as a whole brings us directly before the issue of history, albeit raised in a different way than we find in later Enlightenment historicism. For if the Bible narrates a plot that includes the beginning and end of human history, and if the narrator provides the mediating role between the inside and outside of the text, the question of whether a narrative is tragic or comic will have much to say of its relation to time, history, and "realism."[11] Auerbach's justly celebrated book should thus be a good way of approaching our question, not only because he reintroduces reflection on the Bible's narrative character, but also because in passing he makes a number of observations about this narrative that might lead one to understand it variously as either comic or tragic. What I hope to add is how my own delineation of tragedy and comedy can bring more clarity to his intuitive grasp of the Bible's unique narrative characteristics.

The overall concern of *Mimesis* is, as the subtitle shows, with the representation of reality in Western literature. Through comparing the style of Homer with the style of the Bible, Auerbach raises his concern with history *vis-à-vis* narrative, with "history" functioning for him as the key to this reality. These central texts of the Western tradition represent in their opposition what he calls

---

[11] Only by asking after the Bible's comic or tragic nature, I would argue, with the primary emphasis on narrative this question presupposes, can any question that might be of concern to a historian be adequately answered. Meir Sternberg explains this well when in his *Poetics of Biblical Narrative* he distinguishes between a "source" versus a "discourse" criticism of the Bible (*The Poetics of Biblical Narrative: Ideological Literature and the Drama of Reading* (Bloomington, Indiana University Press, 1985), 7-23). In an argument I will touch on in greater detail in the next chapter, he claims that any adequate research into the "sources," or the historical world laying behind the text must initially be based upon a good reading of the text or "discourse" itself, since that is the source critic's primary body of data. The effect of neglecting a full understanding of the narrative nature of Biblical discourse are skewed conclusions about the sources lying behind it. Our own concern here with the kind of narrative the Bible is, then, should also take us to the heart of the issue of its historicity.

two "basic types."[12] Homer represents the type primarily concerned with "foreground" wherein luxurious description of sensuous detail prevails, while the Bible is a type "fraught with background," with its sparing detail and laconic narrative. Auerbach discusses one of the implications of Homer's "foregrounding" style by taking up the issue of lying:

> The oft-repeated reproach that Homer is a liar takes nothing from his effectiveness; he does not need to base his story on historical reality, his reality is powerful enough in itself; . . . . And this "real world" into which we are lured, exists for itself, contains nothing but itself; the Homeric poems conceal nothing, they contain no teaching and no secret second meaning. Homer can be analyzed, . . . but he cannot be interpreted. Later allegorized trends have tried their arts of interpretation upon him, but to no avail.[13]

Homer's style, in other words, seems to function as would be expected in a tragic narrative, as evidenced by its "realism," mimetic self-subsistence, and imperviousness to interpretation as a "spectacle" unfit for speculation. The "foreground" nature of Homer's works thus links it with the more obvious "showing" of Greek tragic theater, wherein the aesthetic distance of the stage does not invite us "on" or "with" it, but rather only "before" it as we catch every spectacular detail. The very "realism" of Homer, then, seems to foreclose any concern with another (historical) reality behind it, because the centripetal tendencies of its mimetic world leave little room for concerns coming from outside the text. One might even say that the very "ism" quality to "realism" is this role as a surrogate and created substitute for the historically "real," that only works if it is "realistic" enough to allow this very quality to be forgotten. As we shall see, however, what Auerbach calls "realism" will function differently in the ancient world depending upon whether it is connected to what was then classified as the "low"

---

[12] Erich Auerbach, *Mimesis: The Representation of Reality in Western Literature*, trans. William Trask, (Garden City, NY: Anchor Books, 1957), 23

[13] Auerbach, *Mimesis*, 13.

style or the "high" style. In this connection, one of his central arguments will be to show how the narrative style of the Bible transformed the very nature of this "realism."

In contrast with this style in Homer, when we turn to Auerbach's description of the biblical stories,[14] we see something quite different. For, as he says, the religious intent of these stories

> involves an absolute claim to historical truth. The story of Abraham and Isaac is not better established than the story of Odysseus, Penelope, and Euryclea; both are legendary. But the Biblical narrator, the Elohist, had to believe in the objective truth of the story of Abraham's sacrifice—the existence of the sacred ordinances of life rested upon the truth of this and other stories. He had to believe in it passionately; or else (as many rationalistic interpreters believed and perhaps still believe) he had to be a conscious liar— no harmless liar like Homer, who lied to give pleasure, but a political liar with a definite end in view, lying in the interest of a claim to absolute authority.[15]

This concern with "truth" rather than "realism" in the Bible forces us to raise a question that is not necessary to raise in Homer, and that is the status of this narrative *vis-à-vis* its ultimate narrator and narratee and the historical world of which they are both a part. In other words, the Bible raises and thematizes the question of a historical reality that intrinsically transcends the narrative itself. The nature of the "lie" in the Bible, then, if it is a lie, is such that the question cannot be avoided. It is either a deliberate and conscious lie or the very truth—and that is how it asks to be read.

> Far from seeking, like Homer, merely to make us forget our own reality for a few hours, it seeks to overcome our reality; we are to fit our own life into its

---

[14] Auerbach will move elusively up and down the scale from particular stories in the Bible, to the putative "Elohist," to the Bible taken in a very general sense; but I would argue his claims have the most bearing on the Bible taken as whole, as can be seen by his focus on figural interpretation that would seem to presuppose a Bible understood in this way.

[15] Auerbach, *Mimesis*, 14.

world, feel ourselves to be elements in its structure of universal history.[16]

Why is this? What is it about these stories that leads Auerbach to believe it makes such demands upon us as readers?

Simply put, the answer is that the Bible is a comedy. Yet it is not your usual sort of comedy. In fact, it is the very difference between the specific comedy found in the Bible and the more generic comedies found elsewhere that will concern us here. For it is the very uniqueness of the Bible's comedic nature that has led many to read it as a tragedy, including, at times, even Auerbach himself. Nevertheless, the key element that ultimately brings out the comic nature of the Bible is the emphasis upon both narrator and narratee that centrifugally moves from the text to the demand that the world of the text's ultimate narrator—God—become the same world inhabited by the reader. As Auerbach says, these stories seek to subject us, and "if we refuse to be subjected we are rebels."[17] So just as a stage comedy might invite its audience literally or figuratively up on stage to become part of the action, so too in the Bible is the reader not just invited, but compelled, to join the world enunciated in the narrative. This demand would not be compelling, however, without a certain type of narrator who can demand such a thing; so it is here that we see a quality to this sort of comedy that relates it to, and yet sets it apart, from other comedies.

That unique quality is the effacement of any possible human narrator, thereby leaving room only for the Author of the entire world of nature in which the interaction of narrative and audience take place. [18] In contrast with the usual sort of comedy that has

---

[16] Auerbach, *Mimesis*, 15.

[17] Auerbach, *Mimesis*, 15.

[18] This effacement will be manifest quite differently in the Old and the New Testament. The effacement that Sternberg will bring out in what he calls the "narrative persona" throughout most of the Old Testament, will be quite radically altered in the named narrators of the Gospels. Putting both of these narrative styles together leaves us with the question of the Bible's narrative as a whole, and it is that narrative that extends the claims of narrative persona to a higher level, a level that paradoxically allows its particular narratives greater human leeway along with lesser importance. More on this in the next chapter.

very little political effect because its overt created nature under-mines its claim to authority (and even more so in contrast with tragedy, the political role of which Auerbach overlooks by evalu-ating it only aesthetically), the created nature of the comic stories in the Bible can still wield "political" authority (the authority asso-ciated with rebellion or loyalty) because the creativity of the narra-tor is equated with the creativity of the Creator of the world.

Although we must discuss the role of the biblical narrator in more detail later, for now, we can at least say that it is the comic nature of this narrative that causes it to function as Auerbach de-scribes. It is that nature that has also caused it to come into conflict with the notion of "history" in the eighteenth century, thereby set-ting the stage for its final "eclipse" in the nineteenth as described by Hans Frei. For the question raised in the context of nineteenth century historical concerns, was whether or not God was to be read as the ultimate author or narrator of the Bible or whether it should be read in the light of a merely human narrators and hence as a work of human artifice.[19] The decision almost universally taken in the nineteenth century *was* to read it as a work of human

---

[19] God as the author or Scripture does not, of course, preclude human instruments or even involve divine dictation or inscription. Yet as we will see in our later examination of Aquinas and the following discussion of Meir Sternberg's work, because of the centrality of divine inspiration and the distinctive narrative technique of most of the Old Testament (the New Testament is a different matter), it does preclude human authorial license and the usual narrative possibilities of human poets. How this works out is in the details, but Aquinas is quite right to see that both the literal and historical sense of Scripture are making the claim that God is its author, and that this is not merely a theological claim regarding various works of human authorship. I should repeat here my earlier agreement with Robert Funk's claim that "all aspects of narration lie on a single spectrum, from narrators belonging to stories embedded within stories, to authors entirely external to the text" (Sternberg, *Poetics of Biblical Narrative*, 29), with the addition that figuring out the relation between these, and hence whether the "narrator" is comic and overt or tragic and covert, is essentially the issue of discerning what Sternberg will call the function of "intent." Put another way, the question of the author of the Bible is the question of the "who" that goes along with discerning "how" the "what" of the biblical narrative as a whole is narrated. Divine authorship, as the word bears out, is as much a literary as a theological category (and political, as in "authority").

artifice, and so for it still to function, it had to be read as a tragedy wherein its effectiveness derived no longer from the joining together of audience and narrative, but from their separation. This, in turn, allowed the Bible to become an "aesthetic" and "historical" object effecting a "catharsis" by means of this very historical distance. The Bible, in other words, functioned as the tragic scapegoat, and so both revealed and hid the sins of humanity by being cast out, so to speak, from the emerging understanding of "history" as an elaborate artifact founded upon the artifice and the deceit of ideology. The Bible at the height of nineteenth century historical criticism was thus subordinated to the uses of history. In contrast, Auerbach brings out how the Bible was deliberately written not to serve history, but rather to show that our "history" is the illusion and only the "universal history" manifest in this comic narrative of the Bible is truly real.

This connection of history to comedy becomes even clearer when Auerbach, in a way that mirrors Frye's description of the redeeming function of time in comedy, describes the functioning of the characters in the biblical narrative *vis-à-vis* time. In the contrast between biblical heroes and Homeric heroes, Auerbach argues

> [t]ime can touch the latter only outwardly, and even that change is brought to our observation as little as possible; whereas the stern hand of God is ever upon the Old Testament figures; he has not only made them once and for all and chosen them, but he continues to work upon them, bends them and kneads them, and without destroying them in essence, produces from them forms which their youth gave no grounds for anticipating.[20]

Time redeems the Old Testament's characters because the narrative of the Bible as a whole is telling a story that makes all of time, not just that of the story, have a happy ending. "The Old Testament," in other words, "presents universal history: it begins with the beginning of time, with the creation of the world, and will end

---

[20] Auerbach, *Mimesis*, 18.

with the Last Days, the fulfilling of the Covenant, with which the world will come to an end. Everything else that happens in the world can only be conceived as an element in this sequence."[21] The comic nature of the Bible can therefore allow not only every failing on the part of its characters, but also every setback in future events, however tragic and horrible they are to contemplate on their own, to become part of an overarching happy ending wherein all these "horizontally" tragic events are related "vertically" to a larger plot that gives them their final narrative flavor.

Auerbach gives a brilliant analysis of this process in his discussion of "figural interpretation" as the sort of interpretation that he believes is demanded by the open-ended background style of the Bible. Although he does not make the connection between figural interpretation and comedy himself, the comic structure lying behind and making this sort of interpretation possible should by now become apparent. "Figural interpretation," Auerbach says

> establishes a connection between two events or persons in such a way that the first signifies not only itself but also the second, while the second involves or fulfills the first. The two poles of a figure are separated in time, but both, being real events or persons, are within temporality. They are both contained in the flowing stream which is historical life, and only the comprehension, the *intellectus spiritualis*, of their interdependence is a spiritual act.[22]

This spiritual act, I would say, is only the extension on the part of later interpreters of the communal act of a comedy that joins the audience and the poet in the shared world up on stage. When the poet is God, as I think the claim the narrative of the Bible makes of its narrator, then this shared world is also the spiritual world which requires the spiritual act of faith. For just as the poet in a comedy makes all the events work out in the surprise of the plot twist, when God is the poet, the plot twist is not brought about through his strictly poetic artifice, but rather through the artifice

---

[21] Auerbach, *Mimesis*, 16.

[22] Auerbach, *Mimesis*, 73.

of creating and maintaining the entire universe through Divine Providence. Accordingly, when the sacrifice of Isaac is interpreted as prefiguring the sacrifice of Christ

> so that in the former the latter is as it were announced and promised, and the latter "fulfills". . . . the former, then a connection is established between two events which are linked neither temporally nor causally—a connection which it is impossible to establish by reason in the horizontal dimension . . . . It can be established only if both occurrences are vertically linked to Divine Providence, which alone is able to devise such a plan of history and supply the key to its understanding. The horizontal, that is the temporal and causal, connection of occurrences is dissolved; the here and now is no longer a mere link in an earthly chain of events, it is simultaneously something which has always been, and which will be fulfilled in the future; and strictly, in the eyes of God, it is something eternal, something omni-temporal, something already consummated in the realm of fragmentary earthly event.[23]

This lengthy quotation bears out the connection between comedy and figural interpretation. It is almost a direct transposition into the context of the Bible and hermeneutics of both Frye's general account of comedy and Ricoeur's Adamic myth. For in both of them we see a three-part quality to this sort of narrative whereby the entire plot sequence brings out the enduring reality of the final state that was only temporarily covered over in the beginning. All comedy in one way or the other has this vertical and horizontal relationship. But whereas in a merely human comedy, the vertical axis is the transcendent relation of the poet and the audience *vis-à-vis* the plot, in a divine comedy the vertical axis takes part in the intrinsic transcendence of God. Figural interpretation is therefore nothing more than the appropriate way to interpret a comedy that claims God for its author—and interpreted it must be, just as we must "get" the jokes in a human comedy.

---

[23] Auerbach, *Mimesis*, 73-4.

At this point, however, we should remind ourselves of the point raised by Thomas More in Strauss's quotation. The characters in the Bible, especially the main character of Christ, rarely if ever laugh in it—how then can it be a comedy? The importance of this question for the relation between comedy and tragedy in the case of the Bible comes out in Auerbach's discussion of the sublime in relation to "high" or "low" styles. Where his discussion converges and diverges with my own should prove illuminating.

As we have seen in Plato, Aristotle, and Frye, comedy is associated with characters who are on an equal or lower relation to an audience, while tragedy is associated with characters who are on a higher level. Although Auerbach does not connect the differentiation between styles in antiquity directly to this distinction, it is descriptively quite close. The difference lies in Auerbach's connection of these styles to "realistic imitation." Even though his beginning chapter on Odysseus's scar showed that Homer was a glaring exception to this separation of styles because of its realistic details that fill in the "foreground," Auerbach will argue that the stylistic separation took place after Homer and would allow such "realism" only in the low styles of satire or comedy. As he puts it, the antique stylistic rule was that "the description of random everyday life, could only be comic (or at best idyllic)."[24] The reason behind this rule was that in the antique world writers "looked down from above,"[25] and so took seriously subjects at their own level, but laughed at subjects beneath them. Intensely descriptive writing was therefore a form of condescension, and when it appeared it had no serious intent in mind and therefore was quite a bit less than sublime.

The reason Auerbach speaks of this division in terms of realism is that he views the Bible as having led to a fundamental shift in styles, even to the point where in the West, realistic, detailed works can now have serious and tragic consequences.

> In antique theory, the sublime and elevated style was called *sermo gravis* or *sublimis*; the low style was *sermo*

---

[24] Auerbach, *Mimesis*, 44.
[25] Auerbach, *Mimesis*, 46.

remissus or *humilis*; the two had to be kept strictly separated. In the world of Christianity, on the other hand, the two are merged, especially in Christ's Incarnation and Passion, which realize and combine *sublimitas* and *humilitas* in overwhelming measure.[26]

Why then was there this cleavage in antiquity? The reason, he argues, was that antiquity was not concerned with "historical developments" but rather with "ethical judgments," and this difference is manifested in "the stylistic differentiation between the tragic-problematic and realism. Both are based upon an aristocratic reluctance to become involved with growth processes in the depths, for these processes are felt to be both vulgar and orgiastically lawless."[27] What this argument reveals, however, is that Auerbach, as himself heir to this shift, fails to understand what proceeded it. What he misses is that tragic writing is not based upon an avoidance of the "vulgar and orgiastically lawless," but is rather concerned to deal precisely with that "lawlessness." The way it deals with it, however, is to separate it mimetically from the audience by casting it out onto the tragic hero and the plot. The cathartic result of tragedy does indeed coincide with Auerbach's description insofar as it frees and purges the "aristocratic" audience from these elements, but this tragic solution to Dionysian lawlessness is more of an intense preoccupation with it rather than a condescending disdain.

In fact, the reason the typical tragic plot deals with the horrors of "growth" and the questionableness of origins is to provide a product that can, by functioning as their surrogate, provide a way of living with those processes. The antique styles were thus *both* based upon a distrust of anything that "grows" or contingently comes into being. In contrast with the effective hiding of contingent production in a tragedy, in the case of comedy where this contingency is manifest to all, one could also not take such works seriously.

---

[26] Auerbach, *Mimesis*, 151.

[27] Auerbach, *Mimesis*, 38.

The reason Auerbach overlooks this "hiding" quality of antiquity's high style is his own modern trust in "things made": which is to say, the historicist assumption that only things we make ourselves can be understood, and it is to them that we must look to find the "real." What is skewed in his understanding of "realism" is that a comedy only seems "real" to us if we forget the author behind it (which, of course, in a comedy is hard to do), while a tragedy only seems "unreal" if we look to and compare it with the audience. Yet to even make that comparison is itself a sign of a failed tragedy, for it can no longer seem to function as a real world unto itself, which it must do if it is to be tragic. His description of the "realism" in Homer gets this right because there realism is the attempt to make everything plausible; but to equate "realism" with Petronius' *Satyricon* is to confuse things, because in low comedy, plausibility is subject to the whims of the writer, whose smirk we are continually aware of. In other words, if he were to redefine high and low style in terms of the relations of the characters to a putative audience and narrator, Auerbach would be much more persuasive than by connecting them to "realism." Since for him it is ultimately the characters that bear the weight of his description, it falls apart when one brings up and makes central the issue of author.[28]

---

[28] A more fortunate term than "realism" that would describe more adequately what Auerbach is getting at, would be "naturalism"; for in naturalism the descriptions correspond not to something "real" as measured against the text, but rather as something "natural" in which both the text and any other world must take part. In this sense, comedies are much more naturalistic than tragedies because they bring out "human nature" even in midst of wildly contrived and "unrealistic" events. These events, though exaggerated, happen to "natural" characters who are recognized as such because of the immediacy between poet and audience. The goal of the comic poet is therefore to make us believe in the "naturalness" of his narrative, but such writing can not have a long term serious purpose because we cannot forget that this nature appears in the larger context of "make-believe." In modernity, however "nature" has largely disappeared as a concern distinct from artifice, and so comedy can now serve a serious purpose with no questions asked. Yet such comedy becomes in turn hard to distinguish from tragedy. Modern comedies, then, seem to be almost the inverse, secularized image of Auerbach's account of the Bible.

This weakness becomes quite apparent in the two possible ways he accounts for the radical shift in styles manifest in the Bible.

> That the King of Kings was treated as a low criminal, that he was mocked, spat upon, whipped and nailed to the cross—that story no sooner comes to dominate the consciousness of the people than it completely destroys the aesthetics of the separation of styles; it engenders a new elevated style, which does not scorn everyday life and which is ready to absorb the sensorily realistic, even the ugly, the undignified, the physically base. Or—if anyone prefers to have it the other way around—a new *sermo humilis* is born, a low style, such as would properly only be applicable to comedy, but which now reaches out far beyond its original domain, and encroaches upon the deepest and the highest, the sublime and the eternal.[29]

I do prefer it the other way around, and the burden of Part II is to argue for that preference. For it is this second way around that brings out the overarching context of comedy that is manifest supremely in the case of the "King of Kings." For as we see in the prologue of the Gospel of John, he is not only the main character, the hero, but he is also the Poet, the one in charge of the story. It is because of this, and only because of this, that all the other "low" characters take on their serious and sublime quality. The story of Peter's denial, an incident which Auerbach describes as being "entirely realistic both in regard to locale and *dramatis personae*—note their low social station—replete with problem and tragedy," can be described this way only because this event takes place in the middle of the story; just as Christ's tragic crucifixion is only the low point in a three-part plot with a happy ending. [30] All these events are fundamentally tragic only in isolation—as isolated from the entire narrative that functions as it does (as Auerbach has already portrayed famously in his account of typology) because the "vertical" dimension of the narrator has the last word. And that word, because it is the *Logos* who was in the Beginning, and will be

---

[29] Auerbach, *Mimesis*, 72.

[30] Auerbach, *Mimesis*, 41.

in the End, is a comic narrator of a comic narrative. On the other hand, if the narrative comes from a human word, then this narrative is ultimately a failed tragedy or, at best, a noble lie.

The reason Auerbach is ambivalent about whether to describe the Bible as a "new elevated style" or a new "low style" is because there is something about the uniqueness of this sort of narrative that can lead in either of two ways.

> The total content of the sacred writings was placed in an exegetic context which often removed the thing told very far from its sensory base, in that the reader or listener was forced to turn his attention away from the sensory occurrence and toward its meaning. This implied the danger that the visual element of the occurrences might succumb under the dense texture of meanings.[31]

If we replace "sensory base" with the narrative surface of the text (for that is the primary context in which any other "sensory" element would have to be based) we can see from this description that the temptation is to separate the narrative of the Bible from its narrator who gives it its locus of meaning. This is a temptation because the nature of the narrator determines the meaning of the narrative; and so to remove the narrator to a wholly separate realm from the narrative would change significantly the meaning of both. According to Frei's account, we will see that this is exactly what happened, yet Auerbach who himself suffers from the ambivalence of this result, can still describe how it came about as the process of "secularization."

> A real secularization does not take place until the frame is broken, until the secular action becomes independent; that is, when human actions outside of Christian world history, as determined by Fall, Passion, and Last Judgment, are represented in a serious vein; when, in addition to this manner of conceiving and representing human events, with its claim to be

---

[31] Auerbach, *Mimesis*, 48.

the only true and valid one, other ways of doing so
become possible.[32]

The seriousness of this "serious vein" is the tragic quality that
comes about when only a human narrator can be conceived of for
any comedy. In the case of the Bible, critical talk of history and
culture will become code words for the presupposition that God
could not possibly be its narrator. Auerbach with his emphasis on
"history" seems to shares this attitude. Nevertheless, as a brilliant
reader of the biblical narrative he knows that a distinctive understanding of history has somehow accounted for this change even
while somehow standing apart from it. In other words, the weakness of Auerbach is that in his primary use of the categories of
"history" and "development" he has already "eclipsed" the nature
of the narrative he is trying to understand. Hans Frei, who has appropriated these insights of Auerbach, and yet raised this further
question of the role of "history" in eclipsing the biblical narrative,
must now be turned to.

In his *The Eclipse of Biblical Narrative*, Hans Frei, by setting
himself the goal of exploring the reasons for the "power and apt-
ness" of Auerbach's analysis of biblical passages and early Christian biblical interpretation, has in so doing also rediscovered the
narrative nature of precritical biblical interpretation. He describes
this narrative reading of the Bible as "strongly realistic, which is to
say, it is at once literal and historical and not only doctrinal or edi-
fying. The words and sentences meant what they said, and because
they did so they accurately described real events and real truths that
were rightly put only in those terms and no others."[33] This "realistic" reading had three elements to it, all of which are implied by
the traditional connection between a literal and an historical reading of Scripture. The first element was that if a

> biblical story was to be read literally, it followed auto-
> matically that it referred to and described actual his-
> torical occurrences. The true historical reference of a

---

[32] Auerbach, *Mimesis*, 160.

[33] Hans Frei, *The Eclipse of Biblical Narrative: A Study in Eighteenth and Nineteenth Century Hermeneutics*, (New Haven: Yale University Press, 1974), 1.

story was a direct and natural concomitant of its making literal sense. This is a far cry from taking the fact that a passage or text makes best sense at a literal level as evidence that it is a reliable historical report.[34]

The second element has to do with typology. The figural interpretation described by Auerbach is based upon the assumption that "if the real historical world described by the several biblical stories is a single world of one temporal sequence, there must in principle be one cumulative story to depict it." These various stories must therefore fit together into "one narrative" by means of "types" wherein "without loss to its own literal meaning or specific temporal reference, an earlier story (or occurrence) was a figure of a later one." This way of reading turned the variety of the various biblical books into a "single, unitary canon." Figuration was therefore "at once a literary and a historical procedure, an interpretation of stories and their meanings by weaving them together into a common narrative referring to a single history and its pattern of meaning."[35]

In Frei's description of the third element, he accounts for the effect the Bible has upon its readers by describing what I would call its inclusive comic nature with God as its narrator.

> [S]ince the world truly rendered by combining biblical narratives into one was indeed the one and only real world, it must in principle embrace the experience of any present age and reader. Not only was it possible for him, it was also his duty to fit himself into that world in which he was in any case a member, and he too did so in part by figural interpretation and in part of course by his mode of life. He was to see his disposition, his actions and passions, the shape of his own life as well as that of his era's events as figures of that storied world.[36]

In other words, because of the unique type of comedy found in biblical narrative, to read it as it was written was not just to read it,

---

[34] Frei, *Eclipse of Biblical Narrative*, 2.

[35] Frei, *Eclipse of Biblical Narrative*, 2.

[36] Frei, *Eclipse of Biblical Narrative*, 3.

but was rather to allow it to swallow up the entire world "offstage" and make both the narrative and extra-narrative world one under a common Narrator. The process of biblical interpretation was therefore an "imperative need" because of this comic nature, "but its direction was that of incorporating extra-biblical thought, experience, and reality into the one real world detailed and made accessible by the biblical story—not the reverse."[37]

The eclipse of biblical narrative began, however, at the very time the "reverse" started to happen—when the historical world became the measure of the Bible and it was expected to conform to a historical reality fully formed apart from it. This process, which began in the eighteenth century, took place on the part of both detractors and defenders of Scripture. What both had in common was a shared world independently formed prior to that presented in the Bible, a world that would only allow both an historical and literal sense to be had in Scripture if its "literal" level referred outside itself to an extra-biblical "historical" world. The Bible, in other words, was no longer "real," but could at best be "realistic," because it could only imitate, represent, or provide data for the reconstruction of true reality. In comic and tragic terms, the fate of the Bible in the eighteenth century was the displacement of God as the narrator of the scriptures by human narrators. The effect of this displacement was to read it either as a human comedy wherein we get the joke by understanding the detachable meaning intended by the author(s) of the "allegory," or to view it tragically and appreciate its effects with no concern for who narrates it. The power behind both of these approaches is that there is ultimately no other way to read a narrative—unless of course God *is* its narrator. But to not notice that is in fact the very claim of the biblical narrative is not to read it very well. Whether or not that claim is true is another matter, but to not notice the centrality of this claim to this narrative is surely a misunderstanding that can only lead to further misunderstandings.

This new way of reading (or misreading) the Bible, by the time of the nineteenth century, divided the original unitary reading

---

[37] Frei, *Eclipse of Biblical Narrative*, 3.

of Scripture in two different ways—one of which ran with the text, so to speak, and the other with the "meaning":

> Realistic, literal reading of the biblical narratives found its closest successor in the historical-critical reconstruction of specific events and texts of the Bible. The question was: How reliable are the texts? Figural reading, concerned as it was with the unity of the Bible, found its closest successor in an enterprise called Biblical theology, which sought to establish the unity of religious meaning across the gap of historical and cultural differences . . . . Literal and figural reading of the biblical narratives, once natural allies, not only came apart, but the successors looked with great unease at each other.[38]

Higher criticism, one might say, ran with the Bible as comedy in which the intense scrutiny of its putative human narrators resulted from not getting the jokes; and the increasingly aggressive response to this unyielding and fragmentizing text resembles nothing so much as the violence inflicted on a bad stand-up comic. Biblical theology, on the other hand, took the Bible as a tragedy and took its *Heilsgeschichte* dead seriously as a complete world unto itself, independent of its narrative origins, that had salvific impact with no questions asked or even allowed. What looks like obscurantism to one looks like being a spoilsport to the other; but both are inevitably unhappy because the unique nature of the Bible's narrative will not allow either one to rest content without the unwelcome need for the other.

The original narrative vehemence of Scripture was nevertheless still noticed, but only in terms of posing problems to these new sorts of readings. Noticing this problem, however, seems merely to yield a bad conscience. Frei acknowledges that this narrative quality, what he calls its "realistic" characteristic,

> though acknowledged by all hands to be there, finally came to be ignored, or—even more fascinating—its presence or distinctiveness came to be denied for lack

---

[38] Frei, *Eclipse of Biblical Narrative,* 8.

of a "method" to isolate it. And this despite the common agreement that the specific feature was there![39]

What then is the "realistic" character to the Bible? Frei calls it the
"narrative shape" of the biblical accounts, wherein "what they are
about and how they make sense are functions of the depiction or
narrative rendering of the events constituting them—including
their being rendered, at least partially, by the device of chronolog-
ical sequence."[40] He also takes the term "realistic" to imply that

> the narrative depiction is of that peculiar sort in which
> characters or individual persons, in their internal
> depth of subjectivity as well as in their capacity as do-
> ers and sufferers of actions or events, are firmly and
> significantly set in the context of the external environ-
> ment, natural but more particularly social. Realistic
> narrative is that kind in which subject and social set-
> ting belong together, and characters and external cir-
> cumstances fitly render each other. Neither character
> nor circumstance separately, nor yet their interaction,
> is a shadow of something else more real or more sig-
> nificant.[41]

By inheriting this term from Auerbach, Frei has also inherited
some of its congenital defects—the biggest of which is that the
"realistic" quality of a narrative cannot be adjudicated apart from
some sort of reference to a non-narrated "reality." The very object
of describing this sort of reading is thus ultimately defeated by being forced outside its own intrinsic context. In other words, "realistic" comes very close to meaning "history-like"; but if that is the
case, then history is going to win out every time, and its "likeness"
will be dropped.

The bind Frei finds himself in comes out in the context of
miracles, for he will say of them that they are "history-like" even if
not historical and "factually true," because the "depicted action is
indispensable to the rendering of a particular character, divine or

---

[39] Frei, *Eclipse of Biblical Narrative*, 10.

[40] Frei, *Eclipse of Biblical Narrative*, 13.

[41] Frei, *Eclipse of Biblical Narrative*, 13-4.

human."[42] Realistic narrative thus turns out to be narrative *tout court*, and the only strength of this claim to history-likeness will ultimately rest upon the balancing claim that history is narrative-like. This, however, will not get us too far, as evidenced by the circular inconsequence of Ricoeur's *Time and Narrative*.[43]

What I think Frei is trying to say, or should be trying to say, is that the *type* of narrative found in the Bible is what makes all the difference; and because of this peculiar type, if one does not pay attention to how it is written and the terms it sets up for itself, one will miss the point. In other words, because the Bible is the sort of comedy it is, the role played by the narrator in relation to the entirety of events and characters is crucial in giving them the meaning and significance they have. Divorce them from this narratorial context, and you will either change their meaning by limiting them only to the possibilities to be found in a tragedy, or you will have the disappointed and unbelieving irritation of an adult at the happy ending of a children's Disney movie.

The "narrative shape" of the Bible is thus its unique narrative type—its comic type—that demands to be read with God as both

---

[42] Frei, *Eclipse of Biblical Narrative*, 14.

[43] Ricoeur devotes three volumes to the attempt to get out of the circularity of this position, with ever waning confidence as he proceeds. His basic hypothesis is that

> ...between the activity of narrating a story and the temporal character of human experience there exists a correlation that is not merely accidental but that presents a transcultural form of necessity. To put it another way, time becomes human to the extent that it is articulated through a narrative mode, and narrative attains its full meaning when it becomes a condition of temporal existence. (Paul Ricouer, *Time and Narrative*, vol. 1, trans. Kathleen Mclaughlin and David Pellauer (Chicago and London: The University of Chicago, 1984), 52).

Why I call this circularity inconsequential is that in the end Ricoeur's fears that his analysis will prove merely circular rather than spiraling upwards towards "reference," are realized (cf. 72). Reference to what is ultimately of our own making rather than God's or Nature's, however hedged about with sincere ontological intentions, is no more than a continuation of the subtle and tragic "ontogeneses" of German idealism described in his *Symbolism of Evil* (cf. 177).

main character and prime narrator. The very uniqueness of this narrative characteristic has led to the pre-critical conjunction of the three elements of a historical, literal, and typological reading of the Bible, swallowing up merely human history. If we are to retrieve this sort of a reading, or to find a "method" for it, we don't need to read it as "realistic;" rather, one needs only to read it as one would any narrative, and read it well. In sum, one needs only the "methods" of those trained to read well and attentively to rediscover how the Bible has traditionally been read. It is no surprise, then, that readers trained in literary criticism such as Auerbach, Alter,[44] Sternberg, Schneidau,[45] and Josipovici,[46] have gone the furthest in rediscovering what had always been presupposed in connecting the literal sense of Scripture with its historical. What we will do in the next chapter, then, is examine one critic, the best of the lot, I believe, and see how one might read the Bible on its own terms, and raise the questions it asks of us rather than the questions we ask of it.

---

[44] Robert Alter, *The Art of Biblical Narrative* (New York: Basic Books, Inc. Publishers, 1981).

[45] Herbert Schneidau, *Sacred Discontent: The Bible and Western Tradition* (Berkeley: University of California Press, 1976).

[46] Gabriel Josipovici, *The Book of God: A Response to the Bible* (New Haven: Yale University Press, 1988).

X: READING THE BIBLE

ALONG with Auerbach and Frei, the next author who can provide some help in reading the biblical narrative as a whole is Meir
Sternberg, if only because he takes for his Bible the Hebrew scriptures. He has subtitled his provocative[1] book *The Poetics of Biblical*

---

[1] As judged by the many who are provoked into calling his work "polemical," although how one is to distinguish polemics from criticism that is
particularly wholesale and telling I am not sure. What seems to cause the
most offense in those criticisms is Sternberg's emphasis upon divine omniscience, "foolproof narrative" and "ideology." Each of these will be
dealt with as they arise in the following. But at this point it might be
worthwhile to explain why I take Sternberg as seriously as my use of him
in the following discussion will show. The reason is that Sternberg has
gone the furthest, particularly among literary critics writing about the Bible, in giving an account of reading and textual interpretation that steers
clear of the usual and fruitless wrangling that arises out of a mistaken
opposition between meaning being "in" the text and meaning being "in"
the reader. For example, in one review (David Gunn, "Reading Right:
Reliable and Omniscient Narrator, Omniscient God, and Foolproof
Composition in the Hebrew Bible" in *The Bible in Three Dimensions.* (Sheffield: Sheffield Academic Press, 1990)), the reviewer says with a sniff:

> Sternberg is reading for closure—reading, that is, for the
> right meaning. Meaning, on this view, is located in the text,
> which is to say that meaning is essentially a matter of read-
> ing competence. The ideology of the text is stable and re-
> coverable, the ideology of the reader variable and
> discardable. (53)

To the much more tolerant and open-minded Gunn, however:

> Meaning. . . lies (at least) between text and interpreter. To
> assert this position is to assert that readers may validly read
> a text differently. Readers really are in significant part re-
> sponsible for creating the meaning of a text. It is also to

Narrative, with the strange sounding "Ideological Literature and the Drama of Reading." What Sternberg will mean by "ideology" is essentially the end result the narrator is trying to achieve by narrating the Bible as he does. Note, however, the emphasis is on "intent," for to understand the function of a narrative, Sternberg argues, we must understand what it intends to do, and not necessarily whether it in fact succeeds. The importance and fecundity of this subtle distinction comes out clearly in relation to the issue of "realism" and "history-likeness." As Sternberg argues, the intention to write a narrative that is historical *is* what makes it so, and not its success or failure; and so it is to this functional intent that we can attend without committing ourselves either to its success or its "ideology." In other words, by starting with the initial question, "what goals does the biblical narrator set himself?" Sternberg puts his work in the larger context of communication in general, while also paying careful attention to the uniqueness of the Bible's

---

assert that no amount of 'competence' is going to settle substantial questions of meaning. (55)

By setting up this false opposition and then placing Sternberg on one side, Gunn has overlooked the truly remarkable sophistication of Sternberg's account. For Sternberg has deftly avoided all this wrangling over meaning being "in" the text or "in" the reader that derives from the mistaken opposition of a naive realism, by starting with the critical realist position that knowing, particularly in the case of knowing the meaning of a text, is not a case of experiencing (what is "in" the text) or constructing (the making of the reader), but is instead a case of verifying hypotheses. All this talk of "intent" on the part of the text is thus not a case of experiencing that intention, but rather a hypothesis generated in reading that can be verified to a greater or lesser extent through further reading. Readers can and do read texts differently; the question of validity, on the other hand, has to do with how well one has done it. The question of how responsible a reader is, is the question of how well the reading can be validated as responsive to the data in the text. Data is only potential understanding, understanding is only potential knowing. What moves these potencies to act is not a mechanical operation, but the greater or lesser competence of a reader deriving from a greater or lesser knowledge of language, genre, references, as well as a greater or lesser inclination or disinclination to achieve certain results. Who we are, in other words, has a great deal to do with what we can possibly learn or know. Substantial matters of meaning may rarely be settled, but that is far cry from the claim that they are not settleable in principle.

own particular case. This question, however, is itself only a subset of the more "fundamental question," which is

> the question of the narrative as a functional structure, a means to a communicative end, a transaction between the narrator and the audience on whom he wishes to produce a certain effect by way of certain strategies . . . . Hence our primary business as readers is to make purposive sense of it, so as to explain the *what's* and the *how's* in terms of the *why's* of communication.[2]

With this grounding in the functional structure common to all discourse, Sternberg lays a solid foundation for understanding the unique "why" of the biblical narrative. What is more, by following this path determined by "functional structure," he has also gone the furthest in illuminating the Bible's literariness and relation to history, as well as its imperative cognitive demands.

Yet before dealing with the three functional "principles," of biblical narrative, which he calls "aesthetic," "historiographic," and "ideological,"[3] we need to examine more closely what Sternberg means by "function." He takes up this issue in distancing himself from many readers of the Bible who, under the influence of New Criticism, would read the Bible *as* literature, as one among other justifiable ways of reading it. In contrast to this independence of method from its object, Sternberg argues that the decision of how to read a work is determined by the "embodied intention" found in that work. And yet because the "reticent narrator gives us no clue about his intentions except in and through his art of narrative," we must reconstruct these intentions by forming "hypotheses that will relate fact to effect," thereby allowing for differing focuses with varying explanatory power.[4] Yet in all these interpretative explanations, "with the interpreter removed from the Bible's

---

[2] Sternberg, *Poetics of Biblical Narrative*, 1.

[3] Sternberg, *Poetics of Biblical Narrative*, 41.

[4] Sternberg, *Poetics of Biblical Narrative*, 1.

sociocultural context, intention becomes a matter of historical reconstruction," a reconstruction that is nevertheless made possible because of the constants of all human communication. [5]

> [F]or communication presupposes a speaker who resorts to certain linguistic and structural tools in order to produce certain effects on the addressee; the discourse accordingly supplies a network of clues to the speaker's intention. In this respect, the Bible does not vary from any other literary or ordinary message except in the ends and rules that govern the forms of communication . . . "intention" . . . is a shorthand for the structure of meaning and effect supported by the conventions that the text appeals to or devises: for the sense that the language makes in terms of the communicative context as a whole.[6]

These constants of the communicative situation require equal attention to what Sternberg calls "source-oriented" and "discourse-oriented" inquiry, which are distinguished by the types of questions they ask—"the *object* of inquiry, both in the sense of the thing considered and the goal envisaged by its consideration."[7] Equal attention is required to both of these inquiries because all communication is based in the interaction between conventions that can only be known through source inquiry and the innovations upon and usage of those conventions found in the discourse itself. The obvious example of this that should prevent the excesses of New Criticism is the demand to understand the language the discourse is found in; for the more that language is understood apart from particular use in the discourse, the better that discourse can be understood in terms of its continuity and departures from those linguistic norms. This can also apply to the sociocultural norms of the writer's context as well as the literary norms the author might use or discard to telling effect. Nevertheless, once these sorts of things are ascertained to a greater or lesser extent through source inquiry, discourse analysis

---

[5] Sternberg, *Poetics of Biblical Narrative*, 9.

[6] Sternberg, *Poetics of Biblical Narrative*, 9.

[7] Sternberg, *Poetics of Biblical Narrative*, 14-15.

sets out to understand not the realities behind the text but the text itself as a pattern of meaning and effect. What does this piece of language . . . signify in context? . . . What are the rules governing the transaction between storyteller or poet and reader? . . . And, in general, in what relationship does part stand to whole and form to function? . . . To pursue this line of questioning is to make sense of the discourse in terms of communication, always goal directed on the speaker's part and always requiring interpretative activity on the addressee's.[8]

Unfortunately, in the case of the Bible, this intrinsic overlap between source-and discourse-oriented inquiry suffers from one major setback that has caused no end of conflict between the two, and this is the fact that "the independent knowledge we possess of the 'real world' behind the Bible remains absurdly meager."[9] The result of this paucity of "source" information is that most of what we do know must be "culled from the Bible itself, and culling information entails a process of interpretation, where source abjectly waits on discourse."[10] Such abjectness has been rather hard to take, and so in the usual modernist revolt against intrinsic limitations, biblical scholarship has created data where there was little to be found by breaking down the discourse of the Bible into crudely assembled "sources." The price paid for this sort of thing has been the decreasing knowledge of the one body of data necessary to both—the discourse of the Bible as we have it. "For a scholar is only as good as his interpretation" and any hypotheses about source "stand or fall on the cogency of the analysis of discourse."[11]

What Sternberg has done for us in his *Poetics of Biblical Narrative*, then, is given us an interpretation of the biblical discourse, that by illuminating its function in light of the narrator's goals and the narrative techniques used to attain them, has also given us a bril-

---

[8] Sternberg, *Poetics of Biblical Narrative*, 15.

[9] Sternberg, *Poetics of Biblical Narrative*, 16.

[10] Sternberg, *Poetics of Biblical Narrative*, 16.

[11] Sternberg, *Poetics of Biblical Narrative*, 17.

liant interpretation that should prove indispensable for both exegete and historian alike. And as a sort of "first fruit" of this understanding, Sternberg makes a simple, obvious, yet immensely helpful distinction, that should do wonders for clearing the air between historians and exegetes—the distinction between history and fiction in terms of functional intent.

In the context of criticizing a "category-mistake of the first order" that consists of talking about the Bible as though it were a sort of "historicized-fiction" and therefore "realistic" even while not being "real" (a mistake that we have already had occasion to discover in Auerbach and Frei and which Sternberg also finds in Alter and Schneidau), Sternberg points out that

> history-writing is not a record of fact—of what "really happened"—but a discourse that claims to be a record of fact. Nor is fiction-writing a tissue of free inventions but a discourse that claims freedom of invention. The antithesis lies not in the presence or absence of truth value but of the commitment to truth value.[12]

To make claims for either the fictionality or historiography of the Bible apart from attending to its intention, then, is to make a rash judgment about the Bible's nature based upon an inadequate understanding of the various generic possibilities.

> Both historiography and fiction are genres of writing, not bundles of fact or nonfact in verbal shape. In either case, then, it all boils down to the rules of the writing game, namely, to the premises, conventions, and undertakings that attach to the discourse as an affair between writer and audience .... And as a question bearing on a communicative transaction, it can never be answered a priori.[13]

What must be answered *a posteriori*, then, is the question: What is the Bible intending to do? Is its intention to write a fiction with all rights of invention and license allowed? Or is its intention to give

---

[12] Sternberg, *Poetics of Biblical Narrative*, 25.

[13] Sternberg, *Poetics of Biblical Narrative*, 26.

an account of a true history using whatever compositional licenses may be used in subordination to that end? Use of a historical fact does not make *War and Peace* historiography, nor does doubtful history make Herodotus less of an historian, because their relative success or failure is either as a fiction or as history, and not as a genre they have never claimed for themselves.

How, then, does one determine this intention? Sternberg argues that there is nothing on the surface infallibly marking off these two genres. Rather:

> As modes of discourse, history and fiction make *functional* categories that may remain constant under the most assorted *formal* variations and are distinguishable only by their overall sense of purpose .... To establish either mode, therefore, one must relate the forms of narrative to the functions that govern them in context and assign them their role and meaning. In communication, typology makes no sense unless controlled by teleology. And teleology is a matter of inference from clues planted in and around the writing, extending from title and statements of intent to conventions of representation that signal the appropriate narrative contract in the given milieu.[14]

What then is the Bible, history or fiction? Given these *a posteriori* criteria, the answer to Sternberg seems obvious—"Of course the narrative is historiographic, inevitably so considering its teleology and incredibly so considering its time and environment."[15]

Why then has the Bible's historiography ever been doubted? For one, because a convention of writing common to most writings in the ancient world, divine inspiration, has been taken as precluding historicity because it incorporates material not just "undocumented but undocumentable"—such as the hidden acts of God, the secret thoughts of all the participants, and so forth. But as Sternberg reminds us, "the link between history writing and documentation is a rather late arrival," and so an anachronistic application of this criteria to the Bible's unique and historiographic

---

[14] Sternberg, *Poetics of Biblical Narrative*, 30.

[15] Sternberg, *Poetics of Biblical Narrative*, 30.

use of the convention of inspiration has caused many modern readers to overlook the overwhelming quality of the Bible's claim to be historically true, if not *the* historic truth itself.

We must look carefully at the subtle distinction he is drawing here, for if we fail to notice the role the convention of inspiration plays in either fiction or historiographic writing, we will be not be reading the writings of the Bible in terms of the conventions *it* uses, but rather in terms *we* would tend to use, and thereby misreading it.

> As a rule of narrative communication, inspiration amounts to omniscience exercised on history: the tale's claim to truth rests on the teller's God-given knowledge. The prophet assumes this stance (or persona) explicitly, the storyteller implicitly but none the less authoritatively. And its assumption enables him to bring to bear on his world (and his audience) what would elsewhere count as the poetic license of invention without paying the price in truth claim. Herein lies one of the Bible's unique rules: under the aegis of ideology, convention transmutes even invention into the stuff of history, or rather obliterates the line dividing fact from fancy in communication. So every word is God's word. The product is neither fiction nor historicized fiction nor fictionalized history, but historiography pure and uncompromising. If its licenses yet open up possibilities for literary art, they are built into the fabric of the narrative by a special dispensation: a logic of writing equally alien to the world-centered anachronism of historians and the novel-centered anachronisms of literary approaches.[16]

Most important here, however, is the Bible's unique use of inspiration rather than inspiration itself, for inspiration has been almost a constant in ancient literature, both religious and secular, from Homer invoking the Muses to Plato's arguments in *Ion*. The difference in the Bible lies in its use of this convention in such a

---

[16] Sternberg, *Poetics of Biblical Narrative*, 34-35.

way that it allows narratorial omniscience along with the historio-graphic intention to give *the* accurate account of God's dealings with his creation from the beginning. It does this through narrating notable events marked by, but not determined by, historical re-mains, and by the telling of major historical events that demand in turn to be told to their participant's children's children in the same way as they are recorded by the Bible's narrator to be remembered by us. The claim of the biblical narrator to give an accurate history is thus founded not in the authority of research, but in the omni-science of God; and to keep the concern with this God at center stage the narrator must somehow partake in this omniscience even while eschewing the omnipotence of poetic invention.[17] How the

---

[17] Here it might be appropriate to deal with the criticism of Sternberg's view's on the role of omniscience. For example, Lynn Poland in an oth-erwise sympathetic review, claims in her conclusion that "Sternberg's un-complicated acceptance of divine omniscience as the Bible's key theological principle matches his adoption of modernist literary assump-tions so neatly that he limits the range of possible discoveries in advance. Both place relentless stress on the cognitive" (Lynn Poland, "Review of *The Poetics of Biblical Narrative*" in *Journal of Religion* no.68: 426-34). I am not sure about the modernists, but in Sternberg, at least, stressing the cogni-tive seems no more limiting then the stress found in "Hear and hear, but do not understand, see and see, but do not perceive" (Isaiah 6:9), and echoed throughout the gospels as the dominant motif of the history of Israel that leads up to Christ. The "cognitive" in both cases is at once political, ethical and spiritual, and as I have been arguing throughout, the cognitive relation between a narrator and narratee is at the heart of poli-tics, ethics, theology and philosophy, and so has very few limits.

  In the case of David Gunn, however, his much more bilious review overlooks the implications of the omniscient narrator's role as an analog to, but not, God; and presupposes that the traditional reading by both Jews and Christians of an omniscient God in Genesis must have been sheer dogmatism with no textual warrant. For Gunn, the fact that "the narrator plainly narrates at a particular threshold in time, looking back to the known (or I would say, the partially known) and looking forward to the unknown" implies that "the narrator is not all knowing and makes no claim to be so." (Gunn, "Reading Right," 60) The narrator's inside track on God's actions and thoughts during creation is thus a result of the "cre-ative adventure of mind-probing" (59) and not at all a claim to omnisci-ence. Yet this is to overlook that the implicit claim to know the details of creation without also claiming poetic license is at the heart of Sternberg's narrator's omniscience, and that calling this a species of a "creative ad-venture" is to miss the key point of the disconnect between narratorial

biblical narrator accomplishes both of these is to function as an invisible analog to God himself, and as we shall see, it is one of the trickiest maneuvers in all of literature.   So far we have only covered the "historiographic" principle in the light of the reconstructed historical intent of the biblical narrative. But when we turn to the function of the narrator, we can see that the "ideology" he intends to serve is that of advertising the omniscience and omnipotence of the God, who as one of the characters in the plot must also prove to be a "super-agent" who stands outside the narrative as the God of any and every future reader as well. The onus of the narrator is thus described as similar to a "loyal general driven to employ in the vanguard of his army the king for whom he fights. How to play the master while remaining a subject? How to expose the embodiment of one's cause to the dangers of battle without losing the war? How to exercise military command without encroaching on political strategy? How to perform the tasks to which one's sovereign will not stoop?"[18] The burden of the narrator is even more difficult than the general's, however, because of the unique status of God, who in the narrative

> figures as both inspiring originator and individual
> viewpoint, as object and subject of representation, as
> maker of plot and agent, as means and end, as part
> and reason for the whole. In arranging his relations
> with God, therefore, the narrator operates under peculiar restraints.[19]

These peculiar restraints are what led the biblical narrator to function as an analog to God himself. For just as the uniqueness of the biblical God is that he alone is omniscient (as opposed to

---

omniscience and omnipotence. The latter makes the poet god in fact, and "God" a character in his own creation. The challenge to the narrator is to avoid this implication and yet still narrate with historiographic intent. The historiographic intent is why it is narrated from a point in time, but the deliberate absence of specificity allows him to function as an analog. Whether and how this move can ultimately succeed is an issue raised in the New Testament, but I think Sternberg is right in describing the attempt.

[18] Sternberg, *Poetics of Biblical Narrative*, 153.

[19] Sternberg, *Poetics of Biblical Narrative*, 153.

most other gods at the time who were separated from mankind only by their immortality), so also must the biblical narrator show forth this omniscience by exalting God's knowledge at the expense of the ignorance of everyone else, prophets included.

This line of ignorance separating God and humanity is not only uniquely drawn in the Bible, it is also celebrated.

> Far from undercutting or even presupposing divine omniscience, the Bible summons all its craft to dramatize and inculcate it. Precisely here, on the ground of ideological rhetoric, do world-view and narrative technique meet in holy alliance. The Homeric narrator stands above the gods, varying their access to knowledge to suit his own requirements. The biblical narrator and God are not only analogs, nor does God's informational privilege only look far more impressive than the narrator's derivative or second-order authority. The very choice to devise an omniscient narrator serves the purpose of staging and glorifying an omniscient God. The means-end combination typical of ancient literature thus gets practically reversed in the framework of monotheistic art.[20]

Another way of putting this would be to contrast it with Plato's arguments about inspiration in *Ion*. Just as the image of the magnet can work both ways, from gods to men or men to gods, what we can say for sure in Homer or other inspired writings is that the poet is the only omniscient and omnipotent one in point of fact; and that however much the immortal gods may strut upon his stage, the poet has the last word. In contrast, the biblical narrator can claim nothing for himself that isn't itself just a means to promote the very same qualities, possessed in a superlative degree, by the main character in the plot—God himself.

The covertness of Homer the narrator hidden behind his Muses, therefore hides the subversive character of his narration. But the covertness of the biblical narrator allows him to function as God himself to his readers; so the very characteristics of his

---

[20] Sternberg, *Poetics of Biblical Narrative*, 89.

narratorship are not hidden, but rather exalted, as the characteristics of God. Only his person is hidden, but not his prerogatives, which are those of God; and this hiding of his person goes along with forswearing the claim to the license of invention. The overtness of the biblical narrator—what makes it a comedy—is thus the overtness of all his qualities rather than their locus in his person: and those qualities are grounded in the character of God who is both inside and outside the story.

This unique relation of the biblical narrator to his narrative leads to a fundamental choice, just as every comedy leads to the audience's choice of whether or not to laugh. This choice, however, is not a neutral one; rather, all the powers at the poet's disposal are used to advocate and persuade to one rather than the other. Sternberg describes the nature of this choice as follows:

> [I]f God's omnipotence makes history, then a narrator's makes fiction and, where he introduces God, God himself becomes part of the fiction. Ironically enough, only a dealer in make-believe can play God, and what is more, do so without undermining his model's "real-life" authority. Once the heavenly model himself appears on stage, however, the balance of power exacts a clear either/or choice that will reflect the generic and doctrinal premises in the heart of the tale. Fictional or historical writing? Artistic or divine stage management? The whole ontological status of the narrative, as a world-picture and a mode of discourse alike, turns on the answer. Hence the importance of determining with whom lies the control over the biblical world.[21]

How, then, does the biblical narrator seek to persuade us that not he, but God, is in control? Sternberg discusses two primary ways, one of which he calls "asymmetrical" wherein God displays his omnipotence without any audience apart from the reader, and "symmetrical" wherein there is an audience in the story and we, as readers, only look on and hopefully get the point.

---

[21] Sternberg, *Poetics of Biblical Narrative*, 100-101.

The classic example of asymmetrical persuasion is the Creation account, and it is also here that we can see clearly the relation the narrator stands to God. "Let there be light, and there was light." By quoting God's command, and then describing the result, the divine origin of this quotation serves a double role—"performative as well as anticipatory. At the same time as they project an intention within the discourse, they realize it within the world: God's speech is itself a creative act."[22] The omnipotence of the narrator is therefore entirely subordinate to the omnipotent creator of the world. And so, just as we saw in Plato that the comic poet's claim to know nature is undermined by his artifice, in the case of the Bible we can see that starting with the account of God's creation grounds the artifice of the narrator in the overarching artifice of God. The comic narrator is thus free to bring about the "newness" of biblical miracles and plot twists because the entire plot begins with the "quintessence of the new, the story of Creation."[23]

This pattern is continued in the symmetrical relations of God as a character in interaction with other characters. Nothing can be left to chance, so God must continually foreshadow future events and then have the narrator cite their fulfillment. Take the case of Pharaoh.

> Suppose God omitted to preannounce (and the narrator to cite) his intention to harden Pharaoh's heart. Would not the tardiness of the Exodus suggest a discrepancy between will and way? As it is, the potential weakness turns into a source of rhetorical strength, because the advance notice ushers in a double demonstration of omnipotence—over the workings of the heart as well as of nature.[24]

This relation between the performance of God and the narrator's vouching for the performance is repeated time and time again in a

---

[22] Sternberg, *Poetics of Biblical Narrative*, 106.

[23] Sternberg, *Poetics of Biblical Narrative*, 104.

[24] Sternberg, *Poetics of Biblical Narrative*, 105.

sort of quantifying of the qualitative, for "in the hands of the narrator . . . God gives advance notice, then performs, then (often) comments on the performance; and then repeats the sequence all over again."[25] Nevertheless God's omnipotence does not extend over the human heart of all the characters, and the resultant freedom of response is mirrored in the reader's freedom to take or miss the point.

The serial form thus imposed on the action as plotted history is there to be noticed and interpreted by the characters no less than by the reader. But its significance, if not its very presence, is most often lost on them. This opens a variety of perspectival discrepancies among the characters themselves and between them and the reader: the tracing of the hidden God's figure in the carpet becomes a measure of acuteness and faith alike.[26]

The narrative of the Bible is therefore also the story of how it *has* been responded to as well as how it *should* be responded to. Accounts within it of other writings, such as the Ten Commandments written "with the finger of God" himself (Ex. 31:18), function as indications of how this narrative itself should be received. The logic of its composition is thus "an unbroken line from eye through ear to writing." This point, however,

> bears less on factual genesis than on narrative stance, and therefore has little to do with all the scholarly speculation about oral and written antecedents. Whether or not the Israelites actually did remember (witness, hand down, record) wonders past, the narrator presents them as remembering and himself by implication as the sharer and perpetuator of their remembrance.[27]

---

[25] Sternberg, *Poetics of Biblical Narrative*, 109.

[26] Sternberg, *Poetics of Biblical Narrative*, 114.

[27] Sternberg, *Biblical Narrative*, 117. This also answers to Gunn's suspicion that historical positioning implies lack of omniscience. The narrator is omnisciently narrating by analogy a history of God's involvement in a world and people He has himself created.

The biblical narrator is therefore the comic narrator *par excellence* inasmuch as it is his goal to create a common community between himself and audience and audience and characters; and yet he must accomplish this goal without paying the price of creative responsibility. Sternberg sums up the narrator's delicate role in this way.

> Poised between God and people, then, the narrator in effect claims to draw on both sides, to represent both and to have the interests of both at heart, of which the most vital is to bring their viewpoint into alignment. Hence the extraordinary care and skill lavished on the omnipotence effect. This includes the pains taken with the asymmetrical situation, by nature unwitnessible, the alacrity with which the opportunities for symmetry are pounced upon, the imaging of God as master semiotician, psychologist, self-advertiser, together with the consistent reference to whatever helps to forge (perhaps in more than one sense) a chain of narrative transmission on earth.[28]

What Sternberg is claiming for the biblical narrative is that it must be read in terms of both its historiographic and ideological principles; because to understand any written communication one must somehow reconstruct its communicative intent. His arguments about the ideology of the biblical narrative are thus not a sign of religious commitment, but only of interpretative integrity; and this integrity demands of us that we also read the Bible, initially at least, as it intends to be read. The final upshot of Sternberg's argument is that the Bible must be read in a way uniquely different from other forms of literature because of its unique ideology. "If the Bible is ideologically singular" which Sternberg believes is the case,

> then its singularity lies in the world-view projected, together with the rhetoric devised to bring it home. And as long as we adhere to the text's self-definition as religious literature with such and such singularities, we need not even submit to the dictate of identifying

---

[28] Sternberg, *Poetics of Biblical Narrative*, 118.

ourselves as religious or secular readers. Those who
play by the Bible's rules of communication to the best
of their ability can keep their opinions to themselves;
only those who make up their own rules may be required to lay their ideological cards on the table.[29]

If Sternberg has laid out for us the Bible's "rules" in terms of its
historiographic and ideological intent, then we must now examine
in more detail "the rhetoric devised to bring it home." For if comedy is anything, it is at least a species of rhetoric, and so here too
we should see identifying characteristics of the Bible's comedic nature.

By turning to what Sternberg calls the "aesthetic" principles
of the Bible, we will also be attending more specifically to the second half of his subtitle, what he calls the "drama of reading." What
he means by the term "drama" is that the strategy the Bible uses
to bring home its ideological and historiographic points (what he
calls the "art of indirection"), when viewed from the interpreter's
side, creates the "drama of reading."[30] This drama arises from the
fact that the Bible is "literary" even while not being "literature."
Which is to say, "There is abundant material that, without officially
appearing as fiction, yet bears the marks of invention and fulfills
the roles of imaginative enhancement and probing of reality associated with it."[31] So even in the midst of a didactic intent, the biblical narrator will not abandon his aesthetic control. In fact, it is in
contrast to what one might expect in bringing about these historical and ideological goals, that we can see most clearly how consistently the narrator sticks to his aesthetic norms.

> He will leave gaps for the reader to puzzle over—non
> sequitors, discontinuities, indeterminacies, multiple
> versions—while fully aware of the disordering effect
> on the shape and lessons of the past. He will conceal
> and distribute and process meaning to an extent sel-
> dom equaled even by storytellers who could please
> themselves. None of these "incongruous" choices

---

[29] Sternberg, *Poetics of Biblical Narrative*, 37.

[30] Sternberg, *Poetics of Biblical Narrative*, 42-43.

[31] Sternberg, *Poetics of Biblical Narrative*, 41.

was forced, few inherited from neighboring cultures. Rather, most were invented and elaborated in the Israelite tradition of narrative, so that the whole strategy cannot have been less than deliberate . . . . The biblical narrator is determined to operate as an artist even in the radical sense of courting danger and difficulty where he is most anxious for success as a partisan.[32]

Some of these dangers the narrator courts are "gaps in information, neutral-looking posture, complex character-drawing, silent inventiveness, and verbal density."[33] But in all of these the danger is worth courting because the history being recounted

is an affair between heaven and earth, with the heavenly side figuring as a maker and bent on advertising his makership by imposing his will and order on the normal logic of events before the eyes of humanity. Hence the alignment of divine with artistic pattern-making.[34]

The "art of indirection" is therefore licensed by the central status given the character of the Divine Artificer, but what sort of artifice should it be, comic or tragic? To put this another way, should the artifice be experienced but not thematized as in a tragedy, or should it be made central and thematic throughout as in a comedy? The answer can be seen in what makes the "drama of reading" a drama, and that is the unavoidable demand upon the reader to join in and make the drama complete by his active participation—the degree to which even determining how successful and pleasing the drama will be. And just as comedy must deal with the knowledge of its audience because of the effect that knowledge has upon the success of its outcome (hence the concern of comedy with "nature" and who really knows it), so also in the Bible, this concern with knowledge has become so thematic that the uniquely biblical "cognitive antithesis between God and humanity" has been built into the very structure of the narrative.

---

[32] Sternberg, *Poetics of Biblical Narrative*, 33.

[33] Sternberg, *Poetics of Biblical Narrative*, 44.

[34] Sternberg, *Poetics of Biblical Narrative*, 46.

> Not the premises alone but the very composition must bring home the point in and through the reading experience. This exigency calls into sacred play all the choices and techniques mentioned earlier under the rubric of aesthetics, for what they have in common is the effect of twisting, if not blocking, the way to knowledge . . . . Thus insofar as knowledge is information, the ubiquity of gaps about character and plot exposes to us our own ignorance . . . . With the narrative become an obstacle course, its reading turns into a drama of understanding . . . the only knowledge perfectly acquired is the knowledge of our limitations.[35]

If this sounds suspiciously like the effect of a Platonic dialogue, then we need to remind ourselves wherein lies the difference. For the point of all this playful exposé is not just of our limits, but also and more importantly, the revelation of the unlimited knowledge of God. If the point of this narrative artistry is to make it so that it is only "by a sustained effort alone that the reader can attain at the end to something of the vision that God has possessed all along," lest we miss this point, the narrative will reiterate this point in the mouths of its characters, such as the prophet Samuel who says, "Man sees what meets the eye and God sees into the heart" (1 Samuel 16:7 RSV). From the context of this passage, we can see that quite often, "the reader's drama is literally dramatized in and through an analogous ordeal of interpretation undergone by a character," and the resulting "brotherhood in darkness and guesswork and error thus cuts across the barrier separating participant from observer to highlight the barrier separating both from divine omniscience."[36] The comic narrative of the Bible thus pulls us in as audience as a way of exposing ignorance; but in contrast to the philosophical comedies of Plato, the way to avoid the attendant comic ridicule is not to "know thyself" but rather "know thy God."

Yet how is anyone to know of this God if reading the narrative is such a challenge—would not just a few initiates have access

---

[35] Sternberg, *Poetics of Biblical Narrative*, 46-47.

[36] Sternberg, *Poetics of Biblical Narrative*, 48.

to its mysteries? Sternberg argues just the opposite. For just as we see in a comedy that all must be included in the final ending, so also, he argues, the Bible is composed to be "foolproof." By this he means, "the Bible is difficult to read, easy to underread and overread and even misread, but virtually impossible to, so to speak, counterread."[37] In other words, "the essentials are made transparent to all comers: the story line, the world order, the value system," because the Bible's overarching principle of composition is "maneuvering between the truth and the whole truth."[38] The way of accomplishing this end is by means of the absolutely reliable narrator who makes it possible to follow the surface statements and incidents with complete confidence.

> [F]ollow the biblical narrator ever so uncritically, and by no great exertion you will be making tolerable sense of the world you are in, the action that unfolds, the protagonists on stage, and the point of it all. . . . On the other hand, the narrator does not tell the whole truth either . . . . His *ex cathedra* judgments are valid as far as they go, but then they seldom go far below the surface of the narrative, where they find their qualification and shading.[39]

There are jokes and then there are inside jokes, and the Bible always gives you the first as the one thing needful; but it is in pursuit of the other that the Bible reveals its aesthetic mastery and literary depths. Examples of foolproof composition at work are the contrast between the definitive judgments upon character or action and the ambiguous working out of these judgments. Sternberg calls this the rule that "the complexity of representation is inversely proportioned to that of evaluation: the more opaque (discordant, ambiguous) the plot, that is, the more transparent (concordant, straightforward) the judgment."[40] Another example is the "better-late-than-never principle," that "having presented some drama

---

[37] Sternberg, *Poetics of Biblical Narrative*, 50.

[38] Sternberg, *Poetics of Biblical Narrative*, 51.

[39] Sternberg, *Poetics of Biblical Narrative*, 51.

[40] Sternberg, *Poetics of Biblical Narrative*, 54.

without any overt commentary, though with sufficient clues distributed along the way to guide the alert, the narrative will often enlighten the naive or superficial toward the end."[41] In all of these examples, what we see are the precautions the Bible takes against counterreading, even while allowing for the complexity of reading, and it is the "difference between the two, the minimal and maximal pole, that the Bible's art proper lives. But the safeguarding of the minimum truth forms a distinctive mark of its composition and index of its ideological basis."[42] The aesthetic principles used by the Bible are therefore mutually complementary to the historiographic and ideological principles. In fact, the three are so closely linked that one could even draw a link between the history, ideology and the respective aesthetic techniques used to embody them. As I would put it, the decision whether or not to write a comedy was dependent upon the view of the whole that must operate in it, and likewise the comic nature of the narrative ruled in and ruled out certain possibilities as to what kind of sense it could make. Since the overarching aesthetic framework of the Bible is a comedy, when Sternberg elaborates in great detail the particular techniques used by it, he is elaborating upon the narrative possibilities to be found in comedy; and since the general effect of comedy is to connect overtly the narrative means with their ends, a reader can move from his reading to what is portrayed with complete self-consciousness and clarity. Sternberg brings out the theological repercussions of this as follows:

> [E]xcept for a veto on graven images, God does not appear as a critic of art. If anything, his management of the world displays a gift for order, timing, irony, repartee, suspense, peripety, neat closure, dramatic effect, sometimes even a grim sense of fun, all incorporated in the narrative under the most respectable warrant. Not only does God have the instincts of a maker. His very articles of faith easily, almost necessarily translate into aesthetic correlates: the doctrine of free will into complex characterization, the equally

---

[41] Sternberg, *Poetics of Biblical Narrative*, 55.

[42] Sternberg, *Poetics of Biblical Narrative*, 56.

revolutionary concept of omniscience into dramas of perspective, human restrictedness into studies in ambiguity, omnipotence and providence into well-made plots, control of history into cyclical and analogical design imposed on recalcitrant matter, the demand to infer from past to present into ordeal by interpretation.[43]

In all of these doctrinal correlates of aesthetic technique, what we are seeing is the freedom a comedy allows in moving from its effect upon us as readers to the intentions of the poet behind the text. In the case of a human poet, this movement tends toward allegory or what has often been spoken of under the rubric of "esotericism," exemplified in Dante's description of the "allegory of the poets."[44] In tragic writing, on the other hand, because the poet accomplishes his end by obscuring his aesthetic decisions and techniques in light of the result, the temptation to move from the image of the narration to doctrines expressed by means of them would be a sign of aesthetic failure. This is why, as Ricoeur has pointed out, the tragic narratives at the foundation of other religions than the Judeo-Christian one relate to their founding myths through ritual or reenactment rather than interpretation; a difference that also accounts for the unique status accorded doctrines in the Christian tradition.

---

[43] Sternberg, *Poetics of Biblical Narrative*, 156-157.

[44] "[O]ne should know that writing can be understood and must be explained mainly in four senses. One is called the literal [and this is the sense that does not go beyond the letter of the fictive words, as are the fables of the poets. The other is called allegorical] and this is the sense that is hidden under the cloak of these fables, and it is a truth hidden under the beautiful lie, as when Ovid says that Orpheus tamed the wild beasts with his zither and caused the trees and stones to come to him; which signifies that the wise man with the instrument of his voice would make cruel hearts gentle and humble, and would make those who do not live in science and art do his will; and those who have no kind of life of reason in them are as stones. And the reason why this concealment was devised by wise men will be shown in the next to the last treatise. It is true that theologians understand this sense otherwise than do the poets; but since it is my intention here to follow after the manner of the poets, I take the allegorical sense as the poets are wont to take it" (Dante Alighieri, *Convivio*, quoted in Charles Singleton's *Dante's Commedia: Elements of Structure*, (Baltimore: The John Hopkins University Press, 1954), 8).

At this point, however, a new question arises, one that Sternberg would not be very happy with, and yet one which cannot be avoided—and that is the question of the narrative in the Old Testament *vis-à-vis* the later narratives of the New Testament. The question must be asked because it determines what *the* biblical narrative is that we are dealing with, and determines to a great extent what Sternberg's own description of what he calls the biblical narrative (i.e., primarily the narrative of the Hebrew scriptures) has to say of both the narrator and the narrative of the Christian Bible. The very division of the Bible into Old and New would no doubt seem offensive to him and a case of interpretative violence imposed by a lesser narrative upon a greater. Yet it must be admitted that it is the essential interpretative momentum of his own biblical narrative wherein the "truth" attempts to catch up with the "whole truth," that opens up the possibility of a fulfillment and a completion of this movement in the future. Thus, even if the figural interpretations described by Frei and Auerbach are not as possible or as called for if one limits oneself to the Hebrew scriptures (which I do not think is the case), one can at least say that Judaism, even as a religion devoted to the interpretation of past writings, has always been naturally oriented toward some sort of fulfillment in the future, a fulfillment that would complete the not yet completed story told in the past.

Either way, Sternberg is quite right to point out that the narrative technique of the Gospels is different from the earlier narrative of the Old Testament and that the disciplined functioning of the narrator as an analog of God, with inspired rather than verifiable historical authority, does not seem to be the case in the New Testament. What we are to make of this difference is a question we must now explore.

Before doing so, however, we must bring out more directly the continuity of the narrative in the Old Testament argued for by Sternberg. We must, in other words, answer the question of whether there is "a" unity to the first part of the Bible itself, or whether it is merely a miscellany of various types and sorts of different narratives. For if the Bible is merely a *melange*, then any claim to a continuity of narrative type, especially comedy or tragedy, would be mere wishful thinking.

To counter this suspicion, Sternberg contrasts the problematic status of the differing narrative books, seemingly "composed by different hands in different times and conditions," with "all the more remarkable" fact that "this mixed array of writers should have cast themselves in essentially the same role or posture as storytellers."[45] He illustrates what he means by this in the following.

> Take books as far removed from one another—in subject matter and very possibly origin and date of final shaping too—as Genesis, Samuel, and Jonah. In all three, for instance, the storyteller appears only as a disembodied voice, nameless and faceless. In all three, he avoids all reference to the act of storytelling—to himself as maker, recorder, editor or even narrator— nor does he betray the least consciousness of facing an audience by way of direct address and the like . . . . As far as the basic narrative traits and tactics that make up a storyteller's portrait are concerned, they all show an impressive family resemblance or, in diachronic terms, continuity: a unity of artistic persona in a variety of historical person.[46]

This "unity of artistic persona" is therefore the thread that ties together Sternberg's biblical narratives as *the* "biblical" narrative.

Yet already in the case of Ezra and Nehemiah, we can see an exception to this rule and perhaps even a movement away from it across time. In contrast to the single model of narration of all the earlier narratives, "whereby the narrating persona wields powers not just different from but closed to his historical maker, whoever he may be," in Ezra and Nehemiah we see a break with this narrative tradition wherein:

> Looking back on his own career, each narrates in his own name, in his own person, and hence in the eye-witness mode that assumes no special privileges in the treatment of either God or man—including the man

---

[45] Sternberg, *Poetics of Biblical Narrative*, 71.

[46] Sternberg, *Poetics of Biblical Narrative*, 71.

that he himself was as agent and now is as writer. Accordingly, their commissions are the standard biblical teller's omissions, and vice versa.[47]

The exceptions of Ezra and Nehemiah may prove the rule, but they may also open us up to the different narrative possibilities found in the Gospels, and raise the question of their continuity in the midst of discontinuity. Or to put this another way, once the perpetuation of the narrative strategy emphasized throughout most of the Old Testament is no longer possible to maintain (an impossibility that may well have come about because of the changed situation after the exile), how is it possible to still write of the God of Abraham, Isaac and Jacob, without undermining His status as the one true poet who will tolerate no one before Him?

The answer, I think, is the one given in the New Testament, and is the one answer that can deal with incipient skepticism built into Sternberg's use of "ideology" to describe the intent of the biblical narrator. How the Old Testament narrative can be saved from the implicit doubt attendant upon its poetic status comes out in the claim that Christ did all things in order to "fulfill" the scriptures. In this claim we can see that the mundane narration of this one man's history takes on the same prerogatives of Old Testament narration, not by virtue of narrative strategy, but by virtue of its main character and object. One might even go so far as to say that the grounding for the possibility of Sternberg's anonymous narrator who functions as God's analog and uses his prerogatives, has now been named; and, in moving the from the narrative frame of the story to its narrated center, must now finally justify the prerogatives only assumed in the latter.

This, I think, is the point of the Gospel of John's prologue, wherein the *Logos* who was in the "beginning" with God and "was God," is the very same one who could have seconded the asymmetrical acts of creation even as he sees into the hearts of men as freely as he "knows" the Father (Jn 1:1-19). When this Logos "became flesh and dwelt among us," (Jn 1:16) it also seems to have changed the possibilities of narrative license. How a human poet

---

[47] Sternberg, *Poetics of Biblical Narrative*, 73.

could possibly write of God and yet not implicitly subordinate God to human making and power can be seen in the claims of the incarnation. Each time we see the man Jesus identified with the *Logos* who mediated all of creation (cf. Jn. 1:3, Col. 1:15-20) we see the need to identify the divine poet of creation with a man identified as fulfilling the scriptures. Read fulfillment as validation, and it is only the veracity of this man's concrete and historical life that could prevent the scriptures from being just another human fiction.

For now the comic burden has shifted from narrator to plot, and it is the action of the main character in the plot that retroactively fulfills the comic function of the past narrative and thus makes possible a new and different narrative strategy altogether. The continuity of narrative technique is shattered into the four prisms of the Gospels, but the light shining through each is said to be both the same and complete "fulfillment" of the single light shining through the narrative persona of the "scriptures."

Such a claim also radically shifts the priorities of reading. Whereas the effect of the continuity of anonymous narrative persona was to establish a community of truth in his readers as well as the possibility of a fuller "whole truth," in the case of the Gospels, the shift toward direct emphasis upon plot and disregard for narrative technique functions to put the Truth itself on center stage and plot out the reactions to it as part of the story. Sternberg sees the difference but misses its significance when he contrasts the giving of the Law to all of Israel with Jesus' public speaking of the parables that are later privately interpreted for his disciples.

> The gulf dividing these key statements—one addressed to the Twelve far from the crowd, the other to a whole people for all time—epitomizes the mutual incompatibility between two ideologies and between two narrative procedures. The Bible has many secrets but no Secret, many levels of interpretation but all equally accessible, so "very near thee" that, given the will, "thou canst do it."[48]

---

[48] Sternberg, *Poetics of Biblical Narrative*, 49.

What Sternberg overlooks here is that even though the community being built up in his biblical narrative is all-inclusive, that inclusiveness is dependent upon the comic nature of the narrative persona. This inclusiveness is consequently limited to the community of the narrative's readers. In Mark, however, what we are seeing is not an exclusion from that community, but rather the point that community is wholly dependent upon the Truth itself, and that the community does not make truth but rather the Truth makes the community. The "secret" of Mark is thus no more than the application of Isaiah's "Hear and hear, but do not understand; see and see, but do not perceive" (Isa. 6:9 RSV) to the object of that hearing and seeing—which is the Word of God himself who alone is capable of forming a true community. What Sternberg misses is that the inclusion on Mt. Sinai includes only those already called out by God, and even the "sojourner in the gates" sojourns with this "people" united together in this continuity of hearing or reading. The Twelve Disciples are no more than this people hypostasized as characters. Even then, their true "hearing" only comes after the revelation of the Markan secret, which as the "non-sign" or "sign of Jonah," (Mt. 12:38-43) is misunderstood by all, and yet is nevertheless the one act whereby God reasserts that it is on his truth alone that his community shall be built.

To put this another way, the truth of Sternberg's "biblical narrative" ultimately depends upon the unique narrative genius of its writers and their success in instilling an "ideology." Such a success, however, is undermined by the very recognition of it *as* a narrative technique; and Sternberg, whether deliberately or not, signals this subversion by the use of the word "ideology" with its taint of propaganda and political humbug. The Gospels, on the other hand, precisely in their deviation from the narrative norms of the very same "scriptures" they claim to fulfill, may well be providing the one possible antidote to this subversion. For what they relate in varying narrations is one essential story wherein the hero himself, through his actions, gives the historical and human justification for what would otherwise be merely the "ideology" of the biblical narrative. The possibility of rejecting the truthfulness of this gospel story obviously still remains, but that rejection is itself the main and precipitating element built into the story itself. It is thus essentially included in it, and therefore leaves no one outside its limits.

This is what lies behind Auerbach's observation that the Bible "seeks to overcome our reality," or Frei's observation that biblical interpretation's direction was "that of incorporating extra-biblical thought, experience, and reality into the one real world detailed and made accessible by the biblical story—and not the reverse." Yet such claims could only break out of the limits of the specific narrative of the Hebrew scriptures if the narrator's authority was no longer just as an analog of God, but was, in addition, the authority grounded by the merely human narration of that Narrator's own actions themselves—deeds speaking louder than any possible human words. The gospel story must therefore break free of any one specific narrative in order to save (fulfill) the one narrative of the "scriptures" from being a merely human comedy authored "as-if" by God, but by a mere human nonetheless. And since every story must be narrated, the manifold narratives of the Gospels break the connection to their particular narrators by their very diversity and connection to an ongoing community composed of believers rather than readers or rememberers.

The haphazard narrative style of the four Gospels which moves from eyewitness accounts to omnipresent viewpoint, and then even to theological commentary on the inner workings of God, may seem to have no connection to our earlier arguments that the biblical narrative described by Sternberg functions comically—except for the explicit claims these narratives themselves make to be derived from that narrative. Yet in this very claim to fulfill the scriptures, we can see that the Gospels are all at great pains to show their complete dependence upon that narrative; whether it be through explicit reference to Christ's actions and words as fulfillment of the scriptures, or a replaying of narrative themes such as going down and then out of Egypt again, or even a restating of the creation account itself with Jesus at center stage. In all these ways and more, what we are seeing is the interpretative vehemence implicit in the comic nature of Old Testament narra-tive, a vehemence that hurtles itself outside the bounds of its initial narrative frame by making the claim that the story of God's relation to his own creation is itself comic, and that all previous comic writing is retroactively founded upon the comic poet's central, literal, and historical presence in his own poem.

So just as the "omnipotence effect" described by Sternberg tips off the reader that God and the narrator are in complete control of the action, and that the ironic unfolding of events exposes the ignorance of both readers and characters, so also does this ignorance lead to the passion to overcome this ignorance and understand the "whole truth" that relates all these events to the intentions of God. This passion is what leads to typological (or figural) interpretation, and yet this passion itself is no more than the comic eros that seeks to understand how the comic poet is going to make everything work out in the end—the end wherein the "whole truth" will also be the truth of each and every event as a part. The Gospels are therefore in typological continuity with the "what" of Sternberg's "biblical narrative," even if discontinuous with the "how" of the narrative persona's style. Nevertheless, the historiographical intent is still preserved by the typological continuity with the history given through the inspired status of the Old Testament's narrative persona.

When the narrator of Luke thus makes his clear appeal to eyewitness accounts (Lk. 1:2), or when the narrator of John says that there are not enough books in the world to record all the deeds of Jesus' life (Jn. 21:25), what we are seeing is the same historiographic grounding. But instead of being grounded in the unique prerogatives of the narrator, the grounding is now in the historical event that slips the bounds of all possible human narration. The continuity of narrative persona across various narratives is thus replaced with a continuity of historical story across various narrations of it.

This no doubt brings us closer to our modern canons of historiography, but there is still a big difference to be noted, and that is the mediation of that historical memory through the Holy Spirit, the giving of which to the disciples is itself a key part of the story.

In the same way, then, that Sternberg argues the canons of inspiration give the biblical narrator a serious historiographic intent without being an "historian" in our sense of the term, so also in the New Testament we see that the "giving of the Holy Spirit" makes inspiration itself a central part of the common story. The presence of the Holy Spirit in the community of Christ's followers gives the narrative license to make eyewitness appeals (under the rubric of "witness"), and yet also to narrate where no such appeal would be possible (Jesus' prayers to the Father in Gethsemane for example).

Yet, since the Holy Spirit is given to the disciples as an event in the common historical story itself rather than presupposed as the essential prerequisite for the authoritative narrative voice we see in the Old Testament, this "in-Spirit-ation" leads to many and various narrations of a single story. This freedom of narrative emphasis and selection in regards to a common story is epitomized in the Acts of the Apostles, wherein each telling of the gospel contains its own choice of events and thereby makes a different point about a common story.[49] Against the backdrop of the giving of the Holy Spirit, we can see that Acts is also the narrative that both describes *and* justifies the variations across differing written Gospels of the one Gospel. In the Epistles we can also see an extension of this sort of spiritual authority, for the element common to them

---

[49] Robert Funk uses this phenomena in Acts to make clear the distinction between story and discourse; a distinction that takes on much more significance in the New Testament which is no longer tied down to the authority of the particular discourse described by Sternberg.

> If there is more than one version of the same story, it can scarcely be contested that the story of Jesus is to be discriminated from its expression in particular sets of narrative statements. Furthermore, since no two sets of narrative statements appear to be identical (what would be the point of identical sets?), varying narrative statements of the same series of events are to be distinguished from each other. . . . To reiterate, every version of the story is to be distinguished not only from all other versions of the same story, but also from the chain of events, real, legendary, or fictive, to which all versions presumably refer (Robert Funk, *The Poetics of Biblical Narrative* (Sonoma: Polebridge Press, 1988) 43-40).

all is the claim to be written by a main character in a preexisting historical story. Especially in the case of Paul, we can see that the appearance of Christ to him, even if as to one "untimely born" (1 Cor. 15:8) and not an actual a part of a narrated gospel, finally gives him authoritative status because of its connection to the not yet written (until Acts) continuing story of Jesus.

In the Revelation of John, what we see is a proleptic capstone to the entire plot that had its beginning in Genesis and its middle in the Gospels. Revelation, in other words, demonstrates decisively that the Bible is a comic plot, and thus a plot that must tie up all loose ends and reinstate the true natural goodness of all things declared at the very beginning. As proleptic, Revelation also has the historiographical effect of enclosing all of human history within the confines of this story's plot, therefore making history itself a comedy, and its plot coterminous with the Bible's plot.

The conclusion of the New Testament with this apocalyptic revelation, however, also raises the question of the canon. Yet it raises this question in such a way that is rather different than the sort of argumentation Childs makes in his work on canonical criticism—that it is the canonical shape of Scripture that should determine our initial reading of it. Instead, I would argue that in the Old Testament the canon is the external embodiment of the internal impetus given by the continuity of Sternberg's "narrative persona." In the New, the canon is an external, temporary closure, that by ending with Revelation indicates that the plot of history in its entirety has the closure of a comedy, but that we ourselves are in its middle waiting for the reappearance of its comic poet in the final act.

The only canon, or rule, of the New Testament is therefore the story external to the writing of it, and so the lack of anonymity given to the various writings contained in it (in contrast to most of the Old Testament) is itself testimony to its freedom from the writings of men in the face of the ultimate created plot of God. Nevertheless, the story of God (*Logos*) must still remain in contact with the writings of men (i.e., must become flesh and dwell among us), so the plot of God is everywhere plotted against the one discourse actually written down earlier that speaks of God in this way. Figuration (as discussed by Auerbach and Frei) is thus the true "canonical" rule that binds the New together with the Old and makes of them both a complete Canon. The written "narrative persona" of the Old is the type for the antitype of the incarnate *Logos* who is written variously of in the New. The "fulfilling" quality of the New is thus the grounding of the possibility of the Old "writing" in the "unwritten" of the New, which is to say, the taint of ideology can only be overcome by the independence of the story in the New from its various manifestations in human writing.

This returns us to the central characteristic of the Gospels, the great pains they take to write of all the deeds surrounding Jesus' life as "fulfilling" Scripture. Although sometimes this fulfillment is in terms of prophetic passages from the Prophets or Psalms, more often its exact nature is not directly stated (for example the Resurrection in general). A particularly telling fulfillment is played out when a representative of the entirety of the scriptures themselves, John the Baptist, represents the prefiguring and preparatory function of Scripture in relation to the coming of Jesus. Another example is the Mount of Transfiguration, wherein Moses (Law) and Elijah (the Prophets) give place to the direct words of Jesus— "This is my beloved Son, hear *him*" (Mark 9:2-8 RSV).

In our time this sort of statement inevitably arouses our historicist suspicions and we suspect the historical integrity of these accounts in the light of their obvious rhetorical organization. But if we measure them against the manifold renderings of one and the same story in Acts, and if we remember that it is the deeds themselves that fulfill and not the written accounts of them, then we can see that the gospel writers view their rhetorical burden not as a redoing of the biblical narrative, but rather as paying it the compliment of tying their own rhetorical strategy in with the "ideology" already established beforehand by means of the very different strategy used in the scriptures. By fulfilling the type of this "ideology," the deeds of Jesus—above all the deed of his death and resurrection—serve as the historical antitype that grounds the truth of those written human words on the authority of the actions of Truth itself in human history. The mediation of this truth therefore breaks free of an intrinsic connection to human and hence ideo-logical writing by replacing it with a historical mediation to which human writing is only extrinsically connected.

With this movement away from the narrative grounding in the Old Testament in mind, we can see why Auerbach and Frei comment upon the temptation in figural interpretation for the interpreter "to turn his attention away from the sensory occurrence and toward its meaning."[50] Inasmuch as the "sensory base" is the various written narratives of the Gospels, the movement away from this base to a common "meaning" or story is indeed intended. This intention is essentially the historiographical intention of all four Gospels, and their meaning is that the history of Jesus is part of the same history the reader shares in also. To get at this history, then, we are obliged to move beyond the particular gospel accounts to the comic plot enunciated throughout all of them. This temptation is not a temptation at all, except to our own secularized version of this history. Rather, it is the source of our own Western concern with history, for the meaning of the Gospels is the history to be discovered therein. So, however inappropriate figural interpretation may be to the Old Testament on its own, it is no more than the perceptive response to the figural writing of the New.

The equation of the historical and literal meaning of the Bible—united throughout most exegetical history, but sundered in our own—therefore captures exactly the point of the New Testament writing. The literal, narrative meaning is thus also and even more so the historical story that is enunciated through this literal meaning that goes beyond it to include the reader in the same story. In other words, the meaning of the Bible is the history that includes both the text *and* its readers—and self-consciously so. The writing of the Bible therefore demands that its readers live their life in its writing, which is to say, demands that they allow its literal sense to make historical (and we might add, political) sense of themselves. This is, however, just the opposite of Plato's philosophical demand that we *not* live in our writing. Both demands flow from a response to distinctly comic writing; yet nevertheless, the two demands

---

[50] Auerbach, *Mimesis*, 48.

could not be more different—as different as a world in which God has entered into human history and politics and one where he has not.

XI: READING THE BIBLE AS A COMEDY

AT THIS point we will try to consolidate the gains in our understanding of comic and tragic writing, along with our discussion of
the narrative unity of the Bible, by reading the Bible's plot in its
entirety as a comedy. In other words, I will attempt a summary of
the Old and the New Testaments that brings into relief those elements that directly thematize their comic quality and the political
and theological implications that go along with them. And since
comedy is known through its emphasis on the narrator, I will give
a reading of the biblical narrative as a whole that pays attention to
both *what* is narrated and *how* it is narrated to us. This reading will
be at once figural, insofar as it ties the end with the beginning in
terms of its types and antitypes; comic, insofar as it thematizes the
act of creating and artifice; and political, insofar as it brings out the
relation of artifice to the city. The overall goal of such a reading,
however, will be to meet the challenge posed by Leo Strauss, that
claiming both the rightness of philosophy and the Bible would be
a case of having one's cake and eating it too.[1] Such an undertaking

---

[1] "If we compare what More said about Jesus with what Plato tells us
about Socrates, we find that "Socrates laughed twice or thrice, but never
find we that he wept as much as once." A slight bias in favor of laughing
and against weeping seems to be essential to philosophy. For the beginning of philosophy as the philosophers understood it is not the fear of
the Lord, but wonder. Its spirit is not hope and fear and trembling, but
serenity on the basis of resignation. To that serenity, laughing is a little bit
more akin than weeping. Whether the Bible or philosophy is right is of
course the only question that ultimately matters. But in order to understand that question one must first see philosophy as it is. One must not
see it from the outset through Biblical glasses. Wherever each of us may

must, of course, seem highly schematic and selective, but if it is kept in mind that the principles of selection are those relevant to the aspects of comedy and tragedy already discussed, perhaps it will be forgiven. Let us begin, then, at the beginning.

In the first sentences of Genesis we have two sorts of creation side by side that will become fully distinguished only later on. The first of these is what was later termed creation *ex nihilo*—"In the beginning God created the heavens and the earth"—and the second—"The earth was without form and void, and darkness was upon the face of the deep; and the Spirit of God was moving over the face of the waters"—is the sort of creation we are more familiar with from your typical creation myth with its creation of order out of chaos. The first sort is what has given the distinctive quality to the monotheistic religions, and it is this sort that will be uniquely identified with the God believed in by Abraham and his spiritual descendants. This sort of creation is as mysterious as God himself and outstrips all analogies with human making because of the absence of any sort of preexisting material. It is in fact this act itself that sets this sort of God apart from humanity as Creator to creature.

The second sort, the creation of order out of chaos, can be read as either a different event or the redescription of the first. The formless void of the deep, the watery chaos with all its linguistic connections to the murdered corpse of female Babylonian sea-god Tiamat, is something we are already familiar with in the tragic *poesis* of order out of chaos.[2] It is essentially a form of *techne* that, as in all human making, requires some sort of preexisting material. This second sort of creation, then, would be as continuous with human poetry and politics as the first is discontinuous.

But are these two distinct sorts of creation? Or are they one and the same, the second only elaborating what is involved in the first? This is a crucial question, so crucial, that the continuing narrative of the Bible will be centrally concerned with answering it by

---

stand, no respectable purpose is served by trying to prove that we eat the cake and have it." Strauss, *Rebirth*. 206.

[2] On this, see our earlier discussion of Paul Ricoeur's "creations myths" in the chapter "Violence and Tragic Plot as Scapegoat."

holding these two apart and elucidating why they must be. It will do so, however, by means of its figural structure wherein later developments shed light on earlier quandaries and unfold their latent meanings. What is earlier mysterious and yet pregnant with possibilities and oftentimes contradictory options in interpretation will later answer those questions by reinforcing and elucidating one option and excluding the other. What we must do as readers is initially ask those questions and expect that later developments will provide our answers. Consider this structure in the light of the following questions.

In this second description of creation, where did the watery chaos come from? Was it created by God along with the "heavens and earth"? Was it prior to creation and hence as eternal as God? Was it the result of the fall of Lucifer and a third of the angels (cf. Rev. 12:7-9)? None of these questions at this point can be answered completely, but as the story unfolds, the logic of narrative leads us to thematize a third element that will explain as much as possible the difference between it and creation *ex nihilo*, and what is presupposed by creation out of chaos.

If we take creation out of nothing as the characteristic of the uniquely monotheistic God who is the first principle of all that exists, there are certain possibilities opened up in reading these first few lines. For example, if this were indeed the sort of creation spoken of only in the first line, then what must be presupposed by creation out of the "something" of chaos in the next line is the prior creation by created beings who in attempting to act as their own first principle can create only chaos and disorder leading to nonexistence. The spirit of God brooding over the face of the deep would thus intend to bring forth out of this chaos a bubble of order that floats above, through, and within those depths in order to save, preserve, and point to an initial order lost by this creation's own act of disordering. Although the significance of this second-order creation cannot be fully known when it is first described (the same could also be said of creation out of nothing), once we get the narrative of the Fall the distinction between the two becomes underlined and its significance becomes increasingly important.

In fact, it will be between these different types of creation—God's unique creation and then the secondary human creation leading to the need for an emergency secondary divine making—that the Bible will tell the complete story of God's dealing with humanity, a story that does not end until the initial act of creation is reinstated and the secondary acts fall away and disappear. The story begun in Genesis is thus not fully finished until the final vision of John in Revelation wherein he sees a "new heaven and earth" in which, most significantly, "the sea was no more." (Rev. 21:1 RSV).[3] It is only the whole story, the story that ends with Revelation, that makes complete sense of what is ambiguous and yet pregnant with meaning at the very beginning.

"And God said, 'Let there be light': and there was light" (Genesis 1:3 RSV). With this initial fiat of God we are returning to an elaboration of the first act of creation wherein the power of the divine *logos* as speech mediates all of creation. The plurality of the divine agency along with the unnamed narrator who can second these acts set up a mystery as to the nature of this narrative along with the nature of its main character, God, that is not fully resolved until the prologue to the Gospel of John. Yet somehow, the unity in difference of the divine "we" is paralleled by the analogous connection between the actions of God and the narrative persona who shares in the same prerogatives of divine omniscience even while inculcating in us created readers the knowledge of our own relative ignorance.[4]

The evaluation of this act—"and God saw that the light was good"—provides an understanding of this creation that, contrary to the arguments of Leo Strauss, is essentially parallel to the philosophical account of nature. For nature as both intrinsically good and the intelligible structure of all that contingently exists is "seen" to be such by God who, in consulting himself, admits the existence

---

[3] "Sea" here having distinct symbolic connections with the "deep."

[4] Sternberg discusses this in terms of "asymmetrical" demonstrations of God's omnipotence wherein "God works wonders unseen by humanity": he then remains addresseeless, in contrast to the narrator who renders the scene for the benefit of his own addressee, the reader. (*Biblical Narrative*, 103).

of a criteria for goodness and truth, even while finding it only in himself. The question of Socrates in the *Euthyphro*, "Is what is holy (in this case read "good") holy because the gods approve it, or do they approve it because it is holy?"[5] is here answered by the implicit claim that in the case of creation *ex nihilo*, and only then, are both true.[6] Especially here, when light is both the means to see and the

---

[5] Plato, *Euthyphro*, The Collected Dialogues of Plato, trans. Lane Cooper (Princeton: Princeton University Press, 1961), 10a.

[6] What I think is mistaken in the following argument of Strauss, then, is his assumption that knowledge is essentially "taking a good look," in this case, at the "ideas;" rather than knowledge through identity that one finds in Aristotle.

> In other words, if the primary beings are the gods, and not the ideas, whatever is good or just will be good or just because the gods love it, and for no other reason, for no intrinsic reason. The primary act is not knowledge or understanding but love without knowledge or understanding, i.e. blind desire. But is this alternative not overcome in monotheism?. . . . [T]he *Euthyphron* seems to suggest that even the oldest god must be conceived of as subject to the ideas. It is true that if there is only one God, there is no difficulty in thinking that piety consists in imitating God. One must know that God is good or just or wise, i.e., that God complies with the rules of justice. If that rule were subject to God, or dependent upon God, or made by God, if it could be changed by God, it could no longer serve as a standard. God must be thought to be subject to a necessity, an intelligible necessity, which he did not make. If we deny this, if we assume that God is above the intelligible necessity, or not bound by intelligible necessity, he cannot know in the strict sense, for knowledge is knowledge of the intelligible and unalterable necessity. In that case, God's actions would be altogether arbitrary. Nothing would be impossible to him. For example, he could create other gods, and the many gods, who, of course, cannot have knowledge, would fight. (Strauss, *Rebirth of Classical Political Rationalism*, 202)

The notion of "necessity" and "rule following" here seems oddly Kantian. Be that as it may, Aquinas' distinction between our possible knowledge of God's existence and our definite ignorance of his essence, especially in the context of the philosophers, seems to the point here. One only knows strict necessity through the knowledge of one's own ignorance of it, but the striving for that knowledge is the striving for what God knows when he says "the light was good." God's self-knowledge is

object seen, do we see again why light is the paradigmatic image for intellect that allows Plato to say as the light is to eye and the image seen, so too is the Good to the understanding and the object understood.[7] Darkness is merely the absence of light, so only light need be created, for only what is lit and intelligible exists and is good. Darkness, as we shall see, is only a by-product, or secondary result, of what is good. Nevertheless dealing with this darkness soon becomes the Bible's central theme.

After elaborating in the seven days what was involved in God's creation out of nothing, the odd sort of creation that leads to the chaos presupposed by the Spirit's brooding over the deep will now be turned to, starting with Genesis 2:4. In the midst of the garden of Eden, God places the living being he has created who breathes the breath of his very own spirit. In this garden, God has also made to grow "every tree that is pleasant to the sight and good for food," which is to say, created intellect has not yet been divorced from desire. Nevertheless for both to be what they are, that possibility must be allowed; so two other trees are also placed in the garden, the "tree of life" and the "tree of the knowledge of good and evil" (Gen. 2:9). In the instructions that go along with these trees, God says "You may freely eat of every tree of the garden; but of the tree of the knowledge of good and evil you shall not eat, for in the day that you eat of it you shall die" (Gen. 2:16-17). Here then is death introduced for the first time, but only as the consequence of turning away from the source of life—just as darkness is the absence of light. So if this tree is not the tree of life, what is it? What sort of tree is it on its own? The knowledge of good and evil. Is that not a good thing? Do we not know God when we know the Good? Just so, for there is only knowledge and knowledge is always knowledge of God. What then of evil? What

---

thus the only knowledge of necessity, but that means one's own knowledge is always contingent. Unless we ourselves become gods, then (an option Nietzsche would seem to pursues with his eternal recurrence of the same (cf. Friedrich Nietzsche, *Beyond Good and Evil*, trans Walter Kaufman (New York: Vintage Books, 1966), 56), Strauss' criticism is irrelevant because our knowledge is not of "intelligible and unalterable necessity."

[7] Plato, *Republic*, 508c.

that knowledge consists of we shall soon find out, but before doing so, God makes for Adam his Eve: "And the man and his wife were both naked, and were not ashamed" (Gen. 3:25) Knowledge is to know all and leave nothing hid—why then should they not know even evil?

Perhaps because there is nothing to know, because evil is the forgetfulness and occlusion of knowledge, the turning away from the source of all light and creation and the turning toward one's own participation in that created light as to a burning fire or projecting lamp rather than to the sun. With this tree one gains the knowledge of good and evil by *not* eating of it, for evil is only known for what it is by knowing goodness. The irony of eating this tree, of knowing evil through one's own act as independent first principle, is that one now knows neither good nor evil, but only appearances—which is as much a not knowing as a knowing. For the first thing they see upon eating is their own nakedness, and that sight cannot be borne but must be immediately covered over and hid. Let us take a closer look at how this happened.

Something strange has gotten into the garden: the serpent. Where did he come from? Here we get our first indication that creation *ex nihilo* is definitely to be distinguished from the other way of making. For the serpent who brings into the garden the potentiality for chaos and death is himself something created by God. "Now the serpent was more subtle than any other wild creature that the Lord God had made" (Gen. 3:1). Somehow the serpent who was himself made by God brings into the garden something new. What is that new thing?

> He said to the woman, "Did God say, 'You shall not eat of any tree of the garden'?" And the woman said to serpent, "We may eat of the fruit of the trees of the garden; but God said, 'You shall not eat of the fruit of the tree which is in the midst of the garden, neither shall you touch it, lest you die.'" But the serpent said to the woman, "You will not die. For God knows that when you eat of it your eyes will be opened, and *you will be like God*, knowing good and evil." So when the woman saw that the tree was good for food and a delight to the eyes, and that the tree was to be desired

to make one wise, she took of its fruit and ate; and
she also gave some to her husband, and he ate (Gen.
3:1-6, *emphasis added*).

The new thing the serpent brings into the garden is the desire to
be "like God," the desire to possess the wisdom that allows God
to know both how to create and to know his own creation is good.

In other words, the desire to be one's own first principle is
what the serpent brings, for to know good *and* evil is to know everything in the light of its first principle and wisdom consists in just
such knowledge. However, if God alone is truly the first principle
of everything, then knowledge of good and evil is knowledge of
God. To be wise on one's own, then, is to be *like* God but not
God: to be *like* a first principle by making something oneself, but
not truly *the* first principle. The desire to imitate God's creative
power and wisdom is thus the temptation of the serpent, for instead of knowing what is good and a delight to the eyes as a se-
conding of God's creation and judgment, Eve now desires to know
this on her own as a judgment upon her own creation.

To do so, however, would be to overlook the facts if not
downright lie about them—since the facts in this case are that
without God there is no life but only death. The temptation of the
serpent is thus based upon a lie, a deliberate falsification, that leads
to the desire to lie in turn—to appear wise when one is not. When
Adam and Eve eat, their desire is to bring something new into creation that is completely their own—and their desire *is* satisfied.
Throughout the rest of the Bible this new "creation" of the first
humans will thus provide the watery void of chaos and death with
which God must work, the preexisting material, as it were, that
makes this sort of "making" fully analogous to our own.

The first indication of this is as easily overlooked as it is important. Let us pay close attention, then, for here at the very beginning we will see both the essence of tragedy and why men need
it, along with the first faint indication of how that need will be
overcome. "Then the eyes of both were opened, and they knew
that they were naked; and they sewed fig leaves together and made
themselves aprons" (Gen. 3:7). This, then, is the first fruit of their
wisdom, the knowledge of their own nakedness, the knowledge

that they have now become evil. Knowledge of evil is thus knowledge of themselves on their own and in isolation. What then is the knowledge of good? The knowledge that the knowledge of their own evil must be hid. Good thus becomes the "appearance" of good and the hiding of one's evil. When God asks "Who told you that you were naked?" (Gen. 3:11) the answer is no one but themselves. Shame and the desire to hide the truth is the fruit of the knowledge of good and evil. Or, to put this another way, the knowledge gained through eating from the tree of the knowledge of good and evil is only the knowledge of appearances. And since only the Good can truly be known (a knowledge Adam and Eve would have had they obeyed, which shows God is not jealous of this knowledge), what humanity now has is, at best, knowledge of their own ignorance, and at worst, the false knowledge of the lie.

If the price of this new found ignorance is death, what are we to make of Adam and Eve's preservation? There is much cursing, but there seems to be no immediate death. Ah, but there is a death. "And the Lord God made for Adam and for his wife garments of skins, and clothed them" (Gen. 3:21). The first death in creation occurs by God's own hand, offstage and hidden so to speak, when he kills the animals required to cover the nakedness of the human animal. What this first death seems to imply is that the human nakedness and shame of this new found ignorance requires something more drastic than vegetation to be covered over. In other words, this act of God seems to imply that the covering of our nakedness before ourselves and God requires the shedding of blood, some sort of death. Why should this be?

The answer won't become clear until the story of Cain and Abel, but for now we can say that the upshot of succumbing to the temptation of the serpent to be like God is that we make gods of ourselves. Yet since there is only one true God who can both create and know his creation is good, any other creation must remain in ignorance of its own value. The creation of "gods" can thus only claim to be good by means of the facticity of the power to create, but not by means of true knowledge of its goodness. Force and fraud, as we shall see, substitute for knowledge. The creations of gods are thus always in competition for ascendancy, for each god as its own first principle can only be such if it eliminates all other first principles through violence or deceit. Or to put this another way, the creations of different first principles are inherently unshareable and so lead to unavoidable conflict. God, the true first principle, knows this before humanity does, which is why his warning about death is not a threat but merely a prediction about the dire results of this inevitable conflict. Spiritual death is the fruit of being at war with both the true creator and one's own flesh and blood. Physical death is only this war's most obvious manifestation.

When God kills an animal to make the covering for Adam and Eve, he is thus performing the first act that allows humanity to live within their new state of mimetically divine competition and jealousy. Somehow the shedding of blood will allow human beings to live with their nakedness, since the bloodlessness of the vegetable world does not seem adequate. Here then, I think, we see the first pregnant hint of what is involved in the second act of creation wherein the "the spirit of God broods over the face of the waters." God must somehow create order out of the disorder brought about by his creation's own hand. He must create some sort of order that preserves the vestiges of his initial and good creation amidst its own self-obnubilation. And for reasons not yet explained, the second sort of creation requires the shedding of blood and God's own involvement with a death that he did not initially create.

What God did create was Life, and the problem now becomes that in attempting to imitate God in his knowledge of good and evil, mankind has separated wisdom from existence. What is is no longer good for humanity; so life itself becomes unavailable and the only thing we know for sure becomes death. Consider the horror of the unfinished thought in the following.

> Then the Lord God said, "Behold, the man has become like one of us, knowing good and evil; and now, lest he put forth his hand and take also of the tree of life, and eat, and live for ever"—therefore the Lord God sent him forth from the garden of Eden to till the ground from which he was taken (Gen. 3:22-23).

Here *in ovo* we have the essential typological situation of the Bible. The incompletion of God's thought pushes us on as readers to complete it ourselves; and yet as it stands it gives us enough clues to know that it can only be completed when the one Man who truly does know good from evil, brings back the inaccessible "tree of life" by dying on it. Like the gun on the mantelpiece in the first act that must go off in the third, being barred from the Tree of Life at the beginning of the story lets us know that the return of a tree somewhere near the climax of the story is all-important. And when that tree reappears in the form of a paradoxically perverse tree of death, figuring out why there is this inversion proves the point of the entire story.

When we get to the Cain and Abel story we find many of the answers to questions raised earlier. Blood is the theme, envy is the problem, and murder is the result. Yet from out of these elements we are shown the essential backdrop for the founding of the first city. This narrative, one might say, is the foundational text for the political philosophy of the Bible, and it covers some very familiar ground. To begin with, Cain, the first born, is a tiller of the earth while Abel is a keeper of sheep. The importance of this comes out when they offer their respective sacrifices to God—the vegetative offering of Cain and the bloody offering of Abel. "And the Lord had regard for Abel and his offering, but for Cain and his offering he had no regard" (Gen. 4:4-5) Why this difference? Is the Lord arbitrary in his pleasure? For an answer, we get a description of Cain's response that reveals the hidden state of his heart as well as the reason why the bloodshed of Abel's sacrifice seems commensurate with the need for it.

> So Cain was very angry, and his countenance fell. The Lord said to Cain, "Why are you angry, and why has your countenance fallen? If you do well, will you not be accepted? And if you do not well, sin is couching at the door; its desire is for you, but you must master it."
>
> Cain said to Abel his brother, "Let us go out to the field," Cain rose up against his brother Abel, and killed him (Gen. 4:5-8).

Cain's heart is revealed to be murderous, and murderous out of the envy and the desire to be his own judge of the goodness of his actions. The sin couching at Cain's door is the insatiable desire to be one's own first principle, and what this first murder brings out is the competitive frenzy of humankind, who in attempting to imitate God must destroy all others because of the unshareable nature of that desire.

When God thus asks Cain "Where is Abel your brother?" Cain's claim to ignorance and the disclaiming of mutuality is the very truth. This war of all against all is also and essentially at war with creation itself, since it is the nature of creation which gives the lie to its unchecked desire to be Creator rather creature. This is why Abel's blood cries out from the ground, which now becomes a source of cursing to humanity rather than blessing. Cain's true state is thus revealed; he "shall be a fugitive and a wanderer on the earth" because he is at war with both his brothers and the very earth for the same reason: though a creature, he has usurped the prerogatives of the Creator. Cain thus clearly reveals the true result of attempting to be as god knowing good from evil—he is the tyrant-god who, as much as the beast, must live outside the city.

Nevertheless, it is Cain who founds the first city. Why is this? How is it that this fugitive and wanderer becomes the first citizen? Has the Lord made yet another threat and then backed off. Yes and no. Just as death was promised on the day they ate of the tree, and it was God who did the first killing for the skins to cover their nakedness; so too here the truth remains, but it is covered by "appearances" made by the Lord himself. For the truth proclaimed by the ground ("nature" so to speak), which cries out to the Lord with Abel's blood, is that of the *lex talionis* that "whoever sheds blood, by man his blood shall be shed."[8] Cain knows this law implies his

---

[8] The grounding of this law in the nature of things initially created before the Seventh Day comes out in the following blessing given to Noah after the flood: "For your lifeblood I will surely require a reckoning; of every beast I will require it and of man; of every man's brother I will require the life of man. Whoever sheds the blood of man, by man shall his blood be shed; for God made man in his own image" (Gen. 9:4-6). That this "law" of retaliation is grounded in our created nature is borne out in the last

own destruction which is why he cries out that it cannot be borne. "My punishment is greater than I can bear. Behold, thou hast driven me this day away from the ground; and from thy face I shall be hidden; and I shall be a fugitive and a wanderer on the earth, and whoever finds me shall slay me" (Gen. 4:13-14). But the Lord knows that this punishment involves an unending cycle of violence that would destroy not just Cain but the entire human race. Vengeance has no stop, for justice would demand the death of all human beings; so God must somehow intervene if nature itself is not to swallow up the unnatural violence introduced by humanity. The unnatural actions of humanity that lead to our natural destruction must therefore be met by an equally unnatural act of God that protects us from the destructive fruit of true justice.

The Lord's "Not so!" to Cain's complaint is thus a sort of negative fiat, one that corresponds to the second-order artifice that provides for human survival in the midst of their own murderous self-destruction. It is the "not so" to the natural fruits of our own artificial self-destruction, yet this negative fiat also holds out the hope that someday nature will no longer be at war with us and that we can once again be at one with it. Meanwhile, artifice is where we must live, so it is the Lord himself who provides the first and essential act of artifice that makes of us the sort of political creatures we are.

> Then the Lord said to him, "Not so! If anyone slays Cain, vengeance shall be taken on him sevenfold." And the Lord put a mark on Cain, lest any who came upon him should kill him. Then Cain went away from the presence of the Lord, and dwelt in the land of Nod, east of Eden.
> Cain knew his wife, and she conceived and bore Enoch; and he built a city, and called the name of the city after the name of his son, Enoch (Gen. 4:15-17).

The mark of Cain, not there by nature and so the first artificial sign, brings out the essential role of artifice in all human politics.

---

line, which is why Cain can know the results of his action without being told.

Nature in tandem with Cain's violation of It makes of him a wanderer, someone unfit to live together with others. Nonetheless, this artificial mark of God, by instilling mutual fear of God's own vengeance, makes it possible for Cain himself to found the first city.

With this mark of Cain, then, we get the Bible's own account of the nature of the city that is surprisingly similar to that given by Glaucon in the *Republic* and later, Hobbes in the *Leviathan*. Cain, who is in truth a wanderer and unjust, can now appear to be a city dweller and hence, by implication, just. It is, in other words, the "appearances" rather than the truth that allows humans to live together in the city. Unfortunately, true justice would destroy us, so some sort of lie or appearance must be found behind which humanity can hide that truth in order to live together. So just as the Lord covered the nakedness of Adam and Eve with skins from a slain animal, here too the Lord himself must hide humanity's naked murderousness by means of an artificial mark that provides a shield of threatening divine violence behind which humans can hide their own.

The mark of Cain thus seems to be the Bible's way of indirectly revealing the political function of tragedy in much the same way that Plato does in the fifth book of the *Republic*. For the immediate connection between the mark and the founding of the first city, along with the discrepancy of the essential wanderer appearing to be sedentary, brings us before the heart of tragedy that we have seen earlier. The mark of Cain is that work of artifice that provides the foundation of the city by hiding from its citizens and thus making livable the essentially antisocial and violent forces in their hearts. It is that work of artifice that always involves the gods in some way and yet is filled with mutual fear and threatened or actual violence. Yet it is only against this backdrop that it seems possible to either found a city or maintain it. This "mark" thus reveals the essential *nomos* of the city, why convention makes the city what it is, and yet why it is always in tension with what it can only appear to be—"nature" or the "way things truly are."

What is uniquely different about this biblical "mark" as opposed to the usual artifice of tragic narrative is that the artificer and his goals are explicit and center-stage. In this story of the first founding and the artifice of God that makes it possible, we see what is at stake in God's activity of creating order out of the chaos of our own created disorder. We must be saved from ourselves and spared, as of yet, the full knowledge of the truth of our own undoing. Bringing order out of the watery chaos of rebellious human making is thus the essence of all tragedy, which like all tragedies, hides the fullness of the truth in order for us quite literally to live. Most tragedies, however, are merely an extension of the sort of making that led to the problem in the first place: they merely put off the inevitable, which is why they are fundamentally repetitive. In this case, the narrative directionality is linear for its incompletion and stopgap nature is manifest; which is also why each later act of divine making involves a new and responsive element. What stays the same is that these divine "laws," "marks," or "signs" by sparing us the full vision of our nakedness and supplying us instead with a tragic vision of some sort of *nomos*, providing the appearances within which we can alone live. Nevertheless, what is crucially different is their temporal directionality that always anticipates something new because of the manifest inadequacy of the old.

When Agathon in the *Symposium* describes tragedy as the calm at the eye of the storm—or more immediately, when we see in the *Enuma Elish* the tragic theogony of the ordered world being created out of the corpse of the slain sea-goddess Tiamat—we can see that the spirit of God brooding over the face of the watery deep is the Bible's own alternative account of the true workings of tragedy. All are agreed that human politics is a precarious achievement surrounded by threatening chaos and violence, which is why images of the sea, the abyss, and wilderness, along with the various sorts of artificed means of surviving and passing through their respective terrors, are paramount. In the case of the Bible, this motif of rescuing out of the sea or water, by going under or through, will repeat itself in various ways throughout. Whether it be Noah's ark that spares only a few from the destructive and yet just flood, or the crossing of the Chosen through the Red Sea and the Jordan, or the Ark of the Covenant itself that is carried with the Israelites as they pass through the midst of their enemies, all these types are typical of the same "tragic" operation seen in the covering with skins and the mark of Cain. All of these are acts of God's second-order making out of his preexisting human and historical materials that is most akin to our own poetic and technical making.

Yet the difference in the midst of this similarity is all-important. Each of these narrated events is related to one another as types, a relationship that Auerbach connects to both their linear succession and their vertical relationship to the God whose extrinsic relation to space and time is exemplified by his creation *ex nihilo*. The fact of this typological relationship thus brings all these events together in a way that gives them an entirely different quality than the usual founding narratives of cities or religions. They aren't the same old tragic foundings, repeated over and over again; instead, each one is a new event, something different is added and more is learned about the past ones even as something new is anticipated in the future. In other words, what is different about the Bible's sort of tragic making is that it is always founded against the creation *ex nihilo* with which it begins and with which it ends. The tragic motifs of the Bible are thus always found within an overarching comedy, and this bracketing renders them ineffective in the usual way of tragedy, since it is the comedy that gives them their point. They are narratives in which the poet and making, both human and divine, is the main theme rather than what is made—the narrative itself. This thematic centrality of making is precisely what makes these seemingly tragic narratives ultimately comedies.

What we have in the Bible, then, is a comic account of tragedy that is at great pains to explain why tragedy is needed, why it is nevertheless a lie and a mere appearance, and how that need can be overcome. The onus of the Bible is thus to reinstate nature, but in such a way that it exposes the true nature and role of artifice. From the very beginning, with the puzzling dual account of creation, what is being set up is a distinction between the "comic" creation out of nothing and the "tragic" making needed to maintain us here and now. This tension, however, is driven by its forward movement toward a new comic act of creation that will reinstate the original creation by its very newness. That tension, as we will see in the story of Abraham, will be between the outward and historically present sign of God's working, and the invisible and forward looking faith in God's ability to create out of the "nothing" of death and sterility. The reason for this tension is that it leads to a sort of "reality training," wherein the true nature of the human situation becomes progressively more directed toward its source in the creator *ex nihilo* who nonetheless is intimately involved in the political affairs of human making. What God brings forth is always a new development, a new involvement in history that points ahead to an entirely new sort of existence free from the constraints of outer appearances and death. And as we shall see in the story of Abraham, the appropriate response to God's orientation toward this not yet present newness is the act of faith that takes this promised end as more real than outward appearances and seeming facts.

Abraham, who will become the father of an entirely new people, is called by the Lord to exemplify the true homeless and fugitive essence of humanity by being called out from his country and kin to be a wanderer. By thus living out the truth behind the appearances Abraham points the way to overcoming the very need for them. For Abraham as Abram is promised that his descendants shall be as many as the stars in heaven. "And he believed the Lord; and He reckoned it to him as righteousness" (Gen. 15:6). The problem with this promise, however, is that his wife Sarah's womb is sterile and she is past child-bearing years. The object of Abraham's faith is thus no more visible than the stars during the day, yet by believing in spite of both appearances and facts to the contrary, Abraham shows his belief is not in the workings of God who merely brings order out of chaos, but rather in the God who brings something out of nothing—the comic creator *ex nihilo*. As Paul will later describe it in his Epistle to the Romans, the God in whom Abraham believed is the one "who gives life to the dead and calls into existence the things that do not exist" (Rom. 4:17 RSV). So just as a successful comedy always requires the consent of the audience to the comic poet's manipulations to make believable his improbable happy endings, so too here, the faith of Abraham is the essential correlate to the improbable and downright impossible promises of his Creator.

What does not require faith but only presupposes it and points ahead to its fulfillment is the artificial sign or seal of circumcision. This sign, by shedding some blood and tampering with our "unnatural" nature, makes an "appearance" that does not hide but rather points ahead to a new reality that can only truly be grasped by faith. For in its shedding of blood and its connection to our hidden "private" parts (that in their very political and sexual privacy are the locus of both our shame and need to hide in the first place), circumcision speaks to this need to hide in the short term and yet will overcome this need in the long term. The later plea by Moses to "circumcise your hearts" (Dt. 10:16) is thus no more than the elaboration of the true relation between outward sign and appearance and inward substance and truth. Moses, reputed by moderns to be the quintessential law giver, got the point that they all missed—that God's law is not designed to hide, but rather to finally reveal the higher and more "natural" reality of the heart.

And lest we as readers miss the point, in the story of Abraham and Isaac, the relation between blood sacrifice, appearances, types, faith, death and the future are all laid out for us in exemplary detail. The Lord has finally given Abraham a son out of the sterile womb of his wife Sarah—the first fruit of his faith one might say. Yet still God tests Abraham, asks of him an outward burnt offering of his first-born son, Isaac, upon Mount Moriah. In obedience, Abraham takes the fire and the wood along with his son to the mount of sacrifice, whereupon his son asks: "Behold, the fire and the wood; but where is the lamb for a burnt offering?" Abraham said, "God will provide himself the lamb for a burnt offering my son" (Gen. 22:7-8). Abraham has got it right; the sacrifices that have covered humanity's nakedness have been provided by God all along, but the crucial question to be asked here is whether sacrifice is the last word. Is there to be no end to the bloodletting?

Abraham's answer is in the deed itself. He sets his son, the child of promise, upon the altar and raises the knife because the fulfillment of God's promises must be the overcoming of death itself.

> But the angel of the Lord called to him from heaven, and said "Abraham, Abraham!" And he said, "Here

am I." He said, "Do not lay your hand on the lad or
do anything to him; for now I know that you fear
God, seeing you have not withheld your son, your
only son, from me." And Abraham lifted up his eyes
and looked, and behold, behind him was a ram,
caught in a thicket by his horns, and Abraham went
and took the ram, and offered it up as a burnt offering
instead of his son. So Abraham called the name of
that place The Lord will provide; as it is said to this
day, "On the mount of the Lord it shall be provided"
(Gen. 22:11-14).

The willingness of Abraham to act in the present is based upon his
belief in the future—that God will himself provide the sacrifice
and, in so doing, fulfill his promise even from the dead.

The provision of the ram caught in the thicket shows how in
the present God works for Abraham. But the logic of the entire
story in relation to past events and as it looks forward to future
events—both in the prophets and in the Gospels—reveals what is
in store in the future, and how it will restore and make new again
what was there from the very beginning. For what we see in the
provision of the lamb/ram/scapegoat instead of Abraham's own
flesh and blood is the hidden essence of all earlier sacrificial bloodletting; the logic behind the animal skins, the acceptance of Abel's
sacrifice, the mark of Cain, and circumcision. Abraham's faith that
God will provide is thus based upon understanding the "why" of
God's past actions, upon understanding their essentially provisional nature.[9] At the same time, it is based upon an understanding
of the future in the light of God's first act as first principle, which
is the creation of everything out of nothing. In this light, the future
is unbounded, and our own self-imposed limits of death and mutual violence, provided for by God in the present, are believed to
be fully and finally overcome in the future. In fact, it will be

---

[9] In this light, Melchizedek's sacrifice of bread and wine would be Abraham's lesson in the true nature of things wherein blood no longer needs
to be shed because peace is a reality rather than a mere appearance. The
two orders of priesthood based upon either Aaron or Melchizedek mentioned in Hebrews, along with the institution of the Eucharist by Christ
himself which commemorates his own bloody death with bloodless and
deathless vegetable matter would seem to bear this out.

through this belief, especially when believed by that child of Abraham named Jesus, that the promise will fully and finally be fulfilled and all the nations shall be blessed through Abraham's descendants.

The story of Abraham and Isaac is thus the key to the typological structure of the Bible. The one central reversal and plot development that will make sense of all that preceded will be God sending his own Son as *the* bloody sacrifice; for only when the blood shed and the death died is his own, can the return from that death to life fulfill at once the need for covering and the need for an entirely new life. The tragic death of God's own Son, along with his comic resurrection, transforms retroactively all the past tragic sacrifices into comic second act complications that will be fully resolved and untied in the third and final act. So whereas all the earlier signs, marks, laws and artifices hid the audience from the poet and themselves, the final comic revelation of the poet himself, along with the overt overcoming of the need to lie by the overcoming of death, exposes all and makes all future lying and appearances pointless and laughable.

What will be "provided," in other words, is the creator/poet himself—lifted high up upon the mount, speaking for himself, and announcing that all along we haven't known what we are doing. Yet all along the true poet *has* known, and the progress of his poem has been to let his audience in on it. For the return of true knowledge and the life that goes with it is the point of the story. The return of the tree of life with the dying poet upon it who is the fruit that must be eaten if we are finally to know good from evil is the comic reversal, which, in its very unexpectedness and yet fittingness, shows who is in charge of the story.

We, the audience, must either give ourselves over to the comic poet's manipulations because his manipulations are at one with Creation itself, or we must resist because manipulations are just that, manipulations, with only a human hand behind them. Deciding which is true, when the facts seem to bear out only the latter, puts us in the very same position of Abraham. For his willingness to sacrifice his only son can only make sense in light of the God who calls into existence things that do not exist. Otherwise, like all other humans in stories of human beginnings, he is just another spectacular murderer. But since this is a comedy, and since the poet himself is always center stage and the central concern of the narrative, the point of the story is both the internal character's and the external reader's decision regarding his true status—is he the creator of the universe *ex nihilo*, or is he like all human things, as much created as creator? Faith, or the lack thereof, is thus the answer to this question continuously raised from the Bible's first page.

If we turn to the actual giving of the Law to the Israelites upon Mount Sinai, we can now read it in the light of all the earlier artificial conventions given by God since the clothing of Adam and Eve in the skins of slain animals. The very opening, "I am the Lord your God, who has brought you out of the land of Egypt, out of the house of bondage" (Ex. 20:2), reminds us of the grounding of this law in the historical and temporal acts of God that have the seemingly tragic structure of rescuing the few out of the depths of watery chaos. The ordered and chosen few who have been brought through the sea of threatening and disordered waters, rescued from the angel of death by the sign of lamb's blood on the lintel, can now be given the law that is based upon and is a continuation of these provisional founding deeds. Take for example the Passover.

> The blood shall be a sign for you, upon the houses where you are; and when I see the blood, I will pass over you, and no plague shall fall upon you to destroy you, when I smite the land of Egypt . . . . And when in time to come your son asks you, 'What does this mean?' you shall say to him, 'By strength of hand the Lord brought us out of Egypt, from the house of bondage. For when Pharaoh stubbornly refused to let us go, the Lord slew all the first-born in the land of Egypt, both the first-born of man and the first-born of cattle. Therefore I sacrifice to the Lord all the males that first open the womb; but all the first-born of my sons I redeem.' It shall be as a mark on your hand or frontlets between your eyes; for by a strong hand the Lord brought us out of Egypt (Ex. 12:13, 13:14-16).

Blood has been a sign throughout, from the mark put upon Cain, the first born son of Adam and Eve, to the slain ram substituting for the death of first born Isaac. It has continually been the sign of redemption from the death that is God's by right. This artificial sign that spares us from the rightful slaying of the first-born is thus a continuation of the mark of Cain that is put upon the forehead in order to remind us of the words and deeds of the Lord in sparing us. What this mark reminds us of is that, as in all tragedies, civilized order is rescued from the watery chaos by means of some sort of violence and bloodshed; and that it is this very bloodshed as an artificial and mimetic murder that spares us from the plague of actual and unending murder that would otherwise be our lot. As with all human conventions or laws, the law given by God himself will also be founded upon bloodshed; but what is different here is that the need for this foundation is fully revealed along with its ultimate inadequacy and provisional nature. But to make this manifest is also to make all human law suspect as fundamentally unjust, for it is only the true God himself who can righteously take the life of another. It is the one true God, then, who can and must *not* keep his actions hid.

"You shall have no other gods before me. You shall not make for yourself a graven image, or any likeness of any thing that is in heaven above, or that is in the earth beneath, or that is in the water under the earth; you shall not bow down to them or serve them; for I am the Lord your God am a jealous God" (Ex. 20:4-5) In this very first commandment, we have the Creator's competition with human making, making that is disguised under the mask of various divinities. This competition with idolatry will be the central contest of Israel's entire history. The point of this God's deeds is thus shifted from the deeds themselves (all important in tragedy) to the doer of the deed, the God who is a jealous God and will have no other gods before him. Who this God is is the point of both his deeds and his law; and lest that point be missed, the prohibition against graven images sets the deeds of this God in competition with all human making itself and its inevitable connection to the tragic gods worshipped by humanity.

This connection between other gods and graven images is the Bible's agreement with the argument of Plato that gods are made by us to serve our needs, a service that only works if that arrangement is obscured. Consider the reference to the hidden "earth beneath," "heaven above," and "under the water," all three of which imply images of what could not possibly be seen in the first place. The mimetic gods of human making are just as Plato implied they were in his analogy of the mirror—images of the whole that is neither seen nor understood, so is instead made by ourselves as poets. By prohibiting this sort of making, the only image of God allowed is mankind itself, who in being alone created in the image of God is prohibited from finding that image in any thing made rather than themselves as makers. Self-consciousness of ourselves as makers and artificers is thus the only cure for idolatry, for idolatry is the perennial temptation to worship the thing made and forget oneself as maker. By prohibiting this political move *par excellence*, the law that prohibits idolatry thus strips bare the political landscape and the protective covering of human deceit, and leaves behind only the self-knowledge gained through the history of God's stage management rather than our own. His play is a comedy and he expects our applause, but in order to gain it he will let us in on exactly what he is doing even though the end will be beyond our wildest imaginings.

For this law that is placed in an ark, carried across the dried-up Jordan, and later placed inside the temple in Jerusalem continues on in this journey until its outward, artificial appearances are fulfilled in the inward, "natural" deeds of the embodiment of truth itself found in the gospels. The "gospel" is the good news that "newness" is indeed the last word, and that the images provisionally made by God find their fulfillment in the only true image of God, humanity itself. The story of Jesus is thus claimed to be not merely a story, but rather a concretely historical human life that gives completely what was provided for only provisionally in the earlier stories of the Bible. The human body and deeds of Jesus are thus signs that are no longer "signs" at all, of the true reality promised by those signs' provisional and typological character. Jesus' human nature replaces and subsumes the need for all artifice and reveals fully what was self-consciously absent in the animal skins in Eden, the mark of Cain, Noah's ark, circumcision, the ram in the thicket, the Law, and the Ark of the Covenant, to name but a few. In the Gospels of Jesus, the claim is made that his life is the point to the law, its fulfillment, and that his life is the fulfillment of the legal relationship to the actions of God, inculcated since God accepted the sacrifice of Abel and graciously refused the faithful sacrifice of Abraham.

Take, for example, the Gospel According to John. At the very beginning of this gospel we have a rehearsal of the creation story found in Genesis, yet a rehearsal that thematizes and makes explicit the implications of both the "let us make" passages and the narrative persona who can witness and second those acts. The way John's gospel does this is to pick up on the role of the spoken nature of God's fiat, the Word that brings something from nothing.

> In the beginning was the Word, and the Word was with God, and Word was God. He was in the beginning with God; all things were made through him and without him was not anything made that was made (Jn. 1:1-3).

What this introduction does for John's gospel is bring out the overriding and central point that the main character in his narrative and the source of his good news is the divine poet himself who has created all of reality. What was found at the beginning in Genesis is now being witnessed to by John as the source of an entirely new beginning in human history, for all genuine newness can only have its source in the God who creates something out of nothing. The Word that was in the beginning is thus the one artificer who does not create out of existing material but rather brings those very materials into existence through his own utterance.

"In him was life, and the life was the light of men. The light shines in the darkness, and the darkness has not overcome it" (Jn. 1:4-5). Here we have the reiteration and connection between the living breath of God that animates Adam with the first thing created on the first day, light. The Word is both that which gives life to men (and in chapter six we see Jesus claim he must be eaten to live just as the fruit of the Tree of Life was to have been eaten) and the "light that enlightens every man" because in him wisdom is no longer separated from existence. Darkness cannot overcome the light because it still shines in the darkness created by mankind on its own, thereby revealing it for the nullity it is. How that light has continued to shine in man-made darkness is what John will turn to next, for just as in Genesis, once creation *ex nihilo* is established, God's other sorts of working can now have their proper context.

"There was a man sent from God, whose name was John. He came for testimony, to bear witness to the light, that all might believe through him. He was not the light, but came to bear witness to the light. The true light that enlightens every man was coming into the world" (Jn 1:6-9). John the Baptist as a person stands to Jesus as the Spirit of God brooding over the waters stand to creation *ex nihilo*. John is as type to antitype, Israel to Jesus, Old Testament to New Testament, and promise to fulfillment. In other words, he is not the light itself, but rather the lamp that chronologically precedes the true light even though it ontologically follows and is dependent upon it as its source. The logic of light itself to a lamp is the logic of God's provisional workings narrated in the scriptures to the new creation brought about by the Word. As Jesus will later say of John the Baptist:

> He was a burning and shining lamp, and you were willing to rejoice for a while in his light. But the testimony which I have is greater than that of John; for the works which the Father has granted me to accomplish, these very works which I am doing, bear me witness that the Father has sent me. . . . You search the scriptures, because you think that in them you have eternal life; and it is they that bear witness to me; yet you refuse to come to me that you may have life (Jn. 5:35-40).

John the Baptist is thus a stand-in for the entire typological structure of the Old Testament, for both bear witness of what precedes them and will follow them as something new that will put the old into shadow.

When John sees Jesus come before him to get baptized, John exclaims: "Behold, the Lamb of God, who takes away the sin of the world! This is he of whom I said, 'After me comes a man who ranks before me, for he was before me.' I myself did not know him; but for this I came baptizing with water, that he might be revealed to Israel" (Jn. 1:29-31)· The temporal relations that make typology possible are thus laid out for us directly by John, along with their goal of training Israel to recognize their fulfillment when it arrives. When John makes this recognition, "Behold, the Lamb of God!" he is merely reiterating the central statement of Israelite faith, passed down by Abraham to his first son, that "God will provide himself the lamb for the burnt offering" (Gen. 22:8).

And again, why is John a 'baptist' of all things? John came baptizing with water that Jesus might be revealed to Israel, yet he himself recognizes Jesus as "he who baptizes with the Holy Spirit" (Jn. 1:33). This relation of water to Holy Spirit is essentially the relation of provisional tragedy to fulfilling comedy. Baptizing in water is continuous with all the stop gap provisions and rescues from our rightful deaths, epitomized by our rescue from the watery depths surrounding Noah's ark and the local sea-goddesses surrounding the Ark of the Covenant. So whether it is passing through the Red Sea or the Jordan, the artifice of making these "arks" is continuous with the artifice of the mark of Cain and animal skins; for all are the 'tragic' means by which God spares humanity from the full consequences of its own murderousness. Yet by being oriented toward the future and manifesting their artificial and provisional nature, these works of God reveal rather than hide the lying and murderous "nature" that causes us to need them in the first place. Where that "nature" comes from, Jesus claims, is the devil, who from the very beginning (the beginning of the watery chaos that was without form and void?) was both a liar and murderer. "He was a murderer from the beginning, and has nothing to do with the truth, because there is no truth in him. When he lies, he speaks according to his own nature, for he is a liar and the father of lies" (Jn. 8:44). The initial murder and lie of Cain that is covered over by the mark on his forehead is thus the threatening chaos we must be spared from. Yet the way God spares us is through his working rather than our own; for his working, narrated throughout the scriptures, looks forward to the one who will baptize us through the very same Holy Spirit that brooded over the face of the waters. In that baptism, creation will begin all over again, for by suffering the full effects of our own murderousness and deceit upon his own body, when that body rises from the dead, we who rise with him will have a new natural beginning rather than an artificial one.

That is the all-important significance to the climax of John's prologue: "And the Word became flesh and dwelt among us, full of grace and truth" (Jn. 1:14). It is Jesus' very own body, naturally unnatural mortal "flesh" like our own, that by dying and rising again, will provide the new "nature" that will gracefully allow us to live in complete truth. This new nature, manifested in his post resurrection presence of eating and drinking among his disciples, overcomes the need for the artificial conventions of the law entirely, even those given by God to Moses. "For the law was given through Moses; grace and truth came through Jesus Christ" (Jn. 1:17). The temptation to make graven images of the unseen image of God that makes us who we are is also overcome; for the man Jesus as the incarnation of the Word itself reveals that invisible image in the only way it can be. "No one has ever seen God; the only Son who is in the bosom of the Father, he has made him known" (Jn. 1:18).

The body of Jesus is thus the natural fulfillment of the artificial signs given throughout the Old Testament. Just as the temple in Jerusalem was a continuation of the type seen in Noah's Ark and the Ark of the Covenant, Jesus will speak of his own body as a continuation of this same typology. What makes his body the antitype to all these types, however, is that in being raised from the dead, this type hearkens to the creation out of nothing rather than making out of what already is. When it is demanded that Jesus give a sign for his authority in cleansing the money-changers from the temple, his answer, "Destroy this temple, and in three days I will raise it up" (Jn. 2:19), is later remembered by the disciples as speaking of his own body. "But he spoke of the temple of his body. When therefore he was raised from the dead, his disciples remembered that he had said this; and they believed the scripture and the word which Jesus had spoken" (Jn. 2:21-22). This equation of Jesus' words and Scripture, along with their confirmation by the sign that is no longer a 'sign'—the resurrection—leads to the very same belief as that of Abraham because of its connection to an entirely new creation.

Yet even those who do not believe in the God who calls into existence what doesn't exist are part of this story. It is after all a comedy, so in contrast with tragedy, inclusion rather than exclusion is the rule. Even those who don't get the joke or refuse to be taken in are part of a comedy, for the audience's response to the poet is itself the central part of the narrative. In this light consider the ironic role of Caiphas:

> Caiphas, who was high priest that year, said to them, "You know nothing at all; you do not understand that it is expedient for you that one man should die for the people, and that the whole nation not perish." He did not say this of his own accord, but being high priest that year he prophesied that Jesus should die for the nation, and not for the nation only, but to gather into one the children of God who are scattered abroad (Jn. 12:49-52).

In his typical role as the high priest presiding over the once a year sacrifice for the sins of Israel, Caiphas brings out the poetic control God has over both plot and meaning. It is this control that allows for the possibility of typology and the imperative that both internal characters and external readers read between the lines and understand former things in the light of latter things. Caiphas speaks the truth, but the truth is not his own but rather the poet's. Prophecy, as we have also seen in the case of Samuel, is a two-edged sword, for the prophet is as little master over the truth of his words as his hearers. [10] Both are equally subject to the divine stage management that is working toward the long-range educational project climaxing here in the Gospels.

The difference between the truth of Caiphas' utterance and the disciple John who can now grasp the nature of that truth is that

---

[10] Cf. Sternberg's discussion in *Biblical Narrative*, 94-98.

the very same spirit that gives the truth to prophecy is the Holy Spirit that Jesus baptizes in. The access to truth given through prophecy is now available to the disciples and is the source of their ability to witness to and write down events in the life of Jesus that they couldn't possibly have direct access to.

> This is the disciple who is bearing witness to these things, and who has written these things, and we know that his testimony is true. But there are also many other things which Jesus did; were every one of them to be written, I suppose that the world itself could not contain the books that would be written (Jn. 21:24-25).

What is key to the Gospels, then, is that the historical events of Jesus' life and ministry outstrip any human writing about those events. For it is the concrete life of this poet, of both creation itself and the written poem found in the scriptures, that is all important here, and not the various narratives of that life found in the Gospels. By fulfilling the narrative of the scriptures, the life, death, and resurrection of Jesus has also broken free of the need for artifice altogether. The impossible possibility believed in by his disciples is that along with an entirely new nature Jesus' ministry has also given us new access to the truth. And that truth is that what is found in this one man's life is greater than all that could possibly be written about it. Narrative, so to speak, has been swallowed up in victory.

In the proleptic vision of John that ends the New Testament, we find a description of what has been anticipated in faith, at least since Abraham, and experienced directly in the post resurrection appearances of Jesus—a new heaven and new earth.

> Then I saw a new heaven and a new earth; for the first heaven and the first earth had passed away, *and the sea was no more*. And I saw the holy city, new Jerusalem, coming down out of heaven from God, prepared as a bride adorned for her husband; and I heard a loud voice from the throne saying, "Behold, the dwelling of God is with men. He will dwell with them, and they shall be his people, and God himself will be with them (Rev. 21:1-3, *emphasis added*).

In terms of typology, what we see here is what the drive toward "newness" informing the narrative of the Bible has been driving at from the very beginning—the elimination of the watery sea of chaos made on our own as usurpative first agents. Whether created by Lucifer and one-third of the angels described earlier in Revelation, or our own seduced attempt to imitate the divine knowledge of the goodness of our own autonomous creation, the sea, at least since the time of Cain, has been the threatening chaos of death, lies, and murder surrounding the bubble of human civilization. The "sea," in other words, is the human need for tragic narrative in order to found and maintain civilization, so it is fitting that in the comic resolution of the entire plot of human existence the sea of this tragic need should disappear entirely.

To replace it is the city of the new Jerusalem that in its very newness is the city founded upon comedy—a comedy wherein the comic poem reigns, Prospero-like, over the erotic marriage-feast that signals an end that is also an entirely new beginning. What this marriage between Christ and his people also sews up is the missing image of God ("in the image of God he created them, male and female he created them"), not fully seen since Adam and Eve perceived their own nakedness. The natural creativity of humanity is thus restored from its harlotries with artificial idols, through its marriage with the true God and Emmanuel who as comic poet has now permanently married stage and audience.

> And I saw no temple in the city, for its temple is the Lord God the Almighty and the Lamb. And the city has no need of sun or moon to shine upon it, for the glory of God is its light, and its lamp is the Lamb . . . and there shall be no night there . . . . Then he showed me the river of the water of life, bright as crystal, flowing from the throne of God and of the Lamb through the middle of the street of the city; also, on either side of the river, the tree of life with its twelve kinds of fruit, yielding its fruit each month; and the leaves of the tree were for the healing of the nations. There shall no more be anything accursed, but the throne of God and of the Lamb shall be in it, and his servants shall worship him; they shall see his face, and his name shall be on their foreheads. And night shall be

no more; they need no light or sun, for the Lord God will be their light, and they shall reign for ever and ever (Rev. 22:1-15).

Along with this erotic fulfillment goes the political fulfillment of true justice, with no need for appearances and the conventions of law. Justice now flows down like a river from the throne of the one man who in his unity with the Father can truly know the whole and thus render true justice based upon genuine knowledge of good and evil. This river of justice is the living water that replaces the "unplumbed, salt, estranging sea" of appearances and deceit taken for granted in human politics founded upon tragedy.

Along with the disappearance of the tragic sea of appearances there also goes the disappearance of the signs and provisional marks and laws given by God himself. For when the true light appears, all shadows retroactively cast by it and all lamps that provisionally prepare for it disappear in the true light of dawn. Whether it be the temple or the mark on Cain's forehead, all these artificial and provisional works of God are swallowed up by the embodied new creation whose body is the true temple, just as it is his name rather than the mark of Cain that is written upon his servant's forehead. Light as the correlate of wisdom and intelligibility now becomes all in all, with no need of sun or moon, for the creator of both, who has now become flesh, reigns as the one true philosopher who in knowing himself also knows the whole.

The comedy of the Bible, in other words, is that we can indeed have our cake of the love of wisdom and eat it too. The laughter appropriate to this comedy is not seen in the plot itself, for it is the plot of a happy ending. Where the laughter comes is in us, the readers. Should this plot prove to be not just a happy comic plot, but happy for us, then for us it not just preached, but is in fact, the "good news." For to get this joke and laugh at it proves a most unusual form of comedy. It is not ultimately we who get the joke, but the joke who gets us. And that is how it should be, if we are dealing here with the God who is the ultimate maker of all jokes, along with everything else.

XII: THE THEOLOGY OF A COMIC BIBLE

IF READING the Bible as a comedy allows the philosophical life to take seriously the truth of this book and the faith that goes along with it, then we should expect indications of this in the most profound Christian thinkers. In fact, one might expect reflection on how the love of wisdom and the writings of Scripture relate from the very get go. In this chapter we will examine a highly influential Christian theologian who has done just that. For in Thomas Aquinas, doctor of the Catholic Church, we find that he was compelled to begin his *Summa Theologiae* with just this question. Only a God who authored both nature and a comic poem would seem to allow a theologian to remain every bit the philosopher, so Aquinas' entire endeavor hinges on whether God is indeed the author of Holy Scripture. With his use of *techne* and *theoria*, Aquinas' discussion will also remind us of Plato and Aristotle's formulation of the issues, even while pointing us ahead to the problematic emphasis upon "making as knowing" that will become paramount in modern thought. In Aquinas, unfortunately, we may well be dealing with the last great Christian theologian to understand the full import of the genuine challenge philosophy presents to Christian faith and how the Bible must be read if we are to meet that challenge. After him the distinction between the two may have become so attenuated that this question rarely presents itself.

Aquinas begins his *Summa Theologiae*, with the question "whether any teaching is required in addition to philosophy."[1] This question echoes one of the formative questions of this book:

---

[1] Thomas Aquinas, *Summa Theologiae*, ed. Thomas Gilby, O.P., (Garden City, New York: Image Books, 1969), I, q.2, a. 1.

"Whether the Bible or philosophy is right is of course the only question which ultimately matters."[2] This initial question of Aquinas is only the first question to be raised in answering the larger question as to "what Christian theology is and what it covers"; and the last question to be asked in answering this larger question is "whether Scripture can be interpreted in more than one sense."[3] Between these beginning and ending questions, then, we have what is finally at issue between philosophy and theology. For it is how we understand the role of narrative, I believe, that will ultimately determine what our answer to the larger question in theology will be. Let us see, then, how Aquinas understands the narrative of Scripture.

Aquinas answers his first question as to whether we need something besides philosophy by answering, "yes," what we need is "Sacred Doctrine." But to explain this answer, we need to discuss it under two aspects: the first is God himself and the other is Scripture. For it is only because of God that we need something beyond philosophy, and it is only in Scripture that we find an answer that can go beyond the competence of philosophy. The question of God brings out the limits of philosophy inasmuch as in asking the question we discover that our desire to know the whole demands for itself a satisfaction that it is not naturally capable of giving. The life of philosophy, then, is a life lived toward an end that it cannot ever satisfy, and if it in any way possesses that end, it is only in the form of a question, the question Aquinas interprets as the question of God.

This situation of the philosopher (apart from his comic expression of that situation), is what I have argued earlier constitutes the tragic life of the philosopher, inasmuch as what is known in that life is one's own ignorance and the inevitable "fall" awaiting even the greatest heights of theoretic vision. Aquinas, however, explains this situation from a different standpoint—that of a theologian—which is to say, from a vantage point that derives from the writings of the scriptures. As he puts it, "God destines us for

---

[2] Quoted above in the first chapter from Strauss's *Rebirth of Classical Political Rationalism*, 206.

[3] Aquinas, *Summa Theologiae* I, q. 1, a. 10.

an end beyond the grasp of reason . . . . Now we have to recognize an end before we can stretch out and exert ourselves for it. Hence the necessity for our welfare that divine truths surpassing reason should be signified to us through revelation."[4] The claim that Aquinas makes about what our end is is therefore not itself knowledge of that end (the essence of God), but rather the knowledge deriving from that end that we find in Scripture. The knowledge that this end even exists must therefore result from the "effects" of that end, whether natural or gracious, and so in Scripture we can know of this end only because it is itself the gracious effect standing in until we see its author and our God—our true end—"face to face."[5]

What this means for theology is that any claim it makes to be a form of knowing, *theoria*, or science is only the claim one would make for a subalternated science that derives its first principles from a higher science. The science of theology thus stands or falls on the strength of that higher science, which in this case is the knowledge God has of his very own essence. Since there is no higher end than this to our knowing, and since this is the end that Scripture speaks of as promised to the blessed at the end of time, the science of theology, even though subalternated, is still the highest science we are capable of.[6] Philosophy, which knows no principles higher than itself, is therefore lower than theology precisely because of that ignorance. In its own eyes, however, it cannot help being tempted to look upon theology as in the low position of a *techne*, like optics, that obtains its principle from a higher *theoria* such as geometry, or in this case, philosophy itself. Aquinas is aware of this temptation, for he would agree that Sacred Doctrine is analogous to the *techne* of optics that needs a higher theoretical science to give it justification. Nevertheless, he will still argue that in the unique case of theology, the subalternated and technical status of the written scriptures and the Sacred Doctrine that derives from them are higher than the theoretical ignorance of philosophy.

---

[4] Aquinas, *Summa Theologiae* I, q. 1, a. 1, *respondeo*.

[5] Aquinas, *Summa Theologiae* I, q. 1, a 7, ad. 1.1a, Q1, Art. 7.1.

[6] Aquinas, *Summa Theologiae* I. q. 1, a. 2, *respondeo*.

Consider Aquinas' argument in relation to some of the images of Plato. Let us say that a subalternated science is always "erotic," and therefore contrives to mediate between the theoretical world of the divine and the poverty of the human; whereas the divine world of theoretic first principles is as unerotic as Socrates in the eyes of Alcibiades. Whatever science there is to writing, let us say a "poetics," would thus always be subalternated to some sort of theoretical knowing that would function as the "divine" inspiration motivating it. Yet, as we have seen in Plato, comic writing would have the advantage of realizing this subalternated status, while tragic writing must needs obscure it. That is also why tragic writing directly competes with the higher claims the philosopher makes for his unerotic *theoria*. In this light, the oddity of Aquinas' account of theology as a subalternated science is that, in contrast with tragic writers, he is admitting its dependent status, even while directly claiming that this "*techne*" is higher than the *theoria* of philosophy. While the admission is comic, the hubris seems tragic, but this odd appearance makes sense when we realize that the writings of Scripture are "authored" by God himself and so this *techne* is accomplished in the light of the only *theoria* possibly higher than that of the philosopher. The temptation of the philosopher would thus be to see Christianity as another result of tragic writing and thereby overlook that it shares philosophy's same grounds for preferring comic writing—its unrestricted desire for the truth that has no place for the "lie." In the eyes of the theologian, then, philosophy and theology are pursuing the same end; it is only in the eyes of a philosopher that a misunderstanding can take place.

In Aquinas' words, "there is nothing to stop the same things from being treated by the philosophical sciences when they can be looked at in the light of natural reason and by another science when they are looked at in the light of divine revelation"—which is to say, the temptation to exclude comes from the side of natural reason rather than the reverse.[7] Yet because this temptation results from the Aristotelian demotion of both *phronesis* and *techne* in the light of philosophical *theoria*, Aquinas must argue that theology is

---

[7] Aquinas, *Summa Theologiae* I, q. 1, a. 1, ad. 2.

still theoretical even in its dependence upon the technical quality of the written scriptures. He therefore contends that: "every practical science is concerned with what men can do and make, thus ethics is about human acts and architecture about building. Christian theology, however, is about God, who makes men and is not made by them. It is therefore more contemplative [theoretical] than practical."[8] God who has the *techne* to make both humanity and the scriptures, thereby transforms the technical subalternation of theology into a sort of *theoria* that is even higher than that of philosophy because of his dual role of the one true poet of the whole and a particular writing within that whole. "Whereas some among the philosophical sciences are theoretical and others are practical, sacred doctrine takes over both functions, in this being like the single knowledge whereby God knows himself and the things he makes."[9]

It comes as no surprise, then, that it is only in Christian theology, dependent as it is on God as the author of its scriptures, that we find the philosophical notion of God as in a technical relationship to the whole (universal instrumentality), rather than being the whole itself or a significant part of it. It is the God who writes, and who writes comically, that creates a world *ex nihilo*. The question of whether God is transcendent or immanent thus seems to be part and parcel of the "Bible or philosophy" question. If we were to transpose this question of Strauss' to Aquinas' "which is the highest wisdom?" we can see that Aquinas' unconditional reply would be that "Holy teaching should be declared to be wisdom highest above all human wisdoms;" and that, appropriately enough, the analogy he will choose to explain this sort of wisdom is the knowledge the architect has of his own design. [10] The knowledge of the whole desired by the philosopher can thus be known only by something transcendent of that whole, namely the "first and final cause" that knows the whole because it has made the whole. In contrast with Aristotle's "unmoved mover," or Plato's "ideas"

---

[8] Aquinas, *Summa Theologiae* I, q. 1, a. 4, *sed contra*.

[9] Aquinas, *Summa Theologiae* I, q. 1, a. 4, *respondeo*.

[10] Aquinas, *Summa Theologiae* I, q. 1, a. 6, *respondeo*.

or even "demiurge," the highest wisdom is not the contemplation of the highest intelligibility *within* the whole (with the consequent residual unintelligibility that constitutes both the source of the tragic character of the philosophical life and the need for tragic writing's duplicity), but rather the contemplation of the first cause of the whole itself, which makes of the whole a complete intelligibility with no remainder.

This wisdom of Sacred Doctrine is therefore the highest because there is no residual unintelligibility, in the same sense that a comedy ties up all the loose ends at the end of the final act. In both, however, this closure can only come about because of the transcendent, creative role the poet stands in to his creation. Yet if we are to claim that the intelligibility of the whole is indeed that of a comedy, such knowledge can only come about by means of something outside the whole. For us as inextricably part of that whole, then, such knowledge is impossible. This knowledge is only possible if the comic poet of the whole reveals himself within that whole; if he himself trots upon his stage, so to speak, and reveals who created the whole by some means within it. As Aquinas puts it: "Holy teaching goes to God most personally as deepest origin and highest end, and that not only because of what can be gathered about him from creatures (which philosophers have recognized . . .) but also because of what he alone knows about himself and yet discloses for others to share."[11]

And yet this sort of revelation of the whole, even in its claim to being the highest, comes very close to being one of the lowest, for what is claimed to be the whole may be no more than the whole created by a tragic or comic human poet. If such a poetic whole makes a claim to knowledge of the true whole, then it is either tragically hubristic or ridiculously comic. Aquinas would seem to agree, for any argument deriving from the authority of a poet's creation, tragic or comic, is among the weakest, and yet "though weakest when based on what human beings have held, the argument from authority is most forcible when based upon what God

---

[11] Aquinas, *Summa Theologiae* I, q. 1, a. 6, *respondeo*.

has disclosed."[12] The "proper authorities" of sacred doctrine are thus not the "Prophets and Apostles who wrote the canonical books," but rather "the revelation made to" these writers.[13] Which is to say, the authority of Scripture is as the poem authored by God, and although there are indeed human writers of it, none can claim "authorship" because its only and unique claim to authority is that the God of the universe is also its author through revelation.

But what a revelation! Could God truly have authored such writings as these? In Article 9 Aquinas raises this objection seriously, for in asking "Should holy teaching employ metaphorical or symbolical language?" he is asking the equivalent of Plato's question as to whether anything serious should ever be put in writing. This objection to Scripture as revelation has two aspects: the first being that the seriousness of theoretical concerns regarding God and the whole (in other words, the philosophical life) should have no serious dealings with the shadow-world of images and poetry, while the second is the obvious baseness of scriptural content that marks it off as a comedy and thus rules it out as the religiously serious writing of a tragedy. Aquinas puts this first objection as follows: "Now to carry on with various similitudes and images is proper to poetry, the most modest of all teaching methods. Therefore to make use of such similitudes is ill-suited to holy teaching," and then elaborates this in his second objection which consists of the claim that symbols and images obscure rather than clarify the truth. [14] This second objection he puts in the familiar context of relating base characters with play and comedy, and noble characters with seriousness and tragedy. "Again, the nobler the creatures, the closer they approach God's likeness. If then the properties of creatures are to be read into God, then at least they should be chiefly of the more excellent not the baser sort; and this is the way frequently taken by the scriptures."[15]

---

[12] Aquinas, *Summa Theologiae* I, q. 1, a. 8, ad. 2.

[13] Aquinas, *Summa Theologiae* I, q. 1, a. 8, ad. 2.

[14] Aquinas, *Summa Theologiae* I, q. 1, a. 9, arg. 1.

[15] Aquinas, *Summa Theologiae* I. q. 1, a. 9, arg. 3.

In reply to these objections Aquinas provides an indirect defense of the comic nature of Scripture that both sets it apart from philosophy and yet establishes the nature of its claim to be superior to it in comprehensiveness. For when he replies that "Holy Scripture fittingly delivers divine and spiritual realities under bodily guises" since "we are of the kind to reach the world of intelligence through the world of sense," he is making both a political and a philosophical claim because the body is both a cognitive limitation and *the* essential limitation at the heart of all politics. What makes it fitting that Scripture delivers spiritual realities under bodily guises is that the truths of Scripture are accessible not only to the philosopher who is capable of living outside the city, but even more so to everyone else who lives *in* the city and so must have the highest truth made politically accessible. Just as tragic writing can normally supply both the religious and political needs of the city because of its powerful imagery and solidifying impact upon its common audience, so too can Scripture, because of its imagery, make itself politically accessible to one and all and thereby form the foundation of a unique political entity—the kingdom of God, revealed even unto babes. In this way, the "uneducated may then lay hold of them, those that is to say, who are not ready to take intellectual truths neat with nothing else."[16]

Yet what of those who *are* able to take their truths "neat," the philosophers? Does not this distinction itself go to show that Scripture is just another case of tragic writing; politically effective, yes, but no more than an expedient lie? The defense against this suspicion is that, even though political, Scripture is not a case of tragic writing. It is instead the unique case of a politically effective comedy that can and should satisfy the philosopher as well. The reason is that Scripture is written in a similar fashion to Plato's dialogues. The comic nature of both invites us in to discover their meaning, and this meaning must be the joint creation between poet and audience. As Aquinas puts it, "the minds of those given the revelation are not allowed to remain arrested with the images but are lifted up to their meaning; moreover, they are so enabled to

---

[16] Aquinas, *Summa Theologiae* I, q. 1, a. 9, *respondeo*.

instruct others."[17] And in a passage that Sternberg reproduces when he describes Scripture as moving between "the truth and the whole truth," Aquinas continues: "In fact truths expressed metaphorically in one passage of Scripture are more expressly explained elsewhere. Yet even the figurative disguising serves a purpose, both as a challenge to those eager to find out the truth and as a defense against unbelievers ready to ridicule."[18] The comic nature of Scripture thus lures the reader on to greater and greater knowledge in spite of (or better, because of) its playfully comic surface. But this comic exterior also serves the other purpose of exposing (which in the comic world also means to include, as we have seen in Frye's description of the comic role of the clown or fool) those who will have nothing to do with the writings of the poet by their choice to laugh *at* him rather than *with* him. Scripture thus opens itself to ridicule in the same way Socrates did—ironically—in order to reveal others even as it seems to conceal itself. The difference is that what is either revealed or concealed is not the life of the philosopher, but rather the life (and death) of the divine poet himself in relation to the life of his readers.

This also accounts for why the baser characters of Scripture are essential to its comic function. For the juxtaposition and contradiction of base characters with the divine intent throughout Scripture directs the reader to discover and recreate for himself, so to speak, a proper knowledge of the divine; a discovery that does not stay with the initial images themselves (as in a tragedy) but rather ascends beyond them to truths that are every bit as transpolitical as the philosophers'. When Aquinas thus says "the figure of base bodies rather than those of fine bodies more happily serve the purpose of conveying divine things to us," we can see that he is advocating the use of the "low style" of comedy over the "high style" of tragedy; because

> thereby human thinking is the more exempt from error, for the expressions obviously cannot be taken in

---

[17] Aquinas, *Summa Theologiae* I, q. 1, a. 9, ad. 2.

[18] Aquinas, *Summa Theologiae* I, q. 1, a. 9, ad. 2.

the proper sense of their words and be crudely as-
cribed to divine things; this might be more open to
doubt were sublime figures evoked, especially for
those people who can summon up nothing more
splendid than physical beauty. Secondly because un-
derstatement is more to the point with our present
knowledge of God. For in this life what he is not is
clearer to us than what he is; and therefore from the
likenesses of things farthest removed from him we
can more fairly estimate how far above our speech
and thought he is. Thirdly, because thereby divine
matters are more effectively screened against those
unworthy of them.[19]

In other words, the scriptures must essentially be a comedy, because only a comedy recognizes its own contrived quality, brings
to the fore our ignorance, and excludes the proud characters of a
tragedy. And yet what lies behind all these comic qualities is what
Auerbach describes as the temptation for the "sensory" element to
"succumb under the dense texture of meanings," because the trajectory of Scripture's comic narrative is to go beyond itself, toward
both poet and reader. Auerbach's "figuration" then, is an accurate
description of the functioning of Scripture's comic nature, but rather than viewing this as a temptation, Aquinas in his last article of
this section will explain its proper role as both an aspect of the
generic role of comedy in Scripture, and also the unique role it has
as the one divine comedy authored by God.

The heart of what Aquinas says about Scripture, and also the
heart of what I am trying to argue for in describing the comic function of the Bible, is found in Aquinas' central quotation from St.
Gregory.

St. Gregory declares that holy Scripture transcends all
other sciences by its very style of expression, in that
one and the same discourse, while narrating an event,
transmits a mystery as well.[20]

---

[19] Aquinas, *Summa Theologiae* I, q. 1, a. 9, ad. 3.

[20] Aquinas, *Summa Theologiae* I, q. 1, a. 10, *sed contra*.

From this passage we see how "one and the same" comic discourse, by narrating a comic "event," also opens us up to the possibility that it may be transmitting a mystery as well. In other words, there is something about the very nature of biblical discourse, the fact that it is a comic rather than a tragic narrative, that allows it to transcend all other sciences, both technical and theoretical, if, and only if, God is its author. The "style," its comic structure, opens up this possibility; it is not the style but rather its "stylist" that moves it from being a possibility to an actuality that transcends all other sciences.

Aquinas bases this entire article on the belief in God as the author of holy Scripture, and the effect that belief has on interpreting its meaning. As he puts it in his reply: "That God is the author of holy Scripture should be acknowledged"; or again later: "Now because the literal sense is that which the author intends, and the author of holy Scripture is God who comprehends everything all at once in his understanding, it comes not amiss, as St. Augustine observes, if many meanings are present even in the literal sense of one passage of Scripture."[21] In other words, the problem of interpreting the meaning of Scripture is a problem that can only be solved by attending to the role of its author; and yet this attention to its author, or poet, is nothing less than the attention to the poet required in all comedies. The interpretative move to a transcendent author, then, does not overthrow or subvert the literal sense but is rather based upon and arises out of it. Scripture requires of any reader first and foremost a good reading; and it is that reading of its literal and comic sense that demands of us readers that we answer the question as to who its real poet is. For it is only in answering this question, even if we answer that it could not be God, that we can gain full access to its meaning. In typical comic reciprocity, the question as to the poet is equally a question as to the audience. It is only in this full circuit, then, this self-conscious-because-comic-circuit, that the full sense of a comic discourse's meaning can be found.

---

[21] Aquinas, *Summa Theologiae* I, q. 1, a. 10, ad. 1.

Yet, because of the historiographical intent of Scripture, the comic, literal sense must also be connected with what Aquinas calls the "historical" sense of Scripture. The way Aquinas explains the meaning of these juxtaposed terms is to set them off from what he calls the "spiritual senses" of Scripture. The literal and historical sense, he says, is the power of adapting words to convey meanings, a power that is no more nor less than the power of all human written and spoken discourse. Yet in addition to this power, there is the power of adapting "things themselves" to convey meanings, a power that is reserved to God alone. In speaking of Scripture, therefore, he says:

> In every branch of knowledge words have meaning, but what is special here is that the things meant by the words also themselves mean something. The first meaning whereby the words signify things belongs to the sense first-mentioned, namely the historical or literal. The meaning, however, whereby the things signified by the words in their turn also signify other things is called the spiritual sense; it is based on and presupposes the literal sense.[22]

The "specialness" of Scripture is thus the specific qualities of its poet, and those qualities are the unique qualities of the poetic maker of the world who alone can fit things-to-things together in the world to make meaning, just as any human poet can puts words-to-things (and presumably words-to-words) together to make meaning in his own verbal world. The fact that Scripture has both a literal and spiritual sense is thus a result of the nature of its poet, and not a quality of the poem itself.

But what of the poem itself? Is Aquinas here espousing a crude sort of literalism, with a one-to-one correspondence between words and things, thereby making God the only poet who has written anything interesting or worth reading? Not at all, for if we turn to his reply to objection three on the parabolic sense, we will get a clear view of all that he includes under the literal sense: "The parabolic sense is contained in the literal sense, for words can

---

[22] Aquinas, *Summa Theologiae* I, q. 1, a. 10, *respondeo* (emphasis added).

signify something properly and something figuratively; in the last case the literal sense is not the figure of speech itself, but the object it figures."[23] Aquinas goes on to give an example of what he means by this in the following example: "When Scripture speaks of the arm of God, the literal sense is not that he has a physical limb, but that he has what is signifies, namely the power of doing and making."[24] Now we have a better idea of what Aquinas could mean with the literal sense. For what this literal sense must include is the entire range of figurative meanings of the text (which would seem to include both the living and dead metaphors of language). This implies that the parabolic sense of Scripture is the norm rather than the exception, and that the literal sense includes the entire gamut of good readings with all their comic possibilities. On the other hand, it is only the spiritual sense that can include the actuality of meaning found in Aquinas' "Sacred Doctrine" and "articles of Faith"; for this meaning can only flow from the reader's assent to the literal claim that God, rather than any man or men, is in fact the comic poet behind this comic narrative.

The difference between the literal and spiritual senses of Scripture thus seems related to the two poles of Scripture as both a generic and a specific comic narrative. As a generic comedy the literal sense of Scripture does not presuppose the "spirit" but only the usual human understanding that grasps the comic invitation to join in. The specificity of this particular comedy, however, is that the reader must also ask whether God is truly its poet, which means the veracity of its narrative world is entirely dependent upon an affirmative answer to that question. A negative answer still maintains the Scripture's generic comic quality, but it demotes the specific quality to the level of the usual fantastic claims to naturalness in comic artifice that always subvert themselves because of the very nature of that artifice. The rediscovery of nature that the generic artifice of comedy invites one toward, is the discovery of a nature that must be intrinsically independent of narrative and so can be found in the reader alone. The affirmation of God as the poet of

---

[23] Aquinas, *Summa Theologiae* I, q. 1, a. 10, ad. 3.

[24] Aquinas, *Summa Theologiae* I, q. 1, a. 10, ad. 3.

Scripture, on the other hand, leads to an entirely new nature, one wherein the reader must be "born again" and so gain access to a new creation of a supernatural variety.

As a technique, scriptural narrative has its literal sense in common with all other comic narratives; but this technique opens up the unique possibility that the reader will not only inhabit the text's world while reading, but will also become a part of a new world that concretely exists both inside and outside the text. The veracity of that unique world is discerned by the spiritual sense, but the invitation to join that world rather than merely recollect some sort of "nature" is why Aquinas always couples the literal with the historical sense. That the literal sense of Scripture thus always includes a historical sense (in contrast with say, Aristophanes' comedies where an historical intent is nonexistent or in Plato's dialogues where a concern for historical veracity would be to miss the point), ties us in directly with the our discussion of "realism" in Auerbach and Frei. There we determined that the meaning of the Bible is the history that includes both the text and its readers, a history that demands of its readers that they live their lives in its writing and so also demands that they allow its literal sense to make historical (and political) sense of themselves. The equation of the literal and historical sense thus has to do not with the accuracy of its historiography, but rather the accuracy of a literal reading that discovers within the text an historical impetus. The key contrast, then, would be with Plato's dialogues, that if read well, do *not* ask that we live in its writings, but rather ask only that we live outside them in the relatively ahistorical and apolitical life of the philosopher.

The equation between the historical and literal sense in Scripture is therefore what opens up the believing reader to the vertical dimension of Auerbach's "figural interpretation," for the transhistorical connection between "things and things" is at best only a literary conceit apart from faith. If that faith is presupposed, as it is in Aquinas' account of theology, then the grounding of Scripture in its initial historical and literal sense also allows for the three spiritual senses described below.

Now this spiritual sense is divided into three. For, as St. Paul says, *The Old Law is the figure of the New, and the New Law* itself, as Dionysius says, *is the figure of the glory to come.* Then again, under the New Law the deeds wrought by our Head are signs also of what we ourselves ought to do.

Well then, the allegorical sense is brought into play when the things of the Old Law signify the things of the New Law; the moral sense when the things done in Christ and in those who prefigured him are signs of what we should carry out; and the anagogical sense when the things that lie ahead in eternal glory are signified.[25]

What all three of these spiritual senses have in common is the presupposition of a historical continuity between the concrete situation of the believing reader (belief is what makes them "spiritual," for faith is a spiritual rather than natural possibility) and the historical world enunciated in Scripture. Another way of putting this would be to say that if the reader believes his own concretely historical world to be part of the comic world described as beginning with the creation *ex nihilo* in Genesis and ending in the future with the new creation seen in the vision of Revelation, then the spiritual senses are no more than what flows from assenting to the historical and literal sense of Scripture as true. Nothing is added to what is already potentially there, other than the transformation of the reader himself to an already existing, even though "new," reality. The "newness" of the New Law in the allegorical sense is thus part and parcel of the morally new covenant brought about by Christ and the anagogical new creation that will bring this story to full closure. The centerpiece to this entire circuit, however, is the historical life, rather than mere narrative, of the "head," Jesus Christ of Nazareth, who in his unique historical particularity ties in the narrative of the Old Testament with both the literal and concretely historical position of any given reader.

Consider this in the light of Umberto Eco's own account of why the literal and historical are combined in Aquinas:

---

[25] Aquinas, *Summa Theologiae* I, q. 1, a. 10, *respondeo.*

But why should it be that the spiritual senses found in scripture are not equally literal? The answer is that the biblical authors were not aware that their historical accounts possessed the senses in question. Scripture had these senses in the mind of God, and would have them later for those readers who sought in the Old Testament for a prefiguring of the New. But the authors themselves wrote under divine inspiration; they did not know what they were really saying. Poets, by contrast, know what they want to say and what they are saying. Poets therefore speak literally, even when they use rhetorical figures.[26]

Apart from the too historicized account of the historical meaning of Scripture, what Eco brings out well here is that the literal meaning of all other poetry besides the Bible, comic or tragic, is entirely literal even at the heights of its rhetorical and poetic force. Poets *as* poets do not, and cannot, write historically, and it is the Bible alone that makes the unique claim to be historical even while remaining poetic. Such a claim, of course, remains merely a "literal" claim, however unique or odd, if God is not in fact its poet and Jesus is not the Word of God that mediated all of creation.

There are thus two demands that must be distinguished in reading the Bible. The first is the demand to read it well and to discover the uniqueness of its comic narrative structure and the uniqueness of its literal claims to be also historical—a demand upon any reader whatever his or her beliefs are. The second demand, dependent upon the first, is that the reader decide whether or not this poem's claim to be authored by God himself is true; for it is only in the yes or no of that decision that the full circuit of meaning of this text can reach fruition, a fruition that fulfills the "historical" sense, so to speak, along with the spiritual sense.

What happens after Aquinas is that for the most part, "history," as the entire sequence of time and events independent of our making and the result of God's universal instrumentality, gets transformed into the more literary category of a human artifact. To effect this transformation humans, or humanity in general, must

---

[26] Umberto Eco, *The Aesthetics of Thomas Aquinas*, trans. Hugh Bredin, (Cambridge University Press, 1988), 154.

take upon themselves the role of the providential and creator God. In this way, the ultimate question of God's authorship becomes moot, and the spiritual senses of Scripture are added to and inflate the significance of the historical and literal senses. Merely human comedies take on the gravity of "divine" significance, and the divine comedy of Scripture becomes one among many other and competing ideological and poetic products of human manufacture. In the next part we will see how this may have come about and how it has affected our understanding and expectations for both comedy and tragedy.

PART THREE:

MODERN COMEDY AND
TRAGIC NOSTALGIA

XIII: DANTE, MACHIAVELLI, AND THE TECHNOLOGICAL COMEDY OF MODERNITY

One would think that the generation in which I have the honor of living must be a kingdom of god. But this is by no means so; the vigor, the courage, that wants to be the creator of its own good fortune in this way, indeed, its own creator, is an illusion, and when the age loses the tragic, it gains despair. In the tragic there is implicit a sadness and a healing that one indeed must not disdain, and when someone wishes to gain himself in the superhuman way our age tries to do it, he loses himself and becomes comic.

—Søren Kierkegaard, *Concluding Unscientific Postscript*

IN THE transition from the specific comedy of the Bible to the more generic and familiar comedy of modernity, there is a crucial step along the way—Dante's *Divine Comedy*. While looking back and discerning the comic nature of Scripture as elaborated by Aquinas, Dante also looks ahead and blazes a trail for merely human comedies with godlike aspirations. If one might call the Bible a "serious" comedy because of its claim for God as its author, by the time we get to Dante, and even more so his fellow Italian Machiavelli, comedy attempts to be taken seriously in its godlike political and technological aspirations. How one undertakes such a task without affecting our very notion of God will become even more manifest in our later accounts of Hegel and Nietzsche, but for now, let us examine the path blazed by Dante and what I mean by the "technological comedy of modernity."

In Dante's various writings about poetry he has managed to give us two different accounts of allegory that have given later scholars no end of trouble and confusion. The first, the "allegory of the poets" he describes in his *Convivio* as follows:

[O]ne should know that writing can be understood and must be explained mainly in four senses. One is called the literal [and this is the sense that does not go beyond the letter of the fictive words, as are the fables of the poets. The other is called allegorical] and this is the sense that is hidden under the cloak of these fables, and it is a truth hidden under the beautiful lie, as when Ovid says that Orpheus tamed the wild beasts with his zither and caused the trees and stones to come to him; which signifies that the wise man with the instrument of his voice would make cruel hearts gentle and humble, and would make those who do not live in science and art do his will; and those who have no kind of life of reason in them are as stones. And the reason why this concealment was devised by wise men will be shown in the next to the last treatise. It is true that theologians understand this sense otherwise than do the poets; but since it is my intention here to follow after the manner of the poets, I take the allegorical sense as the poets are wont to take it.[1]

Here, Dante is describing the "allegory of the poets" in contrast with the "allegory of the theologians." Yet because the allegory of the theologians is left unexplained there is much room for confusion. In his explanation of the "allegory of the poets," wherein the sense is hid under the cloak of fables and the "truth hidden under the beautiful lie," we can see that Dante is giving a classic account of how a comic poem can be interpreted. For when the artifice of a "beautiful lie" is recognized to be such, this leads one to look for the comic intention of discovering some sort of "nature" on one's own because of its tacit invitation to co-creation. Dante, in other words, is describing for us a reading of Ovid that is both comic and highly influenced by the sort of reading appropriate in the wake of Plato's comic dialogues; one that expects to discover indications about the life of philosophy through the reading of poetic artifice. In giving this account Dante also seems very much aware that this sort of comic allegory is similar to but not the same sort

---

[1] Dante Alighieri, *Convivio*, quoted in Charles Singleton's *Dante's Commedia: Elements of Structure*, (Baltimore, The John Hopkins University Press, 1954), 85.

of allegory described by the theologian Aquinas. For as we have seen in Aquinas, the allegory of the theologians requires God to be the author of its text because it rests upon the connection of things to things that only a divine poet can truly effect.

If we make a loose equation between allegory and comedy (for it is comedies rather than tragedies that generate allegories because of their interpretive vehemence and explicit contrivance), we can say that Dante is also distinguishing two sorts of comedies: the generic comedy of the poets and the specific comedy of Scripture which is of central concern to the theologians. If we recall the role of contrivance in comedy, however, we can see that one of the key problems facing all generic comedies when it comes to taking their allegorical meanings seriously is the obvious fact that the very beauty of their lies casts doubt upon the truth of their meanings. It is this corrosive effect of comic contrivance that renders them much less politically effective than tragedy and makes them useless as a foundation for any sort of lasting political accomplishment. In the case of Scripture, on the other hand, this ineffectiveness is negated by its demand to be received as authored by God. What the comedy found in Scripture gains in specificity also enhances its power to effect political change. When Dante thus distinguishes between his two allegories and claims to be writing only an allegory of the poets, we must keep the political uniqueness of the scriptural comedy very much in mind.

If we remember that the *Convivio* was written prior to Dante's *Commedia*, and that he will later give a startlingly different account of allegory to explain how his own comedy should be read, we should pay close attention to this seeming change of rules in midstream. Consider, then, the very different account of allegory we find in Dante's letter to Can Grande written during or even after he had begun his major work:

> To elucidate, then, what we have to say, be it known that the sense of this work, is not simple, but on the contrary it may be called polysemous, that is to say, "of more senses than one"; for it is one sense that we get through the letter, and another which we get through the thing the letter signifies; and the first is called literal, but the second allegorical or mystic. And

this mode of treatment, for its better manifestation, may be considered in this verse: "When Israel came out of Egypt, and the house of Jacob from a people of strange speech, Judea became his sanctification, Israel his power." For if we inspect the letter alone, the departure of the children of Israel from Egypt in the time of Moses is presented to us; if the allegory, our redemption wrought by Christ; if the moral sense, the conversion of the soul from grief . . . if the anagogical, the departure of the holy soul from the slavery of corruption . . . . And although these mystic senses have each their special denominations, they may all in general be called allegorical, since they differ from the literal and historical. . . . we must therefore consider the subject of this work [his *Commedia*] as literally understood, and then its subject as allegorically intended.[2]

What should leap out immediately from this account is its close modeling after the similar four senses of Scripture we have seen in the last chapter on Aquinas. What should next be noted is the startling divergence from it. For in Dante's account we find no mention of what is all important in Aquinas', the complete dependence of the three spiritual senses upon the authorship of God. In Aquinas it is God alone who can connect "things to things" and so make the allegorical, moral, and anagogical senses genuinely distinct from all the various figural meanings that could be included in the literal sense.

If we ask why Dante should obscure this central element in Aquinas, the suspicion occurs that Dante is single-handedly trying to prepare the way for his own comedy, which, even while self-evidently human, can still share in the prerogatives of the divine comedy of Scripture. On this reading, Dante would seem to be deliberately fudging the distinction between generic comedy and the specific comedy of Scripture in order to give his own *Commedia* the political power of the latter. In applying the above account of allegory rather than his earlier account of the "allegory of the poets" to his own *Commedia*, Dante has chosen an example from the specific comedy of Scripture, explained its allegorical sense in an

---

[2] Dante, *Convivio*, 87.

almost identical way to Aquinas' four senses, and yet then implicitly applied it to his own work by leaving out the crucial element that makes the entire comparison disproportionate and misleading—that God alone can give these four senses to a single literal and historical meaning because of his unique prerogatives as a poet.

Does Dante share those attributes of connecting "things to things"? Obviously not. Why then is he fudging this crucial distinction between Aquinas' allegory of the theologians and what for him can only be an allegory of a poet? The answer, I think, is that Dante is trying to link the comic structure of his national epic with the preexisting comic structure of Scripture and thereby borrow from it the political power that, left to itself, his own comic poem would lack. Dante, in other words, is trying to be the poet of Italy in the way Virgil was the poet of Rome; but whereas Virgil could write a tragedy with its consequent political power, Dante is trying to have the same politically unifying effect in the different world of Christendom by writing a comedy.[3] To succeed in such an endeavor, however, he must tie his own comedy to the coattails of the genuinely "divine" comedy of the Bible, which is why in describing his method of allegorizing he blurs the distinction between the allegory of the theologians and that of the poets, and so lets drop the crucial question as to who the actual author of his poem truly is.

Take, for example, the famous words engraved on the gates of Hell, and ask yourself who they speak of, Dante or the creator God of the Bible.

---

[3] This is admittedly a highly eccentric account of Dante's motivations, but whatever scholarly justification there is for it would come from the work of Ernest Fortin, whose class I attended at Boston College, "Dante and Christianity," opened up all sorts of unusual and yet compelling readings of the *Commedia*. Although his arguments are in no way responsible for my own, they are well worth the reading if only to shake Dante scholarship from its dogmatic slumbers. See, "Dante and Averroism," Actas del V Congreso Internacional de Filosofia Medieval 2: (739-746) 1979. "Dante and the Rediscovery of Political Philosophy," in *Natural Right and Political Right: Essays in Honor of H. V. Jaffa* (Durham: North Carolina Academic Press, 1984). "Dante and the Structure of Philosophical Allegory," Miscellanea Mediaevalia 13:1 (434-440) 1981.

JUSTICE URGED ON MY HIGH ARTIFICER;
MY MAKER WAS DIVINE AUTHORITY,
THE HIGHEST WISDOM, AND THE PRIMAL
LOVE.
BEFORE ME NOTHING BUT ETERNAL
THINGS
WERE MADE, AND I ENDURE ETERNALLY.
ABANDON EVERY HOPE, WHO ENTER
HERE.[4]

In the poem these words seem to speak of the biblical God, and yet it is Dante, the poet in his own poem, who reads them and asks of Virgil their meaning. Why must he do this? Because this gate with its writing is nowhere found in Scripture. Who then authored these verses, and who created everything in them? This very same poet who is in his own poem, and it is his artifice that would lead us to take at face value these artificed Gates of the God who also makes an appearance in his poem. The willing suspension of disbelief in this case is thus made more willing by its repetition of the pattern in Scripture, but the less "willing" this suspension—because unnoticed and instinctively pious—the more Dante can share the godlike power of creating the future "justice" of an entire nation. By conflating his own poetic role with that of God, Dante has paved the way for equating the artificial world of the poet with the natural and historical world of God; and in so doing he has given powers to the comic poet unheard of in the ancient world.

To put this another way, if we contrast Aquinas' account of polysemy with that of Dante's, we can see that Aquinas' view of literal/historical meaning includes all of Dante's' four senses, while Dante's four senses tacitly exclude Aquinas' three spiritual senses and therefore the possibility that God is the author of Scripture. So whereas Dante must piggyback upon Aquinas' account to give credence to his own, the net effect of this tactic is to undermine the very point of Aquinas' distinction and so leave us *de facto* with only the allegory of the poets. It is the sort of distinction endemic

---

[4] Dante, Alighieri, *Inferno*, trans. Mandelbaum, (New York, Bantam Books, 1982), Canto III.

to the early moderns wherein God and supernatural things are distinguished from natural and artificial things in such a way as to
leave room only for a serious concern with the latter.[5]

The overwhelming success of this tactic is exemplified by the
influential article by Charles Singleton, that in recycling the Romantic attack upon allegory, also repeats what is at the heart of this
attack. For in making all human poets divine, the Romantics followed in the footsteps of Dante by erasing the difference between
their own creations and the unique claims of the biblical comedy.
In this light, when Singleton argues that one should have no difficulty making the choice that the *Divine Comedy* is an "allegory of
the theologians" in spite of the continuing efforts to see it as an
"allegory of the poets," we can only wonder what he means when
his explanation runs as follows:

> Whereas, if we take the allegory of the *Divine Comedy*
> to be the allegory of the theologians, we shall expect
> to find in the poem a first literal meaning presented
> as a meaning which is not fictive but true, because the
> words which give that meaning point to events which
> are seen as historically true. And we shall see these
> events themselves reflecting a second meaning be-
> cause their author, who is God, can use events as men
> use words. *But*, we shall not demand at every moment
> that the event signified by the words be in its turn as
> a word, because this is not the case in Holy Scripture.[6]

By saying the "first literal meaning" is presented not as fiction but
as true, Singleton has entirely avoided the question of the difference between words which can be presented *as* true or false, and
things and events, which either do or do not exist, or have or have
not happened. At the level of poetry this distinction is, of course,

---

[5] For example consider Machiavelli's discussion of the Church in *The
Prince*, and the entire structure of Hobbes' *Leviathan* wherein the discussion of the "Christian Commonwealth" that takes up almost a third of
his book serves merely to show why it is entirely irrelevant to Hobbes'
concerns.

[6] Charles Singleton, *Dante's Commedia: Elements of Structure* (Baltimore,
MD: The Johns Hopkins University Press, 1954), 90.

not important; but at the level of philosophy and theology this distinction is absolutely crucial which is why Aquinas has put it at the center of his entire thought as well as his account of Scripture. By resting content with "realism" as a substitute for reality, Singleton has entirely missed the point and fallen for Dante's ruse even while propagating it with sincere arguments of his own. But we should not be too hard on Singleton, for he is suffering from a philosophic confusion that has been endemic to literary criticism at least since Kant, if not before; a confusion which goes back to the equation of poetry and philosophy that Plato worked so hard to keep apart even while recognizing it as the common sense *status quo*. This sort of "natural supernaturalism," which will come to play such a large role in modernity, accounts for why "realistic" can function synonymously with "real"; and why Auerbach and Frei will have such problems making this distinction with respect to the Bible. For when the question of whether God is in fact the poet of Scripture is no longer raised, but is rather tacitly answered in the negative with the assumption that we are all godlike creators, then one of the most important possibilities of meaning in this world has been foreclosed, and the reading of Scripture becomes more and more a case of misreading.

My contention is that Dante has, self-consciously or not, assimilated to himself the world-making powers of the Christian God. What we see here is Dante's radically new approach to poetry that gives to the poet divine powers unheard of in the pagan world. By taking up the prerogatives of Scripture, the poet assimilates himself to the world-making powers of the Christian God through a sleight-of-hand that simultaneously elevates the poet's creativity even while undermining the uniqueness of God's. Such a move is not at all surprising in light of the similar move made by the later Romantics, and the connection that Nietzsche draws between the murder of God and the transformation of reality into fiction would here find its primordial origin. But this sort of move is quite surprising in Dante, at the high-water mark of medieval piety and, seemingly, the poetic embodiment of Thomistic philosophy.

Nevertheless, something odd did seem to happen at this point. Erich Auerbach, in commenting on this and the following period, notes a significant transformation that he is nevertheless loath to blame on Dante. For even though "Dante's work remained almost without influence on the history of European thought; immediately after his death, and even during his lifetime, the structure of literary, cultured society underwent a complete change in which he had no part, the change from Scholastic to Humanistic thinking." Drawing upon the example of Petrarch, Auerbach points out how even though a mere forty years younger,

> he is distinguished from Dante above all by his new attitude toward his own person; it was no longer in looking upward . . . . that Petrarch expected to find self-fulfillment, but in the conscious cultivation of his own nature. Although far inferior to Dante in personality and natural endowment, he was unwilling to acknowledge any superior order or authority; . . . . The autonomous personality, of which Petrarch was to be the first fully typical modern European embodiment, has lived in a thousand forms and varieties; the conception takes in all the tendencies of the modern age, the business spirit, the religious subjectivism, the humanism, and the striving for physical and technological domination of the world . . . . From Christianity, whence it rose and which it ultimately defeated, this conception inherited unrest and immoderation. These qualities led it to discard the structure and limits of Dante's world, to which, however, it owed the power of its actuality.[7]

What Auerbach points out here is the uniquely "Christian," and yet anti-Christian, inheritance following on closely after Dante. "Secularized" Christianity, the deliberate transformation and defanging of Christian doctrines into an immanent historical process, begun by Rousseau and attaining its high-water mark in Hegel, would thus seem no more than the full working out of a possibility built into the first Christian poetic epic and its author's

---

[7] Erich Auerbach, "The Survival and Transformation of Dante's Vision of Reality," *Dante: A Collection of Critical Essays*, ed. John Freccero (Englewood Cliffs, NJ, Prentice-Hall, Inc., 1954) pp. 10-11.

account of what he is doing. In the writings of this position's greatest exponent, Hegel, we can also see an explicit awareness that the understanding of this position must be laid out in terms of comedy and tragedy and the role they play *vis-à-vis* philosophy and Christianity. It is to Hegel, then, as well as the brilliant exception taken by Nietzsche and Kierkegaard, that we must finally turn in order to clarify and confirm how comic and tragic writing are central to the question of the Bible and philosophy, but before doing so, we must examine the new technological comedy that is at the heart of modernity.

If Dante felt that a new national epic that could unify a Christianized Italy must be in the form of a comedy, by the time we get to his fellow Italian Machiavelli, we find that the indirect fruit of Dante's attempt was a new type of comic writing altogether—the technological comedy of modernity. What I mean by this is a sort of comic writing that adopts the focus upon contrivance, the revealed poet, and subversion, from the comedies of Plato and the Bible, and then tries to make all these elements that bring about a happy, because contrived, ending *within* the poem, work *outside* the poem in the political life of both poet and readers. If this sounds similar to the comic effect of the Bible, it is; but what is crucially different is that the poet is every bit as mortal as his readers. The hubristic and yet laughable attempt of modern comedy is thus to create for itself a political unity that doesn't hide what it is doing but rather celebrates and revels in its power to do so. Modern comedy must therefore try to accomplish the same things as tragedy—founding and unifying the city—by somehow dealing with the problems of unshareability and its attendant violence we have seen elaborated in Plato and the Bible. It must do this, however, without hiding its own operations and the central role the poet plays in bringing them about. The poetic *techne* that has always played the foundational role in human politics must now be revealed and the appearances of religion and tradition must therefore be seen through. Nevertheless, religion and tradition must be seen through in such a way that people will still take their political world as seriously as their own individual erotic desires. By not hiding himself, the poet also makes a very different sort of poem—a comedy rather than a tragedy—so the overwhelming challenge of this modern "founder" is how he can reveal his artifice and yet still be taken seriously.

Machiavelli, the author of the comedy *Mandragola* among others, knew intimately how artifice works within a comic poem. More important, Machiavelli in *The Prince* was the inventor of the modern political comedy that attempts to make this sort of manipulation work *outside* of a poem. His "invention" was essentially to erase the difference between the "inside" and "outside" of a poem altogether by making artifice and its technical knowledge all that needs to be known and essentially all that there is. The world of nature grasped by *theoria*, or the knowledge of the creator God (both of which lay outside and above Platonic comedies and the scriptures and thereby subverted the ultimacy of their humanly poetic status), is here replaced by a "nature" that leaves the priority of artifice and poetry intact. "Nature" is now transformed into a sort of raw material out of which the poet, the politician, as well as any prudent man must shape the world in which he lives. In this "nature" the baser instincts of human action are conflated with the vagaries of chance and fortune; and the concern is no longer to know what can and can't be known and what humans tend to do for their own sake, but rather to know those things only as a means to the end of technological mastery. Just as a comic poet might use the manipulation of the predictably base motives of his characters in order to bring about some sort of desirable end, Machiavelli's poet is now the Prince himself or any sufficiently daring individual who is willing to learn the comic "techniques" taught by Machiavelli the master "comedian" of a thoroughly poeticized reality.

The rub, however, comes when the technical knowledge of the comic poet is extended beyond the poem itself, for then the "nature" that must always be presupposed or discovered through a comedy is radically altered. Whereas in most comedies the desirable happy "end" that must be brought about is either presupposed or is discovered in the readers themselves (which is why comedy can point to, but is not, the theoretical knowledge of natural "ends"), in the technological comedy of Machiavelli the knowledge of those ends are completely transformed into the knowledge of the "means." Nature as the raw material that *must* be manipulated does not give any guidance as to how or in which direction it *should* be manipulated, so the poet on his own—"will" and power cut off from reason—becomes the sole arbiter of what constitutes his happy end.

In spite of this incipient nihilism, there is an end continuously sought for by Machiavelli and the moderns; but it is an end that cannot be justified in terms of their own overt account of how to bring it about. It is the end that has always been the goal of tragedy—the control of unending human violence and the livable peace of a unified political entity. Yet because the poet is hidden in a tragedy, his end need not be thematized except insofar as it manifest as the "reality" that is seen by all on stage. In comedy, on the contrary, the manipulations of the poet *are* thematized, and so the happiness of the end must be agreed upon between poet and audience. When comedy has been cut off from any sort of "nature" independent of poetry, however, the only thing the poet can get the audience to agree with him on is the desirability of identifying with himself and his manipulative powers as poet. It is this very ability, then, the *virtù* itself of being able to achieve one's ends that becomes the central theme of modern comedy. The argument of modern technological poetry is that the unrestricted identification with the powers of the comic poet is itself the means to the end of happiness, both individually and collectively. Technical mastery is its own end, for "nature" has been transformed into a "mechanism" that is known only through that mastery.

The hidden belief of the modern thinking inaugurated by Machiavelli is that all of reality is essentially comic; which is to say, things will work out in spite of, or, better because of, every character in the play doing his or her own thing and following his or her individual desires. When Hobbes speaks of the Leviathan as "the machine that runs of itself,"[8] or when Kant speaks of a nation

---

[8] "For seeing life is but a motion of Limbs, the beginning whereof is in some principall part within; why may we not say, that all *Automata* (Engines that move themselves by springs and wheels as doth a watch) have an artificial life?. . . . For by Art is created that great LEVIATHAN

of devils being able to create a peaceful state, "as long as they can calculate,"[9] (i.e., as long as they each emulate the role of the comic poet), we can see this faith in action. This comic faith believes that the violence that must be dealt with in tragedy through catharsis and deception, can now be dealt with by turning it into a series of "mock beatings" that need not be taken seriously because they actually further the comic ends of the play.

How can this comic belief be taken seriously? For two reasons. The first is the essentially tautologous argument that "it works." Comic success is comic success, and if every man is his own poet he alone determines that success. The second reason allows for the intrinsically unlimited and unconstrained quality of the first; the overwhelming fact of death is abstracted from and the power derived from this deliberate avoidance, recoil, and willful act of blindness feeds the "mortal god" of the human comedy since as much as each character may fear death, no one character can ever die and still remain part of the play. Both of these reasons are, of course, ridiculous. But in comedy ridiculousness is part of the fun, and as long as the comic poet seems to know what he is doing, his own ridiculousness is overlooked because of the pleasure he gives us by joining in with him as he ridicules others. It is the very audacity of the modern comic poet that makes us take his poem seriously. Let us look us look more closely, then, at the full nature and extent of Machiavelli's audacity.

Following the arguments of others, I would say that Machiavelli has single-handedly shifted the relation between the philosophical life and the city; a shift that has proved to be a watershed in separating the "ancients" from the "moderns." [10] Hegel described this move as the "lowering of the heavens," but what concerns us here is how this move involved a different relation between philosophy and writing, and more specifically, philosophy

---

called a COMMON-WEALTH, or STATE, (in latine CIVITAS) which is but an Artificial Man" Thomas Hobbes, *Leviathan*, ed. C. B. Macpherson (New York: Penguin Books, 1968), 81.

[9] Immanuel Kant, "Perpetual Peace," from *On History*, trans. and ed. Lewis White Beck (Indianapolis, Bobbs-Merrill, 1957), 112.

[10] Primarily, those of Leo Strauss.

and comic writing. To review a bit, consider what Plato said about the relation between writing and the city. The philosophical life, it seems, involves a reversal in its relation to the city; wherein the truly serious (tragic) life of philosophy conceals and protects that life by playfully writing politically ineffective dialogues (in contrast to politically effective tragic writing) that charmingly dissemble their conclusions under the guise of comic "make-believe." Plato's attack against the poets is thus part of the claim that the philosopher cannot live in his writing (and by extension, the city) except insofar as he writes comically. Tragic living thus involves comic writing, while the comic, because ridiculous, life in the city has its being in the tragic writings of the poets. Lurking behind these reversals is the essential political problem of unshareability and the erotic need to overcome this lack through contrivance. But it is the seriousness or lack thereof with which one takes the contrived solutions of humanity that makes the difference between tragic and comic writing, and by extension, the political life versus the life of philosophy. For the life of the philosopher is ultimately concerned with the nonerotic passivity of *theoria*, while the political life's only concern is with erotically active creations of *techne*. Both are essential and unavoidable in the political and embodied world in which we in fact live, but where we find our "life," so to speak, determines the direction of our movement from one to the other and the seriousness with which we take the unwritten lives we in fact must live.

In Machiavelli's *The Prince* we see him make a move that is all-important in understanding how different modern philosophy is from the ancient philosophy epitomized in Plato. In Chapters 15 and 25 we see him recognize the traditional philosophical relation to the city, and then deliberately replace that relation with another.

> And since I know that many people have already written about these matters, I fear that I shall be considered presumptuous in writing about them, too, the more so because in treating the subject I depart from the rules set down by others. But since it is my intention to write something of use to those who will understand, I deem it best to stick to the practical truth

of things rather than to fancies. Many men have imagined republics and principalities that never really
existed at all. Yet the way men live is so far removed
from the way they ought to live that anyone who
abandons what is for what should be pursues his
downfall rather than his preservation.[11]

What Machiavelli presumes to do here is not only to "depart from
the rules" of classical philosophical writing, but also to write something as "useful" to the city as tragic writing has always been. By
avoiding the "make-believe" of Plato's comic dialogues and the
"charming" conceit of discussing justice in the context of imagined
rather than real cities, Machiavelli seems to be choosing to write
seriously about the serious need of politics.

Yet there is something odd about the way Machiavelli gives
this advice. Whereas in tragic poetry the truth of the human condition is revealed on stage and thereby cathartically hidden for the
audience; Machiavelli here seems bent on revealing all to his audience, especially the need of the city to be lied to. He is honestly
setting forth the need to lie; and however seriously this advice may
be given it is also, unavoidably, rather ridiculous. This serious writing about the serious things of politics is essentially advice to treat
political things as one would a comedy, a comedy in which you are
either the comic poet himself or at least in on his designs. Rather
than using poetic manipulation to set up an ideal regime in writing,
one will instead write about how to manipulate one's fellow citizens as one would characters in a comedy. Otherwise, the "tragic"
facts of the city will include you as a part of its inevitable death and
violence. The joke, of course, is that in the long run we're all dead
anyway, so pursuing one's own preservation above all else is the
sort of quixotic quest that can only succeed within the poetic world
of comedy.

The ridicule that Machiavelli deliberately seems to court is the
same we have already seen heaped on the character of Thrasymachus and the sophist Hippias. For in making Thrasymachus
blush, Socrates has already playfully countered such thinking as

---

[11] Niccolo Machiavelli, *The Prince*, trans. Daniel Donno, (New York:
Bantam Books, 1966), 56.

Machiavelli's with the embarrassment of only knowing one's means while remaining ignorant of one's end. [12] In the mockery of such sophists as Hippias and others, we also see an early exposure of the intrinsic ridiculousness of just the sort of writing Machiavelli is involved in. [13] Nevertheless, just as Socrates braved the ridicule of his own comic proposal of the "three waves," here too Machiavelli braves ridicule and defends his own outrageous proposals by exposing the greater ridiculousness of existing cities and their citizens. Machiavelli gets the last laugh because taking political things seriously always involves some sort of self-deluded blindness. His deliberate exposure of that blindness therefore makes his own exclusion of death and the vagaries of chance seem minor by comparison.

Machiavelli gives an example of this in his comic prologue to the *Mandragola* when he gives an excuse for his comic endeavors that is at once suppliant and threatening.

> And if this material—since it really is slight—does not befit a man who likes to seem wise and dignified, make this excuse for him, that he is striving with these trifling thoughts to make his wretched life more pleasant, for otherwise he doesn't know where to turn his face, since he has been cut off from showing other powers with other deeds, there being no pay for his labors.
>
> The pay he expects is that every man will stand aside and sneer, speaking ill of whatever he sees or hears. This is the reason, beyond all doubt, why from ancient worth the present age in every way is degenerate; for seeing that everybody censures, men do not labor and strain to turn out with a thousand hardships a work that the wind will spoil and the fog conceal.
>
> Yet if anyone supposes that by finding fault he can get the author by the hair and scare him or make him draw back a bit, I give any such man warning and

---

[12] Plato, *Republic*, 350d.

[13] See Plato's *Lesser Hippias*.

tell him that the author, too, knows how to find fault, that it was his earliest art.[14]

Two other things to notice are that Machiavelli implies writing is less desirable than wielding political power directly, and that the present age is noteworthy for its critical spirit that undermines the courage to strive with mortality and fortune. This demotion of writing in relation to political power stands in marked contrast with Plato's demotion of writing in relation to the theoretical life. What this demotion leads to is the *ressentiment* on Machiavelli's part that leads him to invent a comic style of writing that will allow him to become the one unarmed prophet who *does* succeed. Along with overcoming the weakness of comic writing in political things, Machiavelli will also try to overcome the degenerative effects of criticism (a result, no doubt, of the comic atmosphere of Christendom) by making critical technique the greatest weapon of all in beating fortune. The audacity of Machiavelli the comedian is thus to turn comedy's greatest weakness into its greatest asset, for politics will forever be subordinated to comic writing if technique becomes more desirable than virtue, or for those who play the fool, when *virtú* is redefined as technique.

This comic concern with chance and contingency comes out directly when he discusses "Fortuna" in Chapter 25. As we have seen, the difference between tragedy and comedy with regard to chance is that tragedy must convert chance into some sort of inscrutable and yet divine "fate" for the good of the city, while comedy must overcome contingency by making of it an ally within the contrived confines of the comic plot. For his part, Machiavelli starts with the observation (superficially similar to the Xenophonic Socrates' division between what must be divined and what must be thought),[15] that "even if fortune is the arbiter of half our actions,

---

[14] Nicclo Machiavelli, *Machiavelli: The Chief Works and Others*, trans. Allan Gilbert, vol. II (Durham and London: Duke University Press, 1989), 778.

[15] Xenophon, *Memorabilia* I i 7-9.

she still allows us to control the other half."[16] In contrast to Socrates, who suspects madness whenever we confuse which half is which, Machiavelli goes on to say that:

> Therefore, since fortune changes while human beings remain constant in their methods of conduct, I conclude that men will succeed so long as method and fortune are in harmony and they will fail when these are no longer in harmony. But I surely think that it is better to be impetuous than to be cautious, for fortune is a woman and in order to be mastered she must be jogged and beaten. And it may be noted that she submits more readily to boldness than to cold calculation. Therefore, like a woman, she always favors young men because they are not so much inclined to caution as to aggressiveness and daring in mastering her.[17]

Whereas Socrates had *theoria* take up the slack where divination left off, Machiavelli advocates the *techne* appropriate to youth and erotic desire. As we have seen in Aristophanes, this sort of *techne* that involves the "jogging" and "beating" under a controlling mastery is one of the hallmarks of comedy.[18] Machiavelli is therefore describing the control over chance and fortune that one regularly sees in a comedy, but in this case he is expanding this technical control over whatever can be controlled, and not concerning himself with the remainder. He is asking his Prince to play the role of the comic poet in controlling his world, and yet deliberately omitting a serious concern with what cannot be controlled in this way. The lying and manipulation needed to play this role are overtly recommended to move the plot along; even though to the audience that is in on the play (which is to say, both the Prince *and* later readers), such lies cannot be taken seriously. Instead, what is appreciated is the power, forcefulness and ultimately, success, of the manipulator who can pull such things off.

---

[16]Machiavelli, *Prince*, 84.

[17] Machiavelli, *Prince*, 86-7.

[18] Compare the escalating role of beatings in *The Clouds*.

The advice in Machiavelli's *The Prince* thus functions exactly as a comedy and not a tragedy; and the *virtú* praised throughout is the *techne* of a youthful comic poet subverting and manipulating the fruit of tragic writing's and Christian comic writing's past creations. Nevertheless, such a venture must ultimately prove a failure. For just as a merely human comedy cannot be the foundation of any society because it works solely within the confines of the contrived world of joint laughter, a world wherein the contriving poet's role cannot be forgotten, so here the role of Lady Fortuna cannot be forgotten. The conspicuous failure of Cesare Borgia as Machiavelli's prime example is thus an open invitation for the sort of ridicule Machiavelli's advice cannot help but provoke. For the underside of all technical solutions to the political plight of humanity is their ultimate ineffectiveness against contingency and death.

Fully aware of this problem, Machiavelli deals with it at length in the interior monologue of Callimaco, who in the *Mandragola* is awaiting the erotic outcome of his comic scheming.

> How anxious I've been and still am! It's true that Fortune and Nature keep their account balanced; the first never does you a good turn that on the other side something bad doesn't come up. The more my hope has grown, the more my fear has grown . . . . I reproach myself for this excitement and say to myself: "What are you doing? Are you crazy? When you get her, what'll it amount to? You'll recognize your mistake; you'll regret the labor and worry you've gone through. Don't you know how little good a man finds in the things he has longed for, compared with what he expected to find? On the other hand, the worst you can get from it is that you'll die and go to Hell. But how many others have died! And in Hell how many worthy men there are! Are you ashamed to go there? Face your fortune; run away from trouble, but if you can't run away from it, bear it like a man; don't be downcast; don't be a coward like a woman.[19]

This admission of the ultimate failure of all technical solutions to the problem of death gives Machiavelli the last laugh and also

---

[19] Machiavelli, *Chief Works and Others*, 804-805.

aligns him with the manly virtues of courage usually found in tragedy. The joke of this sort of virtue, however, is that it is finally only the base triumph of man over woman, rather than the traditionally more noble triumph of man over man, the gods, or even himself. As much as Machiavelli uses military images, the nature of his new definition of *virtù* would ultimately seem to be that of the scheming slave in a comedy rather than the noble hero of a tragedy.

What Machiavelli has therefore chosen to do about contingency and death in his *Prince* is to incorporate the hidden techniques of tragedy openly as the means to attain and keep power, an incorporation that he also claims will, as a sort of by-product, keep the peace. Machiavelli advises his Prince to deliberately act out in reality what usually only happens on stage in a tragedy. His advice about being feared rather than loved, of strictly applied cruelty and the famous example of Remirro de Orca, are all examples of princes bringing the spectacle of tragic violence concretely into the heart of the city and thereby breaking down the fourth wall that divides audience and stage. The result of the spectacle of de Orca's body, cut in half with a bloody knife and block of wood beside it, is exactly the same as tragic catharsis. "The brutality of this spectacle kept the people of the Romagna for a time appeased and stupefied."[20]

Violence that leads to catharsis and peace is now no longer a poetic technique hidden by the poet within the mimetic process of tragic drama. Instead, it is no longer imitated at all, but rather engaged in directly under the control of the comically manipulative techniques that determine how much, where, and to what effect such violence should be applied. The mock beatings of Aristophanes has been translated into reality by means of questioning the very distinction between the real world and poetry. If all the world is a stage, or if we can only know what we make, then and only then, can the manipulated violence of the poet still bring about the happy ending of a comedy.

It is the Christian world, rather than the pagan world, that can take seriously the ridiculous and hubristic claims of Machiavelli's

---

[20] Machiavelli, *Prince* 58.

modern comedy. For the unique idolatry of a "secularized" Christianity is to worship the powers of man as maker rather than the things made. Such false worship is what gives the seriousness to the comic suggestions of Machiavelli. What Machiavelli would seem to wish for would be that Christendom respond to his writings in the same way Lucretia responds to Callimaco in the *Mandragola* when he succeeds with his outrageous plan and beds with her with the full permission of both the cuckolded husband and the bought-off church.

> Your cleverness, my husband's stupidity, my mother's folly, and my confessors rascality have brought me to do what I never would have done of myself. So I'm forced to judge that it comes from Heaven's wish that has ordered it so, and I'm not strong enough to refuse what Heaven wills me to accept. I take you then for lord, master, guide; you are my father, you are my defender; I want you as my chief good.[21]

Machiavelli is the first modern in thus choosing to write comically for the serious ends of politics, and in so doing he has radically changed our understanding of politics, philosophy, *and* comedy. For the comic writing of the philosophers now has the serious burden of directly and overtly moving from the technical knowledge of their own creation to the technical knowledge of the political whole. And yet the philosopher no longer has at his disposal the mimetic power of the tragic poet who can covertly effect this in his work. So whereas in classical philosophy the erotic need for contrivance in the face of contingency was dealt with by means of the Plato's reversal (i.e., the movement between a serious life of philosophy that knows its own ignorance and the "art of dying," even while playfully writing an expression of that life that laughs at its own powerlessness in the face of death), in the case of modern philosophy there is no longer a reversal because philosophy has wholly given itself over to erotic contrivance. Philosophy now finds its life in its own comic writing, and so is openly revealed as "atheistic" in the face of what it considers the gods of such "tragic"

---

[21] Machiavelli, *Chief Works and Others*, 819.

writings as the Bible. In dropping the distinction between philosophical life and writing, modern philosophy has also dropped the distinction between *theoria* and *techne*, or what is the same, conflated the two—just as it must now conflate the philosopher with God.

Yet by instituting his "new modes and orders"—new in the sense that all comedy is "new" and inevitably "modern"—Machiavelli has only obscured and confused the questions of *theoria* and the philosophical life—a question that his followers must inevitably take up again. [22] For until they do, philosophy is both a "comedy" in its technical reliance and audacity, but also "comic" in its own ignorance and ridiculous hubris. Early modern philosophy in its absolute dependence upon technical science is thus in the same position of Hippodamus, whom Aristotle alone ridicules in his writings because he sought a technical solution for the best regime in the same way one might lay out the streets of a city.[23] Likewise, the joke against the early moderns is that they have not faced up to the tragic problem and need of the city to be lied to, because they have become intoxicated with the technical power of their own "scientific" and comic creations. [24] The moderns have taken on the gods and the lies of the city, yet in such a way that they can never defeat them, for in comedy the deaths are always mock deaths and the lies are only harmless (and painless) "make-believe" (with emphasis on the word "make"). Yet individuals still die and lies still do violence to the soul. So where did this confidence in comic *techne* come from?

Where it comes from is the political power of the Christian comedy. For here is a case where, as we have seen, comic writing can have the same political effect and seriousness as tragedy, without having to rely on tragedy's cathartic and mimetic powers. The political power of the Christian comedy, however, is entirely dependent upon the unique status of God as its poet. But what if humanity can now take on the power of a god? Such a possibility

---

[22] Preface to Machiavelli's *Discourses*.

[23] Aristotle, *Politics* Book 2, Chapter 8.

[24] The scare quotes are here because of the tendency for the early moderns to give a technical account of the theoretic operations of science.

has been brought much nearer in the wake of Dante. To see the full working out of this possibility, however, as well as the most self-conscious attempt to overcome the ridicule attendant upon comic modernity, we must turn to Hegel. For in him we see the full flowering of the movement of modernity into "history," whereby the anchor of historical narrative is detached from its securing in the poetry of God, and reattached to the poetic powers of humanity as a whole. So whereas in Christianity the role of chance and contingency in human affairs is rendered intelligible by its connection to the poetically controlled comedy of the biblical narrative, with the rise of historicism, the contingent universe is wed to the powers of making in all of humanity, spread across time and space, and it is this "poet" who can ultimately affect the comic resolution now demanded. Nevertheless, the genius of Hegel is to realize that this sort of resolution is not comic at all, but is rather the old tragic solution produced on an infinitely larger stage. Let us turn then directly to Hegel's own writing on these themes, and see how he understands comedy and tragedy in the context of his philosophy of history.

XIV: HEGEL'S TRAGIC THEATER

Lastly, there are Idols which have immigrated into men's minds from the various dogmas of philosophies, and also from wrong laws of demonstration. These I call Idols of the Theater, because in my judgement all the received systems are but so many stage plays, representing worlds of their own creation after an unreal and scenic fashion.

—Francis Bacon, *The New Organon*

HEGEL, sitting as he does in the last row, at the last act, of all the reversals of philosophy and theology's plays within plays, tries to give us an explanation of what he has seen. The theater's connection to *theoria* and speculation has returned with a vengeance, and the essential act on stage is a bloody crucifixion more akin to tragedy than comedy. Nevertheless, Hegel is not out to retell the narrative of the Bible. Instead, he is out to transform that narrative into an overarching one that can include the history of philosophy along with the rise of modernity. To do so, however, Hegel must supplant the poetic role of the God of Christianity, especially insofar as it is *that* God who is understood in the Bible to be the poetic maker of history as a cosmic whole.

In the Bible, the climax of its comic structure is the death and resurrection of Christ as the poet who is also the starring actor in his own poem. The God of the Bible is in this way equally the ultimate poet of Scripture and of history. Hegel, if he is to replace this poet with the poetic making of human self-conscious Spirit, must argue that the biblical narrative is no more than another instance, even if the most exemplary, of the free, history-making power of humanity. As he puts it at the conclusion of one of his earlier works criticizing Kant, the "pure concept" must

> re-establish for philosophy the Idea of absolute free-dom and along with it the absolute Passion, the spec-ulative Good Friday in place of the historic Good Friday, Good Friday must be speculatively re-estab-lished in the whole truth and harshness of its God-Forsakenness. Since the [more] serene, less well grounded, and more individual style of the dogmatic philosophies and of the natural religions must vanish, the highest totality can and must achieve its resurrec-tion solely from this harsh consciousness of loss, en-compassing everything, and ascending in all its earnestness and out of its deepest ground to the more freedom of its shape.[1]

These final words of his essay signal Hegel's awareness that he is replacing Christianity with a narrative structure that closely resem-bles the biblical narrative. Nevertheless, it is a replacement of it because the "speculative" rather than "historical" Good Friday takes place in human consciousness, which itself becomes the larger context for history—its "poet," so to speak.

For where Hegel's resurrection comes from is not the final act resolution of a comic narrative; instead, it is "the consciousness of loss, encompassing everything" that ascends with tragic "ear-nestness" to the "serene" freedom of tragedy's cathartic ending. By using terms appropriate to tragedy to describe this "resurrec-tion," Hegel shows that in replacing the comic coupling of historic death *and* resurrection, he was aware that human making—if was to be at all serious—must finally be the tragic making that can only bring about the rememberment of its dismembered parts within the "shape" of something it has itself produced. This "resurrec-tion" is thus not a resurrection at all, but rather something more akin to Ricoeur's "tragic vision" or "cosmogonic myth" wherein the violence and destruction within the narrative is resolved only

---

[1] G. W. F. Hegel, *Faith and Knowledge,* trans. Walter Cerf and H. S. Harris (Albany: State University of New York Press, 1977), 191.

by the totality of the produced narrative itself as product. Consequently, when Hegel's self-conscious Spirit looks upon the totality of all its historical productions, and views them up on the stage as audience to its own tragedy, this "tarrying with" its own shapes of death and negation, "is the magical power that converts it [death] into being."[2] Hegel has thus deliberately replaced Christianity with a tragedy, and in so doing has also replaced the comic "charm" of classical philosophy with the tragic stage "magic" of tragic writing.[3]

Yet in making this substitution, Hegel seems to know full well what is at stake with regard to comedy and tragedy's relation to philosophy and Christianity, for he has many key and pointed observations about the central role tragedy and comedy play. For example, in his essay "Natural Law," published about the same time and in the same journal as *Faith and Knowledge*, Hegel writes two strikingly lucid paragraphs on comedy and tragedy amidst his otherwise impenetrable discussion of natural law. In these sections Hegel gives an account of the role of tragedy in the Absolute that leaves us in no doubt that his philosophy is at bottom a tragic one.

> This is nothing else but the performance, on the ethical plane, of the tragedy which the Absolute eternally enacts with itself, by eternally giving birth to itself into objectivity, submitting in this objective form to suffering and death, and rising from its ashes into glory. The Divine in its form and objectivity is immediately double-natured, and its life is the absolute unity of these natures. But the movement of the absolute contradiction between these two natures presents itself in the Divine nature (which in this movement has comprehended itself) as courage, whereby the first nature frees itself from the death inherent in the other conflicting nature. Yet through this liberation it gives its own life, since that life *is* only in connection with this other life, and yet just as absolutely is resurrected out

---

[2] G. W. F. Hegel, *The Phenomenology of Spirit*, trans. A. V. Miller, (Oxford: Oxford University Press, 1977), 32.

[3] For more on this see Eric Voegelin's "Wisdom and the Magic of the Extreme: A Meditation," *The Southern Review*, Summer 1981.

of it, since in this death (as the sacrifice of the second nature), death is mastered.[4]

Whatever Hegel may be speaking of in particular here, the general image he is using is that of a performance wherein there is between the stage and audience always a doubling of the "beholding" and the "beheld." These two, however sundered, are unified in the entirety of the theater itself. In the movement from audience to stage, "the absolute unity of these two natures," we find the source of the Absolute's life, which is the audience's dying into the otherness and objectivity of the stage, and the cathartic healing which takes place by this very viewing of oneself as indivisible from that otherness and death.

The dying of death that takes place here is thus not that spoken of by St. Paul, but rather that exemplified in Aeschylus' *Eumenides*, wherein the savage nature of human violence and death is never finally removed and eliminated, but rather "pacified" by "the *sight* of Athene enthroned on high on the Acropolis."[5] It is, in other words, the sight of the full gamut of the Absolute's creations, forged in the darkness of the negative and death, that when revealed in the light of a comprehensive tragedy of history, brings out the full glory and life of the human Spirit.

What Hegel has done, we might say, is to have moved the serious and tragic life of the philosopher from the context of a lived human life to the context of writing itself. Our life *is* in our writing, and it is only in the totality of human writing in time, comprehended as such, that we escape from the limitation of this or that particular case of writing and understand the productive nature of writing in itself. The reversals endemic to Hegel are thus recognitions of the reversals endemic to Plato; but what is different here is that poetry has swallowed up philosophy to the point where the life of the philosopher is no more than the productions of a

---

[4] G. W. F. Hegel, *Natural Law*, trans. T. M. Knox (Philiadelphia: University of Pennslyvania Press, 1975), 104.

[5] Hegel, *Natural Law*, 105 (emphasis added).

fully self-conscious poet.[6] The reversals would thus be movement between comic poetic wholes and tragic whole, and their respective playfulness and seriousness is the creating and dispelling of illusions, until finally the sequence of all illusions is revealed as the grand illusion of the Absolute's tragic stage.[7]

This final "grand illusion," however, remains just that, an illusion. For the two of stage and audience, which is to say, humanity's absolute and tragic need to live in the world of its own productions, can only "recollect" the fact and multitude of these productions as its final consummation. The "gallery of images" through which we walk as tragic spectators is thus the walk that is also our "life"; and our life can only be found in our writings. It is

---

[6] Lest this seem too premature an aestheticization of Hegel prior to Nietzsche, consider the following quotations from *Reason and History* (trans. Robert S. Hartman, Indianapolis: Bobbs-Merrill, 1953).

> We have in our universal consciousness two realms, the realm of Nature and the realm of Spirit. The realm of Spirit consists in what is produced by man. One may have all sorts of ideas about the Kingdom of God; but it is always a realm of Spirit to be realized and brought about in man. (20)

> Two things must be distinguished in consciousness, first, *that* I know and, secondly, *what* I know. In self-consciousness the two coincide, for Spirit knows itself. It is the judgment of its own nature and, at the same time, the operation of coming to itself, to produce itself, to make itself (actually) into that which it is in itself (potentially). Following this abstract definition it may be said that world history is the exhibition of spirit striving to attain knowledge of its own nature. (23)

> The very essence of spirit is *action*. It makes itself what it essentially is; it is its own product, its own work. (89).

Production, after all, is the same thing as *poesis*, which is why Hegel's "Reason" is finally a sort of *techne*. Art, religion and philosophy would all thus be species of "writing," as I am using the term from Plato.

[7] "At each stage the *Phenomenology* is a comedy, a part of the *Narrenschiff*, but the true is the achievement of the whole. The whole is a tragedy. But through tragedy is won a kind of peace. It is a peace of the whole like that of which Hegel speaks in the bacchanalian revel—a transparent unbroken calm." Donald Verene, *Hegel's Recollection: A Study of Images in the Phenomenology of Spirit* (Albany: State University of New York Press, 1985), 61.

this claim, that *we* rather than the God of the Bible are the poets of our own narratives and history that converts the Bible into one of the greatest of tragedies rather than the greatest of comedies.

Hegel is thus refusing the invitation to live in and become a part of the poem authored by God. Nevertheless, he knows enough of the nature of that poem to realize this involves a changing of its ending by the transformation of Christ's bodily resurrection into tragic and communal catharsis. When Hegel ends his *Phenomenology of Spirit*, he therefore ends it with his own "Calvary of absolute Spirit" that is a rewriting of Christianity into the tragic writing of human Spirit. This tragic ending he describes as follows:

> The *goal*, Absolute Knowing, or Spirit that knows itself as Spirit, has for its path the recollection of the Spirits as they are in themselves and as they accomplish the organization of their realm. Their preservation, regarded from the side of their free existence appearing in the forms of contingency, is History; but regarded from the side of their [philosophically] comprehended organization, it is the Science of Knowing in the sphere of appearance: the two together, comprehended History, form alike the inwardizing and the Calvary of absolute Spirit, the actuality, truth, and certainty of his throne, without which he would be lifeless and alone. Only
>
> from the chalice of this realm of spirits
> foams forth for Him his own infinitude.[8]

What flows forth from the stage, with the Absolute as the final audience, is thus the infinitude of all its productions, now comprehended in the fullness of their tragic nature, rather than the comic illusions which were limited to the stage itself.[9] For what the *Phenomenology of Spirit* is a phenomenology of is the history of comic delusions, mistaking their own contrived and finite limits for some sort of unlimited truth.

---

[8] Hegel, *Phenomenology*, 808.

[9] "The science of the experience of consciousness is a linguistic science and it is a recollective science. It is an act of recollection carried on in language. But this act is a tragic act because language, even poetic language, never speaks the whole." Hegel's *Recollection*, 111.

One of the greatest of these illusions is the ridiculous illusion of the early moderns, starting as we have seen in Machiavelli and climaxing with Kant, that took with full seriousness the technical powers of comedy. The "individual style of the dogmatic philosophies" mentioned in *Faith and Knowledge* is a case in point, but in order to elucidate this more clearly we must see in more detail what Hegel says of tragedy, and then, more particularly, of comedy.

As we have already seen, the tragedy that is eternally enacted in the Absolute has to do with objectification and alienation, and the overcoming of this type of death within the struggle between two seemingly opposed and irreconcilable forces that are finally reconciled in the vision of their divine unity. For Hegel, then:

> *Tragedy* consists in this, that ethical nature segregates its inorganic nature (in order not to become embroiled in it), as fate, and places it outside itself; and by acknowledging this fate in the struggle against it, ethical nature is reconciled with the Divine being as the unity of both.[10]

What are we to make of this definition, and what does it have to do with what has been said before on tragedy? To begin with, Hegel would agree that the source of the struggle in tragedy has to do with some of the fundamental tensions in the city arising from the problem of shareability. For example, he will say that the "genuine content" of tragic action is supplied by such forces as "love of husband and wife, parents, children, and kinsfolk" and "the life of communities, the patriotism of citizens, the will of those in supreme power."[11] What happens with these various forces is that when embodied in specific characters as ethical demands, although each character on his own is justified, in relation to each other they are "the negation and *violation* of the other" and "consequently in their ethical purport . . . fall under *condemnation*."[12] Even though

---

[10] Hegel, *Natural Law*, 105.

[11] G. W. F. Hegel, *Hegel on Tragedy*, ed. Anne and Henry Paolucci (Doubleday Anchor Original), 46.

[12] Hegel, *Hegel on Tragedy*, 48.

each of these ethical demands on its own is godlike in its inviolability, when embodied in "the definite pathos of a human personality" they cannot help but "render both blame and wrong inevitable."[13]

How are these literally "embodied" tensions to be overcome in order to restore some sort of ethical wholeness? For Hegel, what "is abrogated in the tragic issue is merely the one-sided particularity,"[14] and what tragedy issues *in*, is "the feeling of *reconciliation*, which tragedy affords in virtue of its vision of eternal justice."[15] What must be overcome in tragedy, then, is particularity itself; and the objectification connected with bodies that limits the ultimately unlimited "divine." Ethical nature thus segregates itself from its "inorganic nature as fate," in the sense that fate is whatever cannot be shared within the universalized standpoint of some sort of ethical concern, and the remainder is embodied as its own force standing against and attempting to overthrow this now only "particular" nature. Nevertheless, ethical nature must still be universalized, even though in its confrontation with "fate" this is revealed as impossible.

Where then does a truly unified and shareable unity come from? It comes from the action of the tragedy itself, wherein the struggle against fate brings out the "higher unity" of the Divine which is manifest as the unity of tragic struggle *in toto*. The divine unity of tragedy is therefore the unity of the dramatic art product itself—the unity of beginning, middle and end—that we see up on stage, with emphasis upon "our" seeing of it.

> Inasmuch as then, in conformity with this principle, all that pertains to tragedy pre-eminently rests upon the contemplation of such a conflict and its resolution, dramatic poetry is—and its entire mode of presentation offers a proof of the fact—alone able to make and completely adapt the tragic throughout its

---

13 Hegel, *Hegel on Tragedy*, 49.

14 Hegel, *Hegel on Tragedy*, 49.

15 Hegel, *Hegel on Tragedy*, 51.

entire course and compass, to the principle of the art product.[16]

The "principle of the art product" is therefore also the underlying principle behind the effectiveness of tragedy, what I have called after Girard the "scapegoat mechanism" of tragic catharsis, and so it is no surprise that it is dramatic poetry, with its use of an actual stage, that we see this the most clearly.

Also, because the "principle of the art product" constitutes the divine unity of tragedy, we can see why in the *Phenomenology* Hegel will discuss tragedy, along with epic and comedy, as three forms of the "spiritual work of art," and why in the particular case of tragedy the "actor is essential to his mask." The reason for this is as follows:

> The hero is himself the speaker, and the performance displays to the audience—who are also spectators— *self-conscious* human beings who *know* their rights and purposes, the power and the will of their specific nature and know how to *assert* them . . . they give utterance to the inner essence, they prove the rightness of their action, and the 'pathos' which moves them is soberly asserted and definitely expressed in its universal individuality, free from the accidents of circumstance and personal idiosyncrasies. Lastly, these characters *exist* as actual human beings who impersonate the heroes and portray them, not in the form of a narrative, but in the actual speech of the actors themselves.[17]

What Hegel would seem to be explaining here is what I have called the essential "lie" structure of tragedy, which functions as it does precisely by means of the "mask." The donning of a mask by an actor is in itself the solution to the irreconcilable tensions the actor lives in as a citizen rather than actor. The movement from citizen to actor thus recapitulates the movement from audience to stage, a movement that is essential to the "divine unity" that is the art product itself. That this movement involves the "lying essence"

---

[16] Hegel, *Hegel on Tragedy*, 51.

[17] Hegel, *Phenomenology*, 733.

that Plato speaks of, is brought out further when Hegel goes on to explain that

> Spirit when *acting* appears *qua* consciousness over against the object to which its activity is directed and which, consequently, is determined as the *negative* of the knower; the doer finds himself thereby in the antithesis of knowing and not-knowing. He takes his purpose from his character and knows it as an ethical essentiality; but on account of the determinateness of his character he knows only the *one* power of substance, the other remaining for him concealed. The present reality is, therefore one thing *in itself*, and another thing for consciousness; the upper and the nether law come to signify in this connection the power that knows and reveals itself to consciousness, and the power that conceals itself and lies in ambush.[18]

The struggle against fate is thus also the struggle with the chaos of "not knowing" and even outright deceptions that are attendant upon all forms of human writing, but which are particularly embodied in tragedy. In the case of Hegel, however, whose life is to be found in this writing, this deceptive quality is essential to all of knowing and reality, since, as he says of the Delphic oracle of Phoebus and Zeus who is his father, "the commands of the truth-speaking god and his pronouncements of what *is*, are really deceptive. For this knowing is, in principle immediately a not-knowing, because consciousness, in its action, is in its own self this antithesis."[19]

In this oblique reference to the *Phaedrus'* myth of Theuth as an account of writing's inception, Hegel is also reaffirming Plato's arguments on writing—minus the reversal between life and writing—and thus also anticipating the insights of Derrida on the patricidal tensions built into writing. Tragedy is patricidal in the sense that it is only by the occluding of the father's light, the obscuring

---

[18] Hegel, *Phenomenology*, 737.

[19] Hegel, *Phenomenology*, 737.

by the bad "son" that the true unity of the Absolute can be seen. As a philosopher Hegel sees through this "lie." But because there is no life outside of one's writing, seeing through this lie is itself the discovery of that fact—that our life must be found in our writing—and so the need for the tragic lie is no more than another manifestation of the tragic nature of the Absolute.

Hegel describes this discovery earlier on in the *Phenomenology* as a sort of peeking behind the curtain, only to discover that you are as much on stage as off of it.

> This curtain [of appearance] hanging before the inner world is therefore drawn away, and we have the inner being [the 'I'] gazing into the inner world . . . —self-consciousness. It is manifest that behind the so-called curtain which is supposed to conceal the inner world, there is nothing to be seen unless we go behind it ourselves, as much in order that we may see, as that there may be something behind there which can be seen.[20]

Without going behind the curtain and discovering yourself as also up on stage, there would be no dialectic. For of the two positions in Hegel's dialectic one might say that his *für sich*, or "for itself," can always be understood as an audience, and his *an sich*, or "in-itself," as the stage. The movement toward the Absolute *an und für sich*, or "in and for itself," is thus the movement toward the tragic "Golgotha of absolute Spirit" wherein an infinite drama plays before the only audience capable of viewing it in its entirety for what it is—the whole of history as a tragic drama. All the world is therefore indeed a stage for Hegel, but it is a tragic stage precisely because there *must* be a stage. Nevertheless, along the way to this final stage there is also the discovery involved in peeking behind the curtain, and that discovery is the overarching discovery of the moderns—that we are ourselves our own poets. It is with this discovery of the mere mortal who is also the wizard behind the curtain, that we encounter the importance of comedy.

For what this discovery consists of, and what Hegel also describes as "the general basis of comedy," is "a world in which man

---

[20] Hegel, *Phenomenology*, 165.

has made himself, in his conscious activity, complete master of all that otherwise passes as the essential content of his knowledge and achievement."[21] Yet what makes this mastery comic is that it is also "a world whose ends are consequently thrown awry on account of their own lack of substance."[22] The comic discovery of modernity is therefore the discovery of Machiavelli's *techne* as the means to master all that concerns us; but as Hegel sees it, this discovery lacks all substance because it is truly only the discovery of the subjective "poet" and the power of his own artifice. Hegel is thus recognizing the perennial limitations of comedy and its insubstantiality in the face of tragedy's political solidity. Nonetheless, what comedy *does* lead to—in a big way—is the dissolving and corroding powers of the poetic subject who knows himself as the creator of everything of substance, even tragedy. The reason comedy, especially in its modern form, has traditionally been linked to atheism, is because of this tendency to reveal the man behind the myths of tragedy. Yet once revealed, we find that man is still very much in need of myths even if he is the one making them.

There is then a fine line in modernity between "the merely *ridiculous* [and] and the true comic."[23] In the same way, one might say that the *Wizard of Oz* is ridiculous as long as he doesn't notice Toto nipping at his heels, but if he does, he can again become comic if he knows the jig is up and has no more need to hide behind his curtain. The terms Hegel uses to describe this insubstantiality of comedy is that of the actor and his mask; showing how in comedy it is the taking off of the mask, winking, and putting it back on and off again that increases the powers of the individual self as poet—even while deflating the pretenses of his mask.

> *Comedy* has, therefore, above all, the aspect that actual self-consciousness exhibits itself as the fate of the gods. These elementary Beings are, as *universal* moments, not a self and are not equal. . . . It, the Subject, is raised above such a moment, such a single property, and clothed in this mask it proclaims the irony of such

---

[21] Hegel, *Hegel on Tragedy*, 52.

[22] Hegel, *Hegel on Tragedy*, 52.

[23] Hegel, *Hegel on Tragedy*, 52.

a property wanting to be something on its own account. The pretensions of universal essentiality are uncovered in the self; it shows itself to be entangled in an actual existence, and drops the mask just because it wants to be something genuine. The self, appearing here in its significance as something actual, plays with the mask which it once put on in order to act its part; but it as quickly breaks out again from this illusory character and stands forth in its own nakedness and ordinariness, which it shows to be not distinct from the genuine self, the actor, or from the spectator.[24]

The discovery of comedy is therefore the discovery of the unity of actor, spectator, and "genuine self," not in the sense of the dramatic product (which is the case in tragedy), but rather in the sense of the poetic process itself that knows it is poetic "making" that makes all three. This is why in a comedy the poet in his overtness always corresponds to an equally direct appeal to the audience for participation, for what is always thematic in comedy is the pleasures of creation itself, whether it be the pleasures of writing, watching, or acting.

The unity of comedy is therefore different from the "divine unity" of tragedy insofar as the stage seems to have collapsed in on itself; and all three—actor, spectators, and poet—are all on stage together and have solipsistically unified themselves in terms of their own powers of making.

Through the fact that it is the individual consciousness in the certainty of itself that exhibits itself as this absolute power, this latter has lost the form of something *presented to consciousness*, something altogether *separate* from *consciousness* and alien to it, as were . . . the powers and persons of Tragedy . . . . [O]n the contrary, the actual self of the actor coincides with what he impersonates, just as the spectator is completely at home in the drama performed before him and sees himself playing in it. What this self-consciousness be-

---

[24] Hegel, *Phenomenology*, 744.

holds is that whatever assumes the form of essentiality over against it, is instead dissolved in it—in its
thinking, its existence, and its action—and is at its
mercy. . . . This self-certainty is a state of spiritual
well-being and of repose therein, such as is not to be
found anywhere outside of this Comedy.[25]

The "repose and self-certainty" of comedy, we might say
then, consists in the fact that here self-consciousness exhibits itself
as the fate of the gods. It is in this absence of fate in comedy that
we see clearly how it differs from tragedy.

The absence of fate is thus the presence of the poet; and it is
this overcoming of any sort of otherness or incorrigible opposition
that leads to the usual happy ending and feeling of self-satisfaction
that we find in a comedy. But within this feeling of self-satisfaction
there still lurks the temptation of lapsing back into what Hegel calls
the "merely ridiculousness" instead of the "true comic." For without the consciousness of the negative and dissolving powers of
comedy, the technicians can take their own creations too seriously
and forget that the ever-present Toto nipping at their heels draws
attention away from the smoke and mirrors of the stage to the ordinary "selves" from Kansas who are both behind and in front of
that display.

In the light of this temptation toward ridiculousness, and as
a means of discovering both the insights and fatuousness of modern philosophy, the essay on natural law makes a crucial distinction
between "old" and "modern" comedy.

Comedy, on the other hand, will generally come down
on the side of the absence of fate. Either it falls within
absolute vitality, and thus presents only shadows of
clashes (or mock battles with a fabricated fate and fictitious enemies), or else it falls within non-life and
therefore presents only shadows of self-determination and absoluteness; the former is the old, or Divine, comedy, the latter the modern comedy.[26]

---

[25] Hegel, *Phenomenology*, 747.

[26] Hegel, *Hegel on Tragedy*, 105.

What Hegel means here by "the old, or Divine, comedy" is essentially the comedy of the Bible wherein the "absolute vitality" of God as poet reduces all opposition and sin to the realm of second-act illusions and impotent rebellion and brings "good out of evil" in the final act to the point where this poet-god is "all in all." What Hegel overlooks, however, is the difference the actual "self" of the poet makes. He thus follows in the footsteps of Dante rather than Aquinas in focusing on the structure of comedy in general, rather than focusing on the specificity of the biblical comedy that demands from its audience the concrete choice as to who and what its poet actually is. Obscuring this choice, while one makes a choice nonetheless, inevitably involves an exaggerated and divinized view of the powers of human making.

In seeming recognition of this, however, Hegel does not choose the Bible as his example of "old comedy," but instead, and appropriately, Dante's "divine" comedy. Of this he says:

> Dante's *Divine Comedy* is without fate and without a genuine struggle, because absolute confidence and assurance of the reality of the Absolute exist in it without opposition, and whatever opposition brings movement into this perfect security and calm is merely opposition without seriousness or inner truth.[27]

By choosing Dante as his example here, rather than say Aristophanes or Plautus, Hegel is tipping us off that what he had in mind as the essence of this sort of comedy is the means by which self-consciousness discovers that it is itself the Absolute and Spirit. But such a discovery is on its own still an illusion until it steps off the stage altogether and views the whole history of its past productions as both poet *and* spectator. So while in the short term the awakening to self-consciousness is the comic realization that the "in-itself" of the stage is really the "for-itself" of the audience as poet, in the long-run, the absolute standpoint that is both "in *and* for-itself" is

---

[27] Hegel, *Natural Law*, 105-106.

that of a tragic audience to a stage on which there are smaller audiences and stages reversing themselves from one to the other.[28] But before getting to that final tragic and absolute audience, there is the penultimate comic farce of modernity that must inevitably precede it.

For it is with modern comedy, rather than the old comedy, that we see the sort of ridiculous spectacle exemplified by the likes of Machiavelli, Hobbes and Kant, wherein the absolute vitality of a poetic-god is absent, and what is "shadowy" is not the opposition to this "absolute," but rather the self-determination of absoluteness itself. In other words, in the "other comedy" of modernity, the complications are without "fate" and "true struggle"

> because the ethical nature itself is caught in that fate. Here the climax is reached in conflicts that are not playful but serious for this ethical urge, though comical for the spectator . . . . The ethical urge . . . must, to put it briefly, transmute the existent into the formal and negative absoluteness of law. And thereby it must give its anxious mind the impression that its possessions are secure, must lift all its belongings to safety and certainty by contracts and all imaginable varieties of clause and subclause in the formulary. It must deduce appropriate systems from experience and reason, which are certainty and necessity itself, and base

---

[28] The image being used here comes from the 1797 play by Ludwig Tieck entitled the *Die Verkerte Welt*, or the "Topsy-turvy World," wherein actors climb off stage into the audience, and the audience climbs on stage to be actors, to the point where it climaxes with four plays within plays going on at once. At the end of this play the character Greenfeather, who has been both part of the audience and stage and is left alone in front of the curtain after the "Prologue" has finished introducing the play already finished, exclaims "Ha! Here was a whole Prologue directed at me, namely one of the chief personages in the play, and yet he remained completely unaware of my presence, and yet I'm the only person here! This is a marvel that deserves to be investigated by the philosophers" (Ludwig Tieck, *The Land of Upside Down*, trans. Oscar Mandel (London, Associated University Presses, 1978)). That both Hegel and Kierkegaard are making use of the image deriving from this play can be seen in their constant use of the term "topsy-turvy" in connection with the image of a play within a play. Hegel's entire *Phenomenology* might even be seen as the investigation requested by Greenfeather!

them on the most acute ratiocination . . . the ethical urge here must similarly witness how the next change or even the ascent of the earth-spirit wipes out half, or entire, sciences proved by experience and reason; how one legal system overthrows another; how humaneness here displaces severity, while elsewhere the will to power takes the place of the security of contract; and how in science, as in reality, the most securely acquired and confirmed possessions of principles and laws are ravaged and destroyed.[29]

All the political and ethical accomplishments of modern philosophy, summarized here *in ovo*, are knocked into a cocked hat for us, the laughing spectators, precisely because of the discrepancy between their grandiose claims and their inevitably limited and fugitive accomplishment.

Yet such grand failure seems almost to be a planned part of this sort of play, as we saw in Cesare Borgia's farcical appearance in *The Prince*. Also, it sometimes seems it is the response to that failure. For as Hegel goes on to say:

The ethical urge must either think that these are its own efforts, hovering above fate with reason and will, which work themselves out in such matters and have produced such changes; or it must get perturbed by their unexpected and inappropriate character, and first call on the gods for help against this necessity, and then truckle under to it. In both cases the ethical urge, which seeks an absolute infinity in these finite things, merely performs the farce of its faith and its undying illusion (which is darkest where its brightest), it being already lost and in the wrong when it imagines itself to be resting in the arms of justice, trustworthiness and pleasure.[30]

The farce of the early moderns—which is at least enjoyed by us as spectators to its results—is that in seeking an "absolute infinity in finite things," it has failed to realize the impotence of comedy to effect the same things as tragedy. In the very success of its artifice

---

[29] Hegel, *Natural Law*, 107.

[30] Hegel, *Natural Law*, 107-108.

it has failed to realize that its success is indeed limited *to* that artifice; and that the intractable problems of human unshareability associated with the body and nature can only be periodically purged rather than eliminated by means of tragic writing.

All the postmodern attacks on the Enlightenment—exemplified by Derrida—are in this light no more than the various exposures of the continuing joke behind all modern comedies. Yet as we see here, both Hegel and Plato, in contrast to the Enlightenment, are aware of the political limitations of comic writing. But whereas Plato will choose comic writing as a cover for a truly serious rather than ridiculous life, Hegel will argue for the ultimate science of all, which goes beyond the comic "sciences" of modernity precisely because it is "written" like them, and yet not tied down to one finite and mortal poet. This ultimate science is the tragic science of the Absolute that includes within itself the death and destruction of the negative, even while returning into itself as a "written" and hence "tragic" whole.

The final tragic view of Hegel can thus be found between the *Divine Comedy* of Dante (which is essentially Hegel's view of Christianity interpreted as a comedy) and the modern comedy of the Enlightenment. This tragedy is essentially the equivalent of Plato's serious life of the philosopher—without, of course, the "life." For here life is fully written and writing is life, and this is what the science of the Absolute consists of.

> The comedy so separates the two zones of the ethical that it allows each to proceed entirely on its own, so that in the one the conflicts and the finite are shadows without substance, while in the other the Absolute is an illusion. But the true and absolute relation is that the one really does illuminate the other; each has a living bearing on the other, and each is the other's serious fate. The absolute relation, then, is set forth in tragedy.[31]

---

[31] Hegel, *Natural Law*, 108.

With the death of God as the poet of history, and yet with the continued presence of history (history here as the modern equivalent of Plato's "writing"), the Enlightenment has become the "serious fate" of Christianity as its historical successor; just as the death of this cast out God has become the Enlightenment's "serious fate" that continues to make it possible. It is only with both together that we get the serious tragedy that cathartically reconciles the two; and it is with this tragedy that Hegel concludes his *Phenomenology*, thereby allowing his Absolute Science of Logic to begin.

What is missing from this absolute tragedy, however, is a genuine "life," in the same way, one might say, as there is a missing bodily corpse for his dead God. For what Hegel has done by substituting his cathartic tragic "resurrection" of the absolute "*theoria*" of communal Spirit for the bodily resurrection of the concrete human and divine poet of all creation and history is to have made it impossible to be ultimately concerned with our concretely embodied human lives—either in terms of the Platonic "art of dying" or the Christian "I am crucified with Christ, nevertheless I live." In other words, Hegel covers over the problem of bodily "unshareability" in the usual tragic way of spectacularly distracting us from it. But if we refuse to be distracted by his absolutely tragic stageplay, and demand instead that our insatiable desire for a completely intelligible whole with no remainder not be fobbed off with an idolatrous stand-in, then we must reopen the question, foreclosed at least since Dante, as to whether or not God was in fact the author of the Bible. We must ask whether it was truly a "divine" rather than a merely human comedy.

As we will see in the next two chapters, these are precisely the sort of questions reopened by two of the most far-reaching responses to Hegel's philosophy of the Absolute, that of Nietzsche and Kierkegaard. For Nietzsche the answer is a definite no, but he at least will recognize the rivalry with the poet-God of the Bible implied in that answer. In Kierkegaard, however, we find a sustained attempt to reacquaint ourselves with what it is to live rather than merely to "write" seriously, as the only genuine preparation for the radical demands of the Christian faith to live in the "writing" of God. Both, however, in their own way, will not let us forget that in spite of Hegel's philosophical transformations, the narrative of Christianity is not a tragedy.

XV: NIETZSCHE: FROM TRAGEDY TO COMEDY

Perhaps not many are able to comprehend this conclusion, but then they would not be able to comprehend the tragic, either. If the individual is isolated, then either he is absolutely the creator of his own fate, and then there is nothing tragic anymore but only evil, for it is not even tragic that the individual was infatuated with or wrapped up in himself—it is his own doing; or the individuals are merely modifications of the eternal substance of life, and so once again the tragic is lost.

—Søren Kierkegaard, *Concluding Unscientific Postscript*

THE BRIDGE that stands between the comedies of Plato and the Bible, and most contemporary thinking on the role of tragedy and comedy in philosophy and theology, is not Hegel or Kierkegaard, but rather Nietzsche. Nietzsche, who signaled his radical entry into the philosophical scene by writing *The Birth of Tragedy*, knew full well that his overturning of what he called "Platonism" and Christianity (which he called "Platonism for the people") revolved around the issues of comedy and tragedy. Although most contemporary thought has drunk so deeply from Nietzsche's Dionysian brew that it is now more of a footnote to him than to Plato, we usually do not notice why Nietzsche moved from his early "tragic insight" to his later need to pronounce "holy my laughter." Nietzsche knew full well that his own reversal of Platonism was a renewal of "that ancient quarrel between the poets and the philosophers," and he also knew what side of the quarrel he was coming down on. But he could not avoid the overwhelming change Christianity had made in the nature of that quarrel. The issue was no longer a two-way contest between the philosopher and tragic poetry; it was now a four-way contest between those two and their two new rivals, the divine "comic poet" of the Bible and the comic poets of modernity.

For the most part, however, Nietzsche was in the same position as Hegel; it was his burden to create a tragic philosophy that would rescue him from the leveling and nihilistic effect of modern comedy. Under the influence of what he would later call "Schopenhauerian and Kantian formulas" he would express this early "Dionysian insight" by writing *The Birth of Tragedy*. [1] In later editions, however, he would add an "Attempt at Self-Criticism" that would argue even this expression was at bottom still a form of Christianity. Because of the "metaphysical comfort" it sought in collapsing the individual into some sort of corporate ground or whole, his book, he argues, was ultimately nay-saying and nihilistic insofar as it demanded the obliteration of the individual as such— the collapse of the poet into the poem, so to speak. What Nietzsche desired instead was the exaltation of the poet *as* poet, the poet as the source and god to his own poems. But this would require that the poet become a comic-god who makes himself and everything else as his own comic-poem. The desire to laugh and make holy that laughter is the desire to become a yea-sayer to everything as one's own creation, as did the Christian God after each day of creation.

In the light of this desire, he finally decides his earlier account of tragic philosophy is at bottom romantic and hence, for him, "Christian."[2] The discovery of the "misfortune in the nature of things" that makes life tragic "comforts metaphysically" by putting one, as it were, on the side of the tragic audience rather than the poet. Nietzsche's true desire, however, was to be the "anti-Christ" and direct competitor with the Christian God on his own level, which is the level of comedy. If he were to do this, however, he must become a god, not a pagan god, but the Christian God as comic creator. Overcoming Christianity, which as "Platonism for the people" is as comic as Platonism proper, is not done by turning to tragedy out of resentment for comedy's triumph. Instead, it

---

[1] Nietzsche, *Birth of Tragedy*, 24.

[2] "—in sum, as romantics end, as Christians." Nietzsche, *Birth of Tragedy*, 26.

must be overcome by becoming a comic-god oneself through the "eternal return of the same" that says "yes" to whatever was and is, and in so doing makes that "play and spectacle" necessary "because again and again he needs himself."[3] Is this eternal return the vicious circle of a comic rather than a tragic god? Not exactly. Nietzsche will instead call himself the first *truly* tragic philosopher.[4] Let us see in more detail how he gets to this point.

One of the key aspects to Nietzsche's *early* tragic philosophy is that the individual, questioning or otherwise, is no longer the *locus* for our grasp of the whole. The individual is instead absorbed into a play *not* of his own making, and hence can know himself only by self-forgetfulness, by becoming the illusion projected by the light of the only true reality—the play itself. If there is a "subject" in all this, it is not actually the individual himself, but rather only the subject who is what he is in the totality of this play of appearances, made as if for the subject's own benefit.

> Insofar as the subject is the artist, however, he has already been released from his individual will, and has become, as it were, the medium through which the one truly existent subject celebrates his release in appearance. For to our humiliation *and* exaltation, one thing above all must be clear to us. The entire comedy of art is neither performed for our betterment or education nor are we the true authors of this art world. On the contrary, we may assume that we are merely images and artistic projections for the true author, and that we have our highest dignity in our significance as works of art—for it is only as an *aesthetic phenomenon* that existence and the world are eternally *justified*—while of course our consciousness of our

---

[3] Friedrich Nietzsche, *Beyond Good and Evil,* trans Walter Kaufman (New York: Vintage Books, 1966), 68.

[4] "In this sense I have the right to understand myself as the first tragic philosopher—that is, the most extreme opposite and antipode of a pessimistic philosopher. Before me this transposition of the Dionysian into a philosophical pathos did not exist; tragic wisdom was lacking. I have looked in vain for signs of it even among the great Greeks in philosophy" (Friedrich Nietzsche, *Ecce Homo,* trans Walter Kaufman, (New York: Vintage Books, 1967), 273).

own significance hardly differs from that which soldiers painted on canvas have of the battle represented
on it. Thus all our knowledge of art is basically quite
illusory, because as knowing beings we are not one
and identical with that being which, as the sole author
and spectator of this comedy of art, prepares a perpetual entertainment for itself. Only insofar as the genius in the act of creation coalesces with this
primordial artist of the world, does he know anything
of the eternal essence of art; for in this state he is, in
a marvelous manner, like the weird image of the fairy
tale which can turn its eyes at will and behold itself;
he is at once subject and object, at once poet, actor,
and spectator.[5]

The artistic genius, who is at "once subject and object," "poet, actor and spectator," can be all of these things because in hiding behind his tragic Muse he becomes not himself but rather the
mouthpiece for the gods. Yet in this case it is not exactly the gods,
but rather the "one truly existent subject" who is celebrating his
release into appearance through this artist. Actual concrete works
of art are no longer at issue here, for the prime concern is only that
work of art which is reality itself. Existence and the world have
become an "aesthetic phenomenon."

In Hegel, we saw that this sort of reality was ultimately a tragic
phenomenon, the "Golgotha of Absolute Spirit." Here, however,
it is described as the "comedy of art." Why is that? The reason, I
think, is because we have here two perspectives: that of ourselves
as works of art, and that of the "one truly existent subject." From
the perspective of ourselves as works of art, or even Nietzsche
commenting on the role of the artist, reality is tragic, for in his
Dionysian ecstasy "he is no longer an artist, he has become a work
of art."[6] Think of the soldiers on the canvas. On the other hand,
from the perspective of the "one true subject" who speaks through
that artist, its art cannot help but be a comedy, or even a farce,
because of its own willful caprice in making whatever it wants with
no other criteria than its own powers of creating. Nietzsche is split

---

[5] Nietzsche, *Birth of Tragedy*, 52.

[6] Nietzsche, *Birth of Tragedy*, 37.

between these two perspectives, the first of which can only be tragic if the second is essentially comic.

Hegel had earlier solved this problem by making the movement from one perspective to the other in its totality a tragedy. Tragedy, therefore, had the last word because it was the "rational" tragedy of the Absolute wherein everything was absorbed into its cosmic stage-play. Nietzsche, on the other hand, must deal with the problem of pessimism inherited from Schopenhauer, for his cruder separation between "will" and "representation" makes one no longer happy as the soldier on the canvas because any glimpse of the will of the one true subject who pulls the strings must inevitably cloud his happy self-forgetfulness.

Nietzsche therefore shifts the emphasis of his tragedy from Hegel's audience, which loses itself in the spectacle, to the tragic hero whose "metaphysical comfort" in the face of his own ruin is much more questionable than that of the audience. Having glimpsed the true artist, the blind will behind all appearances, the hero suffers from nausea, the "ascetic, and will-negating mood" that goes along with his own fall. This Dionysian man, or the one who is here actor rather than audience,

> resembles Hamlet: both have looked truly into the essence of things, they have *gained knowledge*, and nausea inhibits action; for their action could not change anything in the eternal nature of things; they feel it to be ridiculous or humiliating that they should be asked to set right a world that is out of joint. Knowledge kills action; action requires the veils of illusion: that is the doctrine of Hamlet . . . . Conscious of the truth he has once seen, man now sees everywhere only the horror or absurdity of existence . . . . he is nauseated.[7]

Taking the perspective of the hero rather than the cathartically purged audience leads to nausea and the raw encounter with the irrational that is otherwise covered over in the aesthetic gap between stage and audience.

As an individual actor rather than the audience, then, salvation through art must come in a different way.

---

[7] Nietzsche, *Birth of Tragedy*, 60.

Here, when the danger to his will is greatest, *art* approaches as a saving sorceress, expert at healing. She alone knows how to turn these nauseous thoughts about the horror or absurdity of existence into notions with which one can live: these are the *sublime* as the artistic taming of the horrible, and the *comic* as the artistic discharge of the nausea of absurdity.[8]

The individual actor must save himself by becoming an artist; but to do so is to step out of the tragedy of reality as an "aesthetic phenomenon" created by another, and into the self-conscious role of being the "sole author and spectator."

In *The Birth of Tragedy*, Nietzsche had not yet fully taken this step, even though we can see all the first moves were already there. Instead, he is both recognizing and struggling to break free of the nihilating effects tragedy has upon the individual. "[A]ll individuals, taken as individuals, are comic and hence untragic—from which it would follow that the Greeks simply *could* not suffer individuals on the tragic stage . . . the one truly real Dionysus appears in a variety of forms, in the mask of a fighting hero, and entangled, as it were, in the net of the individual will."[9] The suffering of the individual is thus the result of striving to be individual, which is why the fall of the hero is also the return of the audience into its purged state of unindividuated unity. Individuation only takes place as an aesthetic moment before it falls into the "aesthetic phenomenon" of reality itself, for the striving for individuation is itself the cause of suffering in this life and hence "objectionable in itself."

This view of things already provides us with all the elements of a profound and pessimistic view of the world, together with the *mystery doctrine of tragedy*: The fundamental knowledge of the oneness of everything existent, the conception of individuation as the primal cause of evil, and of art as the joyous hope that the

---

[8] Nietzsche, *Birth of Tragedy*, 60.

[9] Nietzsche, *Birth of Tragedy*, 73.

spell of individuation may be broken in augury of restored oneness.[10]

The problem here is that the pessimism of the view that knows
individuation must be overcome by means of tragedy, is in tension
with the "joyous hope" that this will happen in reality, as it were,
rather than merely aesthetically.

To put this in terms I have used earlier, the "mystery doctrine
of tragedy" is the political need for catharsis through tragic poetry,
but the "joyous hope" is that life itself will become tragic and there
will be no more need for tragedy as something written rather than
real. Nietzsche was in this sense struggling to disentangle Greek
tragedy (and its essential connection with most religious myths and
the "mysteries") from modern tragic philosophy that romantically
seeks a return to a restored "oneness." The first knows full well
the individual exists and that this is the source for its aesthetic
need; but the second, while comically unable to ignore the individual, seeks to make of him the illusion and unity the reality. The
later discovery of Nietzsche is that he alone is the individual behind
all his aesthetic masks, and that he, and he alone, must individually
become the Dionysus of both tragedy *and* comedy.

Nevertheless, at this point, he is still hesitant to take this step;
for his greatest polemical target throughout *The Birth of Tragedy* is
essentially what I have called "modern," or "technological," comedy, the new creation Nietzsche claims was given birth to by Euripides under the inspiration of the daemonic muse, Socrates. The
mistake Nietzsche makes here is to recognize that tragedy as an art
form has indeed died (however much it may continue as a way of
life) and then mis-identify who the culprits were. Consider the following simile: "Just as Greek sailors in the time of Tiberius once
heard on a lonesome island the soul-shaking cry, 'Great Pan is
dead,' so the Hellenic world was now pierced by the grievous lament: 'Tragedy is dead!'"[11] The laments are in fact one in the same,
but Nietzsche has predated it to the time of Euripides in order to

---

[10] Nietzsche, *Birth of Tragedy*, 74.

[11] Nietzsche, *Birth of Tragedy*, 76.

equate the nihilism of modern comedy with both Socrates *and* Christianity.

For when Nietzsche accuses Euripides of being the suicidal tragic poet, what he overlooks is that Euripides' tragedies with the *deus ex machina* are not tragedies at all, but are rather comedies more akin to Aristophanes than Sophocles. The *Bacchae*, however, *is* a quintessential tragedy, and is as much the source of Nietzsche's understanding of Dionysus as anything written in Greek. When Nietzsche claims this play is merely a recantation in the "evening of his life," the question becomes whether Nietzsche is prophesying his own ambivalent relation to Socrates. Consider this possibility in light of the question Nietzsche puts in the mind of Euripides:

> Is the Dionysian entitled to exist at all? Should it not be forcibly uprooted from Hellenic soil? Certainly, the poet tells us, if it were only possible: but the god Dionysus is too powerful; his most intelligent adversary—like Pentheus is in the *Bacchae*—is unwittingly enchanted by him, and in this enchantment runs to meet his fate . . . . This is what we are told by a poet who opposed Dionysus with heroic valor throughout a long life—and who finally ended his career with a glorification of his adversary and with suicide, like a giddy man who, to escape the horrible vertigo he can no longer endure, casts himself from a tower.[12]

Does Euripides stand to Dionysus as Nietzsche stands to Socrates? Nietzsche cannot let the figure of Socrates go, especially when his own advocacy of a rebirth of tragedy involves a systematic outworking of "Socrates practicing music." Later, when Nietzsche casts himself from his own tower by recanting his desire for "metaphysical comfort," he admits that this earlier need for tragedy was a form of decadence, and that only the new "comedy" of the anti-Christ/Dionysus will do.[13]

---

[12] Nietzsche, *Birth of Tragedy*, 81-82.

[13] In his later edition of *The Birth of Tragedy* that included his "Attempt at a Self-Criticism," Nietzsche re-baptized himself (after the suicide of his earlier self?) and his instincts in a new way.

But before he gets to that point, he quite literally makes Socrates the centerpiece (in German, *mittelpunkt*) of *The Death of Tragedy*:

> "Only by instinct"; with this phrase we touch upon the heart and core [mittelpunkt] of the Socratic tendency. With it Socratism condemns existing art as well as existing ethics. Wherever Socratism turns its searching eyes it sees lack of insight and the power of illusion; and from this lack it infers the essential perversity and reprehensibility of what exists.[14]

Socrates is just as inspired and daemonic as the true tragic poet, but in his case his demon or "instinct" can only say "No!" For Nietzsche this is the heart of Socrates' nihilism and thus the instinctive tendency at the heart of all science.

> While in all productive men it is instinct that is the creative-affirmative force, and consciousness acts critically and dissuasively, in Socrates it is instinct that becomes the critic, and consciousness that becomes the creator—truly a monstrosity *per defectum*.[15]

The argument of my Part I, however, would say that Socrates' (at least the Platonic and Xenophonic Socrates) "demon" is the knowledge of his own ignorance, which is essentially the distinction rather than separation of true knowledge from what is only possibly known in poetry. Socrates' self-knowledge as a philosopher is to know the difference and the importance of this distinction, but that this is not a negation of poetry is seen in the fact that

---

> It was *against* morality that my instinct turned with this questionable book, long ago; it was an instinct that aligned itself with life and that discovered for itself a fundamentally opposite doctrine and valuation of life—purely artistic and *anti-Christian*. What to call it? As a philologist and man of words I baptized it, not without taking some liberty—for who could claim to know the rightful name of the Antichrist?—in the name of a Greek god: I called it Dionysian. (Nietzsche, *Birth of Tragedy*, 24).

[14] Nietzsche, *Birth of Tragedy*, 87, midway through the middle chapter.

[15] Nietzsche, *Birth of Tragedy*, 88.

tragic poetry is criticized in the form of comic poetry. Writing comic poetry is how Plato (if not the "a-music" Socrates), "saved the appearances" of poetry itself.

What Nietzsche is inadvertently describing here, then, is the very different comedy of modernity that makes a division and hostile relation between its own artifice and the unartificed "nature" that it must "beat" and overcome.[16] The "instincts" in this case are the egotistic desires that are alone counted upon in order to create the "machine that runs of itself" of modern democratic liberalism. The "conscious" creator here is the political "scientist" rather than philosopher, epitomized by Hobbes, who would create single-handedly the modern monster and artificial man, the Leviathan. Yet even here Hobbes is doing no more than applying what his mentor, Francis Bacon, was already prescribing for modern natural science. This new science was no longer to be the passive contemplation of nature, but was to become the actively hostile interrogation and manipulation of nature through experiments that were justified through power *over* nature rather knowledge of nature.[17] It is only when *modern science*, then, "turns its searching eyes," that "it sees lack of insight and the power of illusion"; for what it sees is untamed and dangerous nature and what it finds lacking is its own insights into the power of making. It is from nature viewed this way, rather than from the "nature" found in Plato or even Aquinas, that one "infers the essential perversity and reprehensibility of what exists."

The argument of Plato's philosophic comedies, on the other hand, is that knowledge is intrinsically good, but what is not known or even unknowable is neither good nor bad. What is bad, however, is to cover over the difference and to claim knowledge where there is none; but even that is bad only because it stands in the way

---

[16] cf. Machiavelli, *The Prince*, Chapter 25.

[17] "I mean it [his new instauration of science] to be a history not only of nature free and large...but much more of nature under constraint and vexed; that is to say, when by art and the hand of man she is forced out of her natural state, and squeezed and molded...seeing that the nature of things betrays itself more readily under the vexations of art than in its natural freedom" (Francis Bacon, *A Selection of His Works*, ed. Sidney Warhaft (New York: Macmillan Publishing Company, 1985), 320).

of the genuine good of self-knowledge of oneself as both maker *and* knower.

Nietzsche comes close to this insight in his image of the Platonic dialogues as a sort of raft bearing the remains of the shipwrecked "ancients"; but what he misses are the implications of the ancient image of the submissive female *ancilla* rather than modern Machiavelli's beaten *Fortuna*.

> An instance of this is Plato, who in condemning tragedy and art in general certainly did not lag behind the naive cynicism of his master; he was nevertheless constrained by sheer artistic necessity to create an art-form that was related to those forms of art which he repudiated . . . . The Platonic dialogue was, as it were, the barge on which the shipwrecked ancient poetry saved herself with all her children: crowded into a narrow space and timidly submitting to the single pilot, Socrates, they now sailed into a new world, which never tired of looking at the fantastic spectacle of this procession. Indeed, Plato has given to all posterity the model of a new art form, the model of the novel—which may be described as an infinitely enhanced Aesopian fable, in which poetry holds the same rank in relation to dialectical philosophy as this same philosophy held for many centuries in relation to theology: namely, the rank of ancilla. This was the new position into which Plato, under the pressure of the demonic Socrates, forced poetry.[18]

The new art form that Nietzsche claims Plato invented was, by Plato's own account, the old art form of comedy. The reason he chose the comic form for his dialogues was because comedy opened up the possibility of the reader discovering not Socrates, but rather himself; for written comedy turns the reader back upon himself in the same way Socrates' verbal irony turns his interlocutors back upon themselves.

What the reader discovers when he turns to himself is, of course, another matter, a matter over which comedy has no control. Moderns—especially in that appropriately named modern

---

[18] Nietzsche, *Beyond Good and Evil*, 91.

comic genre, the novel—tend to find either their own egotistical self or their own power of making (both of which turn out to be one and the same); while the ancients (at their best) would tend to discover the "theoretical life" which found in the quest for knowledge the highest end of human existence. In this light, modern science and philosophy were the first discovery, albeit dressed up in the prestige and trappings of the ancient discovery.

The Platonic subordination of poetry to philosophy was entirely dependent upon something outside of poetry altogether, and was therefore only a possibility rather than something already actualized within comic poetry on its own. Yet if that possibility were actualized, and the reader took up the life of the philosopher as his highest pursuit, this did not lead to the destruction of, or even hostility to, poetry; but only to the proper subordination that allowed one to say yes to it in the same way as one affirmed one's own ignorance. In the case of theology, subordination functioned essentially the same way. The subordination of philosophy to theology was no more its destruction than was it Mary's when she said "Behold, the handmaid (*ancilla*) of the Lord." It was instead the affirmation of everything in its true place, rather than the attempt at affirmation in one's own place that tempted Eve. The art form that allows for subordination is comedy, even though that subordination is not guaranteed. If it does not occur, however, one loses everything except the nothingness of nihilism that would rather will nothingness itself than not will at all.[19]

In the light of this nihilism that Nietzsche claims was created by Socrates, but which I would argue was a unique creation of modernity, modern science (both of us would agree) finds itself bumping up against a wall created by its essential nay-saying. For in terms reminiscent of Kierkegaard's description in the *Philosophical Fragments* of "reason willing its own downfall," Nietzsche explains how the cheerful optimism of Greek science (more accurately, "modern" science[20])

---

[19] Friedrich Nietzsche, *On the Genealogy of Morals*, trans. Walter Kaufman (New York: Vintage Books, 1967) 163.

[20] Or, more accurately, the cover-story of modern science that mistakes its own practices and describes itself in terms of power when it is actually

speeds irresistibly toward its limits where its optimism, concealed in the essence of logic, suffers shipwreck. For the periphery of the circle of science has
an infinite number of points; and while there is no
telling how this circle could ever be surveyed completely, noble and gifted men nevertheless reach, e'er
half their time and inevitably, such boundary points
on the periphery from which one gazes into what de-
fies illumination. When they see to their horror how
logic coils up at these boundaries and finally bites its
own tail—suddenly the new form of insight breaks
through, *tragic insight* which, merely to be endured,
needs art as a protection and remedy.[21]

This "tragic insight," shared in by such critics of the Enlightenment as Rousseau and Hegel, leads to the attempt to save modern
science by means of art. In a world scoured of the myths created
by tragic poets, who were once hid but are now revealed as fakes
by enlightened and comic Totos, the only hope seems to be some
sort of art form, that without hiding itself, can still have the unifying and consoling effects of tragedy. The claim of philosophy and
Christian theology is that this is possible either through the subordination of poetry to philosophy or the subordination of philosophy to the poetry of God; but the attempt of tragic philosophy is
to do neither and lose itself in the "poetry" of life itself.

The tragic insight into the limits of modern science therefore
leads to a different form of annihilation than that of modernity,
for what it now desires is the annihilation of the egotistical individual himself, who in his petty and subjective desires provided the
foundation for both modern science and politics. Nietzsche himself, when the title for his first edition was still *The Birth of Tragedy
out of the Spirit of Music*, thought that

---

operating in terms of wonder. Science that "knows itself" is in this sense
overwhelmingly compatible with the self-knowledge that must go along
with the "science," or knowing, found desired by Plato, Aristotle and
Aquinas. On this see Lonergan's *Insight*, perhaps the most accurate account of what modern science "does" rather than what it "says" it does
since the two were initially separated by Bacon.

[21] Nietzsche, *Birth of Tragedy*, 97-98.

it is only through the spirit of music that we can understand the joy involved in the annihilation of the individual. For it is only in particular examples of such annihilation that we see clearly the eternal phenomenon of Dionysian art, which gives expression to the will in its omnipotence, as it were, behind the *principium individuationis*, the eternal life beyond all phenomena, and despite all annihilation . . . . In spite of fear and pity, we are the happy living beings, not as individuals, but as the *one* living being, with whose creative joy we are united.[22]

In his later "Attempt at Self Criticism" of this tragic insight, Nietzsche discovered that it was no more than another form of pessimism, and hence Christianly nihilistic because the metaphysical comfort involved hostility toward what "is" and life itself—namely the will to power of the individual.

Thus, whereas the younger Nietzsche would call for a coming generation to form a tragic culture wherein it would be necessary "for the tragic man of such a culture, in view of his self-education for seriousness and terror, to desire a new art form, the *art of metaphysical comfort*, to desire tragedy as his own proper Helen,"[23] the older and wiser Nietzsche exclaims:

"Would it not be *necessary*?"—No, thrice no! O you young romantics: it would *not* be necessary! But it is highly probable that it will end that way, that you *end* that way—namely, "comforted" as it is written, in spite of all self-education for seriousness and terror, "comforted metaphysically"—in sum as romantics end, as *Christians*.[24]

Why would he say this? Would not the tragic man be the opposite of the Christian man? Perhaps Nietzsche saw too well that there was a third possibility here—the democratic man—who, though atheistic, depends for his politics and morality upon a decayed form of secularized Christianity.

---

[22] Nietzsche, *Birth of Tragedy*, 104-105.

[23] Nietzsche, *Birth of Tragedy*, 26.

[24] Nietzsche, *Birth of Tragedy*, 26.

As a case in point, consider the deliberate secularization of Christianity found in Rousseau's "civil religion" which was invented to back up and support his political creation of the "general will."[25] This "general will," I would argue, is at the heart of both tragic philosophy and liberal morality. In this most potent of all political creations, the egotistical individual is absorbed into the general will and "forced to be free." The individual therefore exists only as formal citizen who is "the soldier painted on the canvas" of this entirely artificial and universalized entity. The very universality of this "one living being" is thus the modern substitute for the effects of tragic narrative. Difficulties arise, however, because Rousseau, as the poet of all this, cannot hide himself, and so spills the beans when he gives all true powers of shaping the constitution

---

[25] On the General Will:

> Each of us puts his person and all his power in common under the supreme control of the general will, and we collectively receive each member as an indivisible part of the whole.
>
> In place of the individual persons of the contracting parties, the act of association immediately creates a collective, artificial body, composed of members as the assembly has voters(Rousseau, *The Essential Rousseau*, 17-18).

On Civil Religion:

> There is thus a purely civil creed whose tenets the sovereign is entitled to determine, not precisely as dogmas of religion, but as sentiments of sociability, without which it is impossible to be a good citizen or a loyal subject....The tenets of the civil religion should be simple, few in number, and enunciated precisely, without explanations or commentaries. The existence of a powerful, intelligent, benevolent, foreseeing, and provident Divinity, the life to come, the happiness of the righteous, the punishment of the wicked, the sanctity of the social contract, and the law—these are the positive tenets. As for negative tenets, I limit them to a single injunction: There shall be no intolerance, which is part of the religions we have excluded (Rousseau, *The Essential Rousseau*, 113).

The success of this secularization of Christianity can be see a century later in Harnack's famous book, *The Essence of Christianity*, wherein after the husk of dogmatic Christianity falls away, the kernel is remarkably similar to this religion invented by Rousseau.

of this general will to the outside "lawgiver."[26] Rousseau's "law-giver" is thus the "one" who turns out to be the "one truly existent subject," who, I would say, not only in the early Nietzsche, but also in all Romantic thought, is the source behind the aesthetization of reality *and* politics.

Rousseau's attempt to achieve tragic effects through comic means, however, leads to some problems that came increasingly to Nietzsche's attention. For one, the subversive effects of comedy and laughter, when directed toward the serious ends of tragedy, inevitably get the upper hand and collapse those ends into the one solipsistic end of the power of making and unmaking in itself. A comic and self-conscious approach to a tragic politics and meta-physics, therefore, inevitably collapses into the nihilistic habits of comic modernity—Nietzsche's "Platonism for the people" that leads inevitably to the comic leveling of the "last man." [27]The "herd with no shepherd"[28] is the direct result of the comic nature of the "law-giver" swallowing up the tragic nature of the general will, to the point where each member fancies himself *en masse*, a comic and absolutely unique "inventor of happiness."

---

[26] "The lawgiver is the engineer who invents the machine; the ruler is only the workman who assembles it and keeps it running. . . . Anyone who dares to undertake the task of instituting a nation must feel himself capable of changing human nature, so to speak; of transforming each individual, who by himself is a complete and solitary whole, into a part of a greater whole from which he, in a sense, receives his life and his being. . . . He must, in short, take away man's resources to give him others that are foreign to him and cannot be used without the help of other men.....Therefore, since the lawgiver can use neither force nor reasoning, he must resort to another kind of authority which can lead without compelling and persuade without convincing.

This is what has forced the founders of nations in all ages to appeal to divine intervention and attribute their own wisdom to the gods, so that their people, submitting to the laws of the state as to those of nature, and acknowledging the same power in the formation of man as in that of the body politic, will obey with freedom and bear the yoke of public well-being with docility" (Rousseau, *The Essential Rousseau*, 37-38).

[27] Nietzsche, *Beyond Good and Evil*, 3.

[28] Friedrich Nietzsche, *Thus Spake Zarathustra*, trans. Walter Kaufman (New York: Vintage Books, 1954), 16-19.

After pushing the romantic form of Rousseau's creation as far as he could in the context of his early work on tragedy, the new move of Nietzsche is to turn to the role of this "lawgiver" directly—the lawgiver and creator who remains comically "outside" as the god to his own creation. Instead of remaining romantic and "Christian," then, his response is to say:

> No! You ought to learn the art of *this-worldly* comfort first; you ought to learn to laugh, my young friends, if you are hell-bent on remaining pessimists. Then perhaps, as laughers, you may some day dispatch all metaphysical comforts to the devil—metaphysics in front.[29]

The rejection of metaphysics is the rejection of the essence of German Idealism, which is essentially the metaphysical outworking of Rousseau's political creations. What is "other-worldly" in all this is the destruction of rank and thus life in the leveling process of universalization, so the "this-worldly" comfort is for those few laughers who can assume the rank of who true god is in all this, the "lawgiver" who trans-values all values and overcomes morality.

The overcoming of morality is thus part and parcel of overcoming the nihilism of modern technological comedy *and* romantic tragic philosophy, both of which Nietzsche has now reinterpreted as symptomatic of the inevitable tragic fall of Socrates' philosophy into nihilism. The new sailing of Nietzsche is into a new comic world that makes of himself the creator-god above all moralities, whether of science or religion. As he writes in the *Gay Science*:

> *Homo poeta.*—"I myself, having made this tragedy of tragedies all by myself, insofar as it is finished—I, having first tied the knot of morality into existence before I drew it so tight that only a god could untie it (which is what Horace demands)—I myself have now slain all gods in the fourth act, for the sake of morality. Now, what is to become of the fifth act? From

---

[29] Nietzsche, *Birth of Tragedy*, 26.

where am I to take the tragic solution?—Should I begin to think about a comic solution?"[30]

Nietzsche's comic solution must slay the gods of the old morality in order to become the god who self-consciously creates a new morality; for this sort of mock violence is the subversive quality of comedy that takes nothing seriously outside of its own creation. Nietzsche's comedy must therefore subvert the established tragedy of Western philosophy in its entirety. For when he exposes the fact that (only modern, I would argue) philosophy has been loyal to gods of its own making rather than what truly "is," the collapse of belief in anything at all in the West is no more than "continued proof that the long, real tragedy *is at an end*, assuming that every philosophy was in its genesis a long tragedy."[31] The only thing left after this "death of tragedy," is a new comedy that is no longer nihilistic because it takes as much joy in its creating as in its destroying.

When it comes down to it, however (perhaps in order to separate this comedy from the "optimistic" and "cheerful" comedy of the last man), Nietzsche does not call this a comedy at all, but rather a new form of tragedy, comically discovered by Nietzsche himself. This tragedy no longer seeks to escape from fear and pity, but instead seeks to rise so high above these emotions that it is as serene in its suffering as it is in its creation. "There are heights of the soul from which even tragedy ceases to look tragic; and rolling together all the woe of the world—who could dare to decide whether its sight would *necessarily* seduce us and compel us to feel pity and thus double this woe."[32] This tragedy that is above all fear and pity is the tragedy of a creator-god who is as much a creator as a destroyer. Such a pitiless god redefines the meaning of tragedy entirely, for not only has the emphasis shifted from the poem to the poet, but it has also shifted away from fear and pity to the joy of creating and destroying.

---

[30] Friedrich Nietzsche, *The Gay Science*, trans. Walter Kaufman (New York: Vintage Books, 1974), 197.

[31] Nietzsche, *Beyond Good and Evil*, 37.

[32] Nietzsche, *Beyond Good and Evil*, 42.

In his *Ecce Homo*, he will use a quotation from his own *Twilight of the Idols* to describe how he "found the concept of the 'tragic' and at long last knowledge of the psychology of tragedy."

> "Saying Yes to life even in its strangest and hardest problems; the will to life rejoicing over its own inexhaustibility even in the very sacrifice of its highest types—that is what I called Dionysian, that is what I understood as the bridge to the psychology of the tragic poet. Not in order to get rid of terror and pity, not in order to purge oneself of a dangerous effect by its vehement discharge—Aristotle misunderstood it that way—but in order to be oneself the eternal joy of becoming, beyond all terror and pity—that joy which includes even joy in destroying."
>
> In this sense I have the right to understand myself as the first *tragic philosopher*—that is the most extreme opposite and antipode of a pessimistic philosopher. Before me this transposition of the Dionysian into a philosophical pathos did not exist: *tragic wisdom* was lacking; I have looked in vain for signs of it even among the *great* Greeks in philosophy, those of the two centuries *before* Socrates.[33]

This, then, is the psychology of tragedy: "to be oneself the eternal joy of becoming" and to be "beyond all terror and pity." Yet because Nietzsche claims to have discovered this "tragic wisdom" for the first time, it seems to be something beyond all the traditional characteristics of tragedy, to the point where it appears to be as much comedy as tragedy. It is the attempt to usurp the place of the murdered Christian God who creates comically, but because this usurpation is based upon a murder and destruction, it must still somehow be tragic. Nietzsche therefore calls himself the first "tragic philosopher" because he has discovered the true wisdom of tragedy which is to be beyond good and evil just as it is above terror and pity.

What is the heart of this "tragic philosophy," discovered by Nietzsche, that is as much comic as it is tragic? The answer, I think,

---

[33] Friedrich Nietzsche, *The Twilight of the Idols*, trans. Walter Kaufman (New York: Vintage Press, 1968), 273.

is Nietzsche's teaching on the "eternal recurrence of the same."
For in this teaching we find the most "burdensome thought" that
allows one to become the god who can look down upon all the
pain and suffering in the world and convert this spectacle into joy
and affirmation. It is the act of willing that allows one to become
the comic-god who creates everything that is and was and pro-
nounces all of it good, no matter what suffering is involved.

> Whoever has endeavored with some enigmatic long-
> ing, as I have, to think pessimism through to its
> depths and to liberate it from the half-Christian, half-
> German narrowness and simplicity in which it has fi-
> nally presented itself to our century, namely, in the
> form of Schopenhauer's philosophy; whoever has re-
> ally, with an Asiatic and supra-Asiatic eye, looked
> into, down into the most world-denying of all possi-
> ble ways of thinking—beyond good and evil and no
> longer, like the Buddha and Schopenhauer, under the
> spell and delusion of morality—may just thereby,
> without really meaning to do, have opened his eyes to
> the opposite ideal: the ideal of the most high-spirited,
> alive, and world-affirming human being who has not
> only come to terms and learned to get along with
> whatever was and is, but who wants to have *what was
> and is* repeated into all eternity, shouting insatiably *da
> capo*—not only to himself but to the whole play and
> spectacle, and not only to a spectacle but at bottom
> to him who needs precisely this spectacle—and who
> makes it necessary because again and again he needs
> himself—and makes himself necessary—What? And
> this wouldn't be—*circulus vitiosus deus?*[34]

The "eternal recurrence of the same" is the thought that overcomes the traditional and pessimistic notions of tragedy, by taking
tragedy away from the spectators and their desire to avoid fear and
pity, and putting it into the hands of the tragic-poet who is at once
both hero and creator of his own tragedy. The joy of suffering thus
comes about because it is simultaneously the joy of creating.

---

[34] Nietzsche, *Beyond Good and Evil*, 68.

In comedy the joy of creating is why there is laughter, mock rather than real beatings, and happy endings; but in the usual tragedy, the joy of creating must be hid and experienced only indirectly through catharsis. If one could will everything as it is and was, repeated for all eternity, then and only then, could one experience the godlike pleasures of creativity along with the mortal experiences of suffering at one and the same time. It would be the "vicious circle of a god," because one would be willing oneself and oneself alone, but it would also be the joy of "becoming" because one would also be willing one's own finitude, mortality and suffering in all of its powerlessness.

Instead of Hegel's Absolute that comprehends rationally the tragic whole that must continually rend itself and reconstitute itself out of that rending, Nietzsche's tragic wisdom is that tragedy is an issue of the will rather than of reason. The only true tragedy is thus one of willing as only a god could will—and that is a matter of the individual who has become a god. The *incipit tragoedia* that ends *The Gay Science* thus becomes the individual *incipit Zarathustra* that begins *Thus Spake Zarathustra*.

The passage Heidegger uses from Nietzsche as his *leitmotif* in thinking through the eternal recurrence of the same, should give us more insight into this.[35]

> Around the hero everything turns into a tragedy; around the demi-god, into a satyr play; and around God—what? perhaps into "world"?[36]

The tragic insight of the early Nietzsche is of the hero, the "soldier on canvas" who is part of a tragedy for the sake of the "metaphysical comfort" of the audience. The satyr-play of the demi-god is the "one true existing subject" who is always appearing under the various masks of tragic individuals. But the "world" of God, is it not the tragic world created by oneself through willful affirmation in "the eternal recurrence of the same"? Yet what sort of world would this be, this comic affirmation of a tragic world?

---

[35] Martin Heidegger, *Nietzsche: The Eternal Recurrence of the Same*, trans. David Farrell Krell (San Francisco: Harper and Row Publishers, 1984).

[36] Nietzsche, *Beyond Good and Evil*, 90.

SERIOUS COMEDY

Heidegger attempts to explain it as follows, an explanation that is as much a revelation of his own thinking as Nietzsche's.

> Beings themselves imply torture, destruction, and the "no" as proper to them. In *Ecce Homo*, at the place where he describes the gestation of the thought of eternal return of the same, Nietzsche calls the thought "the highest formula of affirmation that can ever be achieved.". . . Why is the thought of return supreme affirmation? Because it affirms the uttermost "no," annihilation and suffering as proper to beings.[37]

This supreme affirmation of annihilation and suffering is a comic move that creates for itself an entirely tragic world. The joy is in the affirmation and the creation, but what is affirmed is the tragic pain of suffering and destruction. The cathartic reversal that allows the pain and suffering on stage to result in pleasure and unity in the audience is now to be a reversal self-consciously and deliberately effected upon all of reality by willfully choosing and thereby "poetizing" for oneself, everything that was and is into all eternity. The "eternal return of the same" is thus tragic catharsis, albeit one that can only be effected if the world is the stage and you as the audience are its god.

The situation is thus very much akin to that of Hegel, but whereas for him the Absolute Spirit as the tragic audience to the comic spectacle is a corporate entity; in Nietzsche, the god who affirms the eternal return is not corporate at all and so remains in competition with all other gods in their affirmations or negations. And the god he remains in most direct competition with is the God of Christianity. For this is the truly comic God, the god who has no true competitors, who creates everything that is with no remainder and hence no need to affirm again what he has affirmed initially as good.

Who, then, is the god Nietzsche aspires to be? Is it not one of the gods mentioned very early on in Genesis, the "gods" we will become when our eyes are opened, knowing good from evil? Nietzsche knows full well this is the god he aspires to be. In fact, his

---

[37] Heidegger, *Eternal Recurrence*, 30.

386

work entitled *Beyond Good and Evil* is based entirely upon this temptation scene. Here, however, the serpent is Dionysus, the "attempter" and "pied piper" of consciences, and the new Eve is not Mary, but rather Ariadne, the "guide through many a labyrinth." The entire book is a seduction manual for the truth that is "supposed" to be a woman, a seduction that consists of turning her head to a beauty that is "beyond" good and evil.

And yet since one of the greatest forms of competition is to deny the existence of your opponent or even redefine him in the terms of your own making, Nietzsche's final word on the tempter in *Beyond Good and Evil* is that he is in fact God himself—God at leisure and at play on the seventh day.

> Theologically speaking—listen closely, for I rarely speak as a theologian—it was God himself who at the end of his days' work lay down as a serpent under the tree of knowledge: thus he recuperated from being God.—He had made everything too beautiful.—The devil is merely the leisure of God on that seventh day.[38]

This, in a nutshell, is the dramatic history of the world that has led up to Nietzsche. The divine comedy of Christianity has turned into the temptation of the modern nihilistic comedy of modernity; but what it tempts us toward is the new tragic philosophy of Nietzsche wherein not only do the gods philosophize, but one must truly become a god to do so.

The question arises at this point whether Nietzsche's tragic philosophy is as different as he claims from the tragic philosophy of Hegel and others. In the light of George Steiner's following description of the continuity of tragic philosophy after Rousseau, the question for Nietzsche is whether he can truly claim to have understood the psychology of tragedy and discovered tragic wisdom for the first time.

> The major philosophic systems since the French Revolution have been tragic systems . . . . To philosophize

---

[38] Nietzsche, *Ecce Homo*, 311.

after Rousseau and Kant, to find a normative, conceptual phrasing for the psychic, social, and historical condition of man, is to think 'tragically'. It is to find in tragic drama, as did Nietzsche in *Tristan*, the *'opus metaphysicum* par excellence'. This means that formal philosophic discourse, from Kant to Max Scheler and Heidegger, will imply or articulate a theory of tragic effect and that it will draw almost instinctively, on passages from tragedy for decisive illustration.[39]

In this light Nietzsche is not even the last in a long list of tragic thinkers. But Nietzsche can claim credit for putting tragic philosophy in its proper antagonistic relationship to Christianity and the philosophy of Plato, and for seeing that the conflict revolved around the issues of comedy and tragedy. Nietzsche, perhaps even more so than Hegel, consistently worked out of the irrational consequences of living tragically in one's writing, consequences that require lying, violent competition, destruction and willful power to be the ultimate foundations in life. Nietzsche has perhaps most thoroughly and consistently worked through the implications of the philosophic move made by Machiavelli. And where that move leads is not to a comedy with a happy ending, but rather to the imitation of a comic-god, which as an imitation rather than the real thing, can only create tragedy.

A further question that must be asked is whether Nietzsche's "tragic wisdom," because it is based upon a comic affirmation in "the eternal recurrence of the same," can avoid ultimately collapsing into the comic mediocrity of the last man. Just as the tragic philosophy inaugurated by Rousseau finally devolved into the comic leveling of the last man because of the subversive effects of the self-conscious "lawgiver," so we must ask whether Nietzsche's emphasis upon comic affirmation and laughter won't lead to the same thing. Instead of the last man being little Rousseauian "lawgivers" who invent their own happiness, the last men after Nietzsche will be little Nietzscheans who say "yes" to life and become gods for fifteen minutes on talk shows. If Zarathustra cannot in

---

[39] George, Steiner, *Antigones* (New York: Oxford University Press, 1984), 2.

fact become a god through willful affirmation, is not the last man what must inevitably happen instead? This time, however, the last men will be "laughers" instead of "blinkers," and the universalization of mediocrity will consist of the "David Lettermanizing" and reduction of all human endeavor and thought to a "stupid-human trick."

Nietzsche's critique of the tendency toward "last man" decay in his own early tragic philosophy, and my own arguments, raise the possibility that it is truly impossible today to have a tragic philosophy that does not collapse into a form of comedy—a comedy that will be all the worse because it had tragic expectations. The reason for this may well be the simple fact that humans cannot truly live in their own writings. If Platonic philosophy and the Bible have both taken the lid off the scapegoating effects of tragedy and thus made that attempt no longer possible, the only other possibility is to somehow live in comic writing. Yet the nature of comic writing is such that if genuine life is not found elsewhere than in this writing itself—in God, the theoretical life, or both—then the gap that should be filled from without becomes the emptiness of nihilism. The possible fullness of comic writing has today become the actual emptiness of modern nihilism.

Yet because of the hypertrophied self-consciousness of our own powers of making, the "technologization" of our entire lives, the ascendancy of comic writing seems inevitable. This ascendancy will either reduce even the most sustained attempts at tragic philosophy into nihilism, or it will subordinate itself to the only two ways of life that know how to do so—philosophy and Christian faith. When Nietzsche smelt the decay of earlier tragic philosophies into nihilism, he was getting a foretaste of the decay his own tragic wisdom would result in. Jumping off a tower is no way to solve vertigo. In the same way, a deeper plunge into tragic philosophy is no way to solve the dizziness of nihilism. What is needed instead is to climb down off the tower of writing altogether, onto the good solid earth of our own life and the life of God. Such a life is neither comic nor tragic, but it is the life that has been appropriately written about in comedy. For better or worse, then, comedy will have the last written word

XVI: KIERKEGAARD: TRAGIC EXISTENCE AND CHRISTIAN COMEDY

It would be well, if all our lives were a divine tragedy even, instead of this trivial comedy or farce.

—Henry David Thoreau, *Walking*

IN HIS *Concluding Unscientific Postscript to the Philosophical Fragments* Kierkegaard uses the pseudonym of Johannes Climacus to give us what is perhaps one of the most sustained discussions of the relation between what I have called "life" and "writing." Although he will use the terms "subjective existence" and "indirect communication," as a sort of Christian Socrates, Kierkegaard will discipline himself to the implications of writing about life that can only be lived apart from writing at all or in the writing of God. What is different about his own presentation of this relation is that, while still maintaining the central role of Plato's reversal between life and writing, he will no longer relate it primarily to the life of the philosopher. Instead, he will extend it to the fundamental contradiction of all human existence, and hence treat it as a problem for all genuine human communication from one person to the next. According to Kierkegaard, it is because of the demand upon every subjective existence to appropriate individually the truth for him or herself, that there can be no direct communication of that truth from one person to another as something objectively present in writing, narrative, or anything else. So "whereas objective thinking is indifferent to the thinking subject and his existence, the subjective thinker as existing is essentially interested in his own thinking, is existing in it."[1] The subjective thinker is "subjective," then, because "his thinking has another kind of reflection, specifically, that of inwardness, of possession, whereby it belongs to the subject and to no one else."[2] The question is thus not that of the objective truth *per se*, but rather how that truth becomes appropriated by the individual; and because one might overlook this demand for the truth to be appropriated, the seeming presence of the truth in any sort of objective communication tempts one to mistake understanding the communication for appropriating it.

One who *has* appropriated the truth, realizes that a further communication of that truth must somehow avoid the temptation to misunderstand it as something objectively understandable and hence directly communicable. This realization, which Kierkegaard calls "double reflection," leads to a search for some form of communication that *can* communicate what is most important about the truth—that it can only be appropriated subjectively by the individual in inwardness. Wherever this subjective appropriation is of utmost importance, then,

> and appropriation is therefore the main point, communication is a *work of art*; it is doubly reflected, and its first form is the subtlety that the subjective individuals must be held devoutly apart from one another and must not run coagulatingly together in objectivity . . . . Ordinary communication, objective thinking, has no secrets; only doubly reflected subjective thinking has secrets; that is, all its essential content is essentially a secret, because it cannot be communicated directly. This is the significance of the secrecy. That this knowledge cannot be stated directly, because the essential in this knowledge is the appropriation itself, means that it remains a secret for everyone who is not through himself doubly reflected in the same way, but

---

[1] Søren Kierkegaard, *Concluding Unscientific Postscript to Philosophical Fragments*, vol. 1, trans. Howard and Edna Hong (Princeton: Princeton University Press, 1992), 72-3.

[2] Kierkegaard, *Concluding Unscientific Postscript*, 73.

that this is the essential form of truth means that this
cannot be said in any other way.[3]

Subjective communication is thus always "indirect communication"; and the "secret" of all subjective thought is the awareness
that its communication must always be by means of a "work of
art" that creates a barrier separating one subject from another even
while forcing each subject back upon himself for a true understanding. Kierkegaard is thus arguing why *poesis* is unavoidable
when pursuing a life genuinely lived in pursuit of the truth. In so
doing he is also essentially echoing Plato's arguments about writing, but this time in the form of a prescription rather than a complaint.

Kierkegaard gives an account of why we need this poetic
communication by describing the fundamental contradictions that
lead to this gap between life and writing in the first place. "Just as
his communication must in form essentially conform to his own
existence, so his thought must correspond to the form of existence."[4] The form of existence consists of the "subject's synthesis,
in his being an existing infinite spirit."[5] The meaning this has for
existence is as much negative as positive, for whereas the positive
consists of the infinite spiritual element that goes beyond the conditions of space and time, the negative is the fact that such transcendence must be appropriated within the finite limitations of
human life bounded by death and the body.

This contradiction, the problem of becoming and temporal
existence, Kierkegaard equates with Eros in Plato's *Symposium*:

> According to Plato, Poverty and Plenty begot Eros,
> whose nature is made up of both. But what is exist-
> ence? It is that child who is begotten by the infinite
> and the finite, the eternal and the temporal, and is
> therefore continually striving. This was Socrates'

---

[3] Kierkegaard, *Concluding Unscientific Postscript*, 79 (emphasis added).

[4] Kierkegaard, *Concluding Unscientific Postscript*, 80.

[5] Kierkegaard, *Concluding Unscientific Postscript*, 82.

view—therefore love is continually striving, that is, the thinking subject is existing.[6]

Kierkegaard thus uses Eros to discuss the totality of Plato's reversal, the reason why life seems to contradict writing and vice versa.

Existence, for him, is so immersed in this tension that it must unavoidably and always be both comic and tragic, just as writing is either comic or tragic. One is the flip side of the other; and yet their relation is not one of reconciliation but rather one of conflict.

> Existence itself, existing, is striving and is just as pathos-filled as it is comic: pathos-filled because the striving is infinite, that is, directed toward the infinite, is a process of infinitizing, which is the highest pathos; comic because the striving is a self-contradiction. From a pathos-filled perspective, one second has infinite value; from a comic perspective, ten thousand years are but a prank, like a yesterday, and yet the time the existing individual is in does consist of such parts.[7]

Kierkegaard's account of Plato's reversal between life and writing is to understand the contradiction of human existence as being both comic *and* tragic, because the nature of the contradiction is such that each side reverses itself into the other, and neither side can stand alone.

But to understand exactly what Kierkegaard means in his account we need to see why he uses the comic and the tragic to explain the contradiction of existence. To do so, we should imagine human existence as a stage upon which one is both actor and audience, thereby allowing one to bear a differing relation to the "idea," which would seem to be the poetic embodiment of the object of human striving.

> What lies at the root of both the comic and the pathos-filled is the misrelation, the contradiction between the infinite and the finite, the eternal and the

---

[6] Kierkegaard, *Concluding Unscientific Postscript*, 92.

[7] Kierkegaard, *Concluding Unscientific Postscript*, 92.

becoming. A pathos that excludes the comic is therefore a misunderstanding, is not pathos at all. The subjectively existing thinker is therefore just as bifrontal as the existence-situation itself. The interpretation of the misrelation, viewed with the idea ahead, is pathos; the interpretation of the misrelation viewed with the idea behind, is the comic. When the subjective existing thinker turns his face toward the idea, his interpretation of the misrelation is pathos-filled; when he turns his back to the idea, allowing it to shine from behind into the same misrelation, his interpretation is comic.[8]

The image suggested by this bifrontality is that of the play-within-plays already mentioned in relation to Hegel (which in turn is derived from Tieck's *Topsy-Turvy World*), wherein someone from the audience has peeked behind the curtain, only to discover that he is as much in front of the curtain as behind. Or to put it another way, it is a stage upon which another play is being played, and perhaps upon that smaller stage another one, ad infinitum. Such a play within a play can either move centripetally inwards toward the ultimate stage, or centrifugally outwards toward the ultimate audience. But the contradiction of existence for Kierkegaard, in contrast to Hegel, is that there is no final audience any more than there is a final stage; human existence is instead the unsteady and vertiginous going back and forth between the two.

What makes the stage image work, however, is the central role of *poesis* in human existence. The centrality of *poesis* is the demand for an indirect communication involving a double-reflection wherein we create an image of what we have understood, recognizing all the while that the produced image is not fully adequate to that understanding. Producing an image of what is understood and appropriated may be likened to putting a scene or an "idea" on the stage. The gap between audience and stage would be the image of the contradiction between an intelligent grasp of what is intrinsically unconditioned by space and time, and the finite mimesis of that grasp which must be created in space and time as the

---

[8] Kierkegaard, *Concluding Unscientific Postscript*, 89-90.

only means of expressing it to oneself or even another. To look "toward" this idea, then, is to look from one's infinite understanding to its finite expression. The awareness of that discrepancy would therefore be tragic because the reach of audience always exceeds the grasp on stage; and this tragic overreaching would be known and felt precisely in the cathartic gap between audience and stage. To have the idea behind one, on the other hand, is comic because from this perspective one unites both stage and audience within the common idea shared on stage. In this case, the discrepancy between infinite understanding and finite expression is itself part of the expression, and thus not something actually existing apart from that expression.

In the concrete terms that connect with the affective role of tears and laughter, the difference between the comic and tragic has to do with role of pain in encountering the contradiction of our own existence. As Kierkegaard puts it: "The matter is very simple . . . where there is life there is contradiction . . . . The tragic and the comic are the same inasmuch as both are contradiction, but the *tragic is suffering contradiction, and the comic is painless contradiction.*"[9] In terms of actual plot developments, he elaborates this by adding:

> The difference between the tragic and the comic consists in the relation of the contradiction to the idea. The comic interpretation produces the contradiction or allows it to become apparent by having *in mente* [in mind] the way out; therefore the contradiction is painless. The tragic interpretation sees the contradiction and despairs over the way out.[10]

The reason the comic has in mind a way out is because in comedy the "idea" is the fruit of *poesis*, and the work of comic poetry allows it to close the gap of the contradiction by including every element within its created world up on stage, including the audience. The painlessness of this production is thus a result of comedy's ability to include all its struggles and conflicts as second act complications resolved in the comedy as a whole. The idea of comedy, in other

---

[9] Kierkegaard, *Concluding Unscientific Postscript*, 514.

[10] Kierkegaard, *Concluding Unscientific Postscript*, 515-516.

words, is that you are only dealing with the "idea" of contradiction rather than the contradiction itself.

The painful contradiction of tragedy, on the other hand, is painful precisely because the "idea" is the gap itself between stage and audience. We despair over the way out of that gap because what is on stage is a repetition of that very same gulf in the form of the irreconcilable tensions of the tragic plot. It is in tragedy, then, that we feel directly the pain of the contradiction we are. In comedy we see only that we can think or imagine the contradiction reconciled, even though we cannot actually live in those thoughts or imaginations. To "get out" of the contradiction evoked by comedy, is thus to get "back" to the contradiction we in fact are—but that is to leave the play altogether. The reason we "despair over a way out" in tragedy is because the contradiction on stage is the very same contradiction of the existing audience.

From this it might well seem that Kierkegaard is reversing the priorities we saw in Plato by claiming that comedy is more of a "lie" than tragedy. What must be kept in mind, however, is that Kierkegaard is here speaking in his own "indirect" sort of way of what can only be obliquely inferred from Plato, namely, the "tragic" *life* of the philosopher. Just as Plato's dialogues bring out how this serious life can only be apprehended by means of its attendant playful expressions and ironic dissimulations, so too Kierkegaard is here bringing out how tragic existence must always be expressed to others comically. The inwardness of all human existence is thus for Kierkegaard the same thing as the hiddenness of the true lover of wisdom. And just as that philosopher will choose to write in the opposite way he in fact lives, so also will inwardness communicate indirectly through a poetic medium that only "produces" or "manifests" the contradiction of existence and thereby leaves a way out—back to our own subjective existence.

Kierkegaard is thus discussing the crossover between writing and life; but only in terms of the movement from a tragic life to comic writing rather than vice versa. For it is only when the painful contradiction of human existence expresses itself painlessly that we encounter truly subjective existence which appropriates itself

in passionate inwardness apart from its communication, concep-
tualizations, writings, etc. The other possibility, that we might find
our existence in our writing and thereby live a comic rather than
serious life, Kierkegaard calls living "objectively." It is under this
category that he would understand the philosophy of Hegel, insofar as it neglects genuine human existence and has its life in its
writings, which is to say, its "concepts." The final tragedy of Hegel's "Calvary of absolute Spirit" would not be truly a tragic existence because it doesn't "despair over a way out"; there is no one
in that final audience to do so who is not as much a work of *poesis*
as anything going on onstage.

Kierkegaard puts succinctly his opinion of Hegel's *Phenomenology of Spirit* in the following:

> In the world-historical process, the dead are not
> called to life but only to a fantastical-objective life,
> and in a fantastical sense God is the moving spirit in
> a process. In the world-historical process, God is
> metaphysically laced in a half-metaphysical, half-es-
> thetic-dramatic, conventional corset, which is imma-
> nence. What a devil of a thing to be God in that way.[11]

What Kierkegaard complains of here is that by understanding the
contradiction of existence as the "magical" power of the negative
that "converts death into being," Hegel has collapsed the idea of
God into "the moving spirit in a process" otherwise known as
"Absolute Spirit." Such magic is therefore the magic of the sor-
cerer's apprentice, and what he summons to "fantastic-objective
life" is a world-historical process in which God is imprisoned in
the conventions of human writing, thereby making him "half-met-
aphysical, half aesthetic-dramatic."

Taking up the "aesthetic-dramatic" half in terms of comedy
and tragedy, what Kierkegaard seems to be saying is that Hegel's
philosophy is the lie of the tragic-poets, written this time by a philosopher; and the way this lie works is to take as "real" what we
have created on stage rather than the audience watching it. However effective or needed this sort of lie may be, the price one pays

---

[11] Kierkegaard, *Concluding Unscientific Postscript*, 156.

for it is remaining ignorant of the true tragedy of human existence that led to the lie in the first place.

It is this tragedy, the tragic contradiction of human existence, that Kierkegaard does not want to lose sight of. And yet in order even to speak of this life, one must use the narrative possibilities of comedy and tragedy. How to evoke, then, in writing that it is not the "written" but rather life itself one is speaking of? Socrates spoke of the paradoxical nature of his own ignorance, but from "Johannes Climacus" we hear all of human existence in terms of the "God-idea." Existing before the possibility of God means that the human productions of writing, whether comic or tragic, must be understood with built-in limitations. These limitations he speaks of in terms of the theater.

> Accordingly, the individual's ethical development is the little private theater where God certainly is the spectator, but where on occasion the individual also is himself a spectator, although essentially he is supposed to be an actor, not, however, one who deceives but one who discloses, just as all ethical development consists in becoming disclosed before God. But to God, world-history is the royal stage where he, not accidentally but essentially, is the only spectator, because he is the only one who *can* be that. If he fancies himself a spectator there, he is simply forgetting that he himself is supposed to be the actor in that little theater and is to leave it to that royal spectator and poet how he wants to use him in that royal drama, *Drama Dramatum* [The Drama of Dramas].[12]

The "little private theater" of ethical development must, in other words, be conceived of as a stage-play that is itself playing before a larger audience to which the reversing actors and audience on the smaller theater have no access. In contrast to Hegel, then, the central role of narrative in ethics is comical rather than tragic because the point of actor and/or audience on the little theater is not to deceive but to disclose. The disclosure that comedy provides in contrast to the deception of tragedy is that we are both actor *and*

---

[12] Kierkegaard, *Concluding Unscientific Postscript*, 157-8.

audience, the doers *and* observers of our own actions and decisions, who forever lack an immanent standpoint by which to either evaluate or even unify ourselves.

Whatever unity or confidence we do have is therefore always our own produced "idea" of God, the Absolute, the universal or the Spirit. But this produced idea, precisely because it is produced, will in turn be taken up upon stage again—hence comedy's inevitable ironic subversion—as a part of the play that must in turn have another audience produced for itself. What these unending reversals show, then, is how we as the producers of our own audience can never know ourselves *as* producers, can never see ourselves from that perspective however much we must forever strive to do so.

What the actor and audience in Kierkegaard's little theater discloses, then, is the contradiction in human existence between our infinite demand to be fully revealed and fully known, and our finite inability to do so. Such a disclosure is, as I have said, also comic; because such role reversals are indirect communications that merely represent ethical possibilities. If we appropriate such disclosures in subjective inwardness, however, those reversals come to a relative stop, and we become the audience of our own tragic existence that knows and feels its striving as impossible to fulfill because of the contradiction of being unable to get off the stage.

The final disclosure is, of course, our own death, to which we are the final audience; but that is no more than to say that the final realization of all our possibilities is to us, while still existing, *only* a possibility. Until we transcend this play within a play of life by our actual rather than imagined death, there is no final audience to give the entire play a unity. Such is the "little private theater" of immanent existence.

Kierkegaard divides this theater into three representative plays, or what he calls spheres, each characterized by a certain kind of existing audience presented with a certain kind of stage, which he calls *confinium* or border territory, that like stage curtains temporarily divides one sphere from another.

> There are thus three existence-spheres: the esthetic, the ethical, the religious. To these there is respectively corresponding *confinium* [border territory]: irony is the *confinium* between the esthetic and the ethical; humor is the *confinium* between the ethical and the religious.[13]

Now, since these spheres are each in an ordered relationship of increasing inwardness and passionate subjectivity, going from the aesthetic sphere to the religious, the first thing to notice about them is that as existential spheres they must each be essentially tragic, since the tragic has to do with the suffering of existing in the midst of passionate striving. This leads us to the question of the comic, for it is not at all evident how a painless contradiction can find a place in actual existence. For an answer, we must turn to the borders between the spheres. It is here, in the border between different ways of existing, that we can discern not only a realm of sheer possibility, but also a role whereby actual existence in one sphere can play the part of tempting possibility in another. Let us see if we can clarify this by moving in summary fashion through each sphere and border in sequence.

To begin with the aesthetic sphere, we must realize that it is essentially the mode of existence that makes no distinction between actuality and possibility. Since the aesthetic world is the manifestation of the infinite play of human possibilities, it is quite content with the claim that "all the world's a stage." In this sphere there is no conscious distinction between play and audience inasmuch as the pathos of looking toward the idea of infinite possibilities is not countered by the equal pull of finite existence. Choices are made for one on stage, just as suffering is on stage, and creation is looked upon as a self-evident reality completely apart from the demand for an existing, finite creator. The despair over finding a way out in the aesthetic sphere is thus the quiet despair that suffers the loss of its own self in the play of infinite possibility, and yet cannot feel that suffering for lack of a self to feel. As Kierkegaard puts it, "in himself the individual is undialectical and has his dialectic outside himself," which is to say, the individual "finds no

---

[13] Kierkegaard, *Concluding Unscientific Postscript*, 501-502.

contradiction in existing; to exist is one thing, contradiction is something that comes from without."[14] The existing subject has been swallowed up by what is on stage to the point where he can no longer distinguish between the two.

This aesthetic sphere epitomizes how Kierkegaard would characterize Hegel's conflation of writing with life. When we live in our writings the ability to distinguish concrete human life from the world of our own poetic creations becomes practically impossible. Nevertheless, this state has been the typical stance of all human civilizations, especially insofar as they have been founded upon the tragic writings of religion and laws that are for the most part the poetic carvings casting the shadows on the walls of the cave of the city. Aesthetic existence is the existence of the tragic audience that cathartically loses its reality before the more powerful scapegoat reality written "up on stage" for it; and Hegel, by making his last standpoint tragic is concurring with this as the final "actuality, truth and certainty" of humanity watching itself in the form of its own creations. As Kierkegaard puts it, the aesthetic and intellectual principle operative here in Hegel is that no reality is thought or understood until "the *esse* of an actuality is dissolved into its *posse*."[15] To understand an *existing* audience Hegel must therefore understand it as a *possible* audience, and his tragic "Calvary of absolute Spirit" fits this philosophical demand nicely because what is known here is not oneself as audience but only the totality of what is on stage. The actuality of life being a "play within a play" can thus only be understood within the philosophical and dramatic viewpoint that views all of reality as this play within a play of its own making.

But if a particular existing individual in the audience were to ask, "what if I am *in fact* in a play within a play, and this play is also playing in 'the little private theater' of God that is not of my own or anyone else's making?"—then he would have to stop watching and start acting—but that would move him to another sphere. So the real question for Kierkegaard is what sort of "play" would

---

[14] Kierkegaard, *Concluding Unscientific Postscript*, 572.

[15] Kierkegaard, *Concluding Unscientific Postscript*, 324.

prompt that individual to ask this question in the first place and so begin to exist ethically rather than aesthetically.

The answer to that question is an "ironic" play. But irony as a border zone rather than a sphere, or way, of existing. No one can exist ironically, but one *can* exist ethically with irony as an incognito.[16] What this means is that "border zones," like possibility, can only be inhabited temporarily, and even then, only when looking back upon the "idea" of the sphere of existence that preceded it. To be ironical in any other way is merely to be part and parcel of the aesthetic sphere. "Everyone, way down to the lowliest person, dabbles in being ironical, but there where irony actually begins, they all fall away, and this crowd, each one relatively ironic on a descending scale, turns embittered against the genuine ironist."[17] What then is "irony"? "Irony emerges by continually joining the particulars of the finite with the ethical infinite requirement and allowing the contradiction to come into existence."[18]

The ironist is therefore the one who brings it to the attention of a person in the aesthetic sphere that his infinite striving is not a painless play that has left contradiction behind, but that it is instead a painful striving continually contradicted by the demands of finite ethical choice. Yet irony is not sermonizing, it is merely a play with this contradiction which "produces" it rather than allowing us to see it directly, for if we "saw" this contradiction we would also "suffer" it in the ethical sphere. Kierkegaard describes the "play," or comic synthesis of irony, as follows:

> Irony is the unity of ethical passion, which in inward-
> ness infinitely accentuates one's own *I* in relation to

---

[16] This difference is what lies behind the different Socrates of Kierkegaard's masters thesis, *The Concept of Irony*, and the Socrates of the *Fragments* and *Postscript*. The first Socrates embodies "absolute, infinite, negativity", which is to say, embodies nothing at all, and so has no position; but such a Socrates would not truly "exist" either, so Kierkegaard will later describe him as existing ethically, but wearing the incognito of irony. This incognito of irony would thus be a comic mask that Socrates indeed wore, but which was nevertheless "constantly vanishing" in the face of Socrates' ethical, if not religious, existence.

[17] Kierkegaard, *Concluding Unscientific Postscript*, 547.

[18] Kierkegaard, *Concluding Unscientific Postscript*, 502.

the ethical requirement—and culture, which in exter-
nality infinitely abstracts from the personal *I* as a
finitude included among all other finitudes and particulars. An effect of this abstraction is that no one
notices the first, and this is precisely the art, and
through it the true infinitizing of the first is condi-
tioned. Most people live in the opposite way. They are
busy with being something when someone is watching them. If possible, they are something in their own
eyes as soon as others are watching them, but inwardly, where the absolute requirement is watching
them, they have no taste for accentuating the personal
I.[19]

Irony brings to recollection the contradiction between the infinity
of our aesthetic creations, and the fact that we must exist finitely
in the midst of them. Yet *all* irony does is bring out this contradiction, for it is fundamentally comic and so results directly only in a
painless laugh. One can always laugh *with* the ironist, but if one
realizes that one is also being laughed *at*, this contradiction is no
longer painless and so one realizes for the first time that aesthetic
existence is actually pathetic and a suffering of possible infinities
rather than an enjoyment of them. So whether an ironist laughs at
or with you, one can learn nothing from him except what can be
found by looking inwards rather than outwards at the ironist.

   To be truly master of one's own irony, then, an ironist must
have attained such an inward relationship to the ethical requirement that he will not fall victim to his own irony—but that is to
exist no longer in the aesthetic sphere, but rather in the ethical
sphere. This sort of ethical existence wears the incognito of irony
because "the ethicist . . . is sufficiently ironical to be well aware that
what engages him absolutely does not engage the others absolutely.
He himself grasps this misrelation and places the comic in between
in order to be able more inwardly to hold fast the ethical within
himself."[20] Since, however, irony is in itself not any definite sort of
existence, but only a possible existence, "an observer can be fooled

[19] Kierkegaard, *Concluding Unscientific Postscript*, 503.

[20] Kierkegaard, *Concluding Unscientific Postscript*, 505.

if he assumes an ironist to be an ethicist, since irony is only a pos-sibility."[21] To exist truly as an ironist, one must actually exist ethi-cally or religiously and use irony only as an incognito. Any other form of irony is merely a species of aesthetic existence that has no problem imagining it can exist as mere possibility, since that is what the comic is all about.

What then of ethical existence that does wear the incognito of irony, what is its relation to the comic? Is it not comic when it goes incognito? And how will it distinguish between its tragic ex-istence and its comic mask? Kierkegaard's answer to this is as fol-lows: "The ethicist who has irony as his incognito is able in turn to see the comic in irony, but he has legitimation to see it only by continually keeping himself in the ethical and thus sees it only as constantly disappearing."[22] In other words, since the ethical exist-ence that looks forward to the idea of the infinite ethical require-ment demands all of one's passion, the comic relation that can look back on the old "idea" of aesthetic existence and so wear the mask of irony must be a relation that is continually "disappearing" in the light of this higher idea. It "disappears" in the same way a play "disappears" when the curtain goes down—leaving behind, in this case, an audience that must continue to exist in the actuality of its ethical pathos. The tragic pathos of ethical existence consists of the contradiction between the infinite ethical requirement and the finite self-assertion that must be engaged in attempting to fulfill it. The tragedy of this sort of existence is that there is no way this contradiction can be overcome; nevertheless, to exist actually in-stead of only possibly, one must continually keep this contradic-tion unresolved and before one.

It is at this point, in the midst of the pathos of ethical exist-ence, that one encounters the next border zone called "humor." What humor does is bring ethical existence into a relationship with the "God-idea" (not necessarily, in other words, an actual relation-ship with God, but only a relationship with the "possibility" of God); and this relationship presents the possibility of existing in

---

[21] Kierkegaard, *Concluding Unscientific Postscript*, 505.

[22] Kierkegaard, *Concluding Unscientific Postscript*, 521.

an entirely different way in the midst of suffering contradiction. Whereas in ethical existence one suffers the finitude of choosing before an infinite ethical requirement, the God-idea changes this contradiction into that between finite suffering and guilt before an infinite blessed God. Existing before the God-idea thus entails the suffering of guilt, and such an existence Kierkegaard will call the religious sphere. Yet in the same way that ethical existence could only express itself before the less inward idea of the aesthetic sphere in the incognito of irony, so also in the religious sphere it can only express itself before ethical and aesthetic existence through the incognito of humor.

Humor, whether or not the incognito of religious existence, can play with the mere possibility of existing before God and yet also revoke with a jest whatever religious reflections it might thus generate. "The totality of guilt-consciousness in the single individual before God in relation to an eternal happiness is the religious. Humor reflects upon that but in turn revokes it . . . . Humor joins the eternal recollecting of guilt together with everything but in this recollecting does not relate itself to an eternal happiness."[23] The revocation in the jest is thus the comic element in humor that "produces" the contradiction, and yet, since this contradiction is painless for the humorist, also "revokes" it in a jest.

As to what this sort of humor would look like, and how it would be involved with the seemingly foreign matter of religion, we should look at Kierkegaard's following description, that in our own day goes a long way toward describing the religious concerns of such comics as Woody Allen:

> Since an existing humorist is the closest approximation to the religious person, he also has an essential conception of the suffering in which he is, because he does not understand existing as one thing and fortune and misfortune as something that happens to the existing person, but he exists in such a way that suffering stands in relation to existing. But it is then that the humorist make the deceptive turn and revokes the suffering in the form of jest. He comprehends the

---

[23] Kierkegaard, *Concluding Unscientific Postscript*, 554.

meaning of suffering in relation to existing, but he does not comprehend its meaning otherwise than that suffering belongs together with it. The first is the pain the humorous; the second is the jest—and this is why one both weeps and laughs when he speaks. He touches the secret of existence in the pain, but then he goes home again.[24]

The first thought of the humorist is the same idea the existing ethicist sees before him in the suffering contradiction, but because that idea is seen as "behind" the humorist in a painless sort of recollection, he is also able to revoke it in the jest.

Now if this humor is also the incognito of true religious existence, this existence as the highest pathos within immanence must therefore comprehend all other spheres of existence as fundamentally comic insofar as they are all recollected as absolutely relative and equally guilty before the God-idea. This means that the hidden inwardness of religious existence discovers the comic "not because the religious person is different from others but because, although most heavily burdened by sustaining an eternal recollecting of guilt, he is just like everyone else. He discovers the comic, but since in eternal recollecting he is continually relating himself to an eternal happiness, the comic is a continually vanishing element."[25] To exist religiously with the incognito of humor therefore bears the same relation to humor as the ironic incognito did; in other words, it must constantly vanish before actual existence in the same way that an expression disappears in the face of the reality which it expresses.

But with Kierkegaard we also see an understanding of expression that bears a direct relationship to his understanding of inwardness and how it accentuates the crossover between life and writing, for he will want to say that the greater the inwardness, the greater discrepancy there will be between the expression and the existence being expressed.

---

[24] Kierkegaard, *Concluding Unscientific Postscript*, 447.

[25] Kierkegaard, *Concluding Unscientific Postscript*, 555.

Pathos is certainly inwardness, but it is spontaneous and therefore can be expressed. But pathos in the form of contrast is inwardness; it remains with the communicator even when expressed, and it cannot be appropriated directly except through the other's *self-activity*, and the contrastive form is the dynamometer of inwardness. The more consummate the contrastive form, the greater the inwardness; and the less it is present, to the point of being direct communication, the less the inwardness.[26]

This description of what Kierkegaard calls "indirect communication" means that expression as an act of *poesis* is always comic and so must always differ from the pathos of actual existence; that is unless, of course, one exists aesthetically, in which case, the immediacy of inwardness bears little discernible difference from the immediacy of one's surrounding expressive stage machinery. One always expresses possible meanings, and yet one must exist actually. To express one's mode of existence, especially if that mode is inwardly aware of its contradictory relationship with possibility, one must express that existence in such a way that the expression bears within itself that same contradiction, albeit in the mode of possibility.

This is the essence of comedy—the contradiction that is painless because it carries within it contradiction only as a possibility. The vanishing and evanescent quality of humor and irony as incognito is thus the vanishing quality of indirect communication— they both must vanish in the face of what they communicate. Recollection is consequently essential to indirect communication, for whatever content can be communicated lies within the hearer and not within the expression itself. Yet, at the same time, humor is the highest expression within immanence, and so recollects within itself all of immanent existence.

The highest pathos and the greatest inwardness attainable in immanent existence is thus the subjective, existing thinker who exists religiously in infinite guilt before the God-idea. This is the highest sphere of immanent existence and it is a tragic existence.

---

[26] Kierkegaard, *Concluding Unscientific Postscript*, 242.

The highest expression, however, is humor, and it is a comic expression of a tragic existence. But why are these the highest in immanence, and what does immanence mean in this context? To answer this we must look more carefully at the nature of religious existence.

Religious existence is the painful contradiction of relating one's finite existence to the infinite idea of a blessed God, and what this relation results in is the finite individual seeking to become as nothing in the face of this infinite fullness of the God-idea. Nevertheless, that individual still remains as a finite something, and so this irreducible something seeking to reduce itself to nothing in the face of the infinite becomes the source of infinite guilt. Such guilt is the result of the incommensurability of finite existence in relation to infinite blessedness, and, since as long as this individual's existence continues this finitude cannot be done away with, this sort of existence must always remain guiltily and passionately resigned to its immanent suffering. The God-idea is transcendent, but the existing thinker of that idea is immanent, and so the suffering contradiction between the two remains. It is the suffering of immanence insofar as the God-idea can only be an immanent idea for me no matter how transcendent the content may be.

To put this in terms of my stage imagery, the idea of a transcendent God is always on stage, and the immanent audience of that idea can only come close to it by forgetting as much as possible their own existence and letting what is on stage fill all of reality. Nevertheless, the audience and stage are irreducible facts, and for that audience to exist truly, that gap between stage and audience must not be forgotten. The recollection of that fact is therefore the recollection of the suffering and guilt of all finite existence. The more transcendent the idea on stage, the more suffering is involved in the recollection of the finite and immanent existent that can relate itself to that transcendent idea only through the medium of this immanent finitude. Is there no possibility of transcendent existence then? Can the God-idea ever be anything more than an immanent idea?

These are the very questions that prompted Kierkegaard to write the book he did, for these are the questions of the *Philosophical*

Fragments to which the *Concluding Unscientific Postscript* is the postscript. For the question of the *Fragments* is whether an historical
(i.e., immanently existing) point of departure is possible for an eternal consciousness (fully transcendent with no residue of immanent
existence); and what this question is asking is whether there can be
anything higher in passionate existence than the God-idea recollected by religious inwardness. The answer lies in Johannes'
"thought-project," which is the Absolute Paradox of the transcendent God coming into history and giving the condition for the
Truth (the God-idea) in the Moment. In the light of stage and audience, the paradox lies in the fact of the transcendent God leaving
the status of "God-idea" on stage and entering the immanent audience so as to recreate that audience to the point where it can
become equally transcendent. Such a paradox would preserve the
distinction between stage and audience, and yet at the same time,
create perfect equality between them to the point where there was
no longer any contradiction.

The paradoxical nature of this "thought-project" lies in the
consequence that the understanding of the contradiction essential
to existence in both ethical and religious existence would have to
be overcome. For the claim of this paradox is that it would make
this contradiction disappear. In other words, the paradox of Johannes' "thought-project" is that the pathos and tragedy of existence would no longer be contradicted by an idea ahead of it that it
cannot attain, but would instead be met with an idea that is beside
it in existence and yet still equally transcendent—the paradox of
tragic existence being confronted with the comedy of God. The
only sort of relation to this comedy of God that would itself be as
paradoxical as this "thought-project," would be the "happy-pas-
sion" of faith. For this "happy passion" would change the pathos
of existence into a pathos that nevertheless "sees a way out" and
so is also, paradoxically, comic. On the other hand, not to see a
way out in the face of this paradox would be offense, and in that
case the passion would remain, but it would be an unhappy passion
that is content with its own immanence and immanence's proper
understanding of God. The happy passion of faith is what Kierke-

gaard in the *Postscript* will call religiousness B, or Christian religiousness, which is distinguished from religiousness A, or the immanent sphere of religious existence, which in the light of faith is known to be essentially a form of offense.

With this said, what are we to make of the fictional author, Johannes Climacus, and his expression of all these spheres of actual existence in both the *Fragments* and the *Postscript?* Must not the expression of existence be always indirect and comic in relation to tragic existence? This is indeed the case, and for this reason Kierkegaard has Johannes reflect in the *Postscript* upon the nature of expression and its relation to comedy and tragedy and irony and humor. Johannes, the "character" writing these two works is, and must necessarily be, a humorist, since he only expresses, but does not exist, in the sphere of either religiousness A or B. As he says in describing the role he plays in the *Fragments*, his entire thought-project is essentially a humorous joke because:

> Humor, when it uses Christian categories (sin, forgiveness of sin, atonement, God in time, etc.) is not Christianity but a pagan speculative thought that has come to *know* all the essentially Christian. It can come deceptively close to the essentially Christian, but at the point where the decision captures, at the point where existence captures the existing person . . . so that he must remain in existence, while the bridge of recollection and immanence behind is demolished; at the point where the decision comes in the moment and the movement is forward toward the relation to the eternal truth that came into existence in time—at that point humor is not present.[27]

The joke of Johannes' writings is therefore that his "thought-project" is in fact a piece of plagiarism and that what he gives out as his own ideas are in fact only the echoing imitation of Christianity—an "expression" which is in fact not the expression of faith, but instead only a possible condition for recollecting what Christian faith is in the first place.

---

[27] Kierkegaard, *Concluding Unscientific Postscript*, 272.

This means that the true "expression" of genuine Christian existence uniquely precedes what it expresses, which is how it can provide the way out of the contradiction of existence. This expression is the poetic comedy of God becoming an actually existent subject; an expression that Johannes can only humorously imitate by means of his own "poetical venture." For "humor is not faith but is before faith, it is not after faith or a development of faith. In other words, Christianly understood there is no going beyond faith, because faith is the highest—for an existing person . . . . Even when humor wants to try its hand at the paradoxes, it is not faith. Humor does not take in the suffering aspect of the paradox or the ethical aspect of faith but only the amusing aspect."[28] To exist as a Christian, then, to exist in the decisive inward appropriation of Christianity, is an impossibility for the fictional creation "Johannes Climacus"; but it *is* a possibility for Kierkegaard himself or for any actual existing reader of his work—and that possibility is the possibility of faith.

But let us suppose that existing reader does have faith, has that happy passion that paradoxically no longer looks to the God-idea as on a stage while despairing of bridging that gap, how will that existence express itself? The answer is the expression which is itself the Christian drama, the drama which is fundamentally a comedy because it sees a way out of suffering and becomes the expression that, contrary to the understanding, precedes what it expresses and thus unites audience and stage by looking forwards instead of backwards. Yet, at the same time, it can also be a tragedy if its audience is offended and refuses to let that play be an expression of their own existence.

Humor can thus have no decisive place as an expression of Christianity; the expression of Christianity is the gospel narrative of Christ coming into finite history; and the only existence commensurate with that expression is the life of faith that continually must exist looking *forwards* to that expression as the goal that also lies *behind* as the condition. "Humor is always a revocation . . . is the backward perspective: Christianity is the direction forward to

---

[28] Kierkegaard, *Concluding Unscientific Postscript*, 291.

becoming a Christian and becoming that by be continuing to be that."[29]

Now that we have a sense for how Kierkegaard viewed the dynamics between the comic and the tragic and how they interrelate in the different spheres of existence, we can return to the *Philosophical Fragments* to see the significance this has for the question raised earlier regarding the relation of philosophy and the Bible. The philosophical discussion of the comic and tragic in the *Postscript* was meant to illuminate what was already going on in this earlier work, and what was going on in this work was an attempt to keep apart two incompatible marriage partners—the Socratic viewpoint and a humorous account of Christian faith Johannes calls his "thought-project." Kierkegaard in his *Philosophical Fragments* is therefore raising question of "philosophy or the Bible," and raising it in terms that we should by now find familiar.

He begins by explaining the Socratic viewpoint in terms of Socrates and recollection. Recollection entails the demand for indirect communication and the ironic dissimulation that puts up a barrier between Socrates' own life lived in pursuit of the truth and any form of communicating that life. Socrates in this light is the embodiment of our reversal between life and writing. In Johannes' "thought-project" on the other hand, we are presented with something that is deliberately set apart from the Socratic standpoint, because the "teacher," the "moment," and so forth, gain their articulation by being expressly what the Socratic is not. The "thought-project" thus thinks through the possibility that there may no longer be the need for Plato's reversal—the possibility that the truth can be directly communicated and life can be lived in the light of the truth contained in that communication or expression (writing). The figure that Johannes comes up with by these means is, of course, the Jesus of the Bible. When we see Johannes elaborate the difference between these two standpoints, we can see that he is also contrasting two different types of comedy—the irony of Socrates versus the poetic comedy of the gospel. His question is

---

[29] Kierkegaard, *Concluding Unscientific Postscript*, 602.

therefore our question. What is specific to the comedy of the Christian Bible?

In keeping with this question, in the second chapter entitled "The God as Teacher and Savior: A Poetical Venture," Johannes lays out for us a romantic comedy wherein the God as teacher's relationship to his learner is modeled after a prince courting a humble maiden. In this fairy tale (and almost all fairy tales are classic comedies) the complication that requires solution is how the prince will obtain complete equality with his beloved without basing it upon some sort of illusion. "The love, then, must be for the learner, and the goal must be to win him, for only in love is the different made equal, and only in equality or in unity is there understanding."[30] Yet this demand makes for a complication. God must make himself understood, and that "is not so easy if he is not to destroy that which is different."[31] Nevertheless, as in all good comedies, love will find a way, "for erotic love is jubilant when it unites equal and equal and is triumphant when it makes equal in erotic love that which was unequal."[32]

The solution must be out there; that is expected in a comedy. But how it happens is the decision of the comic poet, for it is he who has the craft to surprise us even as he satisfies—the essence of comic peripety. "Thus the task is assigned, and we invite the poet . . . . The poet's task is to find a solution, a point of unity where there is in truth love's understanding."[33] The solution found, as we all know, is the solution of a descent on the part of the prince, rather than an ascent on her part which would be based upon an illusion. The prince must be equal to this maiden in every way, even to the point of dying for her in her world, for it is only in this way that their love can be consummated.

The running joke throughout the *Fragments*, of course, is the accusation that Johannes is engaging in plagiarism with his so-

---

[30] Søren Kierkegaard, *Philosophical Fragments*, trans. Howard and Edna Hong (Princeton, Princeton University Press, 1985), 25.

[31] Kierkegaard, *Philosophical Fragments*, 25.

[32] Kierkegaard, *Philosophical Fragments*, 27.

[33] Kierkegaard, *Philosophical Fragments*, 28.

called "thought-project." When the credit is taken away from him for creating this fairy tale, he defends himself by saying:

> After all, every poet who steals, steals from another poet, and thus we are all equally shabby; indeed my stealing is perhaps less harmful since it is more easily discovered. But who then is the poet? If I were so polite as to regard you, who pass judgment on me, to be the poet, you perhaps would become angry again. If there is no poet when there is nevertheless is a poem—this would indeed be curious, indeed, as curious as hearing flute playing although there is no flute player. Or is this poem perhaps like a proverb, of which no author is known because it seems as if all humanity had composed it . . . [but] . . . if the whole human race had composed it, this might very well be expressed by saying that each and every person was equally close to having composed it . . . . So perhaps it is not a poem at all, or in any case is not ascribable to any human being or to the human race, either.[34]

When he then realizes that this accusation is not just of plagiarism, but rather "blasphemously pretending to be God," he continues by saying:

> Now my dear fellow, I quite understand you and understand that your anger is justified. But then my soul is also gripped with new amazement—indeed, it is filled with adoration, for it certainly would have been odd if it had been a human poem. Presumably it could occur to a human being to poetize himself in the likeness of the god or the god in the likeness of himself, but not to poetize that the god poetized himself in the likeness of a human being . . . And since we both are now standing before this wonder, whose solemn silence cannot be disturbed by human wrangling about what is mine and what is yours, whose awe-inspiring words infinitely drown out human quarreling about mine and thine, forgive me my curious mistaken notion of having composed it myself. It was a mistaken

---

[34] Kierkegaard, *Philosophical Fragments*, 35.

notion, and the poem was so different from every human poem that it was no poem at all but *the wonder*.[35]

The humor of Johannes Climacus' "thought-project" is thus the joke of pretending to write a story that claims for itself no possible human author, and it is this story that also claims to overcome the problem of the "mine and thine" that Plato can only cover over in the decidedly human and comic accomplishment of the "noble lie."[36]

Kierkegaard has thus brought us back to the distinctive claim of Christian Scripture that we have also seen brought out in Aquinas—that God himself is its author. As a poem this poem of God is like and yet unlike all others, so also as a comedy, this comedy is like and yet unlike all others. In each case the specificity lies not in our reading or hearing of it (at this level it is generically connected to all other comedies), but rather in our response to it; a response that is our own "outside" the text and yet is also already found "inside" as the responses, positive or negative, to the poet himself in the Gospels. This internal and external response to this comedy is unique, however, only because of the nature of this poet. For it is only with God as poet that the response to the poet in the story can be directly correlated with the response of the reader (Aquinas' "things to things"), rather than the merely indirect communication of imaginative participation (Aquinas' "words to words").

This difference brings us before the central question of the *Fragments*, which is explicitly asked on the title page:

> Can a historical point of departure be given for an eternal consciousness; how can such a point of departure be of more than historical interest; can an eternal happiness be built on historical knowledge?[37]

This is a question that has already come up in connection with Auerbach and Frei, and it needs to be addressed again here because it is intimately connected with the issue of God as the poet of

---

[35] Kierkegaard, *Philosophical Fragments*, 36.

[36] cf. Plato, *Republic* Book V.

[37] Kierkegaard, *Philosophical Fragments*.

Scripture. If the poet we are dealing with in the Bible is also the poet of creation, then and only then, can this writing have a direct historical connection linking our own period in history with the history of humanity and the cosmos. Otherwise, this writing is as alienated from what has been going on in our own history as is all writing from an actually lived life. This is why the Socratic viewpoint deals in recollection, for what goes along with the reversal between writing and life is the recognition of the incommensurability of a full understanding and any given written form or conceptualization of that understanding. Such understanding would be the full realization of something beyond the very space the understander is in, and the recognition of this tension leads to what has been called the "tragic" life of the philosopher who must suffer this incommensurability. The philosopher's relationship to history is thus the same thing as his relationship to writing, and so to believe he can gain an understanding of something eternally important from temporal history is the same thing as living one's life in one's writing.

The "Absolute Paradox" of the Christian faith is then just this, that there *is* a historical point of departure, that this moment has more than merely historical interest, that an eternal happiness can be built upon it. In this one case of writing the claim is made that one can indeed have one's life in it. In the chapter entitled "The Absolute Paradox," Kierkegaard contrasts the intrinsic paradox of thought with the extrinsic Absolute Paradox. The intrinsic paradox is the paradox of thought itself:

> for the paradox is the passion of thought, and the thinker without the paradox is like the lover without passion: a mediocre fellow. But the ultimate potentiation of every passion is always to will its own downfall, and so it is also the ultimate passion of the understanding to will the collision, although in one way or another the collision must become its downfall. This, then, is the ultimate paradox of thought: to want to discover something that thought itself cannot think.[38]

---

[38] Kierkegaard, *Philosophical Fragments*, 37.

417

What we have here, then, is another way of describing what he calls the contradiction of human existence, but in this case what we see described is also what after Aquinas and Lonergan can be called "the natural desire to see God."[39] The paradox of thought is that it can't help desiring to think (and know) what it is also incapable of knowing. We raise questions that we cannot answer for ourselves, and we know this by knowing the gap between the two, which is the paradox of the thinker as well as his downfall. This paradox is the same as the tragic life of the philosopher, as well as the reason there must be a crossover between that life and writing. In Plato we saw this as the Socratic ignorance that defers to the gods and piety (and poetry and writing) because it at least knows such things cannot be known. Such ignorance must be respected because contempt or hostility would imply a knowledge one doesn't, and indeed can't have.

In order to speak of the relation of this paradox to the Absolute paradox of Christian faith, Kierkegaard again uses the analogy of erotic love. Eros in his intimate connection with the contrivance of writing, and as the link between the gods and men, serves as the best analogy to God's own writing and his direct relation with humanity. To understand erotic love, however, we need also to see its relation to self-love.

> Self-love lies at the basis of love, but at its peak its paradoxical passion wills its own downfall. Erotic love also wills this, and therefore these two forces are in mutual understanding in the moment of passion, and this passion is precisely erotic love. Why, then, should the lover not be able to think this, even though the person who in self-love shrinks from erotic love can neither comprehend it nor dare to venture it, since it is indeed his downfall. So it is with the passion of erotic love. To be sure, self-love has foundered,

---

[39] cf. Bernard Lonergan, "The Natural Desire to See God" in *Collected Works of Bernard Lonergan: A Second Collection*, ed. Robert M. Doran and John Daneil Dadosky (Toronto: University of Toronto Press, 1988).

but nevertheless it is not annihilated but is taken captive and is erotic love's *spolia opima* [spoils of war].[40]

The central question this analogy raises is, why "shouldn't the lover
be able to think this?" For in the asking and answering of that
question we see how the question concerning the relation of philosophy and the Bible can be raised within the context illuminated
by comedy and tragedy. We have already seen, in the case of Hegel,
how "self-love," which is to say the philosophical life lived in pursuit of full intelligibility, can shrink from the erotic love presented
by the Christian faith. In his case this shrinking took the form of
retelling the Christian story as a tragedy. But what of the case
where self-love *doesn't* shrink, where the passion to know the whole
that brings about its own failure meets the passion of the comic
poet who creates a whole out of just those sorts of provisional
failures—what then? How are we to think this?

To begin with, what can't be forgotten is that the possibility
of thinking this is dependent upon the prior existence of the comic
poem of God, for it is the nature of this poem to include both its
willing and unwilling participants as essential parts of its plot. The
happy passion of faith in this poet is thus just as much a result of
this poem as is the unhappy passion of offense that in refusing to
take part in what is not of its own creation negatively defines the
nature of what it is rejecting. In this happy passion, we see what is
going on when self-love is not annihilated but rather taken captive
as spoils of war. In this image we can see how the fullness of philosophy can be incorporated into Christian faith as an essential second act complication that leads to an even greater finale of divinely
poetic resolution—a resolution that satisfies all the desires previously felt, yet in a way that was unthinkable earlier.

But is it thinkable now? Yes and no. Whatever is thinkable
will remain thinkable, which is to say, the higher destroys nothing
that is thought in the lower in the same way that erotic love does
not destroy self-love. But what it does destroy is the poems created
earlier to cover over the problem of the unthinkable. The poem of
God thus chases out the poems of men because what we learn

---

[40] Kierkegaard, *Philosophical Fragments*, 48.

from this poem is that everything thinkable can only be thought in the light of the one by whom it was made. The contradiction of human existence exemplified by Plato's reversal, elaborated only in terms of different kinds of writing in Hegel, and directly described in terms of human existence by Kierkegaard, is thus both accounted for and resolved by the poetic God who has made the intelligible whole with no remainder. The whole is thus fully intelligible precisely because God made it that way. The universe "written" by the Christian God is thus also the very same intelligible whole the philosopher lives his life pursuing. Yet that pursuit need no longer constitute a tragic life, because what was written is a comedy, and in a comedy all serious pursuits have a happy ending.

XVII: CONCLUSION

"Tragedy plus time equals comedy."

—Woody Allen

KIERKEGAARD once wrote of someone transported to Mount Olympus whereupon he was allowed his greatest wish. After considering the possibilities—youth, beauty, power—he asked the following: "May I always have the laughter on my side." In response, all the gods could do is join in with him in laughter, for to solemnly grant his wish would have destroyed it. Here, at the end of the twentieth century, this, too, may be our fondest wish; and yet, it would seem it is the least likely wish to be granted us. For it to be likely, that most influential narrative of the West (and thus, indirectly, the entire world), the Bible, would have to have God as its ultimate comic poet and not one or many human beings. It would, in other words, have to be a "serious comedy." For only a serious comedy, a comedy that has the Creator-god of the entire universe as its comic poet could preserve the claim of "seriousness" in it from becoming a further joke. A major reason this possibly seems "least likely" to us is because of our critical philosophical and ethical habits, habits inherited from the Enlightenment that see through everything and render everything light, and have made unceasing and corrosive laughter our greatest existential burden. In other words, our unbelief in no longer Matthew Arnold's tragic "melancholy, long, withdrawing roar," but is instead the supercilious grin of David Letterman interviewing a bearded rabbi. On the other hand, "least likely" endings have always been the stock in trade of comic plots, so what is unlikely is precisely what would be

expected from a serious comedy. One way or another, we are
bound to laughter and may not have the power within in us either
to make it our enemy or friend.

What does seem within our grasp is to understand why laughter is so important to us, and that I have tried to do here by following this trajectory of comedy and tragedy from Plato to
Nietzsche. As predicted in the introduction, three options should
by now present themselves to us, options of how we can live our
lives and understand ourselves in the midst of our writings. We can
lead a serious life while not taking writing or what we make seriously—as seems to be the case in the ancient political philosophers. Or we can live our life in the writing and "writer" of the
Bible—a life of faith in the poet of the serious comedy of the Bible.
Or we can attempt to live in the writings of our own making, taking
them seriously, while struggling to take seriously our life apart from
them. This last option is where we most often find ourselves, not
least because our inheritance in the Bible-haunted West is to expect that serious lives *can* be lived in writing, and comic writing at
that. Unfortunately the secularization of this biblical inheritance
wherein we no longer believe in the one divine poet who could
make such a serious life possible leaves us with the unshakable suspicion that the laughter is no longer on our side. We are comic to
ourselves, and the discovery of this joke leads only to the further
folly of pride rather than the serious gain of self-knowledge.

Among the various themes that have converged in this trajectory through comedy and tragedy, perhaps the most important
has been the challenge posed in Leo Strauss' question of whether
the Bible or philosophy is right. This is the question posed for us
in the first option, for if we can live a serious life without taking
any writing seriously, then the option of living as the ancient political philosophers did becomes the one serious option to biblical
faith. By keeping this question ever before my eyes, I have also
been led to disagree with Strauss' further claim that we cannot have
the "cake" of biblical faith and eat it along with philosophy. This
would no doubt be true if the Bible were a tragic narrative. But it
is not a tragedy, as I have argued, and so the problem this comic

narrative presented to political philosophy is that it knows and re-veals what the philosopher knows, and yet it cannot let him rest in that knowledge because it torments and tempts him with some-thing more rather than less. If the philosopher could read the bible as a tragedy he might use it and condescend to it as one would a noble lie, but as a comedy that will not let its readers forget them-selves in the reading, the claims of the Bible cannot prove noble or beneficial in any way if they are a lie; but if *not* a lie, if true, the noble or beneficial life of the philosopher is ultimately inadequate.

For this reason, I would suggest, that the first option of clas-sical philosophy has collapsed into the second two. In its wrestling with modernity, political philosophy cannot break free from Chris-tianity in either its secularized or genuine versions, so even Leo Strauss and the Straussians, the most serious claimants to a revivi-fied ancient philosophy, cannot shake the suspicion that Plato is not truly their model but rather Nietzsche. Nietzsche, who in his quarrel with Socrates provided the terrain for a rebirth of Platonic political philosophy in Strauss and the Straussians, has also sup-plied their largely unspoken and hence more constitutive quarrel with Christ as the author of Christian faith. The understated and suspiciously elided objection is not with modernity as such, but with the Christian philosophy of an Aquinas who knows philoso-phy is only a handmaiden to comic biblical writing. What I have called the expectation that one can live in writing finds its source here; and so even the most profound critics of modernity cannot shake the impression that they, too, believe that the poets have triumphed in their quarrel with philosophy.

Which brings us back to tragic narrative. As much as it seems we are doomed or graced to find ourselves in comic narratives, the penultimate state before we laugh at ourselves or others is a pious turn toward tragic narrative that in hushed tones exalts tragedy as the "story" of our philosophical and existential plight. Whether it be Martha Nussbaum who asks, "whether the act of writing about the beauty of human vulnerability is not, paradoxically, a way of rendering oneself less vulnerable and more in control of the con-trolled elements in life," or Alasdair MacIntyre who marks off the limits of how far he will go in his retrieval of classical virtue by describing the intrinsically tragic limits of philosophical narrative traditions, all too much of contemporary philosophy thinks it can borrow gravity from ancient tragedy. Like it or not, we are all too good at "discovering the lie," the irrational limits built into tragedy. For we are the ones who build it in, and desires that make us want to. It we are not to lie to ourselves, then, or if we are of Nietzsche's painfully self-conscious intellectual probity, we must figure out what we are to do in our contemporary comic predicament.

Let me make a bold suggestion. If we cannot ourselves become tragic-comic creator-gods to Nietzsche's liking, and if we can no longer piously believe in tragedies of our own making, and if we can no longer confidently live the life of resigned quiet contemplation without yearning for more, then perhaps the only true satisfaction to all our desires is to rest in a comedy made for us, about us, with tragedy only a second act complication brought about all by ourselves. Perhaps we must be willingly a created participant in the comedy written by the Creator God. Otherwise, the joke and the laughter will ultimately never be on our side. If it is on our side, if we can join in with it and laugh at ourselves and yet still be fully satisfied in doing so, then here and only here, it would seem, would the classical satisfactions of ancient philosophy find their place. Yet this is no more than the good news proposed by the object of Christian faith. And oddly enough, it is the one major faith that boldly proposes to have the cake of everything the philosopher has ever desired in his wildest dreams, and eat it too.

BIBLIOGRAPHY

Aeschylus, *Eumenides*. Translated by Richard Lattimore. Chicago: University of
Chicago Press, 1947.

Alter, Robert, *The Art of Biblical Narrative*. New York: Basic Books, 1981.

The Complete Plays of Aristophanes. Edited by Moses Hadas. New York: Bantam
Books, 1981.

Aristotle, *Nichomachean Ethics*. Translated by Martin Oṣtwald. New York: Macmillan, 1986.

Aristotle, *Poetics*. Translated by Gerald Else. Ann Arbor: University of Michigan Press, 1970.

Aristotle, *The Basic Works of Aristotle*. Edited by Richard McKeon. New York: Random House, 1941.

Aquinas, Thomas. *Summa Theologiae. Vol 1 The Existence of God* Part One: Questions 1-13. General Editor, Thomas Gilby. New York: Image Books, 1969.

Bacon, Francis, *A Selection of His Works*. Edited by Sidney Warhaft. New York:
Macmillan, 1985.

Bigelow, Robert. *Kierkegaard and the Problem of Writing*. Tallahassee: Florida State
University Press, 1987.

Dante Alighieri, *Inferno*. Translated by A. Mandelbaum. New York: Bantam Books, 1982.

Derrida, Jacques, *Dissemination*. Translated by Barbara Johnson. Chicago: University of Chicago Press, 1981.

Eco, Umberto, *The Aesthetics of Thomas Aquinas*. Translated by Hugh Bredin.
Cambridge: Harvard University Press, 1988.

Else, Gerald, *Aristotle's "Poetics": The Argument*. Cambridge: Harvard University Press, 1957.

Euben, J. Peter, *Greek Tragedy and Political Theory*. Berkeley: University of California Press, 1986.

Fortin, Ernest, "Dante and Averroism," Actas del V Congreso Internacional de Fliosofia Medieval 2: (739-46), 1979.

Fortin, Ernest, "Dante and the Rediscovery of Political Philosophy," in *Natural Right and Political Right: Essays in Honor of H.V. Jaffa*. Durham, North Carolina: Academic Press, 1984.

Fortin, Ernest, "Dante and the Structure of Philosophical Allegory," Miscellanea Mediaevalia 13:1 (434-40), 1981.

Frei, Hans, *The Eclipse of Biblical Narrative: A Study in Eighteenth and Nineteenth Century Hermeneutics*. New Haven: Yale University Press, 1974.

Frye, Northrop, *Anatomy of Criticism: Four Essays*. Princeton: Princeton University Press, 1957.

Frye, Northrop, *A Natural Perspective: The Development of Shakespearean Comedy and Romance*. New York: Harcourt Brace Jovanovich, 1965.

Frye, Northrop, *The Myth of Deliverance: Reflections on Shakespeare's Problem Comedies*. Toronto: University of Toronto Press, 1983.

Funk, Robert. *The Poetics of Biblical Narrative*. Sonoma, California: Polebridge Press, 1988.

Georgopoulos, N., ed. *Tragedy and Philosophy*. New York: St. Martin's Press, 1993.

Girard, Rene, *Violence and the Sacred*. Translated by Patrick Gregory. Baltimore, MD and London: Johns Hopkins University Press, 1979.

Hauerwas, Stanley, *Truthfulness and Tragedy*. Notre Dame: Notre Dame University Press, 1977.

Havelock, Eric, *Preface to Plato*. Cambridge: Harvard University Press, 1963.

Hegel, G.W.F. *Faith and Knowledge*. Translated by Walter Perf and H.S. Harris. Albany: State University of New York Press, 1977.

Hegel, G.W.F., *Hegel on Tragedy*. Edited by Anne and Henry Paolucci. Garden City, New York: Doubleday Anchor Original, 1962.

Hegel, G.W.F., *Phenomenology of Spirit*. Translated by A.V. Miller. Oxford: Oxford University Press, 1977.

Hegel, G.W.F., *Reason and History*. Translated by Robert S. Hartman. Indianapolis, Ind.: Bobbs-Merrill, 1953.

Heidegger, Martin, *Nietzsche Vol. 1 The Will to Power as Art*. Translated by David Ferrell Krell. New York: Harper and Row, 1979.

Heidegger, Martin, *Nietzsche Vol. 2 The Eternal Recurrence of the Same*. Translated by David Ferrell Krell. New York: Harper and Row, 1984.

Heidegger, Martin, *The Question Concerning Technology and Other Essays*. Translated by William Lovitt. New York: Harper and Row Publishers, 1977.

Hobbes, Thomas, *Leviathan*. Edited by C.B. Macpherson. New York: Penguin Books, 1968.

Josipovici, Gabriel, *The Book of God: A Response to the Bible*. New Haven: Yale University Press, 1988.

Kant, Immanuel, *On History*. Translated and edited by Lewis White Beck. Indianapolis, Ind: Bobbs-Merrill, 1957.

Kermode, Frank, *The Genesis of Secrecy: On the Interpretation of Narrative*. Cambridge: Harvard University Press, 1979.

Kierkegaard, Søren, *Concluding Unscientific Postscript to Philosophical Fragments*. Translated by Howard and Edna Hong. Princeton: Princeton University Press, 1992.

Kierkegaard, Søren, *Philosophical Fragments*. Translated by Howard and Edna Hong. Princeton: Princeton University Press, 1985.

Kierkegaard, Søren, *The Concept of Irony: With Constant Reference to Socrates*. Translated by Lee Capel. Bloomington and London: Indiana University Press, 1965.

Lindbeck, George, *The Nature of Doctrine: Religion and Theology in a Postliberal Age*. Philadelphia: Westminster Press, 1984.

Lonergan, Bernard, *Insight: A Study of Human Understanding.* New York: Philosophical Library Inc., 1957.

Machiavelli, Niccolo, *The Prince.* Translated by Daniel Donno. New York: Bantam Books, 1966.

Machiavelli, Niccolo, *The Chief Works and Others.* Vol II. Translated by Allan Gilbert. Durham and London: Duke University Press, 1989.

Nietzsche, Friedrich, *Beyond Good and Evil: Prelude to a Philosophy of the Future.* Translated by Walter Kaufman. New York: Vintage Books, 1966.

Nietzsche, Friedrich, *On the Advantage and Disadvantage of History for Life.* Translated by Peter Preuss. Indianapolis, Ind.: Hackett Publishing Company, 1980.

Nietzsche, Friedrich, *On the Genealogy of Morals* and *Ecce Homo.* Translated by Walter Kaufman. New York: Vintage Books, 1967.

Nietzsche, Friedrich, *The Birth of Tragedy.* Translated by Walter Kaufman. New York: Vintage Books, 1966.

Nietzsche, Friedrich, *The Gay Science.* Translated by Walter Kaufman. New York: Vintage Books, 1974.

Nietzsche, Friedrich, *Thus Spake Zarathustra: A Book for All and None.* Translated by Walter Kaufman. New York: Penguin Books, 1966.

Nussbaum, Martha, *The Fragility of Goodness: Luck and Ethics in Greek Tragedy and Philosophy.* Cambridge: Cambridge University Press, 1986.

The Republic of Plato, Translated by Allan Bloom. New York: Basic Books Inc., 1968.

The Symposium of Plato, translated by S. Groden. Boston: University of Massachusetts Press, 1970.

The Collected Dialogues of Plato: Including the Letters. Edited by E. Hamilton and H. Cairn. Princeton: Princeton University Press, 1978.

Plato: Phaedrus and the Seventh and Eighth Letters. Translated by Walter Hamilton. New York: Penguin Books, 1973.

The Roots of Political Philosophy: Ten Forgotten Socratic Dialogues. Edited by Thomas Pangle. Ithaca and London: Cornell University Press, 1987.

The Laws of Plato. Translated by Thomas L. Pangle. Chicago and London: The University of Chicago Press, 1980.

Plato: Philebus. Translated by Robin A.H. Waterfield. New York: Penguin Books, 1982.

Ricoeur, Paul, *The Rule of Metaphor: Multidisciplinary Studies of the Creation of Meaning in Language.* Toronto University of Toronto Press, 1977.

Ricoeur, Paul, *The Symbolism of Evil.* Boston: Beacon Press, 1967.

Ricoeur, Paul, *Time and Narrative.* 3 Vols. Chicago: University of Chicago Press, 1984-1988.

Roche, Mark William, *Tragedy and Comedy: A Systematic Study and a Critique of Hegel.* Albany: State University Press of New York, 1998.

Roochnik, David, *The Tragedy of Reason: Toward a Platonic Conception of Logos.* New York: Routledge, Chapman and Hall Inc., 1990.

Rorty, A.O., ed. *Essays on Aristotle's Poetics.* Princeton: Princeton University Press, 1992.

Rorty, Richard, *Philosophy and the Mirror of Nature*. Princeton University Press, 1979.

Rosen, Stanley, "Platonic Hermeneutics: On the Interpretation of a Platonic Dialogue." *Proceedings of The Boston Area Colloquium in Ancient Philosophy*. Vol. I. 1985, edited by John J Cleary. Lanham, MD: University of Press of American, 1986.

Rosen, Stanley, *Plato's Symposium*. 2nd Edition. New Haven: Yale University Press, 1987.

The Basic Writings of Rousseau. Translated by Donald Cress. Indianapolis, Ind: Hackett Publishing Company, 1987.

Schneidau, Herbert, *Sacred Discontent: The Bible and Western Tradition*. Berkeley: University of California Press, 1976.

Screech, M.A., *Laughter at the Foot of the Cross*. London: Penguin Books, 1997.

Singleton, Charles, *Dante's Commedia: Elements of Structure*. Baltimore, MD: Johns Hopkins University Press, 1954.

Steiner, George, *Antigones*. New York: Oxford University Press, 1984.

Steiner, George, *The Death of Tragedy*. London: Faber and Faber, 1961.

Sternberg, Meir, *The Poetics of Biblical Narrative: Ideological Literature and the Drama of Reading*. Bloomington: Indiana University Press, 1987.

Strauss, Leo, *On Tyranny*. Revised and Enlarged. Ithaca: Cornell University Press, 1968.

Strauss, Leo, *Socrates and Aristophanes*. Chicago: Chicago University Press, 1966.

Strauss, Leo, *The Rebirth of Classical Rationalism: An Introduction to the Thought of Leo Strauss.* Chicago: University of Chicago Press, 1989.

Strauss, Leo, *Xenophon's Socratic Discourse: An Interpretation of the Oeconomicus.* Ithaca: Cornell University Press, 1970.

Tieck, Ludwig, *The Land of Upside Down.* Translated by Oscar Mandel. London: Associated University Presses, 1978.

Verence, Donald, *Hegel's Recollection: A Study of Images in the Phenomenology of Spirit.* Albany: State University of New York Press, 1985.

Voegelin, Eric. "Wisdom and the Magic of the Extreme: A Meditation." *The Southern Review.* Summer 1981.

Xenophon, *Memorabilia.* Loeb Classical Library. Cambridge: Harvard University Press, 1932.

ABOUT THE AUTHOR

Patrick Downey graduated with a Bachelor's degree in Philosophy from the Claremont Colleges, and continued with a Masters from Harvard and a PhD from Boston College. He is also the author of *Desperately Wicked: Philosophy, Christianity and the Human Heart* (IVP Academic, 2009). He is currently Chair and Professor of St. Mary's College of California's Philosophy Department, where he has taught since 1994.

MORE FROM DAVENANT PRESS

RICHARD HOOKER MODERNIZATION PROJECT
Radicalism: When Reform Becomes Revolution
Divine Law and Human Nature
The Word of God and the Words of Man
In Defense of Reformed Catholic Worship
A Learned Discourse on Justification

INTRODUCTION TO PROTESTANT THEOLOGY
Reformation Theology: A Reader of Primary Sources with Introductions
Grace Worth Fighting For: Recapturing the Vision of God's Grace in the Canons of Dordt

VERMIGLI'S *COMMON PLACES*
On Original Sin (Vol. 1)
On Free Will and the Law (Vol. 2)

LIBRARY OF EARLY ENGLISH PROTESTANTISM
The Laws of Ecclesiastical Polity: In Modern English, Vol. 1 (Preface–Book IV)
James Ussher and a Reformed Episcopal Church: Sermons and Treatises on Ecclesiology
The Apology of the Church of England
Jurisdiction Regal, Episcopal, Papal

DAVENANT GUIDES
Jesus and Pacifism: An Exegetical and Historical Investigation
The Two Kingdoms: A Guide for the Perplexed
Natural Law: A Brief Introduction and Biblical Defense
Natural Theology: A Biblical and Historical Introduction and Defense

DAVENANT RETRIEVALS
A Protestant Christendom? The World the Reformation Made
People of the Promise: A Mere Protestant Ecclesiology
Philosophy and the Christian: The Quest for Wisdom in the Light of Christ
The Lord is One: Reclaiming Divine Simplicity

A Protestant Christendom? The World the Reformation Made

CONVIVIUM PROCEEDINGS
For the Healing of the Nations: Essays on Creation, Redemption, and Neo-Calvinism
For Law and for Liberty: Essays on the Legacy of Protestant Political Thought
Beyond Calvin: Essays on the Diversity of the Reformed Tradition
God of Our Fathers: Classical Theism for the Contemporary Church
Reforming the Catholic Tradition: The Whole Word for the Whole Church
Reforming Classical Education: Toward A New Paradigm

DAVENANT ENGAGEMENTS
Enduring Divine Absence: The Challenge of Modern Atheism

OTHER PUBLICATIONS
Without Excuse: Scripture, Reason, and Presuppositional Apologetics
Being A Pastor: Pastoral Treatises of John Wycliffe
Ad Fontes: A Journal of Protestant Letters

ABOUT THE DAVENANT INSTITUTE

The Davenant Institute aims to retrieve the riches of classical Protestantism in order to renew and build up the contemporary church: building networks of friendship and collaboration among evangelical scholars committed to Protestant resourcement, publishing resources old and new, and offering training and discipleship for Christians thirsting after wisdom.

We are a nonprofit organization supported by your tax-deductible gifts. Learn more about us, and donate, at www.davenantinstitute.org.

Made in the USA
Las Vegas, NV
04 January 2023

64839196R00262